Journal of Biblical Literature

Volume 136
2017

GENERAL EDITOR
ADELE REINHARTZ
University of Ottawa
Ottawa, ON K1N 6N5

A Quarterly Published by
SBL Press

JOURNAL OF BIBLICAL LITERATURE

EDITORS OF THE JOURNAL
General Editor: ADELE REINHARTZ, University of Ottawa
Managing Editor: CHRISTOPHER HOOKER, Society of Biblical Literature
Editorial Assistant: CAITLIN J. MONTGOMERY, Society of Biblical Literature

EDITORIAL BOARD

WILLIAM ADLER, North Carolina State University
ELIZABETH BOASE, Flinders University
JO-ANN A. BRANT, Goshen College
DAVID M. CARR, Union Theological Seminary
RICHARD J. CLIFFORD, Boston College
KELLEY COBLENTZ BAUTCH, St. Edwards University
COLLEEN CONWAY, Seton Hall University
TOAN DO, Australian Catholic University
GEORG FISCHER, Leopold-Franzens-Universität Innsbruck
PAULA FREDRIKSEN, Hebrew University
WIL GAFNEY, Brite Divinity School
FRANCES TAYLOR GENCH, Union Presbyterian Seminary
SHIMON GESUNDHEIT, Hebrew University of Jerusalem
MARK GOODACRE, Duke University
MARTIEN A. HALVORSON-TAYLOR, University of Virginia (Charlottesville)
RACHEL HAVRELOCK, University of Illinois at Chicago
ELSE K. HOLT, Aarhus Universitet
DAVID G. HORRELL, University of Exeter
L. ANN JERVIS, Wycliffe College
JONATHAN KLAWANS, Boston University
JENNIFER KNUST, Boston University
BRUCE W. LONGENECKER, Baylor University
MICHAEL A. LYONS, Simpson University
DANIEL MACHIELA, McMaster University
CHRISTL M. MAIER, Philipps-Universität Marburg
JOHN W. MARSHALL, University of Toronto
SHELLY MATTHEWS, Brite Divinity School
NAPHTALI MESHEL, Hebrew University
CHRISTINE MITCHELL, St. Andrew's College, University of Saskatchewan
KEN M. PENNER, St. Francis Xavier University
PIERLUIGI PIOVANELLI, University of Ottawa
MARK REASONER, Marian University
ANNETTE YOSHIKO REED, University of Pennsylvania
THOMAS RÖMER, Collège de France and University of Lausanne
DALIT ROM-SHILONI, Tel Aviv University
JEAN-PIERRE RUIZ, St. John's University (New York)
SETH L. SANDERS, University of California, Davis
KONRAD SCHMID, University of Zurich
WILLIAM M. SCHNIEDEWIND, University of California Los Angeles
CLAUDIA SETZER, Manhattan College
ABRAHAM SMITH, Perkins School of Theology, Southern Methodist University
JOHANNA STIEBERT, University of Leeds
JOHN T. STRONG, Missouri State University
D. ANDREW TEETER, Harvard Divinity School
MATTHEW THIESSEN, Saint Louis University
STEVEN TUELL, Pittsburgh Theological Seminary
EMMA WASSERMAN, Rutgers University
LAWRENCE M. WILLS, Episcopal Divinity School

The Society of Biblical Literature is a constituent member of the American Council of Learned Societies. *President of the Society:* Michael V. Fox, University of Wisconsin–Madison, Madison, WI 53706; *Vice President:* Brian K. Blount, Union Presbyterian Seminary, Richmond, VA 23227; *Chair, Research and Publications Committee:* Gale A. Yee, Episcopal Divinity School, Cambridge, MA 02138; *Executive Director:* John F. Kutsko, Society of Biblical Literature, 825 Houston Mill Road, Suite 350, Atlanta, GA 30329.

The *Journal of Biblical Literature* (ISSN 0021–9231) is published quarterly by the Society of Biblical Literature, 825 Houston Mill Road, Suite 350, Atlanta, GA 30329. The annual subscription price is US$55.00 for members and US$220.00 for nonmembers. Institutional and online rates are also available. For information regarding subscriptions and membership, contact: SBL Press, 825 Houston Mill Road, Suite 350, Atlanta, GA 30329. Phone: 866-727-9955 (toll free) or 404-727-9498. E-mail: sblservices@sbl-site.org. For information concerning permission to quote, editorial and business matters, please see the first issue of the year, p. 2. Periodical postage paid at Atlanta, Georgia, and at additional mailing offices. POSTMASTER: Send address changes to SBL Press, 825 Houston Mill Road, Suite 350, Atlanta, GA 30329. Copyright © 2016 by the SBL Press.

JBL is indexed in the following resources:

Arts and Humanities Citation Index
Scopus
ATLA Religion Database
Religious and Theological Abstracts
New Testament Abstracts (ATLA)
Old Testament Abstracts (ATLA)
Periodicals Index online (Proquest)
European Reference Index for the Humanities

PRINTED IN THE UNITED STATES OF AMERICA

The Aramaic Transition and the Redaction of the Pentateuch

MARK LEUCHTER
mark.leuchter@temple.edu
Temple University, Philadelphia, PA 19122

Virtually all scholars recognize that the Pentateuch was redacted during the Persian period but that its current form highlights the inconsistencies of its sources rather than attempting to harmonize or mediate them. In order to understand this phenomenon, it is important to reconsider the scribal culture of the Persian Empire with special attention to the Aramaic Transition—the widespread training of scribes in the Aramaic language, script, and the ancient classics transmitted in this medium—and its role in the promotion of Persian imperial mythology. In the context of the Aramaic Transition, the incorporation of dissonant sources in the Pentateuch emerges as a hermeneutical statement on the role of these sources and the social universe that produced them. The retextualization of these Hebrew-language traditions in Aramaic script provided an interface with intellectual trends that applied equally across all of the precursor sources utilized by the redactors of the Pentateuch, irrespective of their surface dissonances.

The last few decades of research into the formation of the Pentateuch have seen an increasing polarization on the question of how the redactional enterprise leading to the definitive form of the Pentateuch took place. Opinions remain divided on the source-critical assignments and categories: though some scholars have developed new models for identifying the growth of text units, others have renewed the case for the Documentary Hypothesis with a different approach to studying the compilation of the Pentateuch and the relationship between its

The research for this paper took place while I held the Mandelbaum Visiting Scholar Fellowship at the University of Sydney in August–September 2014; I am grateful to the Mandelbaum Trust and to Professors Ian Young and Suzanne Rutland for their kindness, friendship, and support. An earlier version of this paper was presented at the 2014 meeting of the Australian Fellowship for Biblical Studies (University of Sydney) and at the Old Testament Research Colloquium at Princeton Theological Seminary in December 2014. The present article benefited greatly from the feedback of those in attendance. I also wish to thank Seth Sanders, James Watts, and the anonymous reviewers at *JBL* for their comments and suggestions.

constituent parts.¹ Virtually all researchers agree, however, that the development of the Pentateuch's sources can be traced back to the late monarchic through the exilic eras, leading to the formation of the Pentateuch itself in the Persian period. A mid-fifth-century BCE date is widely accepted, and Neh 8 is often cited as the basis for this dating.² Even if the current form of Neh 8 reflects the hands of fairly late tradents, it preserves a memory of Ezra's mission in the mid-fifth century involving the public reading of a document that defined communal boundaries on religious and ethnic levels (especially in the context of group identity conflicts of *gôlâ* vs. homeland).³ This date seems quite likely in view of the authoritative status

---

[1] For recent overviews of the state of the discussion, see Joel S. Baden, "The Continuity of the Non-Priestly Narrative from Genesis to Exodus," *Bib* 93 (2012): 161–86 (Baden argues in favor of the [neo-]documentarian approach); Konrad Schmid, "Genesis and Exodus as Two Formerly Independent Traditions of Origins for Ancient Israel," *Bib* 93 (2012): 187–208 (Schmid argues against the traditional documentary paradigm). A careful consideration of the issue based on an evaluation of the oral-textual dynamic in scribal transmission of ancient texts is that of David M. Carr, *The Formation of the Hebrew Bible: A New Reconstruction* (Oxford: Oxford University Press, 2011). Carr's discussion of scribal methodology provides a new set of controls and raises important questions (13–101), though the present study will propose an additional matter that may require a reconsideration of the process of compilation Carr subsequently proposes (214–21).

[2] Karel van der Toorn, *Scribal Culture and the Making of the Hebrew Bible* (Cambridge: Harvard University Press, 2007), 248–51; Michael Fishbane, *Biblical Interpretation in Ancient Israel* (Oxford: Clarendon, 1985), 107–23. Alexander Fantalkin and Oren Tal suggest a somewhat later date for canonization of the Pentateuch ("The Canonization of the Pentateuch: When and Why?," *ZAW* 124 [2012]: 1–18, 201–12), though this does not preclude a fifth-century origination for its redaction.

[3] Many scholars date Ezra's mission to 398 BCE during the reign of Artaxerxes II; see Lisbeth S. Fried, "You Shall Appoint Judges: Ezra's Mission and the Rescript of Artaxerxes," in *Persia and Torah: The Theory of Imperial Authorization of the Pentateuch*, ed. James W. Watts, SymS 17; Atlanta: Society of Biblical Literature, 2001), 63–89; Joachim Schaper, "The Temple Treasury Committee in the Time of Nehemiah and Ezra," *VT* 47 (1997): 200–206, here 201; Saul M. Olyan, "Purity Ideology in Ezra-Nehemiah as a Tool to Reconstitute the Community," *JSJ* 35 (2004): 1–16, here 14. The traditional date of 458 BCE, however, can be defended. See Richard C. Steiner, "The *mbqr* at Qumran, the *episkopos* in the Athenian Empire, and the Meaning of *lbqrʾ* in Ezra 7:14: On the Relation of Ezra's Mission to the Persian Legal Project," *JBL* 120 (2001): 623–46, here 628–30; Joseph Blenkinsopp, *Ezra-Nehemiah: A Commentary*, OTL (Louisville: Westminster John Knox, 1988), 144. For Ezra already as a figure of memory in the mid to late fifth century BCE, see also Mark Leuchter, "Ezra's Mission and the Levites of Casiphia," in *Community Identity in Judean Historiography: Biblical and Comparative Perspectives*, ed. Gary N. Knoppers and Kenneth A. Ristau (Winona Lake, IN: Eisenbrauns, 2009), 173–95. For a thorough consideration of scholarship regarding the literary, historical, and ideological character of Neh 8, see Titus Reinmuth, "Nehemiah 8 and the Authority of Torah in Ezra-Nehemiah," in *Unity and Disunity in Ezra-Nehemiah: Redaction, Rhetoric and Reader*, ed. Mark J. Boda and Paul L. Redditt, HBM 17 (Sheffield: Sheffield Phoenix, 2008), 241–62. Reinmuth argues that Neh 8 is a late addition to the corpus that binds together the Ezra and Nehemiah narratives through a Torah-centered orientation, though the chapter may build on an older memory regarding Ezra as both a high-ranking official and a learned sage; see H. H. Schaeder, *Esra der Schreiber*, BHT 5 (Tübingen:

that the Chronicler, writing circa 350 BCE, already affords the Pentateuch in his own work.[4]

The question of *why* the Pentateuch was constructed, however, remains more contested. Persian imperialism is clearly a factor, but research in recent decades has pointed to influences beyond the level of official imperial intervention, as Peter Frei once proposed.[5] Internal pressures in the Aaronide priesthood of Jerusalem to conform to imperial trends and political norms provided a likely motivation for the production of the Pentateuch from extant sources, many clearly steeped in Mesopotamian literary influence.[6] This view, however, carries with it a complication. Seth Sanders has recently observed that, while the Pentateuch's precursor sources have parallels in Mesopotamian classics, their final redacted form does not. The redactors of the Pentateuch created a document that broke sharply with the standards of these Mesopotamian narratives with its sources arranged in sequence but not harmonized into a coherent or consistent whole. According to Sanders,

> What we never find in Mesopotamian scholarly text-making is what virtually defines the Pentateuch: the interweaving of variant versions of parallel events. Whether following each other in blocks, such as the two creations of Genesis 1 and 2–3, or tightly interdigitated as in the two interwoven flood stories of Genesis 6–9, this way of combining parallel variants is the clearest and most distinctive editorial feature of the Pentateuch. This is a process with no significant role in Mesopotamia.... This process is not attested in other ancient Near Eastern texts but is clearly evident in the literary form of the Primeval History. A sort of meta-literary collection, interweaving two or more different stories according to plot, in chronological order, which makes it still readable. This ... reasserts the unity of a single "Israel's story" but in a new way, with a new dominant literary value: now comprehensiveness trumps coherence.[7]

Mohr Siebeck, 1930), 39–51. On group identity conflicts reflected in Ezra-Nehemiah, see Dalit Rom-Shiloni, *Exclusive Inclusivity: Identity Conflicts between the Exiles and the People Who Remained (6th–5th Centuries BCE)*, LHBOTS 543 (New York: Bloomsbury T&T Clark, 2013), 33–47.

[4] See Zipora Talshir, "Several Canon Related Concepts Originating in Chronicles," *ZAW* 113 (2001): 386–403, here 386–90.

[5] Peter Frei, "Zentralgewalt und Lokalautonomie im Achemenidenreich," in Peter Frei and Klaus Koch, *Reichsidee und Reichsorganisation im Perserreich*, OBO 55 (Göttingen: Vandenhoeck & Ruprecht, 1984), 7–43. Various critiques of Frei's proposal may be found in Watts, *Persia and Torah*.

[6] See Anselm Hagedorn, "Local Law in an Imperial Context: The Role of Torah in the (Imagined) Persian Period," in *The Pentateuch as Torah: New Models for Understanding Its Promulgation and Acceptance*, ed. Gary N. Knoppers and Bernard M. Levinson (Winona Lake, IN: Eisenbrauns, 2007), 57–76; Kenton L. Sparks, "Enuma Elish and Priestly Mimesis: Elite Emulation in Nascent Judaism," *JBL* 126 (2007): 625–48.

[7] Seth L. Sanders, "What If There Aren't Any Empirical Models for Pentateuchal Criticism?," in *Contextualizing Israel's Sacred Writings: Ancient Literacy, Orality, and Literary Production*, ed. Brian B. Schmidt, AIL 22 (Atlanta: SBL Press, 2015), 281–304, here 295, 300–301.

Sanders draws attention to an anomaly that hinders attempts to classify the Pentateuch's redaction strictly according to Mesopotamian models on the level of literary mimesis. This raises a different set of questions regarding the conditions whereby the comprehensiveness of a document retaining eclectic and dissonant sources could trump narrative coherence. What standards or trends among the literati of the Persian period may have eclipsed the need for a text to exhibit consistency/coherence? Under what circumstances might the sequence of materials in a text point to meaning beyond the plain sense of its component parts? Finally, what benefit would there be in retaining the precursor sources rather than rewriting and transforming them into a new stream of discourse (e.g., the strategy of the authors of Deuteronomy)?[8] To answer these questions, we must consider the transition to a new standard of intellectual discourse—that of Aramaic sacral scholarship—which accompanied and reified Persian hegemony over Mesopotamian and Levantine literary and intellectual cultures.

I. Persia and the Aramaic Transition

Aramaic was the diplomatic lingua franca of the ancient world as early as the Neo-Assyrian period and was adopted as the language of administrative discourse in both Assyrian and Babylonian contexts.[9] Its adoption under Persia, however, signaled a notable change. In addition to its use as a language of diplomacy and administration, Aramaic was used for the cultivation of secret knowledge and revelation among the learned classes of the empire. This development represents a marked difference from earlier Babylonian and Assyrian cultures, where secret knowledge was transmitted and studied in Akkadian among the closed circles of Mesopotamian scholars.[10] The Aramaic Transition emulated this esotericism but

---

[8] See the conclusion to the present study for further discussion of Deuteronomy's transformation of extant narrative tradition.

[9] Evidence is abundant, but two examples will suffice: SAA 17, 2:13–18, in which Sargon II berates an imperial scribe for preferring Aramaic to Akkadian; see William M. Schniedewind, *A Social History of Hebrew: Its Origins through the Rabbinic Period*, AYBRL (New Haven: Yale University Press, 2013), 84. The second example is the famous moment in 2 Kgs 18:26, when a delegation of officials from Jerusalem attempt to engage the Assyrian officer Rabshakeh by offering to negotiate in Aramaic. This, notably, is also rebuffed. On Aramaic bilingualism and its effects on political stratification and statecraft in both Mesopotamian and Persian contexts, see Paul Alain Beaulieu, "Official and Vernacular Languages: The Shifting Sands of Imperial and Cultural Identities in First-Millennium B.C. Mesopotamia," in *Margins of Writing, Origins of Cultures*, ed. Seth L. Sanders, OIS 2 (Chicago: Oriental Institute of the University of Chicago, 2006), 187–209.

[10] Seth L. Sanders, "'I Was Shown Another Calculation' (חשבון אחרן אחזית): The Language of Knowledge in Aramaic Enoch and Priestly Hebrew," in *Ancient Jewish Sciences and the History of Knowledge in Second Temple Literature*, ed. Jonathan Ben Dov and Seth Sanders (New York:

universalized it as a standard that legitimized priestly-scribal groups throughout the Persian Empire. This included the adoption of Aramaic *script* in the production of native-language texts, the translation of native-language texts into the Aramaic language, and scribal training in the hermeneutical disciplines of Mesopotamian scholars through study of Mesopotamian classics (and, to be sure, others) in Aramaic translation as well.[11] Added to this was the importation of Babylonian scholarly traditions regarding the esoteric and even cosmic nature of script itself. The graphemes constituting a word or phrase were not simply visual strokes but portents of active, divine speech, containing revelatory meaning that a trained scribe-scholar could extract through proper training and skill. In the pre-Persian context, this understanding of the mythonuminous quality of writing had been restricted to the Akkadian script and language;[12] however, the royal architects of Persian sacral intellectualism appropriated this view and transferred it to the languages promoted by the empire, especially Aramaic. Secret, cosmic knowledge, once solely a matter of Akkadian language and scholarship, was now disseminated and cultivated in an Aramaic cultural milieu.[13]

The transition to Aramaic as a language of both the official chancery and revelatory esoteric knowledge left a deep impression on local scribal cultures across the empire. Texts that originated in native languages and scripts became available for esoteric study when reproduced as Aramaic documents. The use of Aramaic script provided conceptual interfaces between these local text traditions and the new standard of scribal enculturation under the auspices of the empire, and this applied to the scribes of Jerusalem as well. Although the Hebrew language survived, a sharp decline characterized the use of Hebrew script as Aramaic script was adopted for the retextualization of Jerusalemite literature.[14] Among the powerful

---

Institute for the Study of the Ancient World, 2014), 69–103, also online at http://dlib.nyu.edu/awdl/isaw/ancient-jewish-sciences/chapter4.xhtml. This persists at least down to the composition of Dan 9 in the mid-second century BCE. Sanders is correct to note that the revelation in Dan 9 is derived *not* from the study of a text but from an angelic intermediary ("Another Calculation," n. 6). But the narrative begins with Daniel attempting to discern the esoteric meaning of an oracle in written form (9:2), which presupposes the commonplace view that textual study yielded revelation (even if the chapter refutes this norm). See further Marian Broida, "Textualizing Divination: The Writing on the Wall in Daniel 5:25," *VT* 62 (2012): 1–13.

[11] The case of Darius's policy in Egypt is instructive. See Reinhard G. Kratz, *Translatio imperii: Untersuchungen zu den aramäischen Danielerzählungen und ihren theologiegeschichtlichen Umfeld*, WMANT 63 (Neukirchen-Vluyn: Neukirchener Verlag, 1991), 250–51; Joseph Blenkinsopp, "The Mission of Udjahorresnet and Those of Ezra and Nehemiah," *JBL* 106 (1987): 409–21. See also more generally van der Toorn, *Scribal Culture*, 104–8.

[12] I thank Professor Seth Sanders for drawing my attention to this in a private conversation.

[13] See below on the Bisitun Inscription.

[14] On the changes in Hebrew script evidencing the increasing influence of Aramaic forms, see William M. Schniedewind, "Aramaic, the Death of Written Hebrew, and Language Shift in the Persian Period," in Sanders, *Margins of Writing*, 141–52, *pace* Joseph Naveh, "Hebrew Texts in Aramaic Script in the Persian Period?," *BASOR* 203 (1971): 31–32.

castes of Yehud, the battle to preserve Hebrew took place on the level of spoken language (e.g., Neh 13:24), not written script.[15] Even if the learned castes in Jerusalem took seriously the responsibility to preserve Hebrew written tradition, the adoption of Aramaic script in the production of these texts was a concession to the role that Hebrew traditions were to play in the context of the Persian Empire. Menahem Haran recognized this long ago when he proposed that, for Jewish scribes living in the Persian period, Aramaic was the primary, not secondary, language and culture in which they were trained.[16] The use of Aramaic script in the production of Hebrew-language texts subordinated the memory of Hebrew culture to the Aramaic culture promoted by the empire.

A *baraita* in the Talmud Bavli contains some ruminations on this era and issue. Sanhedrin 21b–22aα credits Ezra with the introduction of the Torah in Aramaic script ("Assyrian" in rabbinic parlance) replete with a tradition of interpretation to go with it.[17] The matter is broached first with the assignment of different script traditions to the diversity of populations in Ezra's day:

> Originally the Torah was given to Israel in Hebrew characters and in the sacred [Hebrew] language; later, in the times of Ezra, the Torah was given in Assyrian script and Aramaic language. [Finally], they selected for Israel the Assyrian script and Hebrew language, leaving the Hebrew characters and Aramaic language for the *hedyototh*. Who are meant by the "*hedyototh*"? — R. Hisda answers: The Cutheans.[18]

Here, language and script together form ethnographic and theological boundaries. Only the combination of Aramaic script and Hebrew language yielded the Pentateuch that defined Jewish identity, whereas other combinations dissolve into the miasma of foreignness (in this case, the Cutheans = Samaritans).[19] The talmudic writers go on to specify that, of these variant scripts and ethnicities, Ezra is

---

[15] Regarding Nehemiah's concern for the social and religious role of Hebrew as a spoken language, see Katherine E. Southwood, "'And They Could Not Understand Jewish Speech': Language, Ethnicity, and Nehemiah's Marriage Crisis," *JTS* 62 (2011): 1–19.

[16] Menahem Haran, "Book-Scrolls at the Beginning of the Second Temple Period: The Transition from Papyrus to Skins," *HUCA* 14 (1983): 111–22.

[17] The same talmudic unit offers the explanation that because the script is square/upright (מאושרת), it should be identified with Assyria (אשור), an example of the punning hermeneutic derived from far more ancient precedents. Richard C. Steiner, however, suggests that the phrase "Assyrian script" may actually be quite ancient and derive from the Persian period ("*Mbqr* at Qumran," 637 n. 70).

[18] Translation based on *Hebrew-English Edition of the Babylonian Talmud* (London: Soncino, 1935–1948).

[19] Rabbinic tradition refers to the Samaritans as Cutheans on the basis of 2 Kgs 17:24. Ethnic distinctions between Jews and Samaritans were firmly in place already at the outset of the first century CE, as evidenced in John 4:4–42. I am indebted to Professor Stefan Schorch for discussing the significance of the latter text with me.

responsible for assuring that the Torah reached Israel through the proper *teaching* of the Jewish combination:

> Had Moses not preceded him, Ezra would have been worthy of receiving the Torah for Israel.... Concerning Moses, it is stated: And the Lord commanded me at that time to teach you statutes and judgments; and concerning Ezra, it is stated: For Ezra had prepared his heart to expound the law of the Lord [his God] to do it and to teach Israel statutes and judgments. And even though the Torah was not given through him, its writing was changed through him, as it is written: And the writing of the letter was written in the Aramaic script and interpreted into the Aramaic [language].[20]

In this passage, it is the teaching of the Aramaic-scripted Torah that maintains Jewish identity and social integrity. Though the historicity of Ezra's place in this equation is a matter of debate, the passage fits well with prevailing views regarding social diversity and Jewish identity in the fifth century BCE and how earlier traditions could be annexed and claimed by competing groups.[21] In rabbinic rhetoric, Ezra may stand in for the priesthood; in earlier days priests had served as arbiters between groups, mediating and producing sacral instruction that maintained social order and cosmic boundaries. The adoption of Aramaic script in the preservation of authoritative ancient traditions must have factored into how the priesthood navigated claims on Jewish identity in a multiethnic, multilingual, and multicultural imperial universe.

II. The Bisitun Inscription and Imperial Mythology

The key to understanding the place of the Pentateuch and the priesthood vis-à-vis the adoption of Aramaic script is to consider the source for Persian imperial mythology—the royal inscriptions, especially those of Darius I, and in particular the first and most prominent of these, the Bisitun Inscription (DB).[22] This inscription, carved into the face of the enormous Bisitun cliffside in western Iran, details how Darius came to power through several battles in the first year he held the throne (522 BCE). These battles were more than just bloody politics. They were, in Darius's words, his attempt to purge "the Lie," the cosmic enemy of Ahura Mazda, from within the boundaries of the empire. In so doing, the empire became the full expression of divine order, and Darius's establishment of the social order within

---

[20] The use of the term "Aramaic script" rather than "Assyrian script" originating in Ezra 4:7 has been abstracted and reapplied by the authors of b. Sanh. 21b–22a[α]. The phrase refers not to the Pentateuch but to the Aramaic documents embedded in Ezra 4–6, but see further below for additional discussion on this point and its relevance to the Pentateuch.

[21] Rom-Shiloni, *Exclusive Inclusivity*, 33–47.

[22] The abbreviation DB indicates the commissioning ruler (Darius) and the location of the inscription (Bisitun).

the empire was a realization of Ahura Mazda's wishes. What is more, the line between cosmic events and sociopolitical reality was obliterated: Darius's defeat of his enemies constituted Ahura Mazda's expiation of the Lie from the cosmos.[23]

Three things demand our attention with respect to this mythology and the inscription that expresses it. First, DB is written in three languages utilizing cuneiform script: Old Persian, Elamite, and Akkadian. The inscription tips its hat, in a sense, to the linguistic cultures traditionally written in cuneiform (Akkadian and Elamite) but also elevates Old Persian to the same level of prestige through its use of cuneiform as well. While many scholars view the written form of Old Persian as essentially "created" for Persian imperial inscriptions such as DB,[24] Elamite and Akkadian were common languages for the composition of both monumental inscriptions and foundation inscriptions deposited in temples constructed or restored by various Elamite or Mesopotamian rulers in the past. These languages empowered not only the structures into which they were embedded but the dynasties of the monarchs who commissioned them.[25] With the elevation of Old Persian to this same status, the Persian emperors were poised to carry on in the same tradition of royal inscriptions.

Second, DB was not hidden away in the depths of a temple but was boldly displayed on an enormous mountainside.[26] The implication is that DB functioned like the older Elamite and Akkadian foundation inscriptions in connecting the commissioning ruler or dynasty to the heavenly realm (DB sec. 65 4.69–72; 66 4.72–76). The physical Earth itself replaced the specific temples of the earlier inscriptions; DB was boldly on display for all to see.[27] The connection between Darius and the heavenly realm is literally grounded in the Earth, rendering the entire physical world the sacred space claimed by the deity and the emperor. Christine Mitchell appropriately terms this the Achaemenid concept of

---

[23] For a summary and evaluation of DB, see Edwin M. Yamauchi, *Persia and the Bible* (Grand Rapids: Baker, 1990), 31–35. For a full translation of the inscription, see Roland G. Kent, *Old Persian: Grammar, Texts, Lexicon*, 2nd ed. (New Haven: Yale University Press, 1953), 119–34.

[24] See Amélie Kuhrt, "The Achaemenid Persian Empire (c. 550–c. 330 BCE): Continuities, Adaptations, Transformations," in *Empires: Perspectives from Archaeology and History*, ed. Susan E. Alcock et al. (Cambridge: Cambridge University Press, 2009), 93–123, here 98.

[25] A salient example is the foundation inscription of the Nabu Ša Hare temple; see the translation by Nawala al-Mutawalli, "A New Foundation Cylinder from the Temple of Nabu Ša Hare," *Iraq* 61 (1999): 191–94, here 193.

[26] See also Beaulieu, "Official and Vernacular Languages," 204–5, for the Achaemenid break with the conventional use of inscriptions in earlier Mesopotamian imperial settings.

[27] See the treatment of this Achaemenid inscriptional convention by Margaret Cool Root, "Palace to Temple—King to Cosmos: Achaemenid Foundation Texts in Iran," in *From the Foundations to the Crenellations: Essays on Temple Building in the Ancient Near East and Hebrew Bible*, ed. Mark J. Boda and Jamie Novotny, AOAT 366; Münster: Ugarit-Verlag, 2010), 165–210.

"Earth-Empire"; the foundation of one is that of the other.[28] Thus, even if Darius emerged only at a specific moment in history, that moment was now the culmination of the entirety of the world's history. The fullness of the physical world, down to its core, forever and explicitly expresses the significance of that moment (DB sec. 61 4.57–59).

Finally, DB ends with the notice that Darius circulated copies of the inscription throughout the empire on both tablets and parchment scrolls (DB sec. 70 4.88–92). These media were typically used for sacred scholarship in various languages, especially Aramaic, which was traditionally written on parchment scrolls.[29] The making of written Aramaic copies was *part* of the imperial myth, extending and actualizing the myth's efficacy wherever such copies were found.[30] Any copy, therefore, carried with it not simply imperial power but heavenly power—it was a cosmic text.[31] An Aramaic copy of DB is attested among the documents at Elephantine (TAD 3 C 2.1).[32] That the Elephantine version has a fragment of another imperial inscription woven into it suggests that the inscription was not simply a symbolic or iconic text but part of a curriculum of disparate imperial doctrines and textual sources that might be studied in dialogue with each other. This is an important point to which we shall return below.

Something of this is intimated in the biblical record, for the Artaxerxes Rescript in Ezra 7:12–26 makes clear that, according to both the *data* (Persian) of the empire and the divine instruction of the Jewish deity (Ezra 7:13, 21, 25–26), Jewish priests like Ezra were to oversee Jewish affairs.[33] Ezra 7:12 and 14 imply a

---

[28] Christine Mitchell, "Earth-Empire in Haggai-Zechariah and Persian Imperial Inscriptions," paper read at the Concepts of Ancient Jewish Discourse Session, Annual Meeting of the Canadian Society of Biblical Studies (Ottawa, Ontario, May 2009); Mitchell, "Achaemenid Persian Concepts Pertaining to Covenant and Haggai, Zechariah and Malachi," in *Covenant in the Persian Period: From Genesis to Chronicles*, ed. Richard J. Bautsch and Gary N. Knoppers (Winona Lake, IN: Eisenbrauns, 2015), 291–306.

[29] Haran, "Book-Scrolls," 121–22.

[30] I am indebted to Christine Mitchell for bringing this dimension of the inscription to my attention.

[31] The idea of a text as a cosmic portal existed already in eighth–seventh century Neo-Assyrian literature. See Karel van der Toorn, "Mesopotamian Prophecy between Immanence and Transcendence: A Comparison of Old Babylonian and Neo-Assyrian Prophecy," in *Prophecy in Its Ancient Near Eastern Context: Mesopotamian, Biblical, and Arabian Perspectives*, ed. Martti Nissinen, SymS 13 (Atlanta: Society of Biblical Literature, 2000), 71–87; and James W. Watts, "Ancient Iconic Texts and Scholarly Enterprise," *Postscripts* 6 (2010): 331–44, esp. 333–35.

[32] Bezalel Porten and Ada Yardeni, *Textbook of Aramaic Documents from Ancient Egypt* (Winona Lake, IN: Eisenbrauns, 1987).

[33] Though the Rescript appears to be familiar with Persian administrative convention (Kratz, *Translatio imperii*, 225–60), many commentators have noted features that suggest that its current form is the result of literary shaping with an eye to the larger Ezra-Nehemiah corpus. See Hagedorn, "Local Law in an Imperial Context," 71. Sebastian Grätz identifies the royal donations in Ezra 7 for the restoration of the Jerusalem cult against the background of Hellenistic (Ptolemaic)

hybridization of the two (דת אלהך; דתא די־אלה שמיא).³⁴ The connection between Hebrew *tôrâ* and Persian *data*, along with the memory of Ezra's official capacity as a teacher/expounder of the law (via the term לדרוש in Ezra 7:10) echoes what the extrabiblical evidence suggests about the role and reach of the imperial myth as found in DB.³⁵ The myth was external and in fact externalized, writ large—literally— on a mountainside, claiming the entire visible world as a sacred space and thereby subordinating all other sacred spaces to it and its terms. Further, the mythology it related was translated into a Pax Persica on the local level through trained agents like Ezra and, no doubt, other Aaronide priests of the fifth–fourth centuries BCE.³⁶

Since the original DB inscription writes the making of Aramaic copies into its own myth, the Aramaic copies of DB connected local temples (wherein they were likely kept and studied) to the imperial mythology. This contributed to a certain elite emulation among Jewish priest-scribes in terms of harmonizing their own traditions with the prevailing culture surrounding them.³⁷ This is not to suggest that the mythologies sustained in Jewish sacral thought were equated with Persian imperial mythology, but they were most certainly qualified by it. Thus, when the priestly rituals of the Jerusalem temple were enacted to purge impurity from the midst of the community,³⁸ the priests conducting these rituals affirmed and supported, in Jewish terms, Darius's establishment of imperial order throughout the

---

praxis and thus dates the Rescript to the Hellenistic era (*Das Edikt des Artaxerxes: Eine Untersuchung zum religionspolitischen und historischen Umfeld von Ezra 7,12–26*, BZAW 337 [Berlin: de Gruyter, 2004], 134 and passim). Grätz's observations are compelling, though his conclusion that the Rescript en masse must date to the Hellenistic period is open to adjustment. The details of the donations in the Rescript may just as easily point to a Hellenistic-era revision of an earlier Persian-period tradition or source. In any case, even if the Rescript is a Hellenistic composition, this does not preclude the persistent memory of Persian-era conventions within its verses.

³⁴ Rolf Rendtorff argues for separating *tôrâ* from imperial law ("Ezra und das Gesetz," *ZAW* 96 [1984]: 165–84), though a relationship between the two is strongly implied in the text's rhetoric. See Lester L. Grabbe, *A History of the Jews and Judaism in the Second Temple Period*, 2 vols., LSTS 47, 68 (London: T&T Clark, 2004), 1:332–34.

³⁵ On the significance of the term לדרוש for the scribal teaching of *tôrâ*/*data*, see Paul Mandel, "The Origins of Midrash in the Second Temple Period," in *Current Trends in the Study of Midrash*, ed. Carol Bakhos, JSJsup 106 (Leiden: Brill, 2006), 14–25.

³⁶ The details of Ezra's Aaronide lineage (Ezra 7:1–5) are broadly viewed as historically untenable, but the author of the text containing this lineage presupposes Ezra's Aaronide credentials.

³⁷ Konrad Schmid, "Judean Identity and Ecumenicity: The Political Theology of the Priestly Document," in *Judah and the Judeans in the Achaemenid Period: Negotiating Identity in an International Context*, ed. Oded Lipschits, Gary N. Knoppers, and Manfred Oeming (Winona Lake, IN: Eisenbrauns, 2011), 3–26.

³⁸ See the concise discussion of this aspect of the priestly cult in Jon D. Levenson, *Creation and the Persistence of Evil: The Jewish Drama of Divine Omnipotence* (Princeton: Princeton University Press, 1988), 121–24.

Earth. What is perhaps most significant, the fact that these Aaronide priests read texts aloud to temple audiences in Aramaic script[39] supported the Aramaic translations of the foundational mythological document, DB, and its overt declaration of hegemony over the entire natural world, literally, as far as the eye could see.[40]

This point carries serious implications for the growth of Hebrew Scripture in the Persian period. If these Scriptures were reproduced in Aramaic script, in an environment where an Aramaic translation of DB was preserved and studied, then the imperial myth became part of the curriculum of the Jerusalem temple, taught alongside the native Hebrew-language texts and informing the way in which those Scriptures were transmitted.[41] Aramaic translations of these works probably emerged, but the fact that most of the texts of the Hebrew Bible were preserved in the Hebrew language suggests that such translations did not replace Hebrew-language texts as central to ritual and sacral study.[42] Nevertheless, the increased frequency of Aramaic and Old Persian loanwords and linguistic forms in Late Biblical Hebrew shows how deeply Aramaic scribal culture permeated the ranks of the Jerusalem elite.[43] The body of esoteric learning that accompanied Aramaic enculturation became part of the priestly-scribal establishment in Jerusalem; the transmission of Hebrew texts in Aramaic script would therefore constitute an attempt to find a place for Hebrew text traditions within that intellectual horizon.

III. Three Test Cases

This proposed understanding of the Aramaic Transition finds expression in three Jewish scribal products of the Persian period, the first of which is the Aramaic

---

[39] James W. Watts, *Ritual and Rhetoric in Leviticus: From Sacrifice to Scripture* (Cambridge: Cambridge University Press, 2007), 57–62.

[40] Root, "Palace to Temple," 208–10.

[41] For the role of priests in the preservation and production of texts, see David M. Carr, *Writing on the Tablet of the Heart: Origins of Scripture and Literature* (New York: Oxford University Press, 2005), 3–14 and passim; and van der Toorn, *Scribal Culture*, 51–73.

[42] For a concise discussion, see Joshua Berman, "The Narratological Purpose of Aramaic Prose in Ezra 4.8–6.18," *AS* 5 (2007): 166–67. The Qumran texts shed some light on this matter. Comparisons should not be pushed too far in many cases, for Qumran presupposes the authoritative status of scriptural materials in the early Hellenistic era that are not attested in the Persian-era archive at Elephantine (Reinhard G. Kratz, *Historisches und biblisches Israel: Drei Überblicke zum Alten Testament* [Tübingen: Mohr Siebeck, 2013], 46–47, 184–85). Nevertheless, the fact that most of the Qumran texts are Hebrew rather than Aramaic (but still deploy an Aramaic script form!) is instructive with regard to scribal standards that obtained in Jerusalem before the Qumran sectaries split from the Jerusalem establishment.

[43] For the incursion of Persian administrators into Yehudite life, see Aren Wilson-Wright, "From Persepolis to Jerusalem: A Reevaluation of Old Persian–Hebrew Contact in the Achemenid Period," *VT* 65 (2015): 152–67.

copy of DB found at Elephantine mentioned above, which incorporates at §13 lines from a completely separate imperial text, namely, Darius's tomb inscription. Below is the translation, with the tomb inscription material in boldface:[44]

> Thus speaks King Darius: Whoever you are, O king who will come after me, do not be a friend to the man who lies, or to Lawbreakers. Protect yourself from many lies; a servant who lies, do not support him. **Firmly make known how you act and how your conduct is. Let not that be good to you which one says in your ear. Listen to that which one says in public. Let not that be good to you what the freeborn man does. That which he who is not freeborn, look at that. For yourself too … and you will not be insecure in your happiness. An evil young man will not prosper, and in the land he will not live.** Whoever you are, O king who will come after me, our text … completely.… Believe what I did, and tell the truth to the people. Do not conceal it. If you do not conceal it but tell it to the people, Ahuramazda will bless you. He will befriend you and your descendants will be numerous, your days long lasting. But if you do conceal it, Ahuramazda will curse you. And there will not be any offspring for you.[45]

The Aramaic Elephantine DB papyrus is dated to circa 420 BCE, commemorating a century of DB's role as a foundational imperial ideology. The renewed emphasis on DB also may have constituted an attempt to ground the reign of Darius II in the mythology that legitimized the power of Darius I, especially since Darius II, like his namesake, came to power under contested conditions. If this is so, one would expect a royal inscription or decree of such importance to be transmitted and promoted with deep respect for its original form to promote consistency between these two rulers, their subjects, and their policies. There is linguistic, historiographic, and anthropological evidence that copies of DB circulated in the western provinces in the late fifth century BCE and remained fairly faithful to the original version.[46] The use of material from Darius's tomb inscription in paragraph 13 of the Elephantine DB papyrus indicates that other royal inscriptions were circulated for similar purposes, that is, as a redeployment of Darius I's older royal literature to reinforce civic/political sensibilities in the outlying provinces.[47]

Yet the scribe responsible for incorporating the tomb inscription verses into paragraph 13 of the Elephantine DB did so not simply to reproduce imperial propaganda or to copy it as a scholastic exercise. The Aramaizing of these materials unlocked their hermeneutical potential and allowed them to be combined into a larger composite discourse serving a purpose other than simple royal propaganda. In the Elephantine DB papyrus, the purpose appears to be sapiential: the distinct sources are transformed into a sort of hypertextual discourse on wisdom and ethics

---

[44] Translation by Jan Tavernier, "An Achaemenid Royal Inscription: The Text of Paragraph 13 of the Aramaic Version of the Bisitun Inscription," *JNES* 60 (2001): 161–76.

[45] Ibid., 175.

[46] Wilson-Wright, "From Persepolis to Jerusalem," 160–62, 167.

[47] Kratz, *Historisches und biblisches Israel*, 199.

beyond the royal court, establishing parallels between royal succession and the charge to make evaluations of character and ethics. The redaction of these sources into a single document may well reflect the impetus and intentions of the priestly scribes at the Yahu temple where this document was stored and taught.

The dialectic between the plain sense of the text and the implications of the combination of sources is noteworthy. DB implores the royal successor not to conceal the text but to promote it publicly, and the publication in Aramaic presumably constitutes the manner in which this was to take place (DB 70 4.88–92). Yet the Aramaic scribal culture was not steeped in public awareness; the true meaning of a text was a matter of secret revelation within a circle of scribes.[48] The circulation of Darius I's royal literature may well have been a matter of imperial propaganda, but the redaction of Darius's tomb inscription into paragraph 13 of the Elephantine DB reflects an attempt to penetrate into the esoteric level of both Aramaized sources. For the Elephantine priests who produced the papyrus in question, these hidden meanings would constitute secret knowledge that empowered their own authority, but one derived from the imperial world that produced these sources. The document attests to how such priest-scribes steeped in Aramaic scribal culture developed their disparate textual resources into more resonant cultural discourses. Irrespective of the notable theological differences between Elephantine and Jerusalem in the fifth century BCE,[49] the Elephantine redactional/hermeneutical methods evident in the DB papyrus are instructive for understanding how similar methods would have characterized the production of texts in Jerusalem.

The second test case appears in the biblical record, in Ezra 4–6. These chapters purport to contain detailed correspondence between communities hostile to Yehud and the Persian emperors.[50] The correspondence is overtly identified as drawn from an imperial source/archive and subsequently collected and copied onto a scroll in Aramaic. The common translation for the verse relating this information (4:7) is as follows:

---

[48] Van der Toorn, *Scribal Culture*, 65–66, 220.

[49] Kratz's view that the Jewish priests at Elephantine were isolated from the type of Judaism developing in Jerusalem (and resonating in the biblical record) is very likely correct (*Historisches und biblisches Israel*, 192). See also Ernst Axel Knauf, "Elephantine und das vorbiblische Judentum," in *Religion und Religionskontakte im Zeitalter der Achämeniden*, ed. Reinhard G. Kratz, VWGTh 22 (Gütersloh: Gütersloher Verlagshaus, 2002), 187. Nevertheless, both the Jerusalem and Elephantine temples were subject to the norms of imperial policy and the accompanying cultural/intellectual trends. Both sanctuaries might have produced and preserved different texts, but the method of their manufacture, preservation, and function operated within the same intellectual paradigm.

[50] A full treatment of these chapters, with a consideration of earlier proposals, is that of Richard C. Steiner, "Bishlam's Archival Search Report in Nehemiah's Archive: Multiple Introductions and Reverse Chronological Order as Clues to the Origin of the Aramaic Letters in Ezra 4–6," *JBL* 125 (2006): 641–85.

In the days of Artaxerxes, Bishlam, Mithredath, Tabeel, and the rest of his companions wrote to Artaxerxes king of Persia; and the letter was written in Aramaic (וכתב הנשתון כתוב ארמית), and translated into the Aramaic language (ומתרגם ארמית). (Ezra 4:7)

Richard C. Steiner has shown that much of what follows in Ezra 4–6 was previously compiled onto a scroll that served as a source for the author of Ezra 1–6.[51] Steiner concluded that Ezra 4:7—a heading drawn from this source scroll—attests to one of the letters written in Aramaic language (ומתרגם ארמית) while the others were translated from Old Persian into Aramaic as well.[52] This meshes well with the role that Aramaic played in administrative correspondence as well as in larger bilingual speech communities in the Persian period.[53] Steiner's subsequent discussion provides further explanation for why multiple embedded headings appear in these chapters as well, insofar as search reports resulted in the collection of disparate sources onto a common scroll that were ultimately rendered in the common language of official correspondence.[54]

While Steiner's observation regarding the collation of material has much to recommend it, it could be that Ezra 4:7 attests to the use of Aramaic *script* in the original writing of Old Persian–language dispatches before their translation into the Aramaic language. The phrase וכתב הנשתון כתוב ארמית would therefore be read as "and the letter was written in Aramaic script"; this would account for the plain meaning of Ezra 4:7 and also matches the precedent for the use of foreign script media (cuneiform) in the writing of the Old Persian section of the DB inscription.[55]

---

[51] There is general agreement that Ezra 1–6 is a single unit added to an extant Ezra-Nehemiah tradition at a relatively late point in the latter's literary development. Many scholars follow the position of H. G. M. Williamson that the unit reflects the redactional hand of the Aaronide priesthood (or that of a writer sympathetic to that priesthood) and attempts to present these priests as the trustees and leaders of the Yehudite community ("The Composition of Ezra i–vi," *JTS* 34 [1983] 1–30). Juha Pakkala further identifies some passages in these chapters that appear to derive from the Hellenistic period (*Ezra the Scribe: The Development of Ezra 7–10 and Nehemiah 8*, BZAW 347 [Berlin: de Gruyter, 2004], 140–44, esp. 143 n. 27, 172–73). There is no reason to doubt that the transmission of these documents throughout the Hellenistic period saw periodic glosses and revisions added to their contents.

[52] Steiner, "Bishlam's Archival Search Report," 675–76. Sebastian Grätz questions the authenticity of the letters in these chapters ("Die Aramäische Chronik des Esrabuches und die Rolle der Altesten in Esr 5–6," *ZAW* 118 [2006]: 405–22). Yet even if the letters are not authentic, their function in Ezra 4–6 presupposes norms of the conventional use of Aramaic script and official correspondence that Steiner discusses.

[53] Schniedewind, *Social History*, 84; Sanders, "I Was Shown Another Calculation"; see also Frank Polak, "Sociolinguistics and the Judean Speech Community of the Achaemenid Empire," in *Judah and the Judeans in the Persian Period*, ed. Oded Lipschits and Manfred Oeming (Winona Lake, IN: Eisenbrauns, 2006), 589–628, here 591–92.

[54] Steiner, "Bishlam's Archival Search Report," 650–55, 660.

[55] *Pace* Steiner, "Bishlam's Archival Search Report," 660, which remains possible but speculative.

Evidence from the book of Esther (late Persian or early Hellenistic in date) supports this as well: Esther satirizes the epigraphic norms of the empire in relating that official dispatches were sent across the Persian Empire not only in native languages but in native script traditions (Esth 1:22, 3:12, 8:9).[56] The author of Esther thus assumed that the *usual* course of affairs involved the use of Aramaic script in the communication of different languages for official purposes, and the writing of Old Persian letters in Aramaic script such as those in Ezra 4–6 would dovetail with this presupposition. In addition, b. Sanh. 21b–22aα (the *baraita* noted above) applies the notice of Ezra 4:7 to its depiction of the rescripting of the Pentateuch's Hebrew sources in Aramaic script. Late though it may be, this *baraita* preserves some accurate (if telescoped) memories of Persian literary conventions regarding the writing of the Pentateuch in Aramaic script;[57] the fact that it recruits Ezra 4:7 as a qualifying intertext suggests that the verse was long regarded as a testament to the use of Aramaic script in the textualization of non-Aramaic languages.

For the redactor of Ezra 1–6 who inherited and preserved this verse this is an important point. It makes clear that antagonistic letters in Old Persian nonetheless carried a second and implicit meaning by virtue of their textualization in Aramaic script, one that could serve a purpose beyond their plain-sense anti-Jewish antagonism when subjected to scribal study.[58] This is indeed how the author of Ezra 1–6 uses this source scroll, interfacing it with his own Hebrew traditions that were similarly preserved and transmitted in Aramaic script by the time Ezra 1–6 was redacted.[59] This includes allusions to the written oracles of Jeremiah (Ezra 1:1), Haggai and Zechariah (Ezra 5:1–2, 6:14), as well as a restatement of the list of *gôlâ* returnees from Neh 7 (Ezra 2). The Aramaic script rendered the source scroll viable for inclusion into this sacred history, establishing a conceptual parallel between

---

[56] See, among others, Jon D. Levenson, *Esther: A Commentary*, OTL (Louisville: Westminster John Knox, 1997), 8, 24–25. Elsie R. Stern notes that the authors of Esther go so far as to satirize/criticize life in the diaspora en masse ("Esther and the Politics of Diaspora," *JQR* 100 [2010]: 25–53, here 52). On the dating of Esther, see Sara R. Johnson, "Novelistic Elements in Esther: Persian or Hellenistic, Jewish or Greek?," *CBQ* 67 (2005): 571–89, here 584–85.

[57] The persistence of memory from very ancient periods in Judahite/Judean history into the rabbinic era is attested in various texts; see Shaye J. D. Cohen, "The Judaean Legal Tradition and the *Halakhah* of the Mishna," in *The Cambridge Companion to the Talmud and Rabbinic Literature*, ed. Charlotte Elisheva Fonrobert and Martin S. Jaffee, Cambridge Companions to Religion (Cambridge: Cambridge University Press, 2007), 121–34.

[58] See the similar discussion by Jacob Wright, "Seeking, Finding and Writing in Ezra-Nehemiah," in Boda and Redditt, *Unity and Disunity in Ezra-Nehemiah*, 277–304, here 303–4.

[59] Williamson sees these chapters as deriving from the early Hellenistic era ("Ezra i–vi," 29); a late Persian-period provenance is just as likely, however. Williamson's argument presupposes that these chapters were influenced by late Persian additions to Chronicles, a view that has been challenged by more recent research into the composition of Chronicles. In any case, the script convention of the day (late Persian or early Hellenistic) was exclusively Aramaic, as Schniedewind has noted (*Social History*, 160–61).

Jewish prophetic literature and official Persian documents—even those that appear, on the surface, to run counter to Jewish interests.[60]

Finally, the Book of the Twelve (Hosea–Malachi) has some significance for our current discussion. Though most commentators agree that the Book of the Twelve was redacted subsequent to the Pentateuch, it emerged in the same imperial and intellectual scribal paradigm (one that persisted even beyond the Persian period) and thus provides a useful corollary.[61] These texts show evidence of redaction before their inclusion in the Book of the Twelve.[62] Toward the end of the Persian period, however, these independent prophetic sources were redacted by Levite scribes onto a single scroll to create a cohesive (if multivalent) work.[63] The various cross-references among the component parts of the Book of the Twelve provide a textual model for how the oracles therein should be taught, but there is little to suggest that the scribes who redacted the work sought to hide the origins of the individual prophetic sources.[64] All of these discrete prophetic works, however, would have been transmitted in Aramaic script by the time the Book of the Twelve was redacted. We thus find a composite work that retains dissonant Hebrew sources of disparate origin that were transmitted under the aegis of Aramaic scribal standards,[65] compiled as a single, comprehensive document for the purpose of

---

[60] *Pace* Berman, who argues that the Aramaic language of Ezra 4–6 removes it from a network of intertextuality with extant Hebrew scriptural traditions ("Narratological Purpose," 168). This overlooks the point made in the present study that even those Hebrew works were retextualized in Aramaic script and thus grounded in a wider intertextual network.

[61] There is general agreement in contemporary research that the Book of the Twelve received a definitive redaction in the late Persian period. See the recent collection of essays in Rainer Albertz, James D. Nogalski, and Jakob Wöhrle, eds., *Perspectives on the Formation of the Book of the Twelve*, BZAW 433 (Berlin: de Gruyter, 2012). Van der Toorn, however, argues for an early Hellenistic background for the redaction of this work (*Scribal Culture*, 252–55). It seems likely to me that the Book of the Twelve continued to undergo additional reworking in the Hellenistic period, but its penultimate form is substantially a product of the late Persian period.

[62] On the redaction of these texts predating the construction of the Book of the Twelve, see James D. Nogalski, *Literary Precursors to the Book of the Twelve*, BZAW 217 (Berlin: de Gruyter, 1993), 278–80; Aaron Schart, *Die Entstehung des Zwölfprophetenbuchs: Neubearbeitungen von Amos im Rahmen schriftenübergreifender Redaktionsprozesse*, BZAW 260 (Berlin: de Gruyter, 1998), 151–223.

[63] On the Levite redaction of the Book of the Twelve, see James D. Nogalski, "One Book and Twelve Books: The Nature of the Redactional Work and the Implications of Cultic Source Material in the Book of the Twelve," in Ehud Ben Zvi and James D. Nogalski, *Two Sides of a Coin: Juxtaposing Views on Interpreting the Book of the Twelve/Twelve Prophetic Books*, AnGr 201 (Piscataway, NJ: Gorgias, 2009), 40–46; Mark Leuchter, "Another Look at the Hosea/Malachi Framework in The Twelve," *VT* 64 (2014): 249–65.

[64] Ehud Ben Zvi has mounted the most vigorous arguments for this, both in terms of understanding how texts were perceived by ancient readers and in the reception/transmission history of the contents of the Book of the Twelve. See his essay "Is the Twelve Hypothesis Likely from an Ancient Reader's Perspective?" in Ben Zvi and Nogalski, *Two Sides of a Coin*, 47–96.

[65] The dissonances in the Book of the Twelve are found in the variety of geographical and

empowering a particular priestly group (in this case, the Levites).⁶⁶ The differences between the Pentateuch and the Book of the Twelve set them within highly distinct genres (the Pentateuch as a narrative; the Book of the Twelve as an oracular collection). Nevertheless, the points of contact between the two are strongly suggestive.

IV. Conclusion: The Redaction of the Pentateuch as an "Aramaic" Document

The present study sheds light on why the Pentateuch carries its unique narrative shape and structure: it bears the hallmark of an Aramaic text akin to those in the test cases examined above. The various precursor sources woven into narratives with contradictory details (Gen 6–9; 37; Exod 14) or attesting to variant versions of common traditions (Exod 17:1b–7; Num 20:2–13) and legal collections containing diametrically opposed visions of the cult and society (Covenant Code vs. Deuteronomy vs. P/H) are rendered hermeneutically consistent not by virtue of their content but, rather, *by virtue of their retextualization in Aramaic script*. In each of the test cases above, the disparate origins of the various sources are left in plain view as an affirmation of the new meaning derived from Aramaic retextualization. This would explain why the redactors of the Pentateuch also appear to have the unique character/origins of their sources in plain view. It is indeed the very *inconsistencies* in the sources that highlight how the new script transcends distinctions that would otherwise preclude cohesion.⁶⁷ Retextualization in Aramaic script connected all of the Pentateuch's sources to the intellectual cosmos of Aramaic scribal culture irrespective of distinctions in content.

These conclusions have implications for the redaction history of the Pentateuch's precursor sources. If the Aramaic Transition is what led to the Pentateuch possessing a topography favoring "comprehensiveness over coherence,"⁶⁸ then it becomes difficult to propose earlier circumstances whereby dissonant source texts would have been redacted in any like manner. No similar intellectual or political

---

social perspectives arranged in a manner that highlights their distinctiveness. The northern Hosea is followed by Judah-centric oracles in Joel and Amos; the rural voice of Micah is flanked by the international focus of both Jonah and Nahum; the Aaronide-centric Zechariah is prefaced by the royally focused Haggai and followed by the Levite-oriented Malachi.

⁶⁶ On this point, see further Mark Leuchter, *The Levites and the Boundaries of Israelite Identity* (Oxford: Oxford University Press, 2017), 214–47.

⁶⁷ On the redactional strategy regarding the discrepancies in the redacted sources, see Brian Peckham, "Writing and Editing," in *Fortunate the Eyes That See: Essays in Honor of David Noel Freedman in Celebration of His Seventieth Birthday*, ed. Astrid B. Beck et al. (Grand Rapids: Eerdmans, 1995), 364–83. Peckham identifies diachrony as a self-conscious feature of textual orchestration.

⁶⁸ Sanders, "Empirical Models," 301.

context would have led to a late preexilic or exilic combination of dissonant sources (e.g., the putative JE redaction in the eighth–seventh centuries BCE; an exilic non-P redaction, etc.) if the scribal norms of the day were influenced by Neo-Assyrian or Neo-Babylonian models.[69] Indeed, this late preexilic and exilic period sees a good deal of composition guided by a desire for ideological *coherence*, not comprehensiveness. Deuteronomy and Priestly oriented texts such as Ezekiel or H make reference to other traditions for the sake of displacing or exegetically transforming them, not preserving them.[70] It is only with the Aramaic Transition that we find a conceptual framework for seeing dissonant sources such as those undergirding the Pentateuch coming together in a manner that dovetails with what we know of the era's larger scribal culture as both an esoteric doctrine and a binding social force across the empire.

On one level, this compilation of the Pentateuch reflects an abiding support of the Persian imperial mythology. Just as the empire joined together various cultures ensconced in their provinces with native leadership, languages, rites, and traditions, so too did the Pentateuch make consistent a panoply of sources that once stood on their own and which, even redacted, still retain major dimensions of their original character. This lends support to theories regarding the redaction of the Pentateuch as a form of local law and a symbol of cultural or ideological negotiation

---

[69] For scholars who continue to advocate a JE redaction, see Richard Elliott Friedman, *Who Wrote the Bible?* (New York: Summit, 1987), 87–88; Baruch Halpern, "Late Israelite Astronomies and the Early Greeks," in *Symbiosis, Symbolism, and the Power of the Past: Canaan, Ancient Israel, and Their Neighbors from the Late Bronze Age through Roman Palaestina; Proceedings of the Centennial Symposium, W. F. Albright Institute of Archaeological Research and American Schools of Oriental Research, Jerusalem, May 29/31, 2000*, ed. William G. Dever and Seymour Gitin (Winona Lake, IN: Eisenbrauns, 2003), 323–52, here 323 n. 2. While the Deuteronomistic History does preserve disparate traditions, they are not arranged in the same way as the sources in the Pentateuch. The different traditions regarding Saul's rise to prominence (1 Sam 9:1–10:16; 10:17–27; 11) or David's emergence in the royal theater (1 Sam 16–17) are not parallel traditions of the same essential event (such as the flood narratives in Gen 6–9) but collections of diverse lore with evidence of the redactors' attempts to harmonize the sources into a linear and cohesive succession of events (e.g., the redactional additions in 1 Sam 11:12, 14 that attempt to account for the events reported in 1 Sam 10:27).

[70] On Deuteronomy's subversion of older laws (especially the Covenant Code), see Bernard M. Levinson, *Deuteronomy and the Hermeneutics of Legal Innovation* (New York: Oxford University Press, 1997), 144–51 and passim. On H's supplanting of Deuteronomic legislation, see Jeffrey Stackert, *Rewriting the Torah: Literary Revision in Deuteronomy and the Holiness Legislation*, FAT 52 (Tübingen: Mohr Siebeck, 2007), 209–25. Ezekiel's use of Deuteronomistic language reflects a currency of terminology rather than advocacy of a Deuteronomistic ethos. See Mark Leuchter, "The Medium and the Message, or, What is 'Deuteronomistic' about the Book of Jeremiah?," *ZAW* 126 (2014): 208–27, here 210–11. Ezekiel (or his disciples) clearly rejects Deuteronomy's vision of Levite legitimacy (Ezek 44:10–14) and older legal collections (Ezek 20:25–26).

in the formation of a Jewish *ethnos* within the imperial political landscape.⁷¹ It is clear, however, that this negotiation was not a matter of curbing traditional outlooks or attitudes. The Pentateuch served as a local iconic text symbolizing the place of these different and ancient Hebrew ideologies within a single *ethnos* that, in turn, was part of a multiethnic empire.⁷² Here, the rabbinic tradition in b. Sanh. 21b—22aα is remarkably accurate in much of what it preserves: Hebrew language written in Aramaic script constituted an ethnic boundary marker for the Yehudite community and related satellite groups with allegiances to it.⁷³

The details in b. Sanh. 21b–22aα also appears to preserve some accurate memories about the teaching tradition that accompanied the redaction of the Pentateuch or that emerged from it. According to James Watts, the Pentateuch was redacted to possess a rhetorical shape that reinforced the ritual power of the Aaronide priests and to secure their exclusive right to offer sacral instruction regarding its contents.⁷⁴ The reading of a ritual text with disjunctive, contrasting, and contradictory content invariably created opportunities for explanation to accompany the reading of these texts in plenary ceremonial contexts and for those extratextual explanations to take on the same binding authority as the ritual text itself.⁷⁵ Nehemiah 8 suggests as much when it specifies that scribal explanation carried the same authority as the written content itself; Uri Gabbay has argued that the phrase שום שכל in Neh 8:8 is a Hebrew calque of a comparable Aramaic phrase (שם טעם) and should be understood as "to give a (divine) order."⁷⁶ This explains why the additional, non-Pentateuchal provisions later in the chapter are qualified as ככתוב ("as

---

⁷¹ Hagedorn, "Local Law in an Imperial Context."

⁷² See similarly Fishbane, *Biblical Interpretation*, 123, in relation to disparate communities in Persian-period Judaism claiming distinct interpretive traditions of earlier Scripture.

⁷³ These groups would have included the Jews of the eastern diaspora, whence leaders in Persian Yehud repeatedly arose and in which group legitimacy was rooted. See Peter R. Bedford, "Diaspora: Homeland Relations in Ezra-Nehemiah," *VT* 52 (2002): 147–65; Rom-Shiloni, *Exclusive Inclusivity*, 1–29. This may explain why Ezra is commissioned to be the overseer of Jewish affairs not only in Yehud but throughout the entirety of Transeuphrates (Ezra 7:21, 25). Ideology and intellectual investment factored into group identity far more that geographical location.

⁷⁴ Watts, *Ritual and Rhetoric in Leviticus*, passim; Watts, *Reading Law: The Rhetorical Shaping of the Pentateuch*, BibSem 59 (Sheffield: Sheffield Academic, 1999); Watts, "Ritual and Rhetoric in Leviticus: The Case of Leviticus 1–16," in *The Books of Leviticus and Numbers*, ed. Thomas Römer, BETL 215 (Leuven: Leuven University Press, 2008), 305–18; Watts, "Scripturalization and the Aaronide Dynasties," *JHebS* 13 (2013): article 6, DOI: http://dx.doi.org/10.5508/jhs.2013.v13.a6.

⁷⁵ The sectarian work known as the *sefer gezirtah*, mentioned in *Megillat Ta'anit* 4, is an example of such corollary decrees and doctrines and points to an established practice among Aaronide priests whereby well-developed didactic discourses supported the ritual reading of the text.

⁷⁶ Uri Gabbay, "Hebrew *śôm śekel* (Neh. 8:8) in Light of Aramaic and Akkadian," *JSS* 59 (2014): 47–51.

it is written," Neh 8:15)—which might be better translated as "akin to that which is written" or, better, "equal to that which is written."[77]

As a public document, then, the redacted Pentateuch served as an icon of priestly ritual hegemony. But if the test cases noted above are any indication, the countenancing of the Pentateuch's sources also provided these priests with opportunities to cultivate teachings arising specifically from their newly orchestrated, Aramaized form. The relationship to the source scroll of Ezra 4–6 is especially significant: if the Aramaic script used to textualize foreign letters rendered their contents fair game for conceptual harmonization with Jerusalemite temple doctrines and prophetic texts, then—*kal va'chomer*—how much more so the use of Aramaic script in connecting the Pentateuch's Hebrew sources to one another for the same purpose. Teachings about the script itself must have developed within priestly circles, no doubt influenced by the older Babylonian scholarly tradition (promoted alongside Aramaic scribal culture of the era) that written characters could serve as divine portents of their own esoteric significance.[78] The Aramaized sources that were orchestrated into the Pentateuch served as both a pretext for and a prooftext of the Aaronide priests' claims to be able to mediate the new revelation emerging from these combined older texts and to develop a body of oral teaching to accompany it. If this is so, then the redaction of the Pentateuch as an Aramaic document calls for a renewed appreciation of an old rabbinic maxim—that, indeed, the oral Torah and written Torah originated together (b. Giṭ. 60a–b; Exod. Rab. 47:1).

---

[77] The diversity and range of this term's meaning are addressed by Joachim Schaper, "Torah and Identity in the Persian Period," in Lipschits, Knoppers, and Oeming, *Judah and the Judeans in the Achaemenid Period*, 27–38, here 31–33.

[78] Abraham Winitzer, "Writing and Mesopotamian Divination: The Case of Alternative Interpretation," *JCS* 63 (2011): 77–94, here 93; Winitzer, "The Divine Presence and Its Interpretation in Early Mesopotamian Divination," in *Divination and Interpretation of Signs in the Ancient World*, ed. Amar Annus, OIS 6 (Chicago: Oriental Institute of the University of Chicago, 2010), 192.

"Therefore a Man Leaves His Father and His Mother and Clings to His Wife": Marriage and Intermarriage in Genesis 2:24

MEGAN WARNER
meg.warner@kcl.ac.uk
King's College London, London WC2R 2LS, UK

In recent decades the opponents of same-sex marriage have mounted a "second front" in the debate, shifting their focus from the so-called clobber texts to the creation narratives of Genesis. These scholars argue that Gen 2:24 presents a normative definition of marriage that precludes same-sex marriage. I argue that Gen 2:24 offers not a normative definition of the institution of marriage but a description of the powerful draw to relationship that is the result of God's actions in creation. Just as interpreters of Gen 2:24 across centuries and traditions have approached the verse against the background of a wide range of presenting social issues (e.g., divorce, incest, polygamy, bestiality, and, more recently, homosexuality), so the authors of Gen 2:24 were influenced by a pressing social issue, namely, intermarriage. I explore this hypothesis by means of a word study focusing on the verse's two verbs. The results of the word study are further tested by consideration of the historical and literary contexts of the verse and of the earliest instances of reuse of Gen 2:24 in canonical and noncanonical texts. I conclude that, far from presenting a normative definition of heterosexual marriage, Gen 2:24 is an acknowledgment of the powerful attraction that causes human beings to seek relationship in opposition to the wishes of their parents, society, and religion.

I. Reading Genesis 2:24

A "Second Front"?

In the beginning there were the "clobber texts." Conservative Christian scholars have typically turned to this particular group of biblical passages in order to demonstrate biblical opposition to homosexuality and/or homosexual practice.

Although the individual texts in this group may vary from scholar to scholar, one might expect to find included Gen 19 (and perhaps Judg 19), Lev 18:22 and 20:13, Rom 1:26–27, 1 Cor 6:9–10, and 1 Tim 1:8–11.

More recently, perhaps due to a degree of battle fatigue from the entrenched nature of the debate, there has been an attempt to open a "second front" in this conflict. This second front involves an appeal to the creation narrative(s) of Genesis as a kind of foundation or key for the interpretation of these passages and for assessing biblical attitudes to sexuality more generally. Genesis 1:26–28 and 2:24 have received particular attention. The argument is that the creation narrative(s) reveal God's intended plan or blueprint for human sexuality and that this blueprint should be a guide for the exegesis of other biblical material addressing the topic. The views of Robert A. J. Gagnon are at the front line: "The creation stories of Genesis 1–3 do not speak directly to the issue of homosexual practice. However, they do supply us with a general understanding of human sexuality, set within the broader context of God's grand purposes at creation." About Gen 2:24 in particular Gagnon goes on to say:

> It will not do to argue that nothing is said here about the legitimacy of homosexual relationships. Even though an evaluation of same-sex intercourse is not the point of the text, legitimation for homosexuality requires an entirely different kind of creation story. Only a being made from man can be a suitable and complementary counterpart for him.… The story remains authoritative for conveying that the obvious complementarity (and concordant sexual attraction) of male and female witnesses to God's intent for human sexuality. Male and female are "perfect fits" from the standpoint of divine design and blessing. Male and male, or female and female are not.
>
> Hence, already at the start of the canon, in the description of human origins in Genesis 1–3, a justification for male–female union is provided: the physical, interpersonal, and procreative sexual complementarity of male and female. As we shall see, this motif will reappear as a continuous thread in the Old Testament, early Jewish, and New Testament critiques of same-sex intercourse as "contrary to nature."[1]

In recent decades this approach has increasingly gained ground, so that by 2012 Gordon Preece was able to write that the "primary weakness of a collection of Australian essays addressing the so-called clobber texts was its complete lack of a creation theology."[2]

In the face of rapidly changing attitudes toward homosexuality, especially in Western nations, it is easy to lose sight of the fact that Gen 2:24 has not always been

---

[1] Robert A. J. Gagnon, *The Bible and Homosexual Practice: Texts and Hermeneutics* (Nashville: Abingdon, 2001), 56, 61–62.

[2] Gordon Preece, "(Homo)Sex and the City of God: Sexual Ecology between Creation and New Creation," in *Sexegesis: An Evangelical Response to Five Uneasy Pieces on Homosexuality*, ed. Michael Bird and Gordon Preece (Brisbane: Anglican Press Australia, 2012), 25–47, here 25. The volume to which Preece was responding was *Five Uneasy Pieces: Essays on Scripture and Sexuality*, ed. Nigel Gordon McIver Wright (Adelaide: Australian Theological Foundation, 2011).

read with a particular eye toward issues of gender complementarity. In fact, the history of interpretation of Gen 2:24 has long been shaped by a wide range of social concerns. Christian readings are inevitably influenced by the reception of Gen 2:24 in the Gospels and Pauline letters, where the primary presenting issue is that of divorce (i.e., the permanence of marriage). These readings focus on the motif of "one flesh" in Gen 2:24.[3] At the center of the issue was an internal Jewish debate about the interpretation of "indecency" as a justifiable ground for divorce. The school of Hillel allowed divorce for a number of reasons on this ground (some apparently trivial), while the school of Shammai allowed divorce only for "sexual immorality."[4] Early Jewish commentary, on the other hand, features a particular interest in the issue of incest as it relates to non-Jews and tends to emphasize the motif of "leaving" family.[5] This not to say that neither early Christian nor Jewish readings of Gen 2:24 considered issues of gender complementarity; rather, such issues were not to the fore.[6] Across the last two millennia of interpretation of the verse, these two issues, divorce and incest, have dominated, although other readings relating to issues such as intermarriage, polygamy, and bestiality have appeared as these matters have waxed and waned as social issues.

What all of these readings share is an underlying conviction that Gen 2:24 offers a *normative* definition (i.e., what *must* happen) as opposed to a description (i.e., what *does* happen) of marriage. They proceed from an understanding that the

---

[3] What the New Testament writers do with Gen 2:24 (and 1:27) is not at all unlike the interpretive approach of the conservative evangelical scholars cited above but with a focus on *permanence* rather than *gender*. For example, Craig A. Evans writes, "If the intention of the creation of the male and female is for them to be united into ... 'one flesh' ... 'so that they are no longer two,' then God's will cannot be that they divorce. Divorce is tantamount to an undoing of the created order" (*Mark 8:27–16:20*, WBC 34B [Nashville: Nelson, 2001], 84).

[4] Donald A. Hagner, *Matthew 14–28*, WBC 33B (Dallas: Word, 1995), 547. D. E. Nineham notes that this was most likely a Jewish–Christian debate, given the easy availability of divorce in Rome (*The Gospel of St. Mark*, PNTC [Baltimore: Penguin, 1963], 264).

[5] See, e.g., Gen. Rab. P. 18 and the commentary of Rashi, "The Holy Spirit says this, to prohibit forbidden unions to the children of Noah"; translation by Michael A. Signer, "Coming to Consciousness: Knowing, Choosing or Stealing? Approaches to the Story of the Garden (Genesis 2–3) in Medieval Northern French Jewish Exegesis," in *Beyond Eden: The Biblical Story of Paradise (Genesis 2–3) and Its Reception History*, ed. Konrad Schmid and Christoph Riedweg, FAT 2/34 (Tübingen: Mohr Siebeck, 2008), 209–26, here 224. Rashi's commentary rests on b. Sanh. 58a, which cites Gen 2:24 and, like Gen. Rab. P. 18, offers a working out of marriage law for non-Jewish converts to Judaism. Jacob Neusner notes of Gen. Rab. P. 18, "The entire construction is relevant to the setting only because of the use of Gen. 2:24 as a proof text for propositions not related to its own exegesis" (*Genesis Rabbah: The Judaic Commentary to the Book of Genesis; A New American Translation*, 3 vols., BJS 104–6 [Atlanta: Scholars Press, 1985], 196).

[6] For example, Genesis Rabbah considers the application of Gen 2:24 to couplings between husband and wife that are not "normal" (see Neusner, *Genesis Rabbah*, 196), while b. Sanh. 58a, in the context of a larger debate about marriage rules concerning consanguinity for non-Jews, expressly notes that a male convert must not cling to another male. A footnote specifies that it is pederasty that is in view here.

account of God's creation of the first couple in Genesis can be seen, in the light of Gen 2:24, to offer a blueprint for marriage that is applicable today. The relative opacity of the narrative has meant that this normative definition has been sufficiently flexible and comprehensive to respond to a range of presenting social issues relating to marriage, some of which could not have been contemplated at the time when Gen 2:24 was composed.

The Hypothesis

The hypothesis explored here is that Gen 2:24 was never intended by its authors to function as a normative definition of marriage. Instead, the authors of Gen 2:24 were themselves responding to a pressing social issue of their own time, that of "intermarriage" between Israelites and non-Israelites. Their response in Gen 2:24 was not an attempt to legislate or warn against intermarriage. Rather, Gen 2:24 acknowledges the phenomenon and attributes it to God's actions in creation.

Following a brief introduction to Gen 2:24 itself, and to recent interpretive approaches, I will test the hypothesis by means of a word study, focusing especially on the verbs in Gen 2:24. The results of the study will be measured in terms of the interpretive "fit" of the new interpretation with the historical and literary contexts of Gen 2:24. Finally, I will ask whether there are any examples of reuse or interpretation of Gen 2:24 that indicate that the verse's earliest interpreters connected it with the issue of intermarriage.

II. SOME BACKGROUND TO GENESIS 2:24

Genesis 2:24 in Context

The immediate literary context of Gen 2:24, Gen 2:18–25, comprises a narrative about the creation of a "companion" or "helper" (עזר) for the first earth creature (אדם). After the repeated affirmations of the "goodness" of creation in Gen 1 (vv. 4, 10, 12, 18, 21, 25) and the final emphatic "very good" (v. 31), it comes as shock to discover in 2:18 an element of creation, the aloneness of the אדם, that is "not good." YHWH immediately proposes a solution and forms, out of the ground (אדמה), animals and birds and brings them to the אדם to be named. The אדם names all of the animals and birds but does not find among them an עזר to be his companion. YHWH then fashions a new creature from one of the "ribs" of the אדם. The אדם names the new creature "woman" (אשה), thus creating a wordplay connecting the two of them (איש/אשה) that resonates with the wordplay connecting the earth and the earth creature (אדמה/אדם).[7]

Our verse, Gen 2:24, follows, bringing a sense of discontinuity. Here the narrator intrudes for the first time in the narrative to comment on an aspect of the

---

[7] See the extended discussion of the wordplay in Phyllis Trible, "A Love Story Gone Awry," in *God and the Rhetoric of Sexuality* (Philadelphia: Fortress, 1978), 72–143.

action.⁸ The narrator refers to phenomena that are alien to the story world so far described; at this point there are only two humans and no concept of "father" or "mother" as in Gen 2:24. We return to the story in the final verse of the passage, Gen 2:25, in which the couple realize their nakedness without shame.

There is something of a scholarly consensus that Gen 2:24 is additional to its context. In this regard, a 1990 article by Angelo Tosato has been influential.⁹ Tosato noted that there had been many suggestions that Gen 2:24 "represents a secondary addition, an insertion, a gloss" but that there had been no extended exploration of the idea. He went on to examine a number of questions arising from the classification of Gen 2:24 as additional. The most pressing of these, once it is accepted that Gen 2:24 dates from a later period than the surrounding text, is the question of dating of the added verse. Tosato places Gen 2:24 in the (late) postexilic period, and this is a view likely to win considerable support.¹⁰ Unfortunately, pentateuchal scholarship is currently in such a state of flux that no single dating proposal could satisfy all, or even a clear majority of, scholars with an interest in the matter.¹¹ Few European scholars would consider an earlier dating, while a sizable number of Israeli and American scholars might be expected to favor an exilic or even preexilic date. Tosato's own arguments in support of a postexilic dating are of uneven strength. The first runs the danger of circularity; he identifies the postexilic period as a time of a "reforming movement which led among other things to rigorous matrimonial legislation and jurisdiction."¹² Tosato reads Gen 2:24 as reflecting a newly "rigorous" approach to matrimonial understanding that places it naturally in this period. A further reason is stronger. Tosato points to a "total absence of allusions to Gen 2:24 in preexilic and exilic writings" but argues that texts that are very "close" appear in the postexilic period, while references to Gen 2:24 can be found in materials from the Hellenistic period.¹³ This absence of allusion to Gen 2:24 prior to the return from exile is a compelling reason for dating Gen 2:24 in the postexilic period.

The Character of Genesis 2:24

Most commentators agree that Gen 2:24 is, by nature, explanatory or "etiological."¹⁴ Tosato asks whether Gen 2:24 is etiological on a juridical (or normative)

---

⁸Gordon J. Wenham, *Genesis 1–15*, WBC 1 (Waco, TX: Word, 1987), 70: "This is not a continuation of the man's remarks in v23, but a comment of the narrator, applying the principles of the first marriage to every marriage."

⁹Angelo Tosato, "On Genesis 2:24," *CBQ* 52 (1990): 389–409.

¹⁰Ibid., 406–7.

¹¹See Thomas Römer, "The Elusive Yahwist: A Short History of Research," in *A Farewell to the Yahwist? The Composition of the Pentateuch in Recent European Interpretation*, ed. Thomas B. Dozeman and Konrad Schmid, SymS 34 (Atlanta: Society of Biblical Literature, 2006), 9–27.

¹²Tosato, "On Genesis 2:24," 407.

¹³Ibid., 407–9.

¹⁴Robert Alter, *The Art of Biblical Narrative* (New York: Basic Books, 1981), 31. Michaela

level (i.e., what one *must* do) or on a factual (or descriptive) level (i.e., what one *does* do).[15] He concludes, with many others, that the former is the case.[16] On the other side of the debate stand Gerhard von Rad and Claus Westermann, who take the view that Gen 2:24 is *not* a normative statement about the institution of marriage. Instead, they argue, Gen 2:24 presents an explanation of a phenomenon of nature, namely, "the extremely powerful drive of the sexes to each other."[17] This "powerful drive" is the result of the manner in which men and women were created and, in particular, of the fact that women and men were once a single entity, which was divided and which seeks unification. So von Rad goes on to say:

> Whence comes this love "strong as death" (S. of Sol. 8.6) and stronger than the tie to one's own parents, whence this inner clinging to each other, this drive toward each other which does not rest until it again becomes one flesh in the child? It comes from the fact that God took woman from man, that they actually were originally *one* flesh. Therefore they must come together again and thus by destiny they belong to each other.[18]

Similarly, Westermann speaks of the important role taken by parents in the arrangement of marriages for their children, which is evident "from the patriarchal stories right up to the book of Tobit." Nevertheless, he says, "the significance of the verse lies in this, that in contrast to the established institutions *and partly in opposition to them*, it points to the basic power of love between man and woman."[19]

Both von Rad and Westermann make the point that Gen 2:24 does not set up a normative standard but rather explains the extraordinarily strong force that causes those who marry or who otherwise embark in relationship *to do so regardless of the normative standards that parents and society typically aim to enforce*. This is a very different understanding of Gen 2:24 from that held by those who read Gen 2:24 as a normative definition of marriage. Far from being a "conservative" prescription of how things must be (normative), Gen 2:24 becomes a radically honest appraisal of how things actually are (descriptive). *The radical element of the appraisal lies in the*

Bauks expressly follows Alter in describing Gen 2:24 as an "etiological note" ("Text- and Reception-Historical Reflections on Transmissional and Hermeneutical Techniques in Genesis 2–3," in *The Pentateuch: International Perspectives on Current Research*, ed. Thomas B. Dozeman, Konrad Schmid, and Baruch J. Schwartz, FAT 78 [Tübingen: Mohr Siebeck, 2011], 139–68, esp. 145). See also Tosato, "On Genesis 2:24," 409; Gerhard von Rad, *Genesis: A Commentary*, trans. John H. Marks, OTL (Philadelphia: Westminster, 1961), 82 ("entirely aetiological"); and Claus Westermann, *Genesis 1–11: A Commentary*, trans. John J. Scullion S.J. (Minneapolis: Augsburg, 1974), 233 ("etiological motif").

[15] Tosato, "On Genesis 2:24," 405.
[16] Ibid., 409.
[17] Von Rad, *Genesis*, 82; Westermann, *Genesis 1–11*, 233 ("an explanation of 'the basic drive of the sexes to each other'"). See also the analogous comments of David W. Cotter, *Genesis*, Berit Olam (Collegeville, MN: Liturgical Press, 2003), 32–33.
[18] Von Rad, *Genesis*, 82–83.
[19] Westermann, *Genesis 1–11*, 233 (emphasis added).

fact that opposition to parental or societal authority is attributed to God's actions in creation. The drive for the genders to be united, even if inconvenient, is the direct result of the creative activity of God. Which approach is closer to the original intent of the interpolator(s) of Gen 2:24? The first step toward answering that question will be a close consideration of the distinctive language found in Gen 2:24.

III. The Distinctive Language of Genesis 2:24

The opening phrase of the verse, עֽל־כֵּן ("therefore"), demonstrates the connection between the interpolated verse and the preceding narrative. It indicates that the phenomenon being explained in Gen 2:24 is a result of the events recounted in Gen 2:4b–23 and especially 2:18–23. The two most important words of the verse for our purposes are the two verbs, "leave" (עזב) and "cling" (דבק).[20]

עזב—"to leave"

The first of these verbs, עזב, is relatively well attested in the Hebrew Bible, appearing 261 times with a range of meanings. In translations of Gen 2:24 into English it is generally translated with the simple sense "leave." There are other places where עזב, in the qal (as here), takes this relatively simple sense. An example is Gen 39:12, in which Joseph "leaves" his garment in the hand of Potiphar's wife in his urgency to escape her advances. The use of the verb in the Hebrew Bible most closely analogous to Gen 2:24 is found in Ruth 2:11: "But Boaz answered her, 'All that you have done for your mother-in-law since the death of your husband has been fully told me, and how you left [עזב] your father and mother and your native land and came to a people that you did not know before.'" The resonances between Ruth 2:11 and Gen 2:24 are immediately apparent and will be discussed further below. For the moment we can note that עזב is traditionally translated with the same sense in Ruth 2:11 as it is in Gen 2:24.

The verb עזב is more often used in the Hebrew Bible, however, with the more dramatic sense "to abandon" or "to forsake." This is the case, for example, in the many instances in which the verb is used in relation to Israel's propensity to betray YHWH by the worship of other gods. For example:

> It is because they abandoned [עזב] the covenant of the Lord.... (Deut 29:25)

> If you forsake [עזב] the Lord and serve foreign gods, then he will turn and do you harm and consume you, after having done you good. (Josh 24:20)

> Yet you have abandoned [עזב] me and worshiped other gods.... (Judg 10:6)

---

[20] English translations that adopt the translation "leave" owe something to the KJV, which introduced a wordplay between "leave" and "cleave." For biblical quotations in this article, I follow the NRSV with some modifications.

The same term is used in respect of YHWH's commitment to Israel, which YHWH will not break, despite Israel's fickleness:

> It is the LORD your God who goes with you; he will not fail you or forsake [עזב] you. (Deut 31:6)

> I will dwell among the children of Israel and will not forsake [עזב] my people Israel. (1 Kgs 6:13)

The sense in each of these verses is that an act of abandoning somebody in a relational context is a serious matter, with consequences for the ongoing life of the relationship. Moreover, in the context of the divine relationship, an act of עזב is akin to adultery, in which YHWH is betrayed when the Israelites go after other gods.

The rendering of the verb עזב in most English translations of Gen 2:24 as "leaves," then, is a relatively pale rendering. Much of the strength of the Hebrew verb is lost.[21] The verb is generally understood in the sense that the man leaves his parents' *house*. Yet the word "house" does not appear in the text—the man "leaves" or, better, "abandons" his parents themselves. The "abandoning" of one's parents is not generally something encouraged in the Hebrew Scriptures! On the contrary, one of their foundational directives is the injunction to "honor" one's father and one's mother (Exod 20:12; Deut 5:16). In the face of this commandment, the description in Gen 2:24 of "abandoning" parents is surprising. Mark G. Brett goes further: "The idea of 'abandoning' parents represents a potentially scandalous subversion of the conventional Israelite obligations to mother and father."[22] To the same end Samuel Terrien writes:

> In the ancient Near Eastern and most other cultures, patriarchal lineage prevailed in such a way that the primary bond of solidarity was the duty of a man toward his ancestors in general and to his progenitors in particular. To honor one's father and mother was the most sacred obligation of social responsibility (Exod. 20:12; Deut. 5:16). By dramatic contrast, the Yahwist theologian scandalously upsets, even shockingly reverses, this deep-rooted principle of tribal morality.[23]

To conclude this discussion of the use of עזב in Gen 2:24, we note, first, its covenantal overtones. This verb is regularly used in relation to the behavior of Israel, when Israel forsakes its God and follows other gods. Second, in the ancient Near Eastern context and especially in the light of the Sinai/Horeb directive to

---

[21] Mark G. Brett, *Genesis: Procreation and the Politics of Identity*, OTR (London: Routledge, 2000), 31.

[22] Ibid.

[23] Samuel Terrien, *Till the Heart Sings: A Biblical Theology of Manhood and Womanhood* (Philadelphia: Fortress, 1985), 14–15. See also Wenham, *Genesis 1–15*, 71: "In traditional societies like Israel where honoring parents is the highest human obligation next to honoring God, this remark about forsaking them is very striking."

honor "your father and your mother," the idea of "leaving" parents is not as straightforward as the usual English translation of עזב in Gen 2:24 would make it sound.

דבק—"to cling"

The second verb in Gen 2:24, דבק ("to cling"), is attested far less frequently in the Hebrew Bible than עזב. It appears only sixty-one times. Again, this verb has a range of meanings, and a prominent meaning for the verb is covenantal in nature. Probably the most common use of the word is to indicate the proper attitude of the Israelites to YHWH, which is to "cling" or "hold fast" to their God. A good example is Deut 13:4:

> The LORD your God you shall follow, him alone you shall fear, his commandments you shall keep, his voice you shall obey, him you shall serve, and to him you shall hold fast [דבק].

Further examples may be found in Deut 4:4, 10:20, 11:22, 30:20, Josh 22:5, 23:8, 2 Kgs 18:6, Jer 13:11, and Ps 119:31. An inversion of this idea is found in 2 Kgs 3:3, where the evil king Jehoram, son of Ahab, is said to have clung not to YHWH but to the sins of Jeroboam. In this sense, דבק is the opposite of עזב: Israel should not have *forsaken* YHWH but should have *clung* to its God.

One particular covenantal context in which the verb דבק is used, although not frequently, is marriage. Of the sixty-one times that the verb דבק appears in the Hebrew Bible, four instances (apart from Gen 2:24) are clearly associated with marriage:

> And his [Shechem the Hivite's] soul clung [דבק] to Dinah, daughter of Jacob. (Gen 34:3)

> For if you turn back, and join the survivors of these nations left here among you, and cling [דבק] with them, so that you marry their women and they yours ... (Josh 23:12)

> King Solomon loved many foreign women along with the daughter of Pharaoh: Moabite, Ammonite, Edomite, Sidonian, and Hittite women, from the nations concerning which the LORD had said to the Israelites, "You shall not enter into marriage with them, neither shall they with you; for they will surely incline your heart to follow their gods"; Solomon clung [דבק] to these in love. (1 Kgs 11:1–2)

> As you saw the iron mixed with clay, so will they mix with one another in marriage, but they will not hold together [דבק], just as iron does not mix with clay. (Dan 2:43)

The remarkable thing about these verses is that all four concern not just marriage but intermarriage. The issue of intermarriage, although not apparent on the face of Gen 34:3 above, is made explicit in Gen 34:21: "These people are friendly with us; let them live in the land and trade in it, for the land is large enough for them; let us take their daughters in marriage and let us give them our daughters." In Josh 23:12 Joshua warns the Israelites that intermarriage with those remaining in the land will act as a snare, causing the Israelites to perish in the land that God had given them. 1 Kings 11:12 concerns a chronic intermarrier, King Solomon. Finally, in the much later text Dan 2:43, Daniel interprets the dream of King Nebuchadnezzar, likening intermarriage to the mixing of iron with clay—the two will not hold together.

The connection between the idea of intermarriage and the covenantal sense of the verb is most apparent in Josh 23:12; intermarriage acts as a snare so that "clinging" to foreign women may cause Israelite men to fail to "cling" to YHWH as they ought. This link is made also in Exod 34:11–16 and Deut 7:1–6, especially verses 3–4: "Do not intermarry with them, giving your daughters to their sons or taking their daughters for your sons, for that would turn your children away from following me, to serve other gods." The same sense can be seen in 1 Kgs 11, where our two verbs, עזב and דבק, are used in contradistinction (albeit thirty-one verses apart). While verse 2 says that Solomon clung (דבק) to foreign women in love, in verse 33 YHWH says, through Ahijah the prophet, that he is going to tear the kingdom from the hand of Solomon *because* Solomon had forsaken (עזב) YHWH, worshiping other gods and failing to keep the Torah. These verses are, therefore, essentially covenantal in nature, even if focused directly on the particular covenant of marriage. This sense is picked up by Terrien:

> Just as the verb "to forsake" implies the breaking of a covenant, so also the verb "to cleave" designates its maintenance, not only with outward respect for the commitment but also with the inner compulsion of love. The Deuteronomic style favors this notion whenever it refers to the covenant between Yahweh and Israel, especially from the latter's point of view: Israel is asked to *cleave* to Yahweh, *forsaking* all other gods.[24]

There is *only one other place* in the Hebrew Bible where the verb דבק is used in the context of relationships between individual people. In the book of Ruth, the verb appears four times, and each occurrence is concerned with relationships between individuals. In Ruth 1:14, Ruth "clings" (דבק) to Naomi, unlike Orpah who kisses her mother-in-law and leaves her. In Ruth 2:8, Boaz tells Ruth to "stay close" (דבק) to his young women, and in 2:21 Ruth reports this instruction to Naomi, again using דבק. In Ruth 2:23, the narrator reports that Ruth "stayed close" (דבק) to Boaz's young women, just as Boaz had instructed her. While none of these instances is directly related to marriage, the central focus of the book is the unlikely, even scandalous, marriage union between Boaz and the Moabite woman who became the ancestor of King David. We saw above that the verb עזב is also used in Ruth 2:11, so that in this respect Ruth is like 1 Kgs 11, where the verbs are used in contradistinction. In short, in the only other book in the Hebrew Bible in which דבק is used in connection with relationships between individuals, the context is again that of intermarriage.

---

[24] Terrien, *Till the Heart Sings*, 15 (emphasis original).

IV. Does Genesis 2:24 Contain an Allusion to Intermarriage?

What are we to make of the results of this word study? It is certainly striking that the authors of Gen 2:24 use these two distinctively covenantal terms in contradistinction to each other. In fact, Gen 2:24 is unique in that nowhere else in the Hebrew Bible are these two covenantal verbs to be found in the same verse. Even more striking is the fact that *every other instance* of the use of the verb דבק in the Hebrew Bible in the context of relationships between individuals concerns the issue of intermarriage. Further, in two of those five instances the two verbs, עזב and דבק, are used in contradistinction as they are here (even if not in a single verse).

This must raise the issue for us whether Gen 2:24 ought also to be interpreted as alluding to intermarriage.[25] The very least that can be said is that we ought not deny the possibility without further exploration. Three questions in particular can help us to explore further the hypothesis that Gen 2:24 alludes to intermarriage:

1. Is there a time when intermarriage may have been a pressing concern for the authors of Gen 2:24?
2. Does the literary context in which Gen 2:24 has been placed reflect concern with the issue of intermarriage?
3. Has Gen 2:24 been reused in the context of intermarriage?

Is There a Time When Intermarriage May Have Been a Pressing Concern for the Authors of Genesis 2:24?

The short answer to this first question is yes. We have already identified the postexilic period as the most likely time for the composition of Gen 2:24. Witnesses such as Ezra-Nehemiah, Ruth, Tobit, and Malachi point to the issue of intermarriage as having been to the fore during that period.[26] The various texts written during that time also clearly suggest the prevalence of more than a single view about the issue.[27]

---

[25] For a recent discussion of allusion and other intertextual approaches, see Cynthia Edenburg, "Intertextuality, Literary Competence and the Question of Readership: Some Preliminary Observations," *JSOT* 35 (2010): 131–48.

[26] The literature on this topic is extensive. See, e.g., Sebastian Grätz, "The Second Temple and the Legal Status of the Torah: The Hermeneutics of the Torah in the Books of Ruth and Ezra," in *The Pentateuch as Torah: New Models for Understanding Its Promulgation and Acceptance*, ed. Gary N. Knoppers and Bernard M. Levinson (Winona Lake, IN: Eisenbrauns, 2007), 273–87; Mark G. Brett, "Politics of Marriage in Genesis," in *Making a Difference: Essays on the Bible and Judaism in Honor of Tamara Cohn Eskenazi*, ed. David J. A. Clines, Kent Harold Richards, and Jacob L. Wright (Sheffield: Sheffield Phoenix, 2012), 49–59; Christian Frevel, ed., *Mixed Marriages: Intermarriage and Group Identity in the Second Temple Period*, LHBOTS 547 (New York: T&T Clark International, 2011).

[27] See, e.g., Grätz, "Second Temple," 284–87; Gary N. Knoppers, "Intermarriage, Social

As we saw above, Tosato argues that "the appearance and the consolidation, in the Jewish community of the advanced Persian period, of a reforming movement which led among other things to rigorous matrimonial legislation and jurisdiction" support a dating for Gen 2:24 in the (late) Persian period.[28] Tosato includes the following as a "norm" adopted by that movement: "(a) the prohibition of taking as a wife a woman of another race (= of another religion) or in a close degree of relationship or affinity."[29] One of Tosato's conclusions indicates that he considers it possible that intermarriage was in the view of the authors of Gen 2:24:

> The sense of Gen 2:24 is not that of an etiology concerning sexual drive or love, but rather that of an etiology concerning matrimonial legislation adopted in this period; referring to the work of the Creator himself, the glossator intends to explain and thus to found and better justify the new norm which was generically antipolygamous and implicitly antidivorce (Lev 18:18; cf. Mal 2:13–16), and perhaps also the new restrictive norms in the area of incestuous and mixed marriages (Leviticus 18 and 20; cf. Mal 2:10–11).[30]

Tosato's observation about incest and mixed marriages is unsupported apart from the fact that his views about the date of Gen 2:24 and the prevalence of this issue coincide.[31] The real limitation of Tosato's reading, however, is that he takes for granted that any allusion to the issue of intermarriage during this period would be generally supportive of Ezra's exclusivist program. It does not occur to him that an allusion to intermarriage might intend some degree of opposition to that program. This, however, is precisely the view of Brett, who continues his remarks about the translation of עזב in Gen 2:24 with the following:

> In a context where men were being urged to leave their foreign wives, however, the peculiar strength of this language may well be explained by reading the verse as suggesting a priority of commitments: the kinship bond with the wife stands above that of the parents, and in this sense, marriage comes before bloodlines. The notion of the "holy seed" suggests the reverse—that marriage has to conform to the bloodlines.[32]

Complexity, and Ethnic Diversity in the Genealogy of Judah," *JBL* 120 (2001): 15–30; Georg Braulik, "The Book of Ruth as Intra-Biblical Critique on the Deuteronomic Law," *AcT* 19 (1999): 1–20; Michael Fishbane, *Biblical Interpretation in Ancient Israel* (Oxford: Clarendon, 1985), 123.

[28] Tosato, "On Genesis 2:24," 406–7.
[29] Ibid., 407 (parentheses original).
[30] Ibid., 409.
[31] We noted above the circularity of his argument. Some degree of circularity may not be fatal, so long as there are other supporting and collaborative arguments.
[32] Brett, *Genesis*, 31.

Does the Literary Context in Which Genesis 2:24 Has Been Placed Reflect Concern with the Issue of Intermarriage?

In contrast to homosexuality, the issue of intermarriage is one of special interest in Genesis.[33] Despite YHWH's initial call to Abram in Gen 12:1–3 to *leave* his country, his kindred, and his father's house, Abraham takes great care to ensure that a wife for Isaac is found from among his kin (Gen 24:3–4). Isaac, in turn, sends his son Jacob to Abraham's family to find a wife, telling him, "You shall not marry one of the Canaanite women" (Gen 28:1). Similarly, Hagar, the Egyptian mother of Abraham's son Ishmael, gets a wife for him from the land of Egypt (Gen 21:21). Not all the patriarchal sons, however, toe the family line. Isaac's son Esau marries two Hittite women, much to the frustration of his parents. Similarly, Jacob's daughter Dinah becomes entangled with a foreigner (this is one of the four uses of the verb דבק in a marriage context that we saw earlier), setting off waves of interethnic violence.[34]

The rest of Genesis bears witness both to a practice of parents seeking ethnically appropriate partners for their children (usually sons) and to the phenomenon of sons choosing ethnically inappropriate partners, to the frustration of their parents. Brett, returning to this issue in a 2012 essay writes, "In effect, I am suggesting that the pious appearance of endogamy in the characterisation of Abraham, Isaac and Jacob is being relentlessly exposed by the final editors as contrary to divine commands. This suggestion might well be considered preposterous, were it not executed with such consistency in the texts as we have them."[35]

On the other hand, interpretations of Gen 2:24 that argue for a *normative* etiology of marriage *do not* fit well with the rest of Genesis. These interpretations read Gen 2:24 as establishing a normative pattern in which a man leaves his parents' house and clings to his wife. There are two problems with this reading. First, Gen 2:24 does not speak of the איש abandoning/forsaking his parents' *house* but rather his parents. Second, the marriage practice reflected in Genesis is not matriarchal/matrilocal but

---

[33] The one oft-cited exception to the lack of interest in homosexuality in Genesis is in chapter 19, where the men of Sodom seek to have "knowledge of" two male visitors. This narrative is often included as one of the "clobber texts." As many scholars have noted, however, the story concerns gang rape rather than consensual sexual activity between males, and it is entirely probable that the visitors' divine or semidivine natures were of more significance for the authors than their gender. Further, the reception history of the narrative is focused primarily on the issue of inhospitality to strangers. The sexual aggression in the story may be merely an element of this inhospitality. See, e.g., von Rad, *Genesis*, 212–13; Brett, *Genesis*, 68.

[34] In that case, even though the text indicates that the Hivite man in question seduced (perhaps raped) Dinah, the real problem was not the violence of the seduction but the nationality of the suitor. See Lyn M. Bechtel, "What If Dinah Is Not Raped? (Gen 34)," *JSOT* 19 (1994): 19–36; Brett, "Politics of Marriage."

[35] Brett, "Politics of Marriage," 53.

patriarchal/patrilocal.³⁶ In other words, Genesis reflects not a culture in which a man leaves the house of his parents in order to marry but rather one in which a woman leaves the house of her parents to join her husband. For example, when Isaac marries he brings his wife into his mother's tent (Gen 24:67), and after Dinah is seduced by Shechem she is taken by him into his house (Gen 34:26).

Has Genesis 2:24 Been Reused in the Context of Intermarriage?

The short answer to this third question is yes. There are instances of reuse of Gen 2:24 in late biblical, deuterocanonical and pseudepigraphical texts, although the connections have not often been discussed. The texts that I will consider here are Ruth 2:11, Mal 2:10–16, 1 Esdr 3–5 and Tob 6:18.

Ruth 2:11

Having noted already the analogous use in Ruth of our two verbs, עזב in Ruth 2:11 and דבק in 1:14, and 2:8, 21, 23, I discuss here the extent of the parallel between Gen 2:24 and Ruth 2:11. Ruth 2:11 reads:

> But Boaz answered her, "All that you have done for your mother-in-law since the death of your husband has been fully told me, and how you left [עזב] your father and mother and your native land and came to a people that you did not know before."

The verb עזב appears here, as does the motif of leaving father and mother. Ruth left her father and mother and clung first to Naomi and then to Boaz's young women. Interestingly, Ruth 2:11 appears to allude not only to Gen 2:24 but also Gen 12:1; Ruth leaves not only her parents but also the land of her kin (both Gen 12:1 and Ruth 2:11 use מולדת rather than משפחה) to go to an unknown country.³⁷ These parallels are too extensive to be coincidental.³⁸

Ruth's "leaving" is an abandonment in the full sense of the covenant term. Ruth radically abandons not only her parents (who are never elsewhere mentioned) but also her lodging, her people, and her God (Ruth 1:16). Such abandonment is the inevitable consequence of covenantal relationships with foreigners of which Deut 7:1–7 warns. It is presumably also reflective of the extent of the conversion required for a Moabite to be admitted to the status of honorary Israelite. The story

---

³⁶ Wenham, *Genesis 1–15*, 70: "The traditional interpretation 'leaves' suggests that the man moved from his parents and set up home elsewhere, whereas in fact Israelite marriage was usually patrilocal, that is, the man continued to live in or near his parents' home. It was the wife who left home to join her husband." See also A. F. L. Beeston, "One Flesh," *VT* 36 (1986): 115–17.

³⁷ Grätz, "Second Temple," 281–82.

³⁸ Irmtraud Fischer, *Rut*, 2nd ed., HThKAT (Freiburg im Breisgau: Herder, 2005), 86–91; Grätz, "Second Temple," 282. There is, of course, an inversion here, in that it is the foreign woman who "leaves" her family and country.

itself must have been shocking to its earliest readers. The idea that a Moabite woman should gain admission to the extent of becoming part of the genealogy of King David himself (Ruth 4) was dramatically at odds not only with Deut 7:1–7 but also with the prohibition in Deut 23:3–6 against the admission of Moabites to the assembly and the whole tenor of the intermarriage polemic in Ezra-Nehemiah. As Bernard M. Levinson has observed,

> In deriving the legendary founder of the United Monarchy itself from such a union, it becomes clear the extent to which Ruth's assumptions about Israelite identity (the legal and religious status of foreigners, ethnicity, and intermarriage) offer a very different vision of the community and its boundaries than that articulated in Ezra and Nehemiah.[39]

Although it is possible to say with some confidence that the parallel between Gen 2:24 and Ruth 2:11 cannot be accidental, it is not possible to be certain about the direction of dependence running between them. The book of Ruth is now, like Gen 2:24, generally dated to the Persian period.[40] This makes it impossible to say authoritatively which verse is a reuse of the other. It would certainly strengthen our hypothesis if it were possible to establish that Gen 2:24 was the later text and dependent on Ruth 2:11. Nevertheless, even if Ruth 2:11 is a reuse of Gen 2:24, such reuse in the context of a book that "seeks to revise and liberalize the requirements of Deuteronomy regarding ... the exclusion of Moabites from the community (Deut 23:4–5 [English, 23:3–4]); and the laws of levirate marriage (Deut 25:5–10)" certainly supports my hypothesis.[41]

1 Esdras 3–5

Genesis 2:24 is clearly referenced in the Tale of the Three Youths in 1 Esdras.[42] Three of King Darius's bodyguards compete to say what is "the strongest." Zerubbabel's answer, "women," is judged wiser than the other answers—"wine" and "the king." In 1 Esdr 4:20–21 Zerubbabel says, "A man leaves [ἐγκαταλείπει] his own father, who brought him up, and his own country, and clings [κολλᾶται] to his wife.[43] With his wife he ends his days, with no thought of his father or his mother or his country." Then in 4:25, "A man loves his wife more than his father or his mother." Here we see repeated the motif of the man leaving mother and father in order to cling to his wife in such a manner that the kinship with his wife becomes superior

---

[39] Bernard M. Levinson, *Legal Revision and Religious Renewal in Ancient Israel* (Cambridge: Cambridge University Press, 2008), 44.

[40] Ibid., 34.

[41] Ibid., 35. The fact the Ruth 2:11 appears to reference both Gen 2:24 and 12:1 tends to support the idea that it may be later than Gen 2:24.

[42] Zipora Talshir, *1 Esdras: From Origin to Translation*, SCS 47 (Atlanta: Society of Biblical Literature, 1999), 195.

[43] These verbs echo the verbs used in the LXX of Gen 2:24.

to the kinship with his parents, to whom no further thought is given.[44] As in Ruth, the element of leaving one's country is added. Whereas in Ruth this element was reflected in the narrative (Ruth left Moab in order to follow Naomi), here it is unnecessary in terms of the logic of the text.[45] What is particularly interesting here is the *reason* why a man does this. Zerubbabel's winning argument is that women are stronger than wine or kings because of the extraordinary attraction that they have for men. They cause men to do things that they otherwise would not do and of which they might not otherwise approve:

> If men gather gold and silver or any other beautiful thing, and then see a woman lovely in appearance and beauty, they let all those things go, and gape at her, and with open mouths stare at her, and all prefer her to gold or silver or any other beautiful thing.... Many men have lost their minds because of women, and have become slaves because of them. Many have perished, or stumbled, or sinned because of women. (1 Esdr 4:18–19, 26–27)

This kind of draw, or attraction, to women is the precise phenomenon that von Rad and Westermann see reflected in Gen 2:24. 1 Esdras 4 could be considered a midrash on Gen 2:24, further explicating the effects of the process by which woman was created by God from the body of the man.

In contrast to the book of Ruth, the context here is not explicitly that of intermarriage. Two things, however, suggest that intermarriage is in view. The first is Zerubbabel's repeated reference to the fact that women cause men to *leave their country* and to have no further thought for it. Inasmuch as this element is unnecessary in terms of narrative logic, it is quite possible that here the author of 1 Esdras is simply quoting Ruth. On the other hand, the repeated emphatic reference to leaving one's country suggests a deliberate theme. The second thing to bear in mind is that 1 Esdras as a whole is a subversive retelling of Ezra-Nehemiah.[46] The principal subversive element noted by scholars is the magnification of Zerubbabel's role in the restoration of his people, including his replacement of Nehemiah as temple builder.[47] Although the incident of the foreign wives is not part of the Ezra-Nehemiah tradition that 1 Esdras appropriates, nevertheless the issue of intermarriage and

---

[44] William Loader argues that this element of the forgetting of parents "twists the original into something negative, contrary to the Genesis text, and brings it into conflict with values about honouring parents" (*The Pseudepigrapha on Sexuality: Attitudes towards Sexuality in Apocalypses, Testaments, Legends, Wisdom, and Related Literature*, Attitudes towards Sexuality in Judaism and Christianity in the Hellenistic Greco-Roman Era [Grand Rapids: Eerdmans, 2011], 144). This conflict, however, is already present in Gen 2:24.

[45] Although Michael F. Bird notes that this element reflects "the relational and geographical fracture often caused by taking a wife," this need not necessarily reflect the full sense of the reference to "country" here (*1 Esdras: Introduction and Commentary on the Greek Text in Codex Vaticanus*, Septuagint Commentary Series [Leiden: Brill, 2012], 169–70).

[46] See the comments below about the literary relationship between the two texts.

[47] See, e.g., Talshir, *1 Esdras*, 46–47, 54–57.

Ezra's determined opposition to it is integral to the Ezra-Nehemiah tradition as a whole. The author of 1 Esdras, therefore, can hardly be thought to be writing without thought of it. In the context of Ezra-Nehemiah, Zerubbabel's words about men's propensity to be influenced by women so as to act inappropriately, even so as to forget their own country, are inflammatory.[48]

There is no scholarly consensus about the relative dating of Ezra-Nehemiah and 1 Esdras or about the direction of dependence between them.[49] Both are likely to belong to the Persian or Hellenistic periods, but the safest assumption is probably that 1 Esdras is the later document. Nevertheless, this uncertainty about dating leaves open the possibility that 1 Esdras and Gen 2:24 were composed at roughly similar times and that they reflect a single tradition about men, women, and marriage that can also be seen in books such as Ruth and Tobit.

Tobit 6:18

An allusion to Gen 2:24 in Tobit is less clear but has nevertheless been observed.[50] In Tob 6:18, when Tobias learns that his intended wife, Sarah, is "his kinswoman, related through his father's lineage" he loves her and his heart is drawn (ἐκολλήθη) to her.[51] It is obvious, even in this one verse, that the issue of the "appropriate wife" is particularly strong in the book. The influence of the ancestral narratives of Genesis, including the story in chapter 24 of Abraham's procuration of a wife for Isaac from among his kin, is evident. Tobit has been viewed as presenting an "exact opposite" to the allusion to Gen 2:24 in 1 Esdras 4 because here Tobias does not forget his parents.[52]

To be sure, the allusion to Gen 2:24 in Tobit is different from those in Ruth and 1 Esdras. Although the issue of intermarriage is to the fore, the book's general

---

[48] Intriguingly, Talshir argues that 1 Esdras was composed precisely for the purpose of presenting the story of the three youths (*1 Esdras*, 58). Although others have queried whether the story is sufficiently important to warrant such attention, the idea that the story comments on the intermarriage issue in a subversive manner would answer that query handsomely. See, e.g., James C. VanderKam, "Literary Questions between Ezra, Nehemiah, and 1 Esdras," in *Was 1 Esdras First? An Investigation into the Priority and Nature of 1 Esdras*, ed. Lisbeth S. Fried, AIL 7 (Atlanta: Society of Biblical Literature, 2011), 131–43, here 134 n.10.

[49] See the collected essays addressing these issues in Fried, *Was 1 Esdras First?* It is of course possible that neither is directly dependent on the other. Kristen De Troyer argues that 1 Esdras is dependent on a now lost Hebrew-Aramaic rewritten account (*Rewriting the Sacred Text: What the Old Greek Texts Tell Us about the Literary Growth of the Bible*, TCSt 4 [Leiden: Brill, 2003], 92).

[50] See, e.g., John J. Collins, "The Judaism of the Book of Tobit," in *The Book of Tobit: Text, Tradition, Theology; Papers of the First International Conference on the Deuterocanonical Books, Pápa, Hungary, 20–21 May, 2004*, ed. Géza G. Xeravits and József Zsengellér, JSJSup 98 (Leiden: Brill, 2005), 23–40, esp. 33; Loader, *Pseudepigrapha on Sexuality*, 172, 174.

[51] The verb here echoes προσκολληθήσεται, in the LXX of Gen 2:24 (Loader, *Pseudepigrapha on Sexuality*, 172).

[52] Bird, *1 Esdras*, 169–70.

outlook is highly critical of marriage outside (close) kinship bonds.[53] There are hints, however, of an underlying critique.[54]

Malachi 2:10–16

It is arguable that Mal 2:10–16 is the earliest text in which allusion to Gen 2:24 is used to indicate divine opposition to divorce *and* that Mal 2:10–16 became the foundation for the reuse of Gen 2:24 in the New Testament.[55] The text of this passage is notoriously corrupt, but commentators have nevertheless seen in it an allusion to Gen 2:24.[56] Not only the text but also the logic of the passage is difficult. The passage divides naturally into two halves, the first dealing with the problem of intermarriage and the second with divorce. It is not at all clear how these two relate to each other. Possibly Mal 2:10–16 is simply a collation of two unrelated problems concerning marriage.[57] Some have argued, however, that the two halves of the passage are connected. For example, it has been suggested that Israelites were divorcing their Israelite wives in order to marry foreign (Samaritan) women.[58] Alternatively, it is possible, as Smith argues, that Malachi is responding to the

---

[53] "Proper marriage is a major concern in the work" (Loader, *Pseudepigrapha on Sexuality*, 151); see also Thomas Heike, "Endogamy in the Book of Tobit, Genesis and Ezra-Nehemiah," in Xeravits and Zsengellér, *Book of Tobit*, 103–20.

[54] For example, Sarah's first seven husbands, despite being appropriately sourced from among her kin, died prior to the consummation of the marriages. Additionally, the story courts issues of incest as well as intermarriage in the identification of Sarah as Tobias's "sister" (Tob 7:11). There are strong resonances with this same issue in the marriage of Abraham to Sarah's namesake in Genesis (where an underlying critique of opposition to intermarriage is certainly present). Tobias Nicklas has argued that two literary strata in Tobit, GI and GII, present differing approaches to endogamy, with GII evidencing a far stronger (correcting?) opposition to marriage outside kin circles than GI (to which Nicklas assigns Tob 6:18) ("Marriage in the Book of Tobit: A Synoptic Approach," in Xeravits and Zsengellér, *Book of Tobit*, 139–54). Finally, Gary A. Anderson has recently written that the labeling of Tobit as a Deuteronomic novella "badly misses the mark" ("Does Tobit Fear God for Naught?," in *The Call of Abraham: Essays on the Election of Israel in Honor of Jon D. Levenson*, ed. Gary A. Anderson and Joel S. Kaminsky, CJAn 19 [Notre Dame, IN: University of Notre Dame Press, 2013], 115–43, here 138). Anderson sees in Tobit a theme of Joban testing (will Tobit obey God for naught?) that links it with books such as Genesis and Ruth, as well as Job.

[55] So Collins, "Judaism of the Book of Tobit," 33; Ralph L. Smith, *Micah–Malachi* (WBC 32; Waco, TX: Word, 1984), 325.

[56] E.g., Smith, *Micah–Malachi*, 318–25; W. Rudolph, "Zu Malachi 2.10–16," *ZAW* 93 (1981): 85–90. The essence of the allusion is found in the (supposed) reference in 2:15–16 to YHWH's creation of "one" (אחד) man.

[57] John J. Collins, "Marriage, Divorce, and Family in Second Temple Judaism," in *Families in Ancient Israel*, ed. Leo G. Perdue et al., The Family, Religion, and Culture (Louisville: Westminster John Knox, 1997), 124.

[58] E.g., J. M. Myers, *The World of the Restoration* (Englewood Cliffs, NJ: Prentice-Hall, 1968), 98.

events narrated in Ezra-Nehemiah and saying that, although intermarriage is prohibited, divorce is not the answer: "Malachi is speaking about the disastrous effects of mixed marriage and divorce."[59]

Regardless of the relationship between the two halves of the passage, it is striking that the very first text in which Gen 2:24 appears to have been used in a sense meant to convey the impression of divine opposition to divorce should be located in the text in such close proximity to a denunciation of intermarriage. If commentators such as Ralph L. Smith are correct, then this juxtaposition is not a matter of chance. Rather, Mal 2:10-16, no less than the other three texts we have considered, is a passage that is concerned in its entirety with the issue of intermarriage. Only later was it used to support a line of interpretation that focused on the issue of divorce.[60]

Concluding Remarks about the Early Reuse of Genesis 2:24

The purpose of this brief intertextual study has been to measure whether any of the earliest reuses of Gen 2:24 appear to share our hypothesized interest of Gen 2:24 in the issue of intermarriage. I have identified four early instances of reuse in contexts where intermarriage is a central element.[61] The reuse of Gen 2:24 in Ruth suggests an approach to the issue of intermarriage that is at odds with the negative view portrayed in Ezra-Nehemiah. The book of Tobit, in contrast, appears on its face to be supportive of Ezra-Nehemiah's approach, but it contains clues that its relationship with the issue of intermarriage may be more complicated. 1 Esdras 3-5 presents a view of the power of attraction that women exert over men that is highly analogous to our interpretation of Gen 2:24. I have argued that Gen 2:24 observes the phenomenon of Israelite men being drawn by that same attraction into marriage with non-Israelite women, despite the opposition to such marriages that was prevalent in the Persian period. Finally, Mal 2:10-16, despite its association with the Christian tradition that Gen 2:24 speaks to the issue of divorce, is also closely connected with the issue of intermarriage.

In summary, all four early examples of reuse of Gen 2:24 have a connection with the issue of intermarriage.[62] Further, we see reflected here a variety of attitudes toward the issue; it is by no means the case that the passages demonstrate uniform support of Ezra's response to the problem of foreign wives. A similar variety of attitudes toward intermarriage can be identified in the wider text of Genesis. In addition, at least one of the passages reflects the same concept of the power of the

---

[59] Smith, *Micah–Malachi*, 325.

[60] It is tempting to surmise that the apparently strong statement of divine opposition to divorce in Mal 2:13-16 may be at the root of the persistent idea that Gen 2:24 presents a normative definition of marriage.

[61] As noted, it is not always possible to be certain about the direction of dependence. Accordingly, it is safest to take the position least advantageous to our argument and assume that all four are instances of reuse of Gen 2:24.

[62] I have argued that this is true of 1 Esdras 3-5 no less than of the other examples.

attraction of women for men that we have argued is present in Gen 2:24. Each of these findings supports the conclusion of this word study that the authors of Gen 2:24 had in mind the issue of intermarriage. In light of this evidence, Gen 2:24 ought not to be read as if it were *the only instance in the Hebrew Bible* of the use of the verb דבק in a context concerning a relationship between two individuals that does not also concern intermarriage. My hypothesis—that the authors of Gen 2:24 were responding to a pressing social issue of their own time, that of intermarriage between Israelites and non-Israelites—is supported.

V. Conclusion: Genesis 2:24, Intermarriage, and the Problem of Aloneness

I began by observing that conservative Christian scholars have appealed to the creation narratives of Genesis in order to open a "second front" in the battle over homosexuality in the Bible. They argue that Gen 2:24 establishes a normative and prescriptive definition of marriage that precludes homosexual expression and establishes a biblical theology of sexuality that should be brought to bear on interpretation of all subsequent biblical texts. The findings of our study, however, indicate that this "second front" is a dead-end. Although Gen 2:24 certainly presents an etiology, it is not a normative etiology of marriage that precludes homosexuality (or whatever the presenting issue might be at any given time) but a descriptive etiology of the strong draw and attraction that calls men and women into relationship with one another. Far from setting out to regulate and restrict the institution of marriage, Gen 2:24 acknowledges, *without narratorial censure of any kind*, the propensity of men to pursue "inappropriate" marriages that defy the wishes and schemes of their parents and, by implication, society and religious institutions. This study suggests that the particular brand of inappropriate relationship that the authors of Gen 2:24 had in mind was intermarriage. In our day the presenting issue might be homosexual marriage, but the implication is the same: the cause of this propensity is to be located in God's solution to the problem of the aloneness of the אדם.

In the end this "second front" may prove to be something of an own goal for the opponents of same-sex marriage. They are wrong to argue that Gen 2:24 offers a normative definition of marriage that precludes marriage between people of the same gender; nevertheless, they may well be absolutely right in their assessment that Gen 2:24 should be understood as foundational for the interpretation of the entire body of Scripture. It is in Gen 2:24 that we come to understand the power of the need for relationship that is the result of God's actions in creation.

The Visit of Jethro (Exodus 18): Its Composition and Levitical Reworking

JAEYOUNG JEON
jaeyoung.jeon@unil.ch
Université de Lausanne, 1015 Lausanne, Switzerland

The episode of Jethro's visit in Exod 18 consists of two distinct parts, the visit narrative (vv. 1–12, 27) and the account of the establishment of the judicial system (vv. 13–26). The main strand of the narrative is a continuation of the previous Moses–Midianite cycle (Exod 2–4) and belongs to a relatively early stage of the formation of the Pentateuch. The end of the strand (esp. vv. 8–12), however, underwent a phase of reworking by a scribe familiar with the language of late biblical texts usually assigned to the Levites (e.g., Ps 78, Neh 9, 1 Chr 16). The account of the establishment of the judicial system (vv. 13–26) seems to have been added later probably by the same redactor who reworked verses 8–12. The account exhibits close literary affinity to the Chronicler's account of Jehoshaphat's judicial reform and may reflect the sociopolitical interests of the Levites in the Persian period.

The story of Jethro's visit to the mountain of God and the establishment of the judicial system in Exod 18 have long attracted scholarly interest with its unique contents, structural function, and peculiar language. Among the various issues related to this chapter, the literary unity and dating of the material, especially in comparison to P, have given rise to differing opinions among critics in recent discussions. Classical source criticism regarded the whole chapter as part of the E document with minor additions by J or the *Jehowist* (R^JE),[1] a view still supported by some recent advocates of the classical scheme.[2] Some recent views maintain the

---

[1] The term *Jehowist* (Jahwist + Elohist), often used in the previous generations of German scholarship, indicates the redactional combination of J and E

[2] See, e.g., Julius Wellhausen, *Die Composition des Hexateuchs und der historischen Bücher des Alten Testaments*, 3rd ed. (Berlin: Reimer, 1899), 80; Martin Noth, *Exodus: A Commentary*, trans. John S. Bowden, OTL (Philadelphia: Westminster, 1974), 146. Brevard S. Childs, *The Book of Exodus: A Critical, Theological Commentary*, OTL (Philadelphia: Westminster, 1974), 318–26. For recent support of the classical view, see Baruch J. Schwartz, "The Visit of Jethro—A Case of Chronological Displacement? The Source-Critical Solution," in *Mishneh Todah: Studies in Deuteronomy and Its Cultural Environment in Honor of Jeffrey H. Tigay*, ed. Nili Sacher Fox,

unity of the chapter but argue for much later dates of composition, either pre-Priestly or post-Priestly.[3] Other scholars, however, are increasingly doubtful about the unity of the text and find multiple phases in its literary expansion. These critics usually maintain the major redactional division between the episode of Jethro's visit (vv. 1–12, 27) and the establishment of the judicial system (vv. 13–26), with additional stratifications within both, and give various dates for the layers from pre-P to post-P.[4] In terms of chronology relative to P, the question has become even more complicated with the renewed discussion in recent pentateuchal scholarship about the extent of P. The classical notion of P, especially its extent, has lately been challenged, and an ample number of Pentateuch scholars now confine P to the

---

David A. Glatt-Gilad, and Michael J. Williams (Winona Lake, IN: Eisenbrauns, 2009), 29–48; Joel S. Baden, *The Composition of the Pentateuch: Renewing the Documentary Hypothesis*, AYBRL (New Haven: Yale University Press, 2012), 121, 126, 136, etc.; William H. C. Propp, *Exodus 1–18: A New Translation with Introduction and Commentary*, AB 2 (New York: Doubleday, 1999), 627; Axel Graupner, *Der Elohist: Gegenwart und Wirksamkeit des transzendenten Gottes in der Geschichte*, WMANT 97 (Neukirchen-Vluyn: Neukirchener Verlag, 2002), 93–111. It is notable that Frank Crüsemann does not admit the classical documentary scheme but still argues for a pre-Deuteronomistic and preexilic date for the chapter (*Die Tora: Theologie und Sozialgeschichte des alttestamentlichen Gesetzes* [Munich: Kaiser, 1992], 107).

[3] John Van Seters assigns the text to the pre-Priestly, exilic Yahwist (*The Life of Moses: The Yahwist as Historian in Exodus–Numbers* [Louisville: Westminster John Knox, 1994], 208–19). Thomas B. Dozeman assigns the text to a pre-Priestly D-composition (*Commentary on Exodus*, ECC [Grand Rapids: Eerdmans, 2009], 398–410). Erhard Blum formerly attributed the chapter to (pre-P) KD, but he revised his view to post-Priestly "post-Hexateuch redaction" ("Die literarische Verbindung von Erzvätern und Exodus: Ein Gespräch mit neuere Endredaktionshypothesen," in *Abschied vom Jahwisten: Die Komposition des Hexateuch in der jüngsten Diskussion*, ed. Jan Christian Gertz, Konrad Schmid, and Markus Witte, BZAW 315 [Berlin: de Gruyter, 2002], 136–37, 153–54). Similarly, Rainer Abertz attributes the chapter to post-P Hexateuch redaction (*Exodus*, 2 vols., ZBK 2 [Zurich: TVZ, 2012], 1:296–314.

[4] See, e.g., Volkmar Fritz, *Israel in der Wüste: Traditionsgeschichtliche Untersuchung der Wüstenüberlieferung des Jahwisten*, MThSt 7 (Marburg: Elwert, 1970), 13–14; Christoph Berner, *Die Exoduserzählung: Das literarische Werden einer Ursprungslegende Israels*, FAT 73 (Tübingen: Mohr Siebeck, 2010), 406–25; Peter Weimar, *Die Berufung des Mose: literaturwissenschaftliche Analyse von Exodus 2,23–5,5*, OBO 32 (Freiburg, Schweiz: Universitätsverlag; Göttingen: Vandenhoeck & Ruprecht, 1980), 28–31; Eckart Otto, *Das Deuteronomium: Politische Theologie und Rechtsreform in Juda und Assyrien*, BZAW 284 (Berlin: de Gruyter, 1999), 244; Christian Frevel, "'Jetzt habe ich erkannt, dass YHWH grösser ist als alle Götter': Ex 18 und seine kompositionsgeschichtliche Stellung im Pentateuch," *BZ* 47 (2003): 3–22; Thomas Römer, "Provisorische Überlegungen zur Entstehung von Exodus 18–24," in *"Gerechtigkeit und Recht zu üben" (Gen 18,19): Studien zur altorientalischen und biblischen Rechtsgeschichte, zur Religionsgeschichte Israels und zur Religionssoziologie; Festschrift für Eckart Otto zum 65. Geburtstag*, ed. Reinhard Achenbach and Martin Arneth, BZABR 13 (Wiesbaden: Harrassowitz, 2009), 128–54. For further references, see Konrad Schmid, *Genesis and the Moses Story: Israel's Dual Origins in the Hebrew Bible*, Siphrut 3 (Winona Lake, IN: Eisenbrauns, 2010), 235 n. 447; Cornelis Houtman, *Exodus*, 4 vols., COut (Kampen: Kok, 1993), 2:396–402.

narrative of Sinai, from the end of Exodus to the beginning of Numbers. This interpretive environment forces scholars to be more precise in determining a pre- or post-P date of a given text.

In this article, I first discuss the basic narrative of Jethro's visit in connection with Exod 3–4 and then examine the possibility of a late reworking in verses 8–11 by focusing on a linguistic comparison with late biblical texts. Finally, I explore the dating and possible authorship of the second half of the chapter (vv. 13–26) mainly through a comparison with the account of Jehoshaphat's reform in 2 Chr 17 and 19. These comparisons, along with some additional linguistic considerations, suggest that the reworking of Exod 18 was carried out by a Levitical scribe or scribal group.

I. The Story of Jethro's Visit (Exodus 18:1–7, 8–11*, 27)

A Close Connection with Exodus 2–4

Exodus 18 both thematically and structurally completes the Midianite narrative strand from Exod 2–4, functioning as a transitional hinge between the narratives of the wilderness and Sinai.[5] Exodus 2–4 and 18 have a number of corresponding elements that indicate a close literary connection between them. The correspondences include Jethro as a Midianite priest and Moses's father-in-law (Exod 3:1; 18:1); Moses's marriage to Zipporah (Exod 2:16–22; 18:2) and the reference to his sons (Exod 4:20; 18:3–4); the locations of Horeb, the mountain of God (Exod 3:1; 18:5); Jethro's farewell and greeting to Moses with שלום (לשלום לך in Exod 4:18 and לשלום in 18:7); the use of the verb נצל (hiphil, "rescue") combined with מיד מצרים ("from the hand of Egypt") in Exod 3:8 and 18:8–10; and the sacrifices at Horeb (Exod 3:12; 18:12).[6] The connection of Exod 18 with Exod 2–4 is obvious, yet this Moses-Midianite (Jethro) strand finishes at chapter 18 without further narrative consequence. Exodus 18, therefore, should be considered the completion of the Moses-Midianite cycle.[7]

---

[5] See, e.g., Childs, *Book of Exodus*, 326–32; Eugene E. Carpenter, "Exodus 18: Its Structure, Style, Motifs and Function in the Book of Exodus," in *A Biblical Itinerary: In Search of Method, Form and Content; Essays in Honor of George W. Coats*, ed. Eugene E. Carpenter, JSOTSup 240 (Sheffield: JSOT Press, 1997), 91–108, esp. 107–8; Propp, *Exodus 1–18*, 633–34; see also Dozeman, *Commentary on Exodus*, 400–405; Dozeman, "The Midianites in the Formation of the Book of Numbers," in *The Books of Leviticus and Numbers*, ed. Thomas Römer, BETL 215 (Leuven: Peeters, 2008), 261–84; Albertz, *Exodus*, 1:298–99. Antonius H. Gunneweg contrasts the layer of Midianite tradition in Exod 2–4, 18 with the Sinai tradition ("Mose in Midian," *ZTK* 61 [1964]: 1–9).

[6] For further discussions of the literary connection between the two texts, see Frevel, "'Jetzt habe ich erkannt,'" 7–8; Römer, "Provisorische Überlegungen," 146–47.

[7] The contradictory reappearance of Moses's father-in-law (Reuel or Hobab) at the departure from the wilderness of Sinai in Num 10:29 seems not to be a continuation of the current literary

In my previous study of Exod 3–4, I found three pre-Priestly layers of Deuteronomistic composition and redaction that constitute the bulk of the chapters.[8] My redaction-critical analysis concluded that the earliest layer is that of the second commissioning of Moses, which is the basic strand of the commissioning narrative (Exod 3:1–4*, 7–8, 16–17; 4:1–9, 18, 29–31*); this layer has undergone two phases of Deuteronomistic expansion, namely, the addition of the first commissioning (3:9–15*) and a broader redaction that links the commissioning narrative to the following story of the exodus (3:19–22 and 5:22–6:1; 11:1–3; 12:35–36; 12:39; 13:3–10). The commissioning story is further supplemented by the addition of the motif of Aaron (4:10–16, 27–28), followed by post-Priestly insertions of the staff of God motif (4:17, 20b) and the third commissioning (4:21–23). All these layers were inserted between the accounts of Moses's flight to Midian (Exod 2:1–23aα) and his return (4:19) and, in a broader structure, between the Midianite story in Exod 2 and the earlier narrative strand of Exodus, which I define as *proto-Exodus narrative*.[9]

Turning to Exod 18, the episode of Jethro's visit, in the context of the literary layers of chapters 3–4, seems to be a continuation of the first commissioning in 3:9–15*, which is a secondary addition to chapter 3. This additional passage was previously considered to be an originally independent text (E). Yet some linguistic features, such as the rhetorical marker ועתה הנה ("now look") at the beginning of v. 9, which never opens a new topic in speech but is always used in the middle or end to shift the speech to its climax, prove that these verses cannot be independent of their literary context but presuppose previous verses (esp. vv. 7–8).[10] Exodus 3:9–15* deals with the issues of prophetic signs and the name of YHWH, which, according to Deut 18:15–22 and 13:2–6, are the two criteria for distinguishing between true and false prophets. Since Moses is the prophet par excellence in Deuteronomic/Deuteronomistic conceptualization, it was important for the Deuteronomistic redactor to legitimate Moses according to these criteria from the beginning of his career. Exodus 3:9–15 was therefore added to present Moses as a legitimate prophet.[11]

In this vein, the sign mentioned in 3:12, worshiping God on the mountain of God, must be accomplished for the legitimation of Moses; consequently, the sacrifice at the conclusion of the first half of Exod 18 (v. 12) can be understood as the accomplishment of this sign.[12] In terms of literary stratigraphy, the elements

---

tradition but to be rooted in another Hobab tradition (e.g., Judg 1:16; 4:11, 17). For a further discussion, see Dozeman, "Midianites in the Formation of the Book of Numbers."

[8] See Jaeyoung Jeon, *The Call of Moses and the Exodus Story: A Redactional-Critical Study in Exodus 3–4 and 5–13*, FAT 2/60 (Tübingen: Mohr Siebeck, 2013), 73–158.

[9] See ibid., 215–26.

[10] See further ibid., 93–113.

[11] See further ibid., 114–18.

[12] See also Propp, *Exodus 1–18*, 631; Schwartz, "Visit of Jethro," 46–47; Baden, *Composition of the Pentateuch*, 121.

from Exod 2–4 in our text are explained by the text's connection to Exod 3:9–15*, a later addition to chapters 3–4 that presupposes chapter 2 and the major part of chapters 3–4. The Deuteronomistic nature of 18:1–12 is supported by the expression כל אשר עשה יהוה לפרעה ולמצרים ("all that the Lord has done to Pharaoh and to the Egyptians," 18:8 NRSV), which occurs also in Deut 7:18 and 29:1.[13]

In my previous study I concluded that the major layers in Exod 3–4, including 3:9–15, chronologically precede the Priestly commissioning account in Exod 6 and that the latter presupposes the former.[14] Similarly, the first half of chapter 18 (with the exception of some passages that have been reworked later, which I will discuss below) exhibits neither influence nor recognition of the preceding P narrative, nor any trace of a very late date for its composition. For some critics, the problematic contradiction between the location of the mountain of God and the Priestly itinerary note of the arrival at the wilderness of Sinai in Exod 19:1 are regarded as evidence for a post-P date of this text.[15] Nevertheless, the ritual act by Jethro, a Midianite priest, and the participation of Aaron in the meal (18:12) constitute the high point of the story and probably provided the later editor with a good reason to exclude this story from the Sinai pericope.[16] The location outside of the P itinerary scheme therefore does not necessarily argue for the post-P date of our narrative (vv. 1–12 [27]).

Reworking of Jethro's Speech and Its Linguistic Features

Although the basic narrative strand of Exod 18:1–12 (27) can be understood as a pre-Priestly composition, scholars have often identified later additions, especially in the narration and speech about God's salvation in 18:9–10.[17] These verses include redundant repetitions of the formulaic combination of נצל and מיד מצרים, which disturbs the smooth flow of the narrative. In the LXX as well, several similar phrases mentioning salvation from Pharaoh and Egypt follow verses 8 and 9.[18] These pluses in the LXX may indicate that these verses were fluid until a very late date. Furthermore, these verses, as well as the second half of chapter 18, use language that is uncommon in the Pentateuch. This peculiar language indicates that the reworking stemmed from a scribe or scribal circle relatively unrelated to the

---

[13] See Römer, "Provisorische Überlegungen," 146.
[14] See ibid., 188–206.
[15] See, e.g., Blum, "Die literarische Verbindung," 136–37; Berner, *Die Exoduserzählung*, 408.
[16] See Propp, *Exodus 1–18*, 628.
[17] See, e.g., Noth, *Exodus*, 146; Frevel, "'Jetzt habe ich erkannt,'" 10–11.
[18] The LXX has pluses at the end of verse 8, "and that the Lord had rescued them from the hand of Pharaoh and from the hand of the Egyptians" (καὶ ὅτι ἐξείλατο αὐτοὺς Κύριος ἐκ χειρὸς Φαραω καὶ ἐκ χειρὸς τῶν Αἰγυπτίων), and similarly at the end of verse 9, "and from the hand of Pharaoh" (καὶ ἐκ χειρὸς Φαραω).

major phases of composition and redaction of the Pentateuch.[19] With which scribal circle, then, might this reworking be connected? Interestingly, the linguistic peculiarity of these verses reveals similarities with late texts, especially Levitical ones. These linguistic connections may be significant for an identification of the reworking.

Exodus 18:11a contains Jethro's confession, "Now I know that the LORD is greater than all gods" (עתה ידעתי כי גדול יהוה מכל האלהים). This passage has often been understood on a synchronic level in relation to the "recognition formula" in the exodus story, especially beginning with Pharaoh's derogatory question in Exod 5:2, "Who is the LORD, that I should heed his voice and let Israel go?" (מי יהוה אשר אשמע בקלו לשלח את־ישראל) and the consequent declaration, "I do not know the LORD" (לא ידעתי את־יהוה).[20] Nevertheless, the idea that YHWH is greater than other gods is not a typical pentateuchal notion but one that is found in later liturgical texts, such as Ps 135:5 and 1 Chr 16:25.

Exod 18:11a: עתה ידעתי כי גדול יהוה מכל האלהים

Ps 135:5:   כי אני ידעתי כי גדול יהוה ואדנינו מכל אלהים
For I know that the LORD is great: our Lord is above all gods. (NRSV)

1 Chr 16:25:   כי גדול יהוה ומהלל מאד ונורא הוא על כל אלהים
For great is the LORD, and greatly to be praised; he is to be revered above all gods. (NRSV)

All three verses describe the greatness of God using identical phrases, כי גדול־יהוה האלהים (or על כל) מכל. As in our current text, the dominant theme of Ps 135 is the exodus from Egypt, and this psalm is usually regarded as a late composition based on older psalms.[21] Verse 5, however, is not borrowed from other psalms but is probably the wording of the psalmist, which supports the lateness the verse.[22] Walther Zimmerli points out that אני ידעתי at the beginning of the verse is a "later confessional statement."[23]

---

[19] For the linguistic peculiarity, see Benno Jacob, *The Second Book of the Bible: Exodus*, trans. Walter Jacob (Hoboken, NJ: Ktav, 1992) 497–98; Edward L. Greenstein, "Jethro's Wit: An Interpretation of Wordplay in Exodus 18," in *On the Way to Nineveh: Studies in Honor of George M. Landes*, ed. Stephen L. Cook and S. C. Winter, ASOR Books 4 (Atlanta: Scholars Press, 1999), 155–71; Mordechay Mishor, "On the Language and Text of Exodus 18," in *Biblical Hebrew in Its Northwest Semitic Setting: Typological and Historical Perspectives*, ed. Steven E. Fassberg and Avi Hurvitz, Publication of the Institute for Advanced Studies, the Hebrew University of Jerusalem 1 (Winona Lake, IN: Eisenbrauns, 2006), 225–30.

[20] See, e.g., Greenstein, "Jethro's Wit," 165.

[21] See, e.g., Frank-Lothar Hossfeld and Erich Zenger, *Psalms 3: A Commentary on Psalms 101–150*, trans. Linda M. Maloney, Hermeneia (Minneapolis: Fortress, 2011), 492.

[22] See Hossfeld and Zenger, *Psalms 3*, 493.

[23] See Walther Zimmerli, *Erkenntnis Gottes nach dem Buche Ezechiel: Eine theologische Studie*, ATANT 27 (Zurich: Zwingli, 1954), 35. Cf. Artur Weiser, *The Psalms: A Commentary*, OTL (London: SCM, 1982), 789. Weiser suggests a possible preexilic origin of the verse.

First Chronicles 16:25 develops and expands this expression by adding more elements, yet it still maintains the basic notion and syntactic frame of the other two verses. First Chronicles 16:25 is part of a hymn (16:8–36) sung by the Levitical singers, Asaph and his brothers; this hymn is a composite literary work drawn from other biblical passages such as 2 Sam 6, and Pss 96, 105, and 106. Although 1 Chr 16:25 appears in a section of the hymn referred to as the "communal song" (vv. 23–33), which is considered to consist of quotations from Ps 96:1–13,[24] this verse is not from Ps 96. A similar phrase is found in Ps 135:5, but the current form of the passage indicates that 1 Chr 16:25 is unlikely to have been directly borrowed from Ps 135. In view of the hymn's tendency to borrow longer texts (at least three or four verses), it is improbable that such an isolated quotation would be added in the middle of a borrowed passage from another psalm (Ps 96).[25] Supporting this conclusion is the fact that no further similarity to Ps 135 is found elsewhere in the hymn. A literary dependence of 1 Chr 16:25 on Exod 18:11 is even more implausible, given the quite distinct contexts of the two passages. Verse 25 was, therefore, most likely composed by the author of the hymn, who was probably a Levite scribe, developing the basic expression "YHWH is greater than other gods," which was familiar to him, by adding motifs of ומהלל מאד ונורא הוא.

Additional linguistic connections to our passage are found in the Levitical prayer in Neh 9:5–37. The description of Egypt in Exod 18:11b as "acting presumptuously against them [Israel]" (כי בדבר אשר זדו עליהם) is not only syntactically awkward in its context but also unique as a description of Egypt in the Hebrew Bible, with the exception of Neh 9.

Exod 18:11b: כי בדבר אשר זדו עליהם

Neh 9:10b: כי ידעת כי הזידו עליהם
For you knew that they acted insolently against them.

In Neh 9:10b, this phrase is used almost identically as the description of Egypt in the context of the exodus, except for a minor stem variation (*hiphil* instead of *qal*), which represents no semantic difference. The expression in Neh 9:10 is more likely to be the author's own wording rather than derived from Exod 18:11 since the verb זיד is a characteristic expression in Neh 9, used three times in the chapter (9:10, 16, 29).[26] The linguistic affinity between Exod 18 and Neh 9 is further strengthened by

---

[24] See, e.g., Gary N. Knoppers, *I Chronicles 10–29: A New Translation with Introduction and Commentary*, AB 12A (New York: Doubleday, 2004), 654–55. This was pointed out earlier by Edward L. Curtis, *A Critical and Exegetical Commentary on the Books of Chronicles*, ICC (Edinburgh: T&T Clark, 1910), 223–24.

[25] For the general compositional technique of the hymn, see Knoppers, *I Chronicles 10–29*, 654–59; Sara Japhet, *I and II Chronicles: A Commentary*, OTL (Louisville: Westminster John Knox, 1993), 311–12.

[26] In verses 16 and 29 the word describes the treacherous people of Israel in the wilderness and monarchic period, respectively. Among the ten occurrences of the verb in the Bible (Gen

another unusual expression in Exod 18:8, "all the hardship that had come upon them in the way" (כל התלאה אשר מצאתם בדרך). Except for Num 20:14, which has also been regarded recently as a very late text,[27] the expression appears only in Neh 9:32 in the Hebrew Bible.

Exod 18:8b: את כל התלאה אשר מצאתם בדרך

Num 20:14b: את כל התלאה אשר מצאתנו
... all the adversity that has befallen us (NRSV)

Neh 9:32b: את כל התלאה אשר מצאתנו למלכנו ...
... all the hardship that has come upon us, upon our kings ... (NRSV)

In all three verses, "all the hardship" (כל התלאה) is combined with the verb "to find" (מצא) in subordinate phrases introduced by the relative אשר, exhibiting remarkable linguistic similarity. Whereas in both Exod 18:8 and Num 20:14 the hardship is the wilderness wandering, in Neh 9 it is the suffering of the people since the Assyrian period. The use of the expression in Neh 9 in a different context may indicate that the author was so familiar with the expression that he could use it freely rather than that he directly quoted the pentateuchal passages.

It is broadly accepted that the prayer in Neh 9 (esp. vv. 5b–37) is one of the latest texts in Ezra-Nehemiah, often attributed to a Levite editor of Nehemiah.[28] Juha Pakkala, for example, regards the prayer as the Levites' response to Ezra's prayer in Neh 8.[29] If this is the case, the linguistic affinity of the reworking of Exod 18 to Levitical texts finds further support.

25:29; Exod 18:11; 21:14; Deut 1:43; 17:13; 18:20; Jer 50:29; Neh 9:10, 16, 29), three occurrences are concentrated in Neh 9.

[27] For example, Reinhard Achenbach attributes verse 14b to the Hexateuch redaction, which was made in mid-fifth century BCE (*Die Vollendung der Tora: Studien zur Redaktionsgeschichte des Numeribuches im Kontext von Hexateuch und Pentateuch*, BZABR 3 [Wiesbaden: Harrassowitz, 2003], 335–44).

[28] See G. Hölscher, "Die Bücher Esra und Nehemia," in *Die heilige Schrift des Alten Testaments*, ed. E. Kautzsch, trans. A. Bertholet, 4th ed. (Tübingen: Mohr Siebeck, 1923), 544; Sigmund Mowinckel, *Studien zu dem Buche Ezra-Nehemia*, 3 vols. SNVAO.HF 3, 5, 7 (Oslo: Universitetsforlaget, 1964–1965), 52–58; Reinhard G. Kratz, *Die Komposition der erzählenden Bücher des Alten Testaments: Grundwissen der Bibelkritik* (Göttingen: Vandenhoeck & Ruprecht, 2000), 88–89; H. G. M. Williamson, *1 and 2 Chronicles*, NCBC (Grand Rapids: Eerdmans, 1987), 308–9. See also David J. A. Clines, *Ezra, Nehemiah, Esther: Based on the Revised Standard Version*, NCBC (Grand Rapids: Eerdmans, 1984), 12. For the Levitical scribe, see Juha Pakkala, *Ezra the Scribe: The Development of Ezra 7–10 and Nehemia 8*, BZAW 347 (Berlin: de Gruyter, 2004), 181–84; Kyung-jin Min, *The Levitical Authorship of Ezra-Nehemiah*, JSOTSup 409 (London: T&T Clark, 2004), 106–15.

[29] See Pakkala, *Ezra the Scribe*, 184. There are debates among critics concerning the prayer's original location and function in its literary context. Since, however, it is not my purpose to address this issue, I note here the prayer's close relationship with, or even authorship by, the Levitical scribes.

Additional connections to Neh 9 are found in the second half of Exod 18. In Exod 18:16, תורה ("law") and חקים ("statutes") appear as objects of the verb ידע ("to know," *hiphil*), the conjunction of which is unique in the Pentateuch and occurs elsewhere only in Neh 9:14 and Ps 78:5 (without חקים) in the Hebrew Bible.[30]

Exod 18:16b והודעתי את חקי האלהים ואת תורתיו
I make known ... the statutes and instructions of God. (NRSV)

Neh 9:14: ואת שבת קדשך הודעת להם ומצוות וחקים ותורה צוית להם ...
... and you made known your holy sabbath to them and gave them commandments and statutes and a law ... (NRSV)

Ps 78:5: ... ותורה שם בישראל ... להודיעם לבניהם
... and appointed a law in Israel ... to teach to their children. (NRSV)

In Neh 9:14, the direct object of ידע (*hiphil*) is שבת (v. 14a), but חקים and תורה (with מצוות) are mentioned explicitly in the following parallel phrase. In Ps 78:5, תורה is one antecedent of the plural pronominal suffix on ידע (*hiphil*), and the meaning is similar to Exod 18:16. Psalm 78 is central among the so-called Asaph psalms (Psalms 73–83), recently dated to the postexilic period.[31] Moreover, this psalm is usually attributed to a Levitical performer or preacher, in close parallel with the aforementioned Levitical psalm in 1 Chr 16.[32] Kraus maintains that especially verses 5–11 of the psalm represent a "Levitical didactic proclamation."[33]

We have seen thus far that the rare and atypical expressions in Exod 18 are commonly shared by Levitical texts such as 1 Chr 16, Ps 78, and Neh 9. Furthermore, the expressions in these Levitical texts appear to be familiar to the authors rather than directly borrowed from Exod 18, which suggests the existence of a common scribal tradition. The close relationship between the reworked passage in Exod 18 and Levitical texts continues to the second half of Exod 18, not only linguistically but also in reference to the judicial system of Israel.

II. The Establishment of the Administration of Justice

The second half of Exod 18 (vv. 13–26), quite distinct from the preceding story of Jethro's visit, introduces to Israel a new mode for the administration of justice.

---

[30] Another similar case is found in Ezek 43:11, yet the חקים and תורה in this verse indicate the instructions for the new temple rather than the Mosaic law.

[31] See, e.g., Frank-Lothar Hossfeld and Erich Zenger, *Psalms 2: A Commentary on Psalms 51–100*, trans. Linda M. Maloney, Hermeneia (Minneapolis: Fortress, 2005), 292.

[32] Harry P. Nasuti, for example, claims that Ps 78 is associated with a "Levitical performer," closely parallel to 1 Chr 16 (*Tradition History and the Psalms of Asaph*, SBLDS 88 [Atlanta: Scholars Press, 1988], 323–26). Simiarly, Marvin E. Tate assigns the psalm to a Levitical preacher (*Psalms 51–100*, WBC 20 [Waco, TX: Nelson, 1991], 287).

[33] See Hans-Joachim Kraus, *Psalms 60–150: A Commentary*, trans. Hilton C. Oswald (Minneapolis: Augsburg, 1988), 126.

The distinctiveness of this half chapter has led critics to assume, without source-critical division, that behind the passage lies either a tradition distinguished from the first half or a historical reality in the monarchic period.[34] Recently, however, the passage is being viewed as a later literary addition to the earlier story of Jethro and Moses (vv. 1–12, 27).[35] Verses 13–26 differ from the earlier story in a number of ways: the subject matter of the second part of the chapter falls outside of the narrative framework of the "family" story of Exod 2–4 and 18; Jethro's name is not mentioned in the second part;[36] the role of Jethro as wise man or counselor on a national issue is quite different from his role in the previous Moses-Midianite cycle, where he is a family patron; and the elders of Israel, who are still representatives of the people in the first half (v. 12), are ignored in the new system of judicial authority.[37] The second part, therefore, is hardly a smooth continuation of the first half of the chapter and is better understood as a later literary addition.[38] The lateness and secondary nature of the second half of the chapter are supported by its close literary connection with the account of Jehoshaphat's reform in 2 Chr 19:5–11.

A Close Relationship with 2 Chronicles 17:7–9, 19:5–11

The similarity between Exod 18 and 2 Chr 19:5–11 has already been noted by Rolf Knierim, who assumed the historical reality of Jehoshaphat's reform behind the two texts.[39] Setting aside, however, the dubious historicity of the Jehoshaphat account in Chronicles, the remarkable similarity between the two texts can be analyzed on a literary level.[40] The similarity begins with the qualifications of the judges and their tasks. Exodus 18:21 and 2 Chr 19:9 present personal qualifications

---

[34] For the idea of a different tradition behind the text, see, e.g., Childs, *Book of Exodus*, 324–26; Dozeman, *Commentary on Exodus*, 400. For the view that a historical reality lies behind the text, see Hugo Gressmann, *Mose und seine Zeit: Ein Kommentar zu den Mose-Sagen* (Göttingen: Vandenhoeck & Ruprecht, 1913), 174–75; Rolf Knierim, "Exodus 18 und Neuordnung der mosaischen Gerichtsbarkeit," *ZAW* 73 (1961): 146–71, esp. 155–71.

[35] See n. 4 above.

[36] The contrast is striking, considering the frequent mentions of the name Jethro in the first half, mostly with the designation (Moses's) father-in-law (vv. 1, 2, 4, 6, 9, 10, 12; cf. vv. 8, 27).

[37] The revolutionary nature of the reform is obvious, when one considers that in the parallel account in Deut 1:9–18 the new judges are the elders of the tribes (ראשי שבטיכם, v. 15). The account in Exod 18 concerns only the personal quality of the new judges, ignoring their tribal identity (Exod 18:21).

[38] Römer points out that the collective use of תורה and חקים (Exod 18:16, 20) is found only in late texts such as Lev 26:46 and Ps 105:45, and Neh 9:13. Similarly, he notes that זהר (Exod 18:20) and דרש אלהים (Exod 18:15) are all very late expressions. For further discussion, see Römer, "Provisorische Überlegungen," 149–50.

[39] Knierim, "Exodus 18 und Neuordnung," 146–71.

[40] Similarly Römer, "Provisorische Überlegungen," 150; and Werner H. Schmidt, *Exodus, Sinai und Mose: Erwägungen zu Ex 1–19 und 24*, EdF 191 (Darmstadt: Wissenschaftliche Buchgesellschaft, 1983), 118.

that are almost identical: having the fear of God, ביראת יהוה (Chr) and יראי אלהים (Exod); and being loyal and trustworthy, באמונה (Chr) and אנשי אמת (Exod).[41] Another qualification, despising unlawful gain (שנאי בצע, Exod), is similarly found in the warning against taking a bribe (מקח שחד, 2 Chr 19:7). The characteristic of being mighty men (אנשי חיל) for the officers (שרים) in Exod 18:21 reappears similarly in the designation of Jehoshaphat's officers (שרים) as "mighty warriors" (בן־חיל, 2 Chr 17:7; גבורי חיל, 17:13; and גבור חיל, 17:17).[42] In 2 Chr 17:7–9 the officers are expected to teach the law of YHWH; likewise, in Exod 18 the expected role of the officers is to judge the people and teach them God's law as Moses did (חקים and תורה in vv. 16, 20). The idea that military officers can be responsible for the teaching of Torah is unique to these two passages. Exodus 18 combines the military and judicial functions and assigns both to שרים; furthermore, it expects the "officers" to perform religious duties such as educating the people on God's laws and instructions (e.g., v. 20). The qualities and functions of Moses's שרים apparently become divided under Jehoshaphat into שרים, who instruct the people on the law (2 Chr 17), and שפטים (judges), who perform judicial functions (2 Chr 19). These divided roles in Chronicles, however, are again combined in the duties of the Levites. The Levites are to accompany the שרים in teaching the Torah (2 Chr 17:8) and they, who are called שטרים הלוים, are in fact the judges in Jerusalem for both civil and religious matters (2 Chr 19:11). In terms of actual functions, therefore, Moses's שרים are more or less equivalent to the Levites described in Jehoshaphat's reform.[43]

These literary correspondences are also confirmed linguistically. In Exod 18:20, Moses's role of teaching the law is described with the verb זהר ("to warn") in the *hiphil*, with תורה and חקים as objects. This combination is unique in the Pentateuch and recurs in 2 Chr 19:10 with additional elements such as מצוה and משפטים:

Exod 18:20: והזהרתה אתהם את־החקים ואת־התורת
... teach them the statutes and the instructions ... (NRSV)

2 Chr 19:10: ... בין־תורה למצוה לחקים ולמשפטים והזהרתם אתם ...
(whenever a case comes to you ... concerning bloodshed), law or commandment, statutes or ordinances, then you shall instruct them ... (NRSV)

---

[41] The words אמת ("truth") and נאמן ("faithful"; אמן *niphal*, from which is derived אמונה) appear together in Jer 42:5 as a qualification of YHWH as a witness, and in Ps 111:7 they occur in a parallel structure. The word אמונה is a favorite of the Chronicler (1 Chr 9:31; 2 Chr 19:9; 31:12, 15, 18; 34:12).

[42] The designation בן־חיל is normally read as a proper name, Ben-hail, in the MT, but it is better read as a quality of the officers, following the common usage in Chronicles (1 Chr 26:7, 9, 30, 32; 2 Chr 26:17; 28:16). This interpretation is supported also by the LXX and by a Syriac version (Editio Urmiensis). See also Japhet, *I and II Chronicles*, 750; and Ralph W. Klein, *2 Chronicles: A Commentary*, Hermeneia (Minneapolis: Fortress, 2012), 250.

[43] Also in 1 Chr 26:29–32, the Levites are judges.

The combination of this wording and syntactic structure (with זהר [*hiphil*] taking two accusative objects) is found only in these two places in the Hebrew Bible.[44] Furthermore, as Exod 18:20 describes Moses's judicial responsibilities, so also 2 Chr 19:10 illustrates the duties of the judges in Jerusalem. The scribes who composed or redacted these two texts share not only the unusual idea of judging as a process of teaching (or literally "warning") God's law (cf. Deut 1:9–18, 17:8–13) but also similar language and writing style.

As a number of recent studies have indicated, the account of Jehoshaphat's reform has been formulated with the Chronicler's own language and concepts rather than those of another literary source.[45] This is especially true of Jehoshaphat's commands to the judges in 2 Chr 19:6–7 and 9–11 and of the appointment of officers and Levites as teachers of the law in 2 Chr 17:7–9. Most of the similarities with Exod 18 are found in these passages.[46] The books of Chronicles are broadly regarded as a Levitical (or at least pro-Levitical) composition. In addition, the present passages in Chronicles emphasize the role of the Levites in Jehoshaphat's judicial system. We may then assume a common Levitical scribal tradition behind those passages and the late layer of Exod 18, as will be discussed below.

The Levite Scribal Group

My examination thus far of the late editorial passages in Exod 18, namely, the reworking of verses 8–11 and of the entire second half of the chapter (vv. 13–26), supports a strong connection with a Levitical scribal group that had a scribal tradition different from those dominant in the Pentateuch, such as Deuteronomic/Deuteronomistic and Priestly scribal traditions.[47] To be sure, later texts could have been influenced by earlier texts, and the book of Chronicles and other Levitical texts mentioned above exhibit knowledge of earlier pentateuchal and DtrH traditions. Nevertheless, in our case (1) the additions of Exod 18 contain language unique in the Pentateuch, and (2) similar linguistic features are found in a certain group of texts that are usually attributed to Levite scribes. Hence, it is reasonable to assume a stronger link between this text and the Levitical scribal group than with other authors and redactors prominent in the Pentateuch. A number of sociohistorical studies of Persian Yehud have revealed that competing groups and parties

---

[44] See Gary N. Knoppers, "Jehoshaphat's Judiciary and 'The Scroll of Yhwh's Torah,'" *JBL* 113 (1994): 59–80, esp. 77.

[45] See, e.g., Klein, *2 Chronicles*, 272; Knoppers, "Jehoshaphat's Judiciary," 63–64; Japhet, *I and II Chronicles*, 771–72 (with reservation).

[46] Japhet, who assumes the existence of an earlier source for the narrative framework of Jehoshaphat's reform, admits that the current speeches of Jehoshaphat are the Chronicler's own creation (*I and II Chronicles*, 771–72).

[47] For discussion about Levitical scribal groups in Persian Yehud, see Pakkala, *Ezra the Scribe*, 267–68.

were then in existence and produced various texts, including passages in the Pentateuch.[48] It is therefore possible in this vein that the Levitical scribal group also participated in late phases of the formation of the Pentateuch.

What, then, might be the context and purpose of the composition, especially of the second half of Exod 18? Ernst Axel Knauf, followed by Thomas Römer, suggests that this text reflects the decree of Artaxerxes in Ezra 7, in which Ezra is commanded to appoint judges and teach the law of God.[49] Indeed, the appointment of judges following the advice of a foreign patron in Exod 18 is better connected with the situation of Ezra 7 than with any other period in the history of Israel. Even though we cannot be sure of the authenticity of the decree, a more significant aspect of this Ezra text is that it represents the idea that judges are appointed with the support of a foreign authority and that they would teach (תהודעון) the law of God and judge according to it (Ezra 7:25). This idea is most fully shared by the second half of Exodus 18, and it appears in part in the Chronicler's account of Jehoshaphat's reform.[50]

The account of Jehoshaphat's reform in 2 Chr 17 and 19 is a Levitical or pro-Levitical literary composition; the passages examined here, therefore, probably represent the Levites' ambition for, if not reality of, better status and a more significant role in Persian Yehud.[51] In a similar vein, the second half of Exod 18 may be interpreted as a retrojection or legitimation of such ambition into the period of the wilderness, during which major institutions of Israel were established. I briefly mentioned above that Moses's reform in Exod 18 was revolutionary because the newly appointed judicial officers were not among those named as representatives of the people in the pentateuchal context—the leaders of the tribes or the priests. The quality and status of the judicial officers depicted in our passage well correspond to the social status of the Levites in the Persian period. The Levites, at least a part, may have been pious, and probably ambitious, intellectuals, but they were

---

[48] See, e.g., Paul D. Hanson, *The Dawn of Apocalyptic: The Historical and Sociological Roots of Jewish Apocalyptic Eschatology*, rev. ed. (Philadelphia: Fortress, 1979), 209–79; Morton Smith, *Palestinian Parties and Politics That Shaped the Old Testament*, 2nd corr. ed. (London: SCM, 1987), 75–112; Rainer Albertz, *A History of Israelite Religion in the Old Testament Period*, trans. John Bowden, 2 vols., OTL (Louisville: Westminster John Knox, 1994), 2:437–506.

[49] See Ernst Axel Knauf, *Midian: Untersuchungen zur Geschichte Palästinas und Nordarabiens am Ende des 2. Jahrtausends v. Chr*, ADPV (Wiesbaden: Harrassowitz, 1988), 157; Römer, "Provisorische Überlegungen," 150.

[50] Klein recognizes that the situation in Ezra 7:25 and the account of Jehoshaphat's reform (2 Chr 17:7–9, 19:4–11) are "remarkably similar" (*2 Chronicles*, 250). Yet the foreign authorization in Ezra 7 makes the Ezra text more similar to Exod 18.

[51] Such ambitions of the Levites are well presented in Chronicles, where the Levites are described as holding important administrative and judicial positions in the court of Jerusalem: administration managers and judges (1 Chr 23:4, 26:29), warriors (1 Chr 26:31–32), scribes (1 Chr 24:6), teachers (2 Chr 17:7–8), and even prophets (1 Chr 25:5, 2 Chr 29:30, 35:15).

not the elders of the society, who probably constituted their own influential sociopolitical entity,[52] nor did they belong to the dominant priestly circle. Notably, in the Deuteronomistic version of this event (Deut 1:15), the new judicial officers are appointed explicitly from the heads of the tribes. Such an explicit identification of the judges as the tribal leaders stands in sharp contrast to the qualification of the judges in our text, which focuses only on the high caliber of the individuals rather than their social status. The late Deuteronomistic texts in the Pentateuch are often attributed to the heirs of Josiah's court officials who became the lay leaders of Yehud after the exile.[53] This view is in accord with Deut 1:15, which advocates for the interest of the lay leadership by adding the status as tribal leaders to the quality of judges.[54]

Dating and Relative Chronology

Once we admit the influence, though indirect, of Ezra 7 on Exod 18:12–26, the latter can be dated in the middle of the Persian period, considering that Ezra's return can be dated to either 458 BCE or 398 BCE. Such dating of our text is supported also by the fact that the Levites began to gain imperial support in the Jerusalem temple in the time of Nehemiah (after 445 BCE). Levites were very small in number in the memory of the early Persian period (Ezra 2:40–42; Neh 7:43–45).[55] In accordance with the late dating, our text seems to be a post-$P^{(G)}$ addition in terms of the literary stratigraphy of the Pentateuch. As Römer rightly pointed out, the

---

[52] See further Jaeyoung Jeon, "The Zadokites in the Wilderness: The Rebellion of Korach (Num 16) and the Zadokite Redaction," *ZAW* 127 (2015): 381–411, esp. 396–400.

[53] For the close connection between elders and Deuteronomistic literature, on the one hand, and, on the other, between the sociopolitical groups in the Persian period and their literary products in general, see n. 48 above.

[54] Classical source criticism and some newer models note that the account of Deut 1:9–18 is a correction or retelling of Exod 18:13–26. See, e.g., Martin Rose, *Deuteronomist und Jahwist: Untersuchungen zu den Berührungspunkten beider Literaturwerke*, ATANT 67 (Zurich: Theologischer Verlag, 1981), 224–63; Lothar Perlitt, *Deuteronomium,* BKAT 5 (Neukirchen-Vluyn: Neukirchener Verlag, 1990), 61–77; Achenbach, *Der Vollendung der Tora,* 237–66. Others regard these texts as independent traditions (see, e.g., Eckart Otto, *Deuteronomium 1–11,* 2 vols., HThKAT [Freiburg im Breisgau: Herder, 2012], 1:351–52) or assume the opposite direction of influence (see, e.g., John Van Seters, "Etiology in the Moses Tradition: The Case of Exodus 18," in *Biblical and Other Studies in Memory of S. D. Goitein*, ed. Reuben Ahroni, HAR 9 [Columbus: Ohio State University Press, 1986], 355–65; Van Seters, *Life of Moses*, 212–19; Römer, "Provisorische Überlegungen," 149–50).

[55] For further discussion of the increase of the Levites' power and influence, see, e.g., Joachim Schaper, *Priester und Leviten im achämenidischen Juda: Studien zur kult- und sozialgeschichte Israels in persischer Zeit*, FAT 31 (Tübingen: Mohr Siebeck, 2000), 230–68; Kyung-Jin Min, *The Levitical Authorship of Ezra-Nehemiah*, JSOTSup 409 (London: T&T Clark International, 2004), 116–37; Jeon, "Zadokites in the Wilderness," 401–3; Jeon, "The Levites," *EBR* (forthcoming).

unusual combination of תורות and חקים in Exod 18:16, 20 is also found in Lev 26:46 (cf. Ps 105:45, Neh 9:13), which is a late redactional passage that integrates the Holiness Code into the Sinai pericope.[56] A Priestly response to the Levites' ambition to challenge the priests is found in the Korah story (Num 16), which is the latest literary layer in the composite narrative of Num 16. The Korah layer has usually been attributed to a redactional phase later than P[(G)] such as P[(S)], Theocratic Revision (Achenbach), or Zadokite redaction (Jeon).[57] The Korah layer indicates that the ambitious Levites emerged only in a post-P[(G)] stage. This notion is supported by the recent tendency to confine the extent of P[(G)] to Exodus or Leviticus.[58] Before Numbers, the Levites are totally absent from the Priestly ritual process, which indicates that the Levites were not a significant group in the time of the composition of P[(G)].

The appointment of the officers over thousands and hundreds (שרי אלפים and שרי מאות) in Exod 18:21 is presupposed in the account of the vengeance against the Midianites in Num 31 (vv. 14, 48, 54), which has a strong Priestly flavor. The strong anti-Midianite sentiment in Num 31 not only recalls Exod 18 but also possibly contains an opposition to or correction of Exod 18 and the Moses–Midianite connection as a whole. In Exod 18 the officers are appointed on the advice of Moses's Midianite father-in-law, and now the officers attempt to take Midianite women for themselves through capture (Num 31:15). Moses expresses concern that such behavior may evoke God's wrath (Num 31:15–16), and he accuses the Midianite women of leading Israel to betray YHWH (v. 16). Read in connection with Moses's own marriage relationship with the Midianites, this speech could be interpreted as a later Priestly polemic against the non-Priestly Moses–Midianite connection (Exod 2–4, 18).[59]

---

[56] See Römer, "Exodus 18–24," 149.

[57] For the references, see Jeon "Zadokites in the Wilderness," nn. 1–3.

[58] Thomas Pola, *Die ursprüngliche Priesterschrift: Beobachtungen zur Literarkritik und Traditionsgeschichte von Pg*, WMANT 70 (Neukirchen-Vluyn: Neukirchener Verlag, 1995), 213–98; Eckart Otto, "Forschungen zur Priesterschrift," *TRu* 62 (1997): 1–50; Reinhard G. Kratz, *Die Komposition der erzählenden Bücher des Alten Testaments: Grundwissen der Bibelkritik*, UTB 2157 (Göttingen: Vandenhoeck & Ruprecht, 2000), 102–17; Christophe Nihan, *From Priestly Torah to Pentateuch: A Study in the Composition of the Book of Leviticus*, FAT 2/25 (Tübingen: Mohr Siebeck, 2007), 340–94. For further references, see Jeon, "Zadokites in the Wilderness," 403–4.

[59] Similarly, see J. Hutzli, "La fureur divine et son détournement en Nb 25," in *Proceedings of the International Colloquium "Colères et repentir divins," Collège de France, Paris 24.–25. April 2013*, ed. T. Römer and L. Marti (forthcoming). Further, scholars recognize the polemical nature of the story of Phinehas (Num 25:6–15) in the light of Moses's marriage to the Midianite Zipporah, which is closely related to Num 31 (esp. Num 25:16–18 and 31:1–3, 6, 16). See Achenbach, *Die Vollendung der Tora*, 440–42; Dozeman, "Midianites in the Formation of the Book of Numbers," 278–79.

Nevertheless, Num 31, a text evidencing Priestly concerns, does not preclude the post-P date of our text. Since Julius Wellhausen and Abraham Kuenen, followed by Martin Noth, there has been a general consensus that Num 31 is not a P$^{(G)}$ text but a late addition to the Pentateuch.[60] Recently, Reinhard Achenbach has likewise assigned this chapter to the last phase of "theocratic revision," the latest layer of redaction in the Pentateuch.[61] In my view, too, Num 31 is a post-Priestly composition of Zadokites in Jerusalem in the mid- or late Persian period.[62] In sum, therefore, I would date the reworking in Exod 18:8–11 and the establishment of the judicial system in vv. 12–26 as post-Priestly and the basic narrative of Jethro's visit (vv. 1–12*, 27) as pre-Priestly.

If the reworking of Exod 18 belongs to a Levitical scribe or scribal group, is this text contemporary with other Levitical texts mentioned above? In spite of the similarity between our text and 2 Chr 17 and 19, for instance, the Exodus text appears to precede the latter chronologically. The qualities of the judges in 2 Chr 19:7, 9 have their closest parallel in Exod 18, yet these verses were also influenced by other texts such as Deut 10:17 (לא ישא פנים ולא יקח שחד, "is not partial and takes no bribe" [NRSV]); 16:19 (לא תכיר פנים ולא תקח שחד, "you must not show partiality; you must not accept bribes" [NRSV]); and Zeph. 3:5 (לא יעשה עולה, "he does no wrong" [NRSV]). In addition, the description of the hierarchal system in Jehoshaphat's reform (2 Chr 19:10) shows the influence of Deuteronomic regulations for the judicial system (Deut 17:8–9).[63] These literary influences indicate that the Chronicler knew the Deuteronomic passages regarding the judicial system, in addition to the fundamental affinity with Exod 18. Such a mixture of language in the Chronicles texts could be a sign of the relative lateness of the text; the opposite order is not plausible, as Exod 18 does not explicitly employ the Chronicler's vocabulary and ideas. The chronological priority of the redaction of Exod 18 to 2 Chr 17 and 19 is also supported, though indirectly, by pentateuchal stratigraphy. The Zadokite redaction is later than the redaction of Exod 18, yet a text in this layer is presupposed by Chronicles. For instance, the Korach redaction in Num 16–17, which is a pivotal text of the Zadokite redaction layer, emphasizes the exclusive right of priests to sacrifice incense in the temple, and this passage is presupposed

---

[60] See, e.g., Wellhausen, *Die Composition des Hexateuchs*, 115; A. Kuenen, *An Historico-Critical Inquiry into the Origin and Composition of the Hexateuch (Pentateuch and Book of Joshua)*, trans. Philip H. Wicksteed (London: Macmillan, 1886), 99; Martin Noth, *Numbers: A Commentary*, trans. James D. Martin, OTL (Philadelphia: Westminster, 1968), 229; Philip J. Budd, *Numbers*, WBC 5 (Waco, TX: Word, 1984), 327.

[61] See Achenbach, *Der Vollendung der Tora*, 615–22.

[62] The pentateuchal passages that can be attributed, though provisionally, to the Zadokite redaction are found in the later additions and editorial passages in Exod 6, 16, Lev 11, 16, Num 3, 16, 17, 25, 31. See further Jeon, "Zadokites in the Wilderness," 403–10.

[63] Klein, *2 Chronicles*, 276.

in the Chronicler's episode of Uzziah's failed attempt to make an incense offering (2 Chr 26:16–21).[64]

The chronological distinction between the reworking of Exod 18 and the account of Jehoshaphat's reform in Chronicles leads me to assume several stages of development of the Levitical scribal tradition or several generations of the scribal circle. The reworking of Exod 18 probably belongs to an earlier stage of the tradition or an earlier generation of Levitical scribes.

III. Conclusions

Exodus 18 is not a unified literary composition by a single hand but a text with multiple phases of composition and redaction. Although more detailed redaction-critical analyses might yield additional minor stratifications in the chapter,[65] I have concluded so far that a meaningful distinction of literary strata with literary-historical significance can be made between the initial composition of the story of Jethro's visit (vv. 1–12*, 27), its reworking (vv. 8–11*), and the account of the establishment of a new administration of justice (vv. 13–26).

The first half of Exod 18, with the exception of the reworking in vv. 8–11, belongs to the pre-Priestly layer in Exod 3–4 and consequently does not reflect any Priestly texts or language. In the pre-Priestly level, the passage completes the Moses–Midianite cycle from Exod 2–4, especially the motif of prophetic legitimation in Exod 3:9–15*. The reworking of the first half of Exod 18 (vv. 8–11*), as well as the second half, demonstrates close linguistic affinity with late Levitical texts, so that one may assume a common Levitical scribal group or tradition behind them. Nevertheless, considering that this redaction chronologically precedes those Levitical texts, especially the account of Jehoshaphat's reform in 2 Chr 17 and 19, Exod 18 probably belongs to an earlier stage of the Levitical scribal tradition or an earlier generation. In the pentateuchal context, the redaction is later than P, but it is not the latest layer. Exodus 18 is presupposed by Num 31, which is part of a thorough redaction of Exodus through Numbers by the Zadokite scribes.

---

[64] See Jeon, "Zadokites in the Wilderness." In addition, Achenbach assigns the passages in Num 16–17 to a post-Priestly "theocratic revision" (*Die Vollendung der Tora*, 37–140). This episode is regarded as the Chronicler's own explanation for the Deuteronomistic report of Uzziah's leprosy (2 Kgs 15:5). See Japhet, *I and II Chronicles*, 876; Klein, *2 Chronicles*, 370. The declaration of the Aaronite priests' exclusive right of the incense offering (2 Chr 26:18) presupposes the series of pentateuchal passages about incense offering (e.g., Lev 10:1–3; 16*, and esp. Num 16*, 17*), which all belong to the post-Priestly Zadokite redaction layer.

[65] See, e.g., Weimar, *Die Berufung des Mose*, 27; Berner *Die Exoduserzählung*, 406–29; Römer, "Provisorische Überlegungen," 147.

The literary stratigraphy of Exod 18 in the pentateuchal context indicates the complexity of the later phases of the composition of the Pentateuch. Attempting too much stratification in bibical texts with only literary criteria, however, often places one at risk of writing a sophisticated scholarly work that is not historically realistic. In order to avoid this hazard, scholars should consider the scribal groups who produced these texts, as well as their activities and their sociohistorical contexts, in any reconstruction of a literary history of these texts.

JBL 136, no. 2 (2017): 307-321
doi: http://dx.doi.org/10.15699/jbl.1362.2017.156575

Rebuke, Lending, and Love: An Early Exegetical Tradition on Leviticus 19:17-18

MATTHEW GOLDSTONE
msg444@nyu.edu
New York University, New York, NY 10003

In this article I posit the presence of an early Jewish exegesis of Lev 19:17-18 preserved in the Tannaitic midrash known as Sifra, which is inverted and amplified in Did. 1:3-5, Q 6:27-35, Luke 6:27-35, and Matt 5:38-44. Identifying shared terminology and a sequence of themes in these passages, I argue that these commonalities testify to the existence of a shared exegetical tradition. By analyzing the later rabbinic material I delineate the contours of this Second Temple period interpretation and augment our understanding of the construction of these early Christian pericopae. In commenting on Lev 19:17, Sifra articulates three permissible modes of rebuke: cursing, hitting, and slapping. In its gloss on the subsequent verse, Sifra exemplifies the biblical injunction against vengeance and bearing a grudge through the case of lending and borrowing from one's neighbor. The Didache, Matthew, and Luke invert the first interpretation by presenting Jesus as recommending a passive response to being cursed or slapped, and they amplify the second interpretation by commanding one to give and lend freely to all who ask. The similar juxtaposition of these two ideas and the shared terminology between Sifra and these New Testament period texts suggest a common source. By reading these early Christian sources in light of this later rabbinic work I advance our understanding of the formation of these well-known passages and illustrate the advantages of cautiously employing rabbinic material for reading earlier Christian works.

Significant scholarly attention has been devoted to the use of Lev 19:18b ("love your fellow as yourself") in early Christian literature. Few scholars, however, have emphasized how the full biblical unit of Lev 19:17-18 may also be present in some of these instances. Leviticus 19:17 (concerning rebuke) and 19:18

The preparation and publication of this article were made possible by a grant from the Memorial Foundation for Jewish Culture.

(regarding vengeance and bearing a grudge) constitute a single unit: verse 17 (a) you shall not hate (לא תשנא) your kinsfolk in your heart; (b) reprove (הוכח תוכיח) your kinsman; (c) but incur no guilt because of him; verse 18 (a) you shall not take vengeance or bear a grudge against your countrymen; (b) love your fellow as yourself: I am the Lord (Lev 19:17–18 NJPS).[1] Revenge and resentment represent two problematic expressions of the hatred that one might harbor in one's heart. One is therefore cautioned to channel feelings of animosity into proper reproof (rather than revenge) and encouraged to love the other as oneself.[2] In what follows, I suggest the presence of an early exegetical tradition on Lev 19:17–18 that was employed in different forms in a Tannaitic midrash known as Sifra, as well as in the Didache, Q, Luke 6:27–35, and Matt 5:38–44.[3] These early interpretations involve a series of actions (cursing, slapping, etc.) linked to Lev 19:17 and the exemplum of giving/lending connected to Lev 19:18. While Sifra directly glosses the biblical verses with these ideas, the early Christian sources largely disconnect themselves from the Levitical context. Furthermore, the Christian sources invert the first interpretation by presenting Jesus as recommending a passive response to being cursed or slapped and amplify the second interpretation by commanding one to give and lend freely to all who ask. The parallels between the key terms and their order in these rabbinic and early Christian works offer a new window into the building blocks of these sources and highlight the value for future cautious comparative research.

---

[1] On this biblical couplet, see Baruch A. Levine, *Leviticus* ויקרא: *The Traditional Hebrew Text with the New JPS Translation*, JPS Torah Commentary (Philadelphia: Jewish Publication Society, 1989), 129 n. 17. Even during the late Second Temple period it appears that the close relationship between these two verses was maintained at Qumran, where the Damascus Document (CD IX, 2–8) discusses them in reverse order (Michael O. Wise, Martin G. Abegg Jr., and Edward M. Cook, *The Dead Sea Scrolls: A New Translation*, rev. ed. [San Francisco: HarperSanFrancisco, 2005], 66–67).

[2] James L. Kugel has argued that during the Second Temple period there were two distinct exegetical approaches to Lev 19:17, one moralizing or externalizing and the other judicial ("On Hidden Hatred and Open Reproach: Early Exegesis of Leviticus 19:17," *HTR* 80 [1987]: 43–61). Recently, Christopher Chandler has downplayed the moralistic interpretation, contending that the majority of interpretative traditions surrounding Lev 19:17 frame it in a judicial context ("Blind Injustice: Jesus' Prophetic Warning against Unjust Judging [Matthew 7:1–5]" [Ph.D. diss., University of St. Andrews, 2009], chapter 3).

[3] While this article will explore the differences between Sifra's version and the version found in early Christian works, I will not directly engage the question of the relationship between the various Christian texts themselves (i.e., priority and reworking between Matthew and Luke) even though the early exegetical tradition on Lev 19:17–18 may have been adopted from one of these texts to another, rather than from a more "original" form of the tradition.

I. COMPARISON OF TEXTS

Sifra Qedoshim 4

In the early rabbinic midrash known as Sifra we find the following interpretative gloss on Lev 19:17:

> Do not hate your brother in your heart [Lev 19:17a]. One might think you should not curse him, hit him, or slap him [יכול לא תקללנו לא תכנו ולא תסטרנו]. The Torah therefore says: *in your heart.* I only said hatred which is in the heart. And from where do we know that if he rebukes him four or five times that he should rebuke again? The Torah therefore says *you shall surely rebuke* [Lev 19:17b]. One might think even if he rebukes him and he is embarrassed, the Torah therefore says, *and do not bear sin upon him* [Lev 19:17c]. (Sifra Qedoshim 4; my translation)

The prohibition in Lev 19:17a of hating in one's heart is ostensibly redundant. Where else would one harbor hatred if not in one's heart? In good rabbinic fashion, Sifra seeks novelty underlying the superfluous scriptural qualification of such hatred.[4] If hatred in the heart is what is specifically prohibited, the verse must be worded thus in order to permit other expressions of hatred, namely, cursing, hitting, or slapping.[5] These types of actions are permitted as a valid form of response so long as one is not expressing hatred but rather attempting to chastise. Similarly, the repetition of the root יכח (*hiphil* "rebuke") in the infinitive absolute plus imperfect structure (הוכח תוכיח) captures rabbinic attention as a source for the obligation to repeat the action several times. Finally, the last section of the verse, Lev 19:17c, defines the limitations to this potentially unbounded expression of rebuke at the point when one embarrasses another.[6] Within this series of interpretations the first

---

[4] The exegetical interpretation of ostensibly superfluous material is characteristic of the midrashim attributed to the school of Rabbi Akiva. See Menahem Kahana, "The Halakhic Midrashim," in *Midrash and Targum, Liturgy, Poetry, Mysticism, Contracts, Inscriptions, Ancient Science and the Languages of Rabbinic Literature*, vol. 2 of *The Literature of the Sages*, ed. Shmuel Safrai, CRINT 2.3 (Philadelphia: Fortress, 2006), 17–26.

[5] The listing of these three acts likely appears in increasing order of intensity and humiliation, building up to the gloss on Lev 19:17c that one should desist at the point of humiliation. For another rabbinic example of slapping engendering a particularly high level of humiliation, see m. B. Qam. 8:6. It is also possible that the three actions described correspond to different types of interpersonal relationships: superiors, peers, and inferiors (see Walter Wink, "Neither Passivity nor Violence: Jesus' Third Way [Matt. 5:38–42 Par.]," in *The Love of Enemy and Nonretaliation in the New Testament*, ed. Willard M. Swartley [Louisville: John Knox, 1992], 105).

[6] Sifra implies that one should not rebuke a person to the point of embarrassment, lest this result in sin. This view stands in contrast to an interpretation preserved in Targum Pseudo-Jonathan, which emphasizes that one does not bear guilt for embarrassing one's fellow. For several

clause concerning cursing, hitting, or slapping is striking; these measures seem somewhat extreme, particularly in contrast to the obligations enumerated in the rest of Sifra on Lev 19. Accordingly, the continuation of this section in Sifra presents the views of several prominent rabbis that no one in their generation is able to give proper rebuke.

Following the exegesis of Lev 19:17 and the pronouncement of several Tannaim that no one is able to give rebuke, Sifra presents the prohibition against vengeance and bearing a grudge in Lev 19:18a through a set of examples revolving around lending and borrowing:

> Until what point is vengeance? He said to him, "Lend me your sickle" and he did not lend it. The next day he said to him, "Lend me your axe" and he said to him "I will not lend you just as you did not lend me your sickle"; thus it says *do not take vengeance* (Lev 19:18a). Until what point is bearing a grudge? He said to him, "Lend me your axe" and he did not lend it. The next day he said to him, "Lend me your sickle" and he said to him, "Behold! I am not like you who did not lend me your axe"; thus it says *do not bear a grudge* (Lev 19:18a). *Do not take vengeance or bear a grudge to your people*, but you can to others. *Love your neighbor as yourself* (Lev 19:18b). Rabbi Akiva says, "This is a great principle of the Torah." Ben Azzai says, "*This is the book of generations of man*—this is a greater principle than that one." (my translation)

The prohibition against vengeance and bearing a grudge is illustrated by the case of one who requests a tool from his fellow, having previously refused to lend something himself. Vengeance would be refusing to lend to the other party because they refused you, while bearing a grudge would be lending to them but making it clear that you are morally superior for doing what they refused to do. This illustration is followed by a gloss on the words "to your people," which is interpreted to mean that the verse allows one to take vengeance or bear a grudge against those who are not part of the rabbinic "in-group." The conclusion of this section of the gloss includes statements by Rabbi Akiva and Ben Azzai regarding a great principle of the Torah, where Rabbi Akiva believes Lev 19:18b to be of considerable import.

We find a close parallel to Sifra's comments on Lev 19:18 in the Amoraic midrash Genesis Rabbah (Parshat Vayera 55).[7] In this text, Rabbi Abin presents a parable of a student asking a teacher why the teacher is lending at interest when he himself specifically forbade such a practice. This scenario is then directly compared

---

Second Temple period interpretations of the nature of this sin, see Kugel, "On Hidden Hatred," 56–57.

[7] See J. Theodor and Chanoch Albeck, *Midrash Bereshit Rabba*, 3 vols. (Jerusalem: Wahrmann, 1965), 2:586–87. Kugel introduces this source into his discussion of the reception history of Lev 19:17, although he offers little analysis and primarily focuses on the use of Nah 1:2, which functions similarly in CD IX, 2–8—a Qumran source dealing with Lev 19:17–18 (James L. Kugel, *In Potiphar's House: The Interpretive Life of Biblical Texts* [San Francisco: HarperSanFrancisco, 1990], 233–34).

to Israel's questioning God about vengeance and a reference to Lev 19:18. The midrash thus connects the case of lending (particularly at interest) with the prohibition on vengeance in Lev 19:18. In addition, the parable makes a distinction between lending at interest to Jews as opposed to non-Jews, just as we find in Sifra's gloss on "to your people," which allows vengeance against those who are not of your people.[8]

There is another important parallel to our Sifra passage in the late work Ecclesiastes Rabbah (ch. 8) that also contains the correlation between vengeance and taking interest.[9] The relevant section in Ecclesiastes Rabbah is immediately preceded by another homily that discusses the so-called rebuke sections of the Pentateuch and concludes with Prov 3:11 ("Do not reject the discipline of the Lord, my son; do not abhor His rebuke" [תוכחתו] NJPS). Here we clearly see the juxtaposition between a discussion of rebuke and the parable comparing vengeance to lending.

In sum, Sifra interprets Lev 19:17 as allowing cursing, hitting, and slapping as appropriate forms of rebuke and glosses Lev 19:18 as encouraging lending to other "insiders" in cases where one may be initially disinclined. This tradition has several echoes in later rabbinic sources and, as we shall see, appears in an altered form in several early Christian texts.

Didache 1:3–5

The Didache mentions rebuke explicitly in two contexts. The first appears in chapter 2 following a list of several prohibitions that parallel a number of biblical injunctions (particularly in the Ten Commandments).[10] The second comes in the fifteenth chapter following a command to appoint bishops and deacons, where the people are admonished to rebuke one another in peace rather than anger.[11] Aside from these two definitive statements, there is a strong parallel in the beginning of

---

[8] It is also potentially relevant that the section of the midrash that precedes the passage quoted here discusses parables of a potter hitting a vessel or a flax maker beating flax as analogous to God's testing of the righteous. The imagery of physically hitting these objects in order to improve their quality may remind us of the hitting and striking actions suggested in Sifra for Lev 19:17a. If so, then this section of Genesis Rabbah puts the link between Lev 19:18 and lending immediately after this hitting imagery, just as we find the order of material discussed in Sifra. The section that precedes the passage quoted here, however, also appears elsewhere in Genesis Rabbah without the above section (see Theodor and Albeck, *Midrash Bereshit Rabba*, 1:290, 314; see also Song of Songs Rabbah 2).

[9] On the dating of Ecclesiastes Rabbah, see H. L. Strack and G. Stemberger, *Introduction to the Talmud and Midrash*, trans. Markus Bockmuehl (Minneapolis: Fortress, 1992), 345–46.

[10] See John S. Kloppenborg, "The Transformation of Moral Exhortation in Didache 1–5," in *The Didache in Context: Essays on Its Text, History, and Transmission*, ed. Clayton N. Jefford, NovTSup 77 (Leiden: Brill, 1995), 99 n. 45.

[11] "Correct one another not in anger but in peace, as you have it [written] in the gospel; and let no one speak to anyone who wrongs another—let him not hear [a word] from you—until he

the Didache (1:3b–1:5a) to the themes in Sifra, which suggests that the passage in the Didache may also be related to rebuke.[12]

There is almost unanimous agreement among scholars that Did. 1:3b–2:1 (often referred to as the *sectio evangelica*) constitutes a late interpolation in the development of this text.[13] This does not necessarily mean that the tradition it preserves is of late provenance, but it does allow for the possibility that the material in this section constitutes a coherent unit that was adopted from elsewhere.[14] The placement of this section at the beginning of the Didache was likely motivated by the resonance between its focus on love and the second command of the way of life—to love one's neighbor as oneself—which is a direct reference to Lev 19:18b. An analysis of this section reveals that this unit may derive from the same exegetical tradition that we find underlying Sifra:

1:3b   Bless those who curse you [τοὺς καταρωμένους ὑμῖν] and pray for those who hate you [τῶν ἐχθρῶν ὑμῶν], fast for those who persecute you [τῶν διωκόντων ὑμᾶς].

1:3c   What kind of favor is it when you love those who love you? Do not even the nations do that?

1:3d   Just love those who hate you [τοὺς μισοῦντας ὑμᾶς] and you will not have any enemy [οὐχ ἕξετε ἐχθρόν].

1:4a   Avoid the fleshly and bodily passions.

1:4b   If someone strikes [δῷ ῥάπισμα] you on your right cheek, turn your other one to him too, and you will be perfect.

1:4c   If someone presses you into one mile of service, go along with him for two.

---

has repented" (Huub van de Sandt and David Flusser, *The Didache: Its Jewish Sources and Its Place in Early Judaism and Christianity*, CRINT 3.5 [Minneapolis: Fortress, 2002], 15).

[12] There are numerous allusions in the Didache to Lev 19, which strengthens the possibility that the particular theme of rebuke from Lev 19:17 also appears in the Didache (Kloppenborg, "Transformation of Moral Exhortation," 103).

[13] See Kurt Niederwimmer, *The Didache: A Commentary*, Hermeneia (Minneapolis: Fortress, 1998), 68. Scholars have noted that Did. 1:3b–2:1 is a particularly "Christian" section (see, e.g., John S. Kloppenborg, "The Use of the Synoptics or Q in Did. 1:3b–2:1," in *Matthew and the Didache: Two Documents from the Same Jewish-Christian Milieu?*, ed. Huub van de Sandt [Minneapolis: Fortress, 2005], 113; Niederwimmer, *Didache*, 68–69).

[14] Sandt and Flusser suggest that this section "undoubtedly derives from more recent sources" (*Didache: Its Jewish Sources*, 40). As summarized by Kloppenborg, Helmut Koester posits that the compiler of the Didache took the already edited *sectio evangelica* and included it "more or less without alteration" (Kloppenborg, "Use of the Synoptics," 114; cf. Koester, *Synoptische Überlieferung bei den apostolischen Vätern*, TUGAL 65 [Berlin: Akademie, 1957], 239). That this particular section is missing from other versions of the Two Ways traditions and other parallel texts indicates that Did. 1:3b–2:1 is a late interpolation into the Didache as we possess it, but this is not proof that the material is necessarily of late provenance. My hypothesis is that the material underlying Did. 1:3b–1:5 derives from an early exegetical tradition that has likely been reworked and incorporated into the Didache at a late stage in its composition history.

1:4d If someone takes [ἄρῃ] your cloak [τὸ ἱμάτιόν σου], give him your tunic [τὸν χιτῶνα] as well.
1:4e If someone takes away from you what is yours, do not demand it back since you cannot do so anyway.
1:5a Give to everyone what he asks of you, and do not ask for it back.
1:5b For the Father wants people to share with everyone the gifts that have been freely granted to them [ἐκ τῶν ἰδίων χαρισμάτων].[15]

This section opens in Did. 1:3b by recommending the countermeasures of blessing, praying, and fasting against those who curse (τοὺς καταρωμένους ὑμῖν), hate (τῶν ἐχθρῶν ὑμῶν), and persecute you (τῶν διωκόντων ὑμᾶς). Of these three, only the first corresponds directly to the cursing (תקללנו) that we find in Sifra. Yet the multiple references to hatred (ἐχθρῶν/ἐχθρόν in Did. 1:3b, d and μισοῦντας in 1:3d) hark back to the beginning of Lev 19:17—"You shall not hate [לא תשנא] your kinsfolk in your heart." In addition, Did. 1:3c–d implies that all three of the negative actions described are understood as the types of actions carried out by one who hates you. Thus, both Sifra and the Didache suggest three negative responses as manifestations of hatred. For the Didache, these are the actions taken by one's enemy to which one must respond positively, while for Sifra these are potential actions one might take as an expression of anger/rebuke rather than harboring it in one's heart. Beyond this parallel, Did. 1:3c–d, which focuses on loving not only those who love you, stands in contrast to Sifra's interpretation of "your people" as limiting the prohibition of vengeance and bearing a grudge. The tradition preserved in the Didache specifically rejects the internalistic gloss of Lev 19:18 and encourages one to love precisely those whom one would desire to exclude—one's enemies.

Following Did. 1:4a, which appears somewhat interjectory, the text continues to introduce the proper response to one who slaps you. Slapping (ῥάπισμα) parallels the appearance of slapping [תסטרנו] in Sifra on Lev 19:17a, the latter employing a root used only infrequently in rabbinic texts.[16] Next we see the command to go an extra mile with one who compels you in Did. 1:4c, after which the Didache turns to three parallel statements regarding giving things to others. The first two discuss giving more to someone taking your cloak or other possession, while the last is a general statement to give to anyone who asks. While none of these examples explicitly uses a word for lending or borrowing, the occurrences do reflect the themes of Sifra's interpretation of vengeance and bearing a grudge. Sifra understands vengeance to be refusal to lend, and the *sectio evangelica* goes beyond simply avoiding vengeance, commanding that one must give without any expectation of return.[17] The Didache then goes on in 1:5b to address the mental state of the giver—that he

---

[15] Translation based on Sandt and Flusser, *Didache: Its Jewish Sources*, 10.

[16] It is possible that the use of ῥάπισμα here and ῥαπίζει in Matt 5:39 may be influenced by the LXX's translation of Lev 19:18, which includes the word "hand" (χείρ).

[17] This added level of not asking for or expecting an item to be returned may be why the Didache avoids the language of borrowing/lending, which implies return.

should give of his own free gifts (ἐκ τῶν ἰδίων χαρισμάτων). The term used for "free gifts" (χαρισμάτων) implies something "freely and graciously given" without any resentment.[18] Sifra understood bearing a grudge to be characterized by the expression of moral superiority while lending, and the Didache once again goes beyond simply not expressing resentment with the directive to give away possessions freely.

The similar language of negative actions associated with hatred (particularly cursing and slapping), the juxtaposition of a command to give freely that addresses both the action and mental state of the actor, and the placement of this section directly following a reference to Lev 19:18 cumulatively suggest that this pericope may have derived from the same exegetical tradition that we see in Sifra. The Didache, however, inverts the example of one who curses or hits by recommending corresponding positive responses and amplifies the command to lend by promoting free giving without expectation of return.

Q 6:27–30

Scholars have noted the similarities between Q 6:27–30 and the *sectio evangelica* in the Didache. Scholarship on this issue, however has revolved mainly around questions of priority and dependence among the Synoptic traditions, the Didache, and other related texts such as the Epistle of Barnabas.[19] Few have tried to reach behind the curtain to question the source of the juxtaposition of the different traditions underlying these pericopae. In light of the preceding analysis, it appears that this material in Q stems from the early exegetical tradition on Lev 19:17–18 that stands behind Sifra and the Didache. The critical reconstructed edition of Q reads as follows:

> Love your enemies [[and]] pray for those [[persecuting]] you, so that you may become sons of your Father, for he raises his sun on bad and [[good and rains on the just and unjust]]. [[The one who slaps]] you on the cheek, offer [[him]] the other as well; and [[to the person wanting to take you to court and get]] your shirt, [[turn over to him]] the coat as well. [[«And the one who conscripts you for one mile, go with him a second.»]] To the one who asks of you, give: and [[from the one who borrows]], do not [[ask]] back [[«what is»]] yours. And the way you want people to treat you, that is how you treat them. If you love those loving you, what reward do you have? Do not even tax collectors do the same? And if you [[lend «to those» from whom you hope to receive, what <reward do> you <have>?]] Do not even [[the Gentiles]] do the same?[20]

---

[18] BDAG, s.v. χάρισμα.

[19] See the discussion in Kloppenborg, "Use of the Synoptics."

[20] James M. Robinson, Paul Hoffmann, and John S. Kloppenborg, *The Critical Edition of Q: Synopsis Including the Gospels of Matthew and Luke, Mark and Thomas with English, German, and French Translations of Q and Thomas*, Hermeneia Supplements (Minneapolis: Fortress, 2000), 56–71.

This reconstruction of Q by James M. Robinson, Paul Hoffmann, and John S. Kloppenborg excludes the Didache's reference to those who curse you but mentions those who hate you (τοὺς ἐχθροὺς ὑμῶν) and persecute you (τῶν [[(διωκ)]]όντων ὑμᾶς). The reconstruction by Harry T. Fleddermann, however, retains the full verse as it appears in Matthew, together with verse 27, although he repositions it after verses 30 and 31.[21] Regardless of whether the explicit language of cursing appeared in Q, it is highly likely that the juxtaposition of the themes of slapping and taking/giving was present, lending credence to the idea that these were two sequential glosses on Lev 19:17–18. In addition, both major reconstructions of Q include the verb meaning to borrow/lend (δανίζω). Based on Luke 6:34, the critical reconstruction includes this verb in Q 6:34 with the force of lending (δανίσητε), while Fleddermann reconstructs Q 6:30 using this verb in the middle voice with the force of borrowing (δανίσασθαι). While neither Q nor the Synoptic Gospels employ the element of a freely given gift (χάρισμα) that appears in the Didache, they do include some form of not asking for lent objects to be returned. Thus, we once again find an inversion of Sifra's slapping theme followed by a discussion of lending—amplified to giving without anticipation of return.

The golden rule of doing to others as you want them to do to you follows the discussion of giving and lending according to both reconstructions. A negative formulation of the golden rule appears in the beginning of the Didache in direct connection with the reference to Lev 19:18, which suggests that Q may also have associated the golden rule with Lev 19:18. If so, then the passage discussing giving and lending/borrowing is directly followed by a reference to Lev 19:18, strengthening the parallel between Q and the exegetical tradition presented in Sifra. Furthermore, the theme of loving one's enemies and not simply those in one's close circle (noted above in connection with the Didache as a rejection of Sifra's exclusionary gloss) also appears in Q at this point.

Based on the ordering of material in Luke, this passage, which juxtaposes the several negative actions inspired by hatred with the command to give/lend, is followed by another injunction not to judge that includes the famous parable of the speck and the beam (Q 6:37–42): "why do you see the speck in your brother's eye, but the beam in your own eye you overlook?"[22] This section has been understood by many to refer to the issue of rebuke. In light of our analysis it becomes clear that this section is actually a second rebuke-related text that appears at this point in Q in conjunction with the first passage.[23]

---

[21] Harry T. Fleddermann, *Q: A Reconstruction and Commentary*, BTS (Leuven: Peeters, 2005), 877–78.

[22] Robinson, Hoffmann, and Kloppenborg, *Critical Edition of Q*, 80.

[23] Whether Q 6:27–30 or Q 6:37–42 was the original passage that triggered the inclusion of the other is less relevant for our purposes than recognizing that the juxtaposition of these two traditions stems from the fact that they are both directly engaging with rebuke.

Luke 6:27–35

In seeking to identify sources for material that underlies the Sermon on the Mount and the Sermon on the Plain, scholars such as F. Gerald Downing have pointed primarily to parallels in the work of the Cynics and sapiential sources.[24] While many of these similarities can help explain the appearance of individual dicta, however, they do not always elucidate the juxtaposition and ordering of material that we find in the Gospels. By contrast, the early Jewish exegetical tradition that I am positing correlates both thematically and sequentially with these New Testament passages. Luke 6:27–35, from the Sermon on the Plain, presents perhaps the clearest parallel to the interpretative tradition preserved in Sifra:

> 27 But I say to you that listen, Love your enemies, do good to those who hate you, 28 bless those who curse you, pray for those who abuse you. 29 If anyone strikes you on the cheek, offer the other also; and from anyone who takes away your coat do not withhold even your shirt. 30 Give to everyone who begs from you; and if anyone takes away your goods, do not ask for them again. 31 Do to others as you would have them do to you. 32 If you love those who love you, what credit is that to you? For even sinners love those who love them. 33 If you do good to those who do good to you, what credit is that to you? For even sinners do the same. 34 If you lend to those from whom you hope to receive, what credit is that to you? Even sinners lend to sinners, to receive as much again. 35 But love your enemies, do good, and lend, expecting nothing in return. Your reward will be great, and you will be children of the Most High; for he is kind to the ungrateful and the wicked. (Luke 6:27–35 NRSV)

In this passage we find three major themes reiterated in a consistent order and summarized in verse 35 as "love your enemies, do good, and lend, expecting nothing in return."[25] Luke 6:27 opens with the command to love one's enemies by doing good for those who hate you. The explication of those to whom one should positively respond despite their negative actions includes language that strongly resonates with Sifra's gloss on Lev 19:17–18. Specifically, Luke refers to those who *hate* you (τοῖς μισοῦσιν ὑμᾶς), *curse* you (τοὺς καταρωμένους ὑμᾶς), *mistreat* you (τῶν ἐπηρεαζόντων ὑμᾶς), *strike* you (τῷ τύπτοντί σε), and *take* something from you (τοῦ αἴροντός σου). In the Didache, the discussion of cursing, hating, and persecuting is separated from the one who slaps by Did. 1:4a (abstaining from desires of the flesh), and 1:4c (going an extra mile) separates slapping from giving. By contrast, Luke records these actions in closer juxtaposition, although the first three appear in the

---

[24] F. Gerald Downing, *Cynics and Christian Origins* (Edinburgh: T&T Clark, 1992), 127–30; Downing, *Christ and the Cynics: Jesus and Other Radical Preachers in First-Century Tradition*, JSOT Manuals 4 (Sheffield: JSOT Press, 1988), 23–30.

[25] See A. J. P. Garrow, *The Gospel of Matthew's Dependence on the Didache*, JSNTSup 254 (London: T&T Clark, 2004), 225: "In the next three verses (6.32, 33, 34) Luke then elaborates on three positive actions, 'love, do good, lend', that arise from the actions approved of in Lk. 6.27–31. These three actions are then reinforced once again, in this same order, in Lk. 6.35a."

second person plural while the last two are in the singular. This list of negative actions parallels the biblical prohibition of not hating (לא תשנא) in one's heart and the three categories that we find in Sifra's presentation of actions *not* biblically prohibited as actions of rebuke: cursing (תקללנו), hitting (תכנו) and slapping (תסטרנו). In contrast to the Didache and Matthew, which use the word ῥαπίζει/ ῥάπισμα, Luke uses τύπτοντι ("striking"), which may correlate with the word hitting (תכנו) in Sifra.[26] If so, then among these witnesses we have the presence of all three verbs that appear in Sifra.

The next thematic cues, referring to one who takes something from you (Luke 6:29b, which some understand as referring to robbery) and giving to all who ask (Luke 6:30), are tempered by the corresponding rhetorical question: "If you lend to those from whom you hope to receive, what credit is that to you? Even sinners lend to sinners, to receive as much again." Here the issue of lending (δανίσητε; δανίζουσιν) corresponds to Sifra's exemplification of Lev 19:18a. Yet once again the Christian text amplifies the early Jewish interpretation by promoting lending without expectation of return rather than simply lending without resentment. Additionally, the theme of doing good and lending to all challenges the exclusionary reading of Lev 19:18b that we saw in Sifra as referring only to the "in-group."[27]

Matthew 5:38–44

The majority of scholars who seek a connection between Lev 19:17–18 and the Gospel of Matthew have turned to Matt 7:1–5 and 18:15–20. Neither of these sections explicitly cites the Levitical verses. Based on the general understanding of

---

[26] With regard to the connection between hitting and Lev 19:17–18, Mekhilta de-Rabbi Shimon bar Yoḥai employs Lev 19:18c twice in relation to striking and killing, glossed as "select for him a quick death!" See J. N. Epstein and E. Z. Melamed, *Mekhilta de-Rabbi Shimon bar Yochai* (Jerusalem: Mekize Nirdamim, 1979), 169, 172; W. David Nelson, *Mekhilta de-Rabbi Shimon bar Yoḥai* (Philadelphia: Jewish Publication Society, 2006), 277–78, 281–82. On the relationship between Matthew and the Didache, see the debate between Christopher M. Tuckett and Aaron Milavec: Aaron Milavec, *The Didache: Faith, Hope, & Life of the Earliest Christian Communities, 50–70 C.E.* (New York: Newman, 2003); Milavec, "Synoptic Tradition in the Didache Revisited," *JECS* 11 (2003): 443–80; Milavec, "A Rejoinder," *JECS* 13 (2005): 519–23; C. M. Tuckett, "Synoptic Tradition in the Didache," in *The Didache in Modern Research*, ed. Jonathan A. Draper, AGJU 37 (Leiden: Brill, 1996), 92–128; Tuckett, "The Didache and the Synoptics Once More: A Response to Aaron Milavec," *JECS* 13 (2005): 509–18. For a brief summary of the various possible connections between the Didache and the Synoptics and recent trends toward seeing the Didache as independent of the Gospels, see Kloppenborg, "Use of the Synoptics," 105–6.

[27] In contrast to the two garments that are taken in the New Testament texts, in Sifra the objects lent or borrowed are a sickle and an axe. The discrepancy between these objects can be understood as representing some of the standard possessions for each group. Agricultural tools appear frequently among utensils discussed in Tannaitic literature, and, given the ideally transient nature of the early apostles, clothing would be one of the few possessions they would be assumed to own (thus, e.g., Matt 10:9–10 and Luke 9:3).

the parable of the speck and the beam, however, as well as on an important parallel in 1QS V, 24–VI, 1, these two passages have been accepted as standing in dialogue with Lev 19:17–18. Several of the parallel themes that we find in Sifra and Luke appear in Matt 5:38–44, which indicates that this section should also be considered among the Matthean verses that engage with Lev 19:17–18 despite not referencing Lev 19:17 explicitly:

> 38 You have heard that it was said, "An eye for an eye, and a tooth for a tooth." 39 But I tell you, do not resist an evil person. If anyone slaps you on the right cheek, turn to them the other cheek also. 40 And if anyone wants to sue you and take your shirt, hand over your coat as well. 41 If anyone forces you to go one mile, go with them two miles. 42 Give to the one who asks you, and do not turn away from the one who wants to borrow from you. 43 You have heard that it was said, "You shall love your neighbor and hate your enemy." 44 But I say to you, Love your enemies and pray for those who persecute you. (Matt 5:38–44 NRSV)

Matthew incorporates slapping (ὅστις σε ῥαπίζει) as well as the idea of giving to one who wishes to borrow from you (τὸν θέλοντα ἀπὸ σοῦ δανίσασθαι) in his fifth antithesis. In addition, Matthew actually cites part of Lev 19:18, albeit as the opening of the sixth antithesis.[28] Given that the antithesis form and quotation from Exodus do not appear in Luke—and presumably not in Q as well—it is possible that this block of material was originally associated with Lev 19:17–18 and then appropriated by Matthew or the editor of the antitheses as a gloss on Exod 21:24, leading directly into a separate gloss on Lev 19:18.[29] If this line of reasoning is correct, then the particular counterbiblical message that Matthew records Jesus promoting aligns more closely with the issue of retaliation than with rebuke, likely prompting the use of Exod 21:24 as opposed to Lev 19:17. The resonance between these biblical

---

[28] Kugel suggests that the enigmatic quotation in Matthew of "you shall love your neighbor and hate your enemy" is a response to the exegetical traditions on Lev 19:18 that we see in the Damascus Document and the limiting phrase "to your people" in Lev 19:18 (which is understood in Sifra as only your people and not others) (*In Potiphar's House*, 236–38).

[29] See Richard A. Horsley, "Ethics and Exegesis: 'Love Your Enemies' and the Doctrine of Nonviolence," in Swartley, *Love of Enemy*, 72–101, here 90. The question of whether the antithesis form in the Sermon on the Mount is Matthean or pre-Matthean has been a subject of scholarly debate; see Hans Dieter Betz, *The Sermon on the Mount: A Commentary on the Sermon on the Mount, Including the Sermon on the Plain (Matthew 5:3–7:27 and Luke 6:20–49)*, Hermeneia (Minneapolis: Fortress, 1995), 212–14. Even if this form predates the redaction of Matthew, it is still possible that the compiler of the antitheses section based himself upon a source for antitheses 5 and 6 that was originally tied to Lev 19:17–18. Another possible intertext, however, may be found in Hos 4:2–4, where we find several of the themes of the antitheses in verse 2, followed by an admonition against striving or rebuking: "[False] swearing, dishonesty, and murder, and theft and adultery are rife; crime follows upon crime! For that, the earth is withered: Everything that dwells on it languishes—beasts of the field and birds of the sky—even the fish of the sea perish. 'Let no man rebuke, let no man protest!' For this your people has a grievance against [you], O priest!" (NJPS).

passages is supported by J. W. Doeve's correlation between the verses from Exodus that Jesus comes to reject with material in the Holiness Code in Leviticus. Specifically, Doeve believes that the "eye for an eye" passage (Exod 21:24) lines up with Lev 19:15-18a, which "also speaks of judgment and forbearing vengeance."[30]

Testament of Gad 6:1

Before concluding it is important to note that T. Gad 6:1 preserves a tradition that appears to be independent of Sifra and the aforementioned early Christian sources but nevertheless summarizes some of the common themes: "And now, my children, each one of you love his brother and banish hate from your hearts, loving one another in action and in speech and in the soul's thought" (ἐν ἔργῳ καὶ λόγῳ καὶ διανοίᾳ ψυχῆς).[31] Kugel has argued that the author of this line (as well as the several subsequent verses) is "thinking specifically of Lev 19:17-18."[32] The admonition to remove hatred from the heart recalls Lev 19:17, while the element of love links to Lev 19:18. Specifically, the three means by which one should love others—in deed, word, and intent—map onto some of the themes illustrated above. We find the verbal and physical axes in the verbal and physical acts of cursing, slapping, and so on that gloss Lev 19:17. The notion of lending without resentment in Sifra's example of not bearing a grudge and the "freely given gifts" of the Didache present another instance of a physical act, this time along the axis of intention. While T. Gad 6:1 does not employ the details that we find in any of the other traditions, it offers an independent witness to the broad ideas that underlie the early exegesis of Lev 19:17-18 in the other sources.[33]

II. AN EARLY EXEGESIS OF LEVITICUS 19:17-18

The key words highlighted above of hitting, cursing, and slapping are used in the Christian works in ways significantly different from the usage in Sifra. In Sifra

---

[30] J. W. Doeve, *Jewish Hermeneutics in the Synoptic Gospels and Acts* (Assen: Van Gorcum, 1954), 193. Also see J. Duncan M. Derrett, "Christ and Reproof (Matthew 7.1-5/Luke 6.37-42)," *NTS* 34 (1988): 271-81, here 277; Dennis C. Duling, "Matthew 18:15-17: Conflict, Confrontation, and Conflict Resolution in a 'Fictive Kin' Association," *BTB* 29 (1999): 4-22, here 13-14.

[31] Louis H. Feldman, James L. Kugel, and Lawrence H. Schiffman, eds., *Outside the Bible: Ancient Jewish Writings Related to Scripture*, 3 vols. (Philadelphia: Jewish Publication Society, 2013), 2:1807.

[32] Kugel, *In Potiphar's House*, 221.

[33] It is notoriously difficult to date the Testaments of the Twelve Patriarchs. Most scholars agree, however, that they preserve Second Temple period material, even if composed in a later Christian milieu. See Robert A. Kugler, *The Testaments of the Twelve Patriarchs*, Guides to Apocrypha and Pseudepigrapha (Sheffield: Sheffield Academic, 2001); James R. Davila, *The Provenance of the Pseudepigrapha: Jewish, Christian, or Other?*, JSJSup 105 (Leiden: Brill, 2005).

they appear as permitted modes of rebuking one's fellow. By contrast, in the Christian material these actions are ascribed to a third party who performs them, against whom one is encouraged to adopt a nonretaliatory response. Similarly, while Sifra speaks of lending without resentment to one's fellows, the Christian texts amplify this directive by promoting free giving to all without expectation of return.

One possibility for understanding these differences is to posit that the editor of Sifra was aware of the interpretive direction of the Jesus tradition and was actively polemicizing against it. There is insufficient evidence, however, to justify the claim that the editor of Sifra was aware of any early Christian works. Furthermore, as Sifra's gloss applies directly to the biblical verses, it is more likely that this interpretation originally appeared as such rather than as a polemical response to an already polemical challenge to the biblical material. A more likely alternative for understanding the different manifestations of the early exegetical tradition among these sources is that Sifra reflects a more accurate portrait of the original tradition, which explains the nature of the commandment of rebuke. The early Christian versions represent a divergent interpretation attributed to Jesus that undermines the Levitical command to rebuke as well as the limited and exclusionary command to lend.

Sifra as a whole comprises multiple literary layers including material from the pre-rabbinic period that may be preserved with minimal reworking.[34] Particularly in this instance I am inclined to date Sifra's gloss on Lev 19:17 to a time before the emergence of the rabbis, as it is immediately followed by the comments of several early rabbis who explicitly reject rebuke.[35] Ostensibly, the desire to transmit an accurate formulation of the received tradition outweighed any motivation to change it in response to later attitudes toward the content.[36] By contrast, the authors of the

---

[34] Despite the late dating of Sifra, this work appears to preserve significantly older Jewish traditions. Günter Stemberger suggests that the "simple commentary" (of which our glosses are a part) is the earliest layer of Sifra and "is to be dated to the decades after Bar Kochba (parts of it may be earlier)" ("The Redaction and Transmission of *Sifra*," in *Melekhet Mahshevet: Studies in the Redaction and Development of Talmudic Literature*, ed. Aaron Amit and Aharon Shemesh [Ramat Gan: Bar-Ilan University Press, 2011], 66*). Similarly, Jacob Epstein (Jacob Nahum Epstein and E. Z. Melamed, *Mevoʾot le-sifrut ha-Tanaʾim: Mishnah, Tosefta u-midreshe-halakhah* [Jerusalem: Magnes, 1957], 513) and Yonatan Sagiv ("Studies in Early Rabbinic Hermeneutics as Reflected in Selected Chapters in the Sifra" [Ph.D. diss, Hebrew University, 2009], 253) note that anonymous material in the Tannaitic midrashim (as well as material brought in the name of late Tannaim) can be of much earlier provenance. For more on the dating of Sifra, see Strack and Stemberger, *Introduction to the Talmud and Midrash*, 285–87.

[35] Rabbis Tarfon, Elazar ben Azaryiah, and Akiva all proclaim rebuke to be inapplicable in their day, due either to the ineptitude of potential rebukers or potential recipients of rebuke (see Sifra Qedoshim 4).

[36] I am not suggesting, however, that this preserved tradition is entirely free from slight reworking in the process of transmission. As Sifra was likely compiled sometime during the third century CE, there may be some transformation of the earlier tradition. The significant time differential precludes seeking too precise a formulation of the earlier Jewish exegesis in Sifra, but it does not detract from the comparative possibility with early Christian texts. I believe that the

Gospel passages felt no compunction about adapting and reworking the tradition, particularly in the case of Matthew's antitheses, which are explicitly formulated as challenges to inherited ideas. It seems plausible that the key commandment of Lev 19:18 of loving others encouraged the authors behind these early Christian versions to negate any trace of the negative components of hatred, rebuke, vengeance, or grudge bearing. Rereading the received tradition in light of the obligation to love one's fellow, these texts radically inverted the command of not hating one's brother into loving one's enemy and the admonition against refraining from lending into giving freely.[37]

By bringing Sifra's comments on Lev 19:17–18 into dialogue with several prominent early Christian texts, I hope not only to have advanced our understanding of the genesis of these particular pericopae but to have illustrated the potential for future cautious comparison between early rabbinic and Christian material.

---

interpretation in Sifra retains the core ideas and perhaps even some terminology of the original tradition.

[37] For different reflections on the genesis and role of this emphasis on loving enemies, see John Piper, *"Love Your Enemies": Jesus' Love Command in the Synoptic Gospels and in the Early Christian Paraenesis; A History of the Tradition and Interpretation of Its Uses*, SNTSMS 38 (Cambridge: Cambridge University Press, 2012); Gordon M. Zerbe, *Non-Retaliation in Early Jewish and New Testament Texts: Ethical Themes in Social Contexts*, JSPSup 13 (Sheffield: JSOT Press, 1993), chapter 5; and Swartley, *Love of Enemy*.

New and Recent Titles

HANDBOOK OF CLASSICAL RHETORIC IN THE HELLENISTIC PERIOD (330 B.C.–A.D. 400)
Stanley E. Porter, editor
Paperback $99.95, 978-1-62837-180-2   918 pages, 2017   Code: 069580
Brill Reprints 80

THE ART OF VISUAL EXEGESIS
Rhetoric, Texts, Images
Vernon K. Robbins, Walter S. Melion, Roy R. Jeal, editors
Paperback $69.95, 978-1-62837-172-7   540 pages, 2017   Code 064819
Hardcover $89.95, 978-0-88414-214-0   E-book $69.95, 978-0-88414-213-3
Emory Studies in Early Christianity 19

WHEN TEXTS ARE CANONIZED
Timothy H. Lim, editor
Paperback $29.95, 978-1-946527-00-4   188 pages, 2017   Code: 140359
Hardcover $44.95, 978-1-930675-95-7   E-book $29.95, 978-1-930675-99-5
Brown Judaic Studies 359

SEX, CHRIST, AND EMBODIED COGNITION
Paul's Wisdom for Corinth
Robert H. von Thaden Jr.
Paperback $47.95, 978-1-62837-181-9   358 pages, 2017   Code: 064820
Hardcover $62.95, 978-0-88414-228-7   E-book $47.95, 978-0-88414-227-0
Emory Studies in Early Christianity 16

THE RABBULA CORPUS
Comprising the *Life of Rabbula*, His Correspondence, a Homily Delivered in Constantinople, Canons, and Hymns
Robert R. Phenix Jr. and Cornelia B. Horn
Paperback $99.95, 978-0-88414-078-8   768 pages, 2017   Code: 061617
Hardcover $119.95, 978-1-58983-127-8   E-book $99.95, 978-0-88414-077-1
Writings from the Greco-Roman World 17

SBL Press • P.O. Box 2243 • Williston, VT 05495-2243
Phone: 877-725-3334 (toll-free) or 802-864-6185 • Fax: 802-864-7626
Order online at www.sbl-site.org/publications

Reinventing Mosaic Torah in Ezra-Nehemiah in the Light of the Law (*dāta*) of Ahura Mazda and Zarathustra

YISHAI KIEL
yishai.kiel@gmail.com
Yale University, New Haven, CT 06520

In this study I examine the linguistic and theological contours of the term תורה (*tôrâ*) in Ezra-Nehemiah—particularly the identification of תורה with the law (דת\דתא) of God promulgated by Ezra (Ezra 7:14)—through the lens of Old Persian and Avestan notions of "the law set down (*dāta*)" by Ahura Mazda and revealed through Zarathustra. While the basic notion of divine revelation of laws through the mediation of Moses emerges already in preexilic biblical texts, I posit that the innovative link drawn by the authors of Ezra-Nehemiah between the Old Persian and Avestan term *dāta* (via Aramaic דת\דתא) and the Hebrew תורה reflects a broader and more comprehensive impact of Avestan traditions, mediated by Achaemenid ideology, on the construction and conceptualization of Mosaic תורה in Ezra-Nehemiah. Weighing in on the ongoing debate over the range of imperial authorization of local legislation and cult in Judea, Egypt, and Asia Minor, I argue that the Achaemenids, who were probably involved in certain aspects of the codification and canonization of textual, legal, and theological manifestations of Zoroastrianism, functioned as agents (whether actively or passively) in facilitating and reinforcing the adaptation by the Babylonian-Judean scribes of Avestan notions of divine revelation of the law and scriptural unity linked to personal authority.

Scholars have long debated the theory of imperial authorization of the codification and promulgation of pentateuchal law by Ezra, in the context of the broader policy of the Achaemenids vis-à-vis local laws and cults in Asia Minor and Egypt.[1]

I would like to thank John Collins, Christine Hayes, Prods Oktor Skjærvø, and Yakir Paz for their illuminating comments.

[1] The literature is vast. See, e.g., Peter Frei, "Zentralgewalt und Lokalautonomie im Achämenidenreich," in *Reichsidee und Reichsorganisation im Perserreich*, ed. Peter Frei and Klaus Koch, 2nd ed., OBO 55 (Freiburg, Schweiz: Universitätsverlag, 1996), 8–113; Erhard Blum, *Studien zur*

In this context, scholars have examined possible evidence for imperial authorization and self-ascription of local laws and cults in the inscription of Udjahorresnet, the Passover letter from Elephantine, the document on the verso of the Demotic Chronicle, the trilingual inscription from Letoon, the Gadatas letter (of questionable authenticity), a Greek inscription from Miletus, and the purported imperial proclamation of Artaxerxes preserved in Ezra 7:12–26.[2] Of particular interest to Ezra's alleged mission in terms of the codification and promulgation of pentateuchal law is the parallel mission of Udjahorresnet, the Egyptian scribe and priest, which is likewise said to have been promoted by the Persian authorities.[3]

I will argue that, regardless of how one reconstructs the historical role of the Persian authorities in the process of the codification and consolidation of

---

Komposition des Pentateuch, BZAW 189 (Berlin: de Gruyter, 1990), 346–56; Kenneth G. Hoglund, *Achaemenid Imperial Administration in Syria-Palestine and the Missions of Ezra and Nehemiah*, SBLDS 125 (Atlanta: Scholars Press, 1992), 207–40; Joseph Blenkinsopp, *The Pentateuch: An Introduction to the First Five Books of the Bible*, ABRL (New York: Doubleday, 1992), 239–42; Blenkinsopp, "Was the Pentateuch the Civic and Religious Constitution of the Jewish Ethnos in the Persian Period?," in *Persia and Torah: The Theory of Imperial Authorization of the Pentateuch*, ed. James W. Watts, SymS 17 (Atlanta: Society of Biblical Literature, 2001), 41–62; Jon L. Berquist, *Judaism in Persia's Shadow: A Social and Historical Approach* (Minneapolis: Fortress, 1995), 138–39; James W. Watts, *Reading Law: The Rhetorical Shaping of the Pentateuch*, BibSem 59 (Sheffield: Sheffield Academic, 1999), 137–44; Joseph Wiesehöfer, "'Reichsgesetz' oder 'Einzelfallgerechtigkeit'? Bemerkungen zu P. Freis These von der Achämenidischen 'Reichsautorisation,'" *ZABR* 1 (1995): 36–46; Udo Rütersworden, "Die persische Reichsautorisation der Thora: Fact or Fiction?" *ZABR* 1 (1995): 47–61; Hans-Christoph Schmitt, "Die Suche nach der Identität des Jahweglaubens im nachexilischen Israel: Bemerkungen zur theologischen Intention des Pentateuch," in *Pluralismus und Identität*, ed. Joachim Mehlhausen (Munich: Kaiser, 1995), 259–78; Jean Louis Ska, *Introduction à la lecture du Pentateuque: Clés pour l'interprétation des cinq premiers livres de la Bible*, Le livre et le rouleau (Paris: Cerf, 2000), 310–21; Pierre Briant, "Histoire impériale et histoire régionale: À propos de l'histoire de Juda dans l'empire achéménide," in *Congress Volume: Oslo, 1998*, ed. A. Lemaire and M. Sæbø, VTSup 80 (Leiden: Brill, 2000), 235–45. See also the articles collected in Watts, *Persia and Torah*.

[2] See esp. the sources collected and discussed in Frei, "Zentralgewalt und Lokalautonomie," 8–113. For a fresh reassessment of the evidence see Kyong-Jin Lee, *The Authority and Authorization of Torah in the Persian Period*, CBET 64 (Leuven: Peeters, 2011).

[3] Alan B. Lloyd, "The Inscription of Udjahorresnet: A Collaborator's Testament," *JEA* 68 (1982): 166–80; Joseph Blenkinsopp, "The Mission of Udjahorresnet and Those of Ezra and Nehemiah," *JBL* 106 (1987): 409–21; Karel van der Toorn, *Scribal Culture and the Making of the Hebrew Bible* (Cambridge: Harvard University Press, 2007), 249–51, here 249: "The parallel between the mission of the Egyptian priest Udjahorresnet and that of the Jewish priest Ezra is striking. Ezra was sent from Babylonia to Jerusalem to reorganize the province of Judah in accordance with the rules of the Law. The Persian authorities referred to Ezra's law code as 'the Law of your God that is in your hand' (Ezra 7:14). Since Ezra was an expert in the Law of Moses (literally, a 'proficient scribe of the Law of Moses,' Ezra 7:6), it is legitimate to equate the 'Law of your God' with the Torah of Moses. The Persian king explicitly endorsed the mission of Ezra by adopting Jewish national law as the law of the Persian king (Ezra 7:26)." But cf. Donald B. Redford, "The So-Called 'Codification' of Egyptian Law under Darius I," in Watts, *Persia and Torah*, 135–60.

pentateuchal law in the time of Ezra,[4] the Achaemenids—who were, in all probability, involved in certain aspects of the codification and canonization of textual, legal, and theological manifestations of the Zoroastrian tradition —inspired and facilitated, whether actively or passively, the Babylonian-Judean adaptation of Iranian notions of "scriptural unity" of the Avesta as a revealed text and the codification of the law set down by Ahura Mazda and revealed through Zarathustra.[5]

The connections suggested here do not rest solely on thematic parallels and historical proximity but also on terminological affinity. The study centers on the semantic range of the term תורה in Ezra-Nehemiah,[6] and particularly the identification of the תורה with the law (דת\דתא) of God, through the lens of Old Persian and Avestan notions of the law (dāta).[7] While the term דת\דתא is itself attested

---

[4] Konrad Schmid has correctly observed that a distinction must be made between responses of the Persian authorities (whether on an imperial or a local basis) to local initiatives via authorization and even self-ascription of local laws, on the one hand, and the notion of a central system of codification of local laws integrated into imperial law, on the other hand. While there seems to be insufficient evidence for a broad codification both on the imperial and the local levels, it is difficult to deny that the Achaemenids indeed seem to have authorized, albeit nominally perhaps, local initiatives of cultic codification. See Konrad Schmid, "The Persian Imperial Authorization as Historical Problem and as Biblical Construct: A Plea for Differentiations in the Current Debate," in *The Pentateuch as Torah: New Models for Understanding Its Promulgation and Acceptance*, ed. Gary N. Knoppers and Bernard M. Levinson (Winona Lake, IN: Eisenbrauns, 2007), 22–38.

[5] For the involvement of the Achaemenids in the consolidation of the Zoroastrian tradition, see below in detail. For now see Albert de Jong, "Religion in the Achaemenid Court," in *Der Achämenidenhof/The Achaemenid Court: Akten des 2. Internationalen Kolloquiums zum Thema "Vorderasien im Spannungsfeld klassischer und altorientalischer Überlieferungen," Landgut Castelen bei Basel, 23–25 Mai 2007*, ed. Bruno Jacobs and Robert Rollinger, Classica et Orientalia 2 (Wiesbaden: Harrassowitz, 2010), 533–58. By "scriptural" I do not necessarily mean "written." Although the Pentateuch can properly be described as "holy writ," the Avesta was largely an oral form of "scripture." For the orality of the Avestan tradition, see, e.g., Philip Kreyenbroek, "The Zoroastrian Tradition from an Oralist's Point of View," in *K. R. Cama Oriental Institute, 2nd International Congress Proceedings (5th to 8th January, 1995)*, ed. H. J. M. Desai and H. N. Modi (Bombay: Cama Oriental Institute, 1996), 221–37; Prods Oktor Skjærvø, "The Importance of Orality for the Study of Old Iranian Literature and Myth," *Nāme-ye Irān-e Bāstān* 5 (2005–2006) [2007]: 1–23; Skjærvø, "The Zoroastrian Oral Tradition as Reflected in the Texts," in *The Transmission of the Avesta*, ed. Alberto Cantera, Iranica 20 (Wiesbaden: Harrassowitz, 2012), 3–48.

[6] As we shall see, the term תורה initially referred to particular legal instructions and, subsequently, to specific legal codes (e.g., the laws of Deut 12–26). It is only in the postexilic period, however, that תורה begins to refer to the totality of pentateuchal law (perhaps even the Pentateuch as a whole) as a codified unity, the consolidation of which was achieved through the authoritative and authorial role of Moses.

[7] See Ezra 7:12 (דתא די אלה שמיא, "the law of the God of heaven"), 26 (דתא די אלהך, "the law of your God"), 14 (כל־קבל די מן־קדם מלכא ושבעת יעטהי שליח לבקרא על יהוד ולירושלם בדת), אלהך די בידך, "For you are commissioned by the king and his seven advisers to regulate Judah and Jerusalem according to the law of your God, which is in your care").

The word *dāta* is the Old Iranian term for "law" (from the root *dā-*, "to put, set in place,"

elsewhere in the Bible in a more general sense of "law, custom" (see, e.g., Esth 3:8, Neh 8:36), the use of the term in Ezra 7 seems to trigger a particular meaning attached to the term *dāta* and its cognates in the Old Persian and Avestan context. Thus, beyond emphasizing the obvious employment of the Aramaic term for "law" in a document that purports to be a royal proclamation issued by Artaxerxes, I will endeavor to illuminate the particular significance of this term for Ezra's alleged mission of promulgating the תורה of Moses.[8]

The basic notion of divine revelation of the law mediated through the figure of Moses emerges already in preexilic texts—as can be gathered from the revelation of the Covenant Code according to E, the laws of Deut 12–26 according to D, and the laws of the tabernacle and the cultic and purity regulations according to P—and is paralleled in part by several ancient Near Eastern traditions, in which instructions are similarly ascribed to deities via the mediation of scribal authorship.[9] For

---

thus "[the law] set/laid down"), attested both in Avestan (Old and Younger Av. *dāta-*) and in Achaemenid royal inscriptions (Old Pers. *dāta-*). See, in general, Rüdiger Schmitt, "Dāta," in *EIr* 7.1:114–15 (originally published 15 December 1994; last updated 18 November 2011).

[8] On the debate over the authenticity of the proclamation, see the summary of scholarship in Joseph Blenkinsopp, *Ezra-Nehemiah: A Commentary*, OTL (Philadelphia: Westminster, 1988), 146–47.

[9] In the ancient Near East, the gods were, by and large, perceived as guardians of justice and dispensers of truth who authorized the kings by establishing them and conferring upon them the principles of justice and the wisdom essential to their rule. The particular laws, however, were produced by the kings themselves and were known by the kings' names. Although similar ideas can be found in the Bible, Deuteronomy seems to reflect the paradigm of a "disempowered king" who is subject to God's revealed law and its interpretation by the priests. For the three dominant biblical models of kingship and the relationship between the king and the law, see Yair Lorberbaum, *Disempowered King: Monarchy in Classical Jewish Literature*, Kogod Library of Judaic Studies 9 (New York: Continuum, 2011), 1–36. But cf. Michael LeFebvre, who argues that, in line with the prevailing ancient Near Eastern model, according to Deuteronomy and the Deuteronomistic History the king is not instructed to consult the Torah as prescriptive revealed legislation but rather to rely on the wisdom and discernment granted by YHWH (*Collections, Codes, and Torah: The Re-characterization of Israel's Written Law*, LHBOTS 451 [New York: T&T Clark, 2006], 88–94). See recently Christine Hayes, *What's Divine about Divine Law? Early Perspectives* (Princeton: Princeton University Press, 2015), 31–36. For ascription of instructions to deities in the ancient Near East, see, e.g., van der Toorn, *Scribal Culture*, 207–11. Perhaps the example closest to the biblical model of revelation can be found in the Mesopotamian Catalogue of Texts and Authors. See, e.g., frag. VI, line 16, which states that Ea spoke these texts and "Adapa wrote them down at his dictation." See Wilfred G. Lambert, "A Catalogue of Texts and Authors," *JCS* 16 (1962): 59–77, esp. 66–69; Peter Machinist and Hayim Tadmor, "Heavenly Wisdom," in *The Tablet and the Scroll: Near Eastern Studies in Honor of William W. Hallo*, ed. Mark E. Cohen, Daniel C. Snell, and David B. Weisberg (Bethesda, MD: CDL, 1993), 146–51, here 146–47; and, most recently, Uri Gabbay, "Akkadian Commentaries from Ancient Mesopotamia and Their Relation to Early Hebrew Exegesis," *DSD* 19 (2012): 267–312. These similarities notwithstanding, Bernard M. Levinson notes that "Israelite scribes introduced into the ancient world a *new* idea: the divine revelation of law. Accordingly, it was not the legal collection as a literary genre but the

the most part, however, these instructions were perceived not as prescriptive revealed legislation but rather as descriptive, academic, or pedagogical forms of nonlegislative instruction.[10]

Although there is some debate over the transition from descriptive to prescriptive perceptions of divine law in ancient Israel, it would seem that the Persian period constituted an important milestone in this regard.[11] One way or another, the distinctiveness of Ezra-Nehemiah's conceptualization of תורה lies not in inventing the idea of divine revelation of instructions mediated through Moses but in the literary use of the figure of Moses so as to achieve the textual unity of the Pentateuch (or, at least, pentateuchal law).[12] In this context, Moses functions not merely as a mediator of a single law code revealed by God but as the scarlet thread that unifies and consolidates the various law codes contained in the Pentateuch. In fact, it is this comprehensive construal of Mosaic תורה that serves to justify the very redactorial endeavor purportedly undertaken by Ezra of weaving discrete law codes into a single unity. Below we shall see that a strikingly similar conception is embedded in the Avestan construction of the "law [dāta-] of Zarathustra" set down by Ahura Mazda, which serves to unify, consolidate, and subsume distinct elements

---

voicing of publicly revealed law as the personal will of God that was unique to ancient Israel" (*Legal Revision and Religious Renewal in Ancient Israel* [Cambridge: Cambridge University Press, 2008], 27). The similarities between biblical and Avestan notions of divine revelation of the law, however, were by and large overlooked by scholars. But see recently Yaakov Elman, who briefly observes that "in vital respects Israelite religion and Zoroastrianism stood apart from Sumero-Akkadian religion even in Achaemenid times. Both had become, or were in the process of becoming, scriptural religions, that is, religions whose central doctrines were embodied in a revelation vouchsafed to a prophet in the form of a long compilation, though it would be more than a millennium before Zoroastrianism's 'scripture' would be written down" ("Contrasting Intellectual Trajectories: Iran and Israel in Mesopotamia," in *Encounters by the Rivers of Babylon: Scholarly Conversations between Jews, Iranians, and Babylonians in Antiquity*, ed. Shai Secunda and Uri Gabbay, TSAJ 160 [Tübingen: Mohr Siebeck, 2014], 7–106, here 13–14).

[10] For the nonlegislative and nonprescriptive nature of ancient Near Eastern law and the essential conformity of biblical law to this model, see LeFebvre, *Collections, Codes, and Torah*, 1–30; Raymond Westbrook, "What Is the Covenant Code?," in *Theory and Method in Biblical and Cuneiform Law: Revision, Interpolation and Development*, ed. Bernard M. Levinson, JSOTSup 181 (Sheffield: Sheffield Phoenix, 2006), 15–36. But, in the same volume, cf. Sophie Lafont, "Ancient Near Eastern Laws: Continuity and Pluralism," 91–118, esp. 96.

[11] Cf. LeFebvre, according to whom the authors of Ezra-Nehemiah do not yet perceive the תורה as prescriptive legislation but rather see it as an authoritative ideal (*Collections, Codes, and Torah*, 3–8, 96–145). Perhaps LeFebvre's reluctance to read Ezra-Nehemiah's concept of תורה maximally as the beginning of prescriptivism in ancient Israel derives from his erroneous assumption that Persian concepts of divine law do not differ from those found among other cultures in the ancient Near East (see the assertion of Anne Fitzpatrick-McKinley, *The Transformation of Torah from Scribal Advice to Law*, JSOTSup 287 [Sheffield: Sheffield Academic, 1999], 48, quoted by LeFebvre, *Collection, Codes, and Torah*, 5).

[12] What exactly is meant by the term תורה in Ezra-Nehemiah will be discussed below in detail.

of the Zoroastrian tradition under an indivisible and coherent notion of scriptural revelation.

Hindy Najman applies Friedrich Nietzsche's discussion of the Homeric corpus and Foucauldian conceptions of authorship to the Pentateuch and the question of its Mosaic authority. On that basis, she attempts to reconstruct the "Mosaic discourse" that pervades postbiblical works (especially Jubilees and 4 Ezra). She argues that these ancient works aim not only to tie a discourse to a founding figure (as can be said of other figures in antiquity such as Enoch) but also to ascribe personal authority and authorship to a literary corpus, thus contributing to its textual unity.[13]

A similar case, I posit, should be made for the concept of תורה in Ezra-Nehemiah and the literary role reserved for the figure of Moses in affirming the textual unity of the Pentateuch and its perception as revealed legislation. By broadening the semantic range of the term תורה to encompass the entirety of pentateuchal law (and perhaps even the Pentateuch as a whole) and depicting Moses as the ultimate promoter of this law, the authors of Ezra-Nehemiah essentially project the consolidation and promulgation of the תורה (which they attributed to Ezra) back onto the authoritative figure of Moses.[14] In that respect, the authors seem both to affirm the process of interweaving and consolidating distinctive codes into a single textual unity in the time of Ezra[15] and, at the same time, to subvert this very

---

[13] In his inaugural lecture at the University of Basel, Nietzsche readdressed the long-debated "Homeric question"—the problem of reconstructing the "original" Homeric texts and identifying the figure of Homer as their "original" author. In a radical and much-criticized move, he wondered, "Was the person created out of a concept or the concept out of a person?," arguing that, the question of the historicity of Homer as a person notwithstanding, the conception of a full-blown author responsible for the composition and production of the Homeric corpus is the product of a long process of textual consolidation, which came into its familiar form only in late antique Alexandria. See Friedrich Nietzsche, "Homer and Classical Philology" (inaugural lecture, Basel University, 28 May 1869), in *The Complete Works of Friedrich Nietzsche: The First Complete and Authorized English Translation*, ed. Oscar Levy, trans. John McFarland Kennedy, 18 vols. (Edinburgh: T. N. Foulis, 1910), 3:145–70, here 155.

For Foucault, see esp. Michel Foucault, "What Is an Author?," in *Aesthetics, Method, and Epistemology*, ed. James D. Faubion, trans. Josué V. Harari, modified by Robert Hurley, vol. 2 of *The Essential Works of Foucault, 1954–1984*, 3 vols. (New York: New Press, 1997–2000), 205–22.

See Hindy Najman, *Seconding Sinai: The Development of Mosaic Discourse in Second Temple Judaism*, JSJSup 77 (Leiden: Brill, 2003); and, more recently, Najman, "Traditionary Processes and Textual Unity in 4Ezra," in *Fourth Ezra and Second Baruch: Reconstruction after the Fall*, ed. Matthias Henze and Gabriele Boccaccini, JSJSup 164 (Leiden: Brill, 2013), 99–117.

[14] For a history of the term תורה, see below.

[15] That Ezra's activity is the most plausible historical context for the consolidation of the Pentateuch was suggested already in Spinoza's *Theological-Political Treatise* (1670). For a recent discussion on the matter, see Baruch J. Schwartz, "The Torah—Its Five Books and Four Documents," in *The Literature of the Hebrew Bible: Introductions and Studies* [in Hebrew], ed. Zipora Talshir, 2 vols. (Jerusalem: Ben Zvi, 2011), 2:161–226, here 215–16. Although this suggestion is plausible, I do not insist on the historical association of the formation of the Pentateuch with Ezra,

same process by ascribing the תורה, in the broadest sense possible, to Moses.¹⁶ Here I hope to illuminate the linguistic and comparative context underlying this process by recourse to the Avestan notion of the "law [*dāta-*] of Zarathustra" set down by Ahura Mazda and its Old Persian subversion in Xerxes's royal inscription. This connection is arguably alluded to in the distinctive association made in Ezra 7 between the תורה of Moses and the דת\דתא of God promulgated by Ezra.

Scholars have previously noted the similarity between the dual system of imperial and divine law reflected in Artaxerxes's alleged proclamation (Ezra 7:26; דתא די אלהך ודתא די מלכא, "the law of your God and the law of the king")¹⁷ and Xerxes's allusions both to the law set down by Ahura Mazda and the law established by the king (although, never in the same context).¹⁸ The Old Persian inscriptions generally discuss "religious" matters only inasmuch as they pertain to the political ideology of the Achaemenids (e.g., the mention of "creation" by Ahura Mazda is intended, first and foremost, to support the idea of divine enthronement of the sovereign¹⁹). Thus, Xerxes's mention of the law set down by Ahura Mazda is

---

as my argument concerns mainly the literary reconstruction of Ezra (and Moses) according to the authors of Ezra-Nehemiah.

¹⁶ See Frank Crüsemann, *The Torah: Theology and Social History of Old Testament Law*, trans. Allan W. Mahnke (Minneapolis: Fortress, 1996), 102–7. Crüsemann remarks that "in the postexilic period Moses was just an image, but an extremely effective one for the correlation of tradition and autonomy. He stood for the possibility and necessity to bring together the interests and traditions of divergent groups, especially between priests and laity" (107). Jean Louis Ska similarly observes that "Moses is the only figure who can unify the different groups and different tendencies within the postexilic community, especially the priestly families and the landlords of the civil and lay authorities of Judah" ("Persian Imperial Authorization: Some Question Marks," in Watts, *Persia and Torah*, 161–82, here 177–78). Moses, therefore, is presented in Ezra-Nehemiah as the authority behind the תורה (in the inclusive sense of the entirety of pentateuchal law), so as to account for the process of hybridization and consolidation of the pentateuchal documents, thus enabling the representation of different social groups in the legal canon. Regardless of whether Ezra was historically responsible for the consolidation of the Pentateuch as many scholars maintain, he is *depicted* in Ezra-Nehemiah as a "second Moses." See, e.g., Klaus Koch, "Ezra and the Origins of Judaism," *JSS* 19 (1974): 173–97. Compare also the rabbinic statement in t. Sanh. 4:7; b. Sanh. 22a.

¹⁷ This does not mean that the law of the king and that of YHWH are perceived as identical by way of royal self-ascription of the religious law or the like, but rather that Ezra assumed authority over both. On this point, see Blenkinsopp, *Ezra-Nehemiah*, 151 (cf. Ska, "Persian Imperial Authorization," 166–67). That Ezra occupied both a religious and an official position has been widely accepted since the suggestion of Hans Heinrich Schaeder, *Esra der Schreiber*, BHT 5 (Tübingen: Mohr Siebeck, 1930), 39–59. Blenkinsopp correctly notes, however, that this theory relies heavily on the language of the firman itself, which describes Ezra as both scribe and priest (Ezra 7:12, 21) (*Ezra-Nehemiah*, 137). Since this is how Ezra is also described in the narrative (e.g., Neh 8:9, 12:26), it is more likely that this terminology reflects the perspective of the authors of Ezra-Nehemiah that influenced the formulation of the firman.

¹⁸ The sources are discussed below.

¹⁹ See, e.g., Darius at Naqsh-e Rostam (DNa 1–8): "The great god is Ahuramazdā, who set in place this earth [*haya imām būmim adā*], who established that heaven [*haya avam asmānam*

intended, at least in part, to portray the king as an agent of the supreme god. If we seek, however, to understand the significance of the identification of תורה and *dāta* according to Ezra-Nehemiah—a claim that is essentially religious in nature—we must direct our attention beyond the political agenda of the Old Persian inscriptions to the Avestan underpinnings of Xerxes's allusion to "the law set down by

---

adā], who established man [*haya martiyam adā*], who established happiness [*šiyātim*] for man, who made Darius king." Similarly, in the Old and Young Avestan texts, Ahura Mazda is said to have "established" or to have "set in place" (Avestan and Old Persian *dā*-; Old Indic *dhā*-) Order (Avestan *aṣa*-). This verb is reflective of a notion not of creation *ex nihilo* (contra the arguments of Mary Boyce, *A History of Zoroastrianism* [HdO 8; Leiden: Brill, 1982; repr. as *A History of Zoroastrianism II: Under the Achaemenians* [Leiden: Brill, 1996], 2:43–47) but rather of enforcing order upon the domain of chaos. For the meaning of the verb *dā*-, see Jean Kellens, "Ahura Mazdā n'est pas un dieu créateur," in *Études irano-aryennes offertes à Gilbert Lazard*, ed. C. H. de Fouchécour and Phillip Gignoux, StIr.C 7 (Paris: Association pour l'avancement des études iraniennes, 1989), 217–28; Prods Oktor Skjærvø, "Truth and Deception in Ancient Iran," in *Ātaš-e dorun—The Fire Within*, vol. 2 of *Jamshid Soroush Soroushian Commemorative Volume*, ed. Farrokh Vajifdar and Carlo G. Cereti (n.p.: 1st Books Library, 2003), 383–434, esp. 407–16; Skjærvø, "Zoroastrian Dualism," in *Light against Darkness: Dualism in Ancient Mediterranean Religion and the Contemporary World*, ed. Armin Lange et al., JAJSup 2 (Göttingen: Vandenhoeck & Ruprecht, 2011), 55–91, here 59–62. Albert de Jong observed that "the discussion of this particular subject of ancient Zoroastrianism has been muddied by the suggestion of Jean Kellens that Ahura Mazdā was not a creator god at all. This suggestion was based on a characteristically learned and detailed analysis of passages from the Gāthās in which the verb 'to create' occurs and it has made quite an impression on a number of scholars. Others, fortunately, have been quick to point out that the whole exercise was futile in being based on a very particular notion of 'creation' as *creatio ex nihilo*, which is currently thought to be a Christian philosophical invention of the second century" (de Jong, "Ahura Mazdā the Creator," in *The World of Achaemenid Persia: History, Art and Society in Iran and the Ancient Near East; Proceedings of a Conference at the British Museum 29th September–1st October 2005*, ed. John Curtis and St. John Simpson [London: I. B. Tauris, 2010], 85–89, here 88). The ordering of the cosmos by Ahura Mazda is described in several places in Old and Young Avestan texts as well as in Old Persian inscriptions, e.g., Yasna haptaŋhāiti 37.1: "So, in this way we are sacrificing to Ahura Mazdā, who set (in place) both the cow and Order, (who set in place) both the (good) waters and the good plants, (who set in place) both the lights and the earth and all good (things in between)." Yasna 44.3–4: "Who, I wonder, (is), by (his) engendering, the first father of Order? Who, I wonder, (first) set (in its place) the road of the sun and of the stars? Who is he by who(se agency) the moon is first waxing then waning?… Who, I wonder, (first) held (up) the earth down below and the clouds (above keeping them) from falling? Who (fashioned) the waters and the plants? Who yoked the two fleet (coursers) to the wind and the clouds?" The answer to these rhetorical questions is "Ahura Mazda." On several occasions, Ahura Mazda is said to have produced certain elements merely by thinking them (through *mantā*, Yasna 31.7, 31.19). One of the oldest cosmogonic accounts in Zoroastrianism is that of a "weaving" myth, for which see Prods Oktor Skjærvø, "Poetic and Cosmic Weaving in Ancient Iran: Reflections on Avestan vahma and Yasna 34.2," in *Haptačahaptāitiš: Festschrift for Fridrik Thordarson on the Occasion of His 75th Birthday*, ed. Daug Haug and Eirik Welo (Oslo: Novus, 2005), 267–79. For a comparison of Yasna 44 and the rhetoric of Second Isaiah, see Morton Smith, "II Isaiah and the Persians," *JAOS* 83 (1963): 415–21.

Ahura Mazda." Thus, while the references in the inscriptions of Darius and Xerxes to the law of the king upheld and authorized by Ahura Mazda are not significantly different from the rhetorical paradigm that pervaded the ancient Near Eastern law codes, the notion of a law distinct from that of the king, which was set down and established by Ahura Mazda, differs from this paradigm and appears to be derived from the Avestan concept of divine revelation.

Though there is hardly a consensus on the dating of the Avesta, the regnant scholarly position maintains that the Avestan works were composed (or rather crystallized) orally between the late second and early first millennium BCE, before the advent of the Achaemenids.[20] It has further been demonstrated by Prods Oktor Skjærvø that the Achaemenids were, in all probability, familiar with parts of an Old Persian *zand* (translation-cum-commentary) of the Avesta, which they in turn paraphrased and incorporated into their Old Persian inscriptions.[21]

In a recent article, Albert de Jong posited that the Achaemenids played a significant role as agents in the centralization, consolidation, and canonization of the textual, ritual, and theological manifestations of Zoroastrianism.[22] While

---

[20] For a pre-Achaemenid dating of the Avesta (even the later parts) and the rejection of previous suggestions, see, e.g., Prods Oktor Skjærvø, "The *Videvdad*: Its Ritual-Mythical Significance," in *The Age of the Parthians*, vol. 2 in *The Idea of Iran*, ed. Vesta Sarkhosh Curtis and Sarah Stewart (London: I. B. Tauris, 2007), 108–12; Jean Kellens, *Essays on Zarathustra and Zoroastrianism*, ed. and trans. Prods Oktor Skjærvø (Costa Mesa, CA: Mazda, 2000). See also Ilya Gershevitch, "Approaches to Zoroaster's Gathas," *Iran* 33 (1995): 1–29; Gherardo Gnoli, "Once More Zoroaster's Time: A Manichaean Dating," *East and West* 45 (1995): 313–19; Gnoli, *Zoroaster in History*, Biennial Yarshater Lecture Series 2 (New York: Bibliotheca Persica, 2000); Shaul Shaked, "Zoroastrian Origins: Indian and Iranian Connections," in *Axial Civilizations and World History*, ed. Johann P. Arnason, S. N. Eisenstadt, and Björn Wittrock, JSRC 4 (Leiden: Brill, 2005), 183–200. Biblicists seem to have largely ignored the significance of the Avestan evidence for postexilic biblical material, not only for reasons of language obscurity but also because it was erroneously assumed that the Avesta (or at least its later parts) was composed during the Parthian period. Thus, for example, Blenkinsopp writes, "We know of no Persian compilation of laws prior to the collection of instructions in the Videvdad or Vendidad (Anti-demonic Law) from the Parthian period" ("Was the Pentateuch the Civic and Religious Constitution?," 42). As we shall see below, however, this dating has long fallen out of favor among Iranists.

[21] See Prods Oktor Skjærvø, "Avestan Quotations in Old Persian? Literary Sources of the Old Persian Inscriptions," in *Irano-Judaica*, vol. 4, ed. Shaul Shaked and Amnon Netzer (Jerusalem: Ben-Zvi, 1999), 1–64; Skjærvø, "The Achaemenids and the Avesta," in *Birth of the Persian Empire*, vol. 1 of *The Idea of Iran*, ed. Vesta Sarkhosh Curtis and Sarah Stewart (London: I. B. Tauris, 2005), 52–84.

[22] De Jong, "Religion in the Achaemenid Court," 533–58. In this article, de Jong supplements his prior assertion (de Jong, "The Contribution of the Magi," in Curtis and Stewart, *Birth of the Persian Empire*, 85–99) regarding the role of the magi (as recorded in the Greek and Latin sources) in the process of consolidating Zoroastrianism, which suggests that the Achaemenids themselves were the main agents behind this process. In this context, he discusses a tradition (preserved in the much later Pahlavi corpus) describing the attempt of the Achaemenids to collect, retrieve, and canonize the Avestan tradition. One such version of this tradition appears in the fourth book of

remaining somewhat skeptical regarding the intelligibility of the Avesta to the Old Persian–speaking Achaemenids and the plausibility of its use as a "source" in their consolidation of Zoroastrianism,[23] he proposes nonetheless that the Achaemenids encouraged and enforced the collection and codification of their laws and sacred traditions, which must have intersected, at least in part, with the Avesta.[24] It is thus in the light of the Avestan tradition that we should attempt to read Xerxes's advancement of "the law set down by Ahura Mazda."

That the Avestan concept of the law of Ahura Mazda mediated through the figure of Zarathustra could have reached the Judean scribes via Achaemenid agency is possible on several grounds. Whether, as the authors of Ezra-Nehemiah would have us believe, the Achaemenids actively endorsed or authorized the consolidation and promulgation of pentateuchal law (and other local endeavors) is difficult to ascertain. Even if they did not, this hardly excludes the possibility that the Judean scribes were inspired by Zoroastrian models of canonization, codification, and revelation mediated by the Achaemenids.[25]

This assumption can be supported by several attempts to demonstrate the existence of Zoroastrian impact on postexilic biblical texts.[26] Of particular interest

---

the Dēnkard: "Dārāy, son of Dārāy, having committed to writing the entire Avesta and Zand as it had been received by Zarathustra from Ohrmazd, commanded two copies to be made—one to be kept in the gubernatorial treasury and one in the Fortress of Books" (Dēnkard 4.15 [ed. Madan, 412; ed. Dresden, 321–22]; *The Spirit of Zoroastrianism*, ed. and trans. Prods Oktor Skjærvø, Sacred Literature Series [New Haven: Yale University Press, 2011], 41). Compare Carlo G. Cereti, *La letteratura Pahlavi: Introduzione ai testi con riferimenti alla storia degli studi ed alla tradizione manoscritta* (Milan: Mimesis, 2001), 59–61; Alberto Cantera, *Studien zur Pahlavi-Übersetzung des Avesta*, Iranica 7 (Wiesbaden: Harrassowitz, 2004), 106–13. For a discussion of this tradition and its Hebrew and Arabic parallels, see Mansor Shaki, "The Dēnkard Account of the History of the Zoroastrian Scriptures," *ArOr* 49 (1981): 114–25; Shlomo Pines, "A Parallel between Two Iranian and Jewish Themes," *Irano-Judaica* 2, ed. Shaul Shaked and Amnon Netzer (Jerusalem: Ben Zvi, 1990), 41–51; Kevin T. van Bladel, *The Arabic Hermes: From Pagan Sage to Prophet of Science*, Oxford Studies in Late Antiquity (Oxford: Oxford University Press, 2009), 30–63; Shai Secunda, "The Talmudic Bei Abedan and the Sasanian Attempt to 'Recover' the Lost Avesta," *JSQ* 18 (2011): 343–66; Yishai Kiel, "The Authority of the Sages in the Babylonian Talmud: A Zoroastrian Perspective," *Shnaton Ha-mishpat Ha-ivri* 27 (2012–2013): 157–58. While there are many anachronisms in this tradition—most notably the improbable notion of a written Avesta in the Achaemenid period, which most likely stems from late Sasanian times and reflects a Sasanian projection back onto the Achaemenid period—it has been argued (convincingly in my mind) that this Pahlavi tradition preserves a memory, however faint and distorted, of Achaemenid times.

[23] De Jong, "Religion in the Achaemenid Court," 537–40.

[24] Ibid., 541.

[25] For the various social venues through which such interactions were made possible, see recently Jason Silverman, "Iranian-Judaean Interaction in the Achaemenid Period," in *Text, Theology, and Trowel: New Investigations in the Biblical World*, ed. Lidia D. Matassa and Jason M. Silverman (Eugene, OR: Wipf & Stock, 2011), 133–68.

[26] Notable contributions include Smith, "II Isaiah and the Persians," 415–21; James R. Russell, "Zoroastrian Elements in the Book of Esther," in Shaked and Netzer, *Irano-Judaica* 2:

is the existence of structural and compositional affinity between postexilic biblical texts and the Avesta, a fact that points to similar redactorial activity. It has been posited in this context that, at a somewhat earlier point after the conquest of Babylonia in 539 BCE, the very same process of Achaemenid mediation facilitated the composition of the Priestly source (P) by the Judean priesthood in the image of the Videvdad, a Young Avestan work probably known to the Achaemenids.[27]

I. A Semantic History of תורה

The Pentateuch itself makes no self-referential claim for Mosaic authorship. While the precise manner by which Mosaic authorship of the Pentateuch came to be the authoritative view in rabbinic Judaism and early Christianity is not entirely clear, some evidence regarding this process can be gleaned from the

---

33–40; Russell, "Ezekiel and Iran," in *Irano-Judaica*, vol. 5, ed. Shaul Shaked and Amnon Netzer (Jerusalem: Ben Zvi, 2003), 1–15; Joseph Fleishman, "The Rebuilding of the Wall of Jerusalem: Neh. 2:1–9 and the Use of Zoroastrian Principles," *JNSL* 34 (2008): 103–26; Jason M. Silverman, *Persepolis and Jerusalem: Iranian Influence on the Apocalyptic Hermeneutic*, LHBOTS 558 (London: T&T Clark, 2012); Boyce, *History of Zoroastrianism*, 2:43–47); S. David Sperling, "Pants, Persians, and the Priestly Source," in *Ki Baruch Hu: Ancient Near Eastern, Biblical, and Judaic Studies in Honor of Baruch A. Levine*, ed. Robert Chazan, William W. Hallo, and Lawrence H. Schiffman (Winona Lake, IN: Eisenbrauns, 1999), 373–85. For possible connections between the biblical and Avestan purity laws, see Yishai Kiel, "Zoroastrian and Hindu Connections in the Priestly Strata of the Pentateuch: The Case of Numbers 31:19–24," *VT* 63 (2013): 577–604; Reinhard Achenbach, *Die Vollendung der Tora: Studien zur Redaktionsgeschichte des Numeribuches im Kontext von Hexateuch und Pentateuch*, BZABR 3 (Wiesbaden: Harrassowitz, 2002), 500–504; Thomas Kazen, *Issues of Impurity in Early Judaism* (Winona Lake, IN: Eisenbrauns, 2010), 5–8. See also Christian Frevel and Christophe Nihan, "Introduction," in *Purity and the Forming of Religious Traditions in the Ancient Mediterranean World and Ancient Judaism*, ed. Christian Frevel and Christophe Nihan, Dynamics in the History of Religion 3 (Leiden: Brill, 2013), 40–43; Carsten Colpe, "Priesterschrift und *Videvdad*: Ritualistische Gesetzgebung für Israeliten und Iranier," in *Meilenstein: Festgabe für Herbert Donner zum 16. Februar 1995*, ed. Manfred Weippert and Stefan Timm, ÄAT 30 (Wiesbaden: Harrassowitz, 1995), 9–18.

[27] Yishai Kiel, "A Young Avestan Model for the Composition of P," in *Proceedings of the Eighth Symposium of the Melammu Project Held at the University of Kiel, Germany, November 11–15, 2014* (forthcoming). The study argues that, in both P and the Videvdad, the sacrificial and purity laws, which form the body of the legislative part, are preceded by and theologically facilitated through a creation narrative (exhibiting the initial taming of chaos by God); a flood story (reflecting the persistence of chaos and evil); a "history" of divine revelation, entailing God's communication with certain individuals prior to the ultimate revelation of his law; and finally the revelation of the law (consisting primarily of purity and cultic regulations) to Moses and Zarathustra, respectively. P and the Videvdad are similarly marked, moreover, by a theological watershed that divides the pre-nomian era of pre-Mosaic and pre-Zarathustrian communication with the deity—a period in which no positive divine law existed and no sacrifices were offered—from the period that unfolded with the imparting of divine law to humans through the mediation of Moses and Zarathustra.

biblical use of the term תורה in the postexilic strata. The semantic development of this term need not be rehearsed here in detail,[28] so I will restrict myself to a brief summary of the evidence, highlighting the distinctive use of the term תורה in the postexilic strata.[29]

The term תורה essentially means a "teaching" or "instruction." Often it refers to a specific instruction, such as the decisions given by a judge (Exod 18:16, Deut 17:11) or the instructions given by God to Abraham (Gen 26:5).[30] In P, תורה generally refers not to a specific decision or instruction but rather to a body of instructions pertaining to a specific ritual rite.[31] This usage of תורה may be rooted in priestly ritual instructions recorded in short scrolls, each carrying a specific body of instructions pertaining to a particular topic and marked by a colophon.[32]

D represents the first attempt to apply the term תורה more broadly to encompass a "code" or collection of laws (but cf. Exod 24:12), as the term seems to refer specifically to the legal part of Deuteronomy (chs. 12–26), which is said to have been delivered by Moses to the Israelites on the plains of Moab.[33] It is in this context

---

[28] On the term תורה, see Michael Fishbane, "Torah" [in Hebrew], *Encyclopaedia Miqra'it* (Jerusalem: Bialik, 1971–1988), 8:469–83; Félix García López, "תורה torah," *ThWAT* 8:597–637; Moshe Greenberg, "Three Conceptions of the Torah in Hebrew Scriptures," in *Die Hebräische Bibel und ihre zweifache Nachgeschichte: Festschrift für Rolf Rendtorff zum 65. Geburtstag*, ed. Erhard Blum, Christian Macholz, and Ekkehard W. Stegemann (Neukirchen-Vluyn: Neukirchener Verlag, 1990), 365–78; Jonathan Ben-Dov, "Writing as Oracle and as Law: New Contexts for the Book-Find of King Josiah," *JBL* 127 (2008): 223–39, esp. 225–29; Schwartz, "Torah—Its Five Books," 162–63. See also Joel S. Baden, *The Composition of the Pentateuch: Renewing the Documentary Hypothesis*, AYBRL (New Haven: Yale University Press, 2012), 14–16.

[29] I am less interested here in the "secular" dimensions of the term תורה used in several passages in the wisdom literature (e.g., Prov 1:8, 4:2, 6:20, 13:14, Job 22:22; see Fishbane, *Encyclopaedia Miqra'it* 8:480) than in the religious and legal connotations that govern the vast majority of its occurrences. I will also not be addressing some of the prophetic uses of the term תורה as a divine oracle (e.g., Isa 1:10, 2:3), which are naturally closer to Mesopotamian conceptions of "revelation." See, e.g., Fishbane, *Encyclopaedia Miqra'it* 8:473; Ben-Dov, "Writing as Oracle," 226.

[30] Using the plural form תורות (*tôrôt*) in Exod 18:16 and Gen 26:5.

[31] See, e.g., Exod 12:49 ("there shall be one law [תורה אחת] for the native and for the alien who resides among you"), which refers only to the preceding instruction as well as the constructs typical of P: תורת המנחה ("the law of the cereal offering"), תורת החטאת ("the law of the purification offering"), תורת האשם ("the law of reparation"), תורת היולדת ("the law of a woman who bore a child"), and תורת המצורע ("the law of scale disease"). See Lev 6:2, 7, 18; 7:1, 7, 11, 37; 11:46; 12:7; 13:59; 14:2, 32, 54, 57; Num 5:29, 30; 6:13, 21; 15:16, 29; 19:2, 14; 31:21.

[32] García López, *ThWAT* 8:605–6; Jacob Milgrom, *Leviticus 1–16: A New Translation with Introduction and Commentary*, AB 3 (New York: Doubleday, 1991), 382–83.

[33] See, e.g., Deut 4:8: "And what other great nation has statutes and ordinances as just as this entire law [כל התורה הזאת] that I am setting before you *today*," which seems to refer only to the laws of Deut 12–26, which were delivered on *that very day*. See also Deut 4:44; 17:18, 19; 27:3, 8, 26; 28:58, 61; 29:20, 28; 30:10; 31:9, 11, 12, 24, 26; 32:46. I tend to agree with Joel Baden that the term תורה in D by and large refers only to the laws of Deut 12–26 and not to the book as a whole

that the term תורה begins to acquire a more central religious place, and it is here that it begins to reflect a sense of canonical composition.³⁴ While there is some precedent in E, it is mainly in Deuteronomy that the term תורה is applied to a written document in particular, a fact that can be gleaned from the frequent use of the phrases ספר התורה ("book of the תורה") and ספר הברית ("book of the covenant") as well as various instructions relating to writing.³⁵

The Deuteronomistic History uses the phrases ספר תורת משה, ספר התורה, תורת משה, and the like to refer not merely to the laws of Deut 12–26 but rather to the literary book of Deuteronomy, including its historical and rhetorical introductions. This can be gleaned from references to the תורה that paraphrase or allude to parts of Deuteronomy that are not limited to the law code of chapters 12–26. Thus, for example, Josh 8:31 describes the building of the altar on Mount Ebal: "as Moses, the servant of YHWH, had commanded the Israelites, as is written in the book of the תורה of Moses [בספר תורת משה]." This is an allusion not to the law collection of Deuteronomy but to Deut 27:2–8.³⁶

It is only with the postexilic works (mainly in Ezra-Nehemiah and Chronicles³⁷) that the term תורה assumes a broader semantic range encompassing most,

---

(including its rhetorical and historical parts). But cf. Najman (*Seconding Sinai*, 29–31) and Schwartz ("Torah—Its Five Books," 163), who argue that the term may refer to the entire book of Deuteronomy, including the historical introductions and rhetorical exhortations. Deuteronomy 1:5 seems to support the latter position.

[34] See Yehezkel Kaufmann, *The Religion of Israel: From Its Beginnings to the Babylonian Exile*, trans. and abridged Moshe Greenberg (Chicago: University of Chicago Press, 1960), 174–75; Barnabas Lindars, "Torah in Deuteronomy," in *Words and Meanings: Essays Presented to David Winton Thomas on His Retirement from the Regius Professorship of Hebrew in the University of Cambridge, 1968*, ed. Peter R. Ackroyd and Barnabas Lindars (Cambridge: Cambridge University Press, 1968), 117–36. here 131. Also noteworthy in this context is the negative mention of תורת יהוה in Jer 8:8, which may be a reference to an early edition of Deuteronomy, perhaps the one linked to the reform of Josiah in 622. See the classical treatment in Karl Marti, *Der Prophet Jeremia von Anatot* (Basel: Detloff, 1889), 18–20; and more recently van der Toorn, *Scribal Culture*, 143.

[35] Several scholars have attempted to distinguish "proto-sources" in Deuteronomy by their distinctive use of ספר התורה as opposed to ספר הברית. See, e.g., the discussion and summary in van der Toorn, *Scribal Culture*, 143–72, and the literature cited on 322–24. That there are two distinctive historical and rhetorical introductions to the laws of Deuteronomy is broadly acknowledged. See, e.g., Baden, *Composition of the Pentateuch*, 129–39; Moshe Weinfeld, *Deuteronomy 1-11: A New Translation with Introduction and Commentary*, AB 5 (New York: Doubleday, 1991; repr., AYB 5 [New Haven: Yale University Press, 2008]), 13–14; Alexander Rofé, *Deuteronomy: Issues and Interpretation*, OTS (London: T&T Clark, 2002), 9; Richard D. Nelson, *Deuteronomy: A Commentary*, OTL (Louisville: Westminster John Knox, 2002), 8; Werner H. Schmidt, *Old Testament Introduction* (Berlin: de Gruyter, 1995), 126; Ska, *Introduction à la lecture*, 5. For instructions related to writing, see, e.g., Deut 17:18; 28:61; 29:20; 30:10; 31:9, 24, 26.

[36] See also Josh 1:7–8; 8:31–32, 34; 22:5; 23:6; 1 Kgs 2:3; 2 Kgs 14:6; 22:8; 23:25.

[37] For the ongoing debate over the relationship between the authorship of Ezra-Nehemiah and that of Chronicles, see, e.g., Sarah Japhet, "The Supposed Common Authorship of Chronicles and Ezra-Nehemiah Investigated Anew," *VT* 18 (1969): 330–71; H. G. M Williamson, *Israel in the*

if not all, of the pentateuchal law, as it alludes not merely to the laws contained in a single document but, at the very least, to the Deuteronomic and Priestly law codes (including the Holiness legislation).[38] The question of the exact corpus designated by the term תורה in these works remains, however, somewhat obscure. Since Wellhausen, many scholars have endorsed the proposition that it is the entire Pentateuch (or Hexateuch), or at least a relatively mature version of it, that Ezra is said to have mastered (Ezra 7:6, 10) and promulgated in the seventh month (Neh 8:2).[39] Others maintain that the term תורה should be identified mainly with a single code, either with the laws of D or those of P (with or without the Holiness legislation). Most scholars agree, however, that the combination of Deuteronomic and Priestly legislation under the same rubric of תורה suggests that the term corresponds, at the very least, to some form of fusion of pentateuchal law.[40] Of particular

---

Book of Chronicles (Cambridge: Cambridge University Press, 1977). Cf. Blenkinsopp, *Ezra-Nehemiah*, 47–54.

[38] Thus, according to Ezra 3:2 the building of the altar conformed to what is "written in the תורה of Moses, the man of God" (ככתוב בתורת משה איש האלהים), alluding to Deut 27:6. Similarly, Ezra 9:11–12 and Neh 10:31, 13:25 allude to Deut 7:3, while Neh 13:1–2 alludes to Deut 23:3–4. Other references to the תורה are more closely related to the Priestly laws; for example, Ezra 3:3 alludes to Exod 29:38–42 and Num 28:3–8; Ezra 6:19–22 alludes to Exod 12:1–6, 19, 45; Lev 23:5–6; and Num 9:3, 5. For a comprehensive list of such references, see Blenkinsopp, *Ezra-Nehemiah*, 152–57; Blenkinsopp, "Was the Pentateuch the Civic and Religious Constitution?," 56–62; Judson R. Shaver, *Torah and the Chronicler's History Work: An Inquiry into the Chronicler's References to Laws, Festivals, and Cultic Institutions in Relationship to Pentateuchal Legislation*, BJS 196 (Atlanta: Scholars Press, 1989). Blenkinsopp asserts that "it is therefore tolerably clear that the author of Ezra 7 was familiar with what is now known as Deuteronomic and Priestly legislation, and the Holiness Code too if it is thought to be a distinct compilation" ("Was the Pentateuch the Civic and Religious Constitution?," 57–58).

[39] Julius Wellhausen, *Prolegomena to the History of Israel, with a Reprint of the Article "Israel" from the Encyclopaedia Britannica* (New York: Meridian, 1957), 384–85, 405–7. On the connections between Ezra 7–10 and Neh 8, see Blenkinsopp, *Ezra-Nehemiah*, 44–45.

[40] For the ongoing debate concerning the exact identity of the תורה and law of Ezra, see, e.g., Ulrich Kellermann, "Erwägungen zum Esragesetz," ZAW 80 (1968): 373–85; Ralph W. Klein, "Ezra and Nehemiah in Recent Studies," in *Magnalia Dei, The Mighty Acts of God: Essays on the Bible and Archaeology in Memory of G. Ernest Wright*, ed. Frank Moore Cross, Werner E. Lemke, and Patrick D. Miller Jr. (Garden City, NY: Doubleday, 1976), 361–76, esp. 366–68; Cees Houtman, "Ezra and the Law: Observations on the Supposed Relation between Ezra and the Pentateuch," in *Remembering All the Way: A Collection of Old Testament Studies Published on the Occasion of the Fortieth Anniversary of the Oudtestamentisch Werkgezelschap in Nederland*, ed. Bertil Albrektson et al., OtSt 21 (Leiden: Brill, 1981), 91–115; Sigmund Mowinckel, *Die Ezrageschichte und das Gesetz Moses*, vol. 3 of *Studien zu dem Buche Ezra-Nehemia*, SNVAO.HF NS 7 (Oslo: Universitetsvorlaget, 1965), 124–41; Frank Crüsemann, "Israel in der Perserzeit: Eine Skizze in Auseinandersetzung mit Max Weber," in *Max Webers Sicht des antiken Christentums: Interpretation und Kritik*, ed. Wolfgang Schluchter, Stw 548 (Frankfurt: Suhrkamp, 1985), 205–32, here 216–17; H. G. M. Williamson, *Ezra, Nehemiah*, WBC 16 (Waco, TX: Word, 1985), xxxvii–xxxix; Williamson, "The Concept of Israel in Transition," in *The World of Ancient Israel: Sociological, Anthropological, and*

interest in this regard are cases in which the תורה in Ezra-Nehemiah refers specifically to a hybrid version of laws contained elsewhere in the Pentateuch.[41]

The implications of this semantic shift are far-reaching. Whether the תורה of Ezra-Nehemiah alludes to an early version of the Pentateuch or merely to a fusion of pentateuchal law, the innovative conceptualization of תורה that underlies this semantic shift contributes, from a literary perspective, to the textual unity of the Pentateuch as revealed legislation. The figure of Moses, to whom the תורה is emphatically ascribed, is likewise transformed in this framework, in the sense that Moses is no longer the mediator of a single law code—as the notion of "Mosaic Torah" seems to imply in Deuteronomy and the Deuteronomistic History—but also the personal authority that "justified" the authorial fusion of distinct pentateuchal codes into a single textual and legal unity. In this context, the authors of Ezra-Nehemiah projected the consolidation of the תורה, which they ascribed to Ezra, back onto the figure of Moses.

Further insight into the literary and theological significance of this semantic shift can be gathered from the distinctive association of תורה and *dāta* according to Ezra 7. In what follows, I examine the implications of this cross-cultural "translation" in the light of Avestan traditions mediated by Achaemenid royal ideology.

II. The *dāta* and *daēnā* of Zarathustra

In the Achaemenid inscriptions, the Old Persian term *dāta* most often refers either to a specific decree or to a general notion of the law imposed by the

---

Political Perspectives; Essays by Members of the Society for Old Testament Study, ed. Ronald E. Clements (Cambridge: Cambridge University Press, 1989), 141–61, here 154; Jacob M. Myers, *Ezra-Nehemiah: A New Translation with Introduction and Commentary*, AB 14 (New York: Doubleday, 1965), lix; van der Toorn, *Scribal Culture*, 250; Baden, *Composition of the Pentateuch*, 15; Blenkinsopp, *Ezra-Nehemia*, 152–57; Blenkinsopp, "Was the Pentateuch the Civic and Religious Constitution?," 56–62.

[41] See, e.g., Jacob Milgrom, *Leviticus 23–27: A New Translation with Introduction and Commentary*, AB 3B (New York: Doubleday, 2001), 2426, regarding the laws of tithes: "From Ezra's time, the entire body of pentateuchal literature was considered to be a unity (the Torah of Moses), and the people were expected to comply with the Torah as a whole. This required that the various attitudes toward the tithe, as reflected in the different sources (especially in the Priestly Code, on the one hand, and Deuteronomic Code, on the other), be combined in a way that reconciled contradictions. Thus, for instance, the two types of tithes prevalent at this period, 'the first tithe' and 'the second tithe,' are the outcome of the contradiction between Numbers 18:21–24 and Deut. 14:22–27." Along similar lines, Baden observes, "The famous example from 2 Chronicles 35:12–13 serves to demonstrate this. While in Deuteronomy 16:7 the Passover sacrifice is to be 'boiled' (ובשלת), in Exodus 12:8–9 it is to be 'roasted in fire' (צלי-אש), and definitely not boiled (אל תאכלו ממנו נא ובשל מבשל במים); 2 Chronicles 35:12–13 says that the Israelites 'boiled the Passover sacrifice in fire' (ויבשלו הפסח באש)—thereby combining the two pentateuchal laws—'as is written in the book of Moses'" (*Composition of the Pentateuch*, 15).

sovereign.[42] While in the inscriptions of Darius I (522–486 BCE) all of the occurrences of *dāta* refer to the king's law,[43] Xerxes also mentions the "law set down by Ahura Mazdā" (XPh 46–56):

*tuva ka haya apara yadi-maniyāiy šiyāta ahaniy jīva utā mr̥ta r̥tāvā
ahaniy
avanā dātā parīdiy taya auramazdā nīyaštāya
auramazdām yadaišā r̥tācā br̥zmaniy
martiya haya avanā dātā pariyaita taya auramazdā nīštāya
auramazdām yadataiy r̥tācā br̥zmaniy
hauv utā jīva šiyāta bavatiy utā mr̥ta r̥tāvā bavatiy*

If you who come hereafter should think, "May I be blessed/happy [*šiyāta*] while alive
and one with Order [*r̥tāvā*; cf. Avestan *ašauua*] when dead!"
then behave according to the law which Ahuramazdā set down.
You should sacrifice to Ahuramazdā *according to the Order up on high*.
The man who behaves according to the law which Ahuramazdā set down and sacrifices to
Ahuramazdā *according to the Order up on high*,
he will both be blessed while alive and one with Order when dead.[44]

---

[42] See, e.g., Roland G. Kent, *Old Persian: Grammar, Texts, Lexicon* (New Haven: American Oriental Society, 1950), 189; Schmitt, *EIr* 7.1:114–15.

[43] See, e.g., DB 1.23; DNa 21–22 (compare DSe 20–21 and XPh 18–19); DSe 37–39. Darius at Behistun (DB 1.23) (transcription and translation in Skjærvø, "Achaemenids and the Avesta," 69):

*vašnā auramazdāha imā dahayāva tayanā manā dātā apariyāya
yaθā-šām hacā-ma aθahaya avaθā akunavayantā*

By the greatness of Ahura Mazdā, these lands which behaved according to
my established law as was said to them by me, thus they would do.

Darius at Naqsh-e Rostam (DNa 16–22) (transcription and translation in Skjærvø, "Achaemenids and the Avesta," 69):

*vašnā auramazdāha imā dahayāva tayā adam agr̥bāyam apataram hacā
pārsā adam-šām patiyaxšayaiy manā bājim abaraha
taya-šām hacā-ma aθahaya ava akunava dātam taya manā avadiš adāraiya*

By the greatness of Ahura Mazdā, these lands which I seized beyond Pārsa,
I ruled over them, they bore me tribute.
What was said to them by me, that they did. It was my established law that held them.

[44] Xerxes at Persepolis (XPh 46–56); Skjærvø, *Spirit of Zoroastrianism*, 181; Skjærvø, "Achaemenids and the Avesta," 73; cf. Kent, *Old Persian*, 151–52. Compare Yasna 71.15–16 and Yašt 10.105, which reflect lexical and grammatical parallels to this proclamation (see Skjærvø, "Avestan Quotations in Old Persian," 2). For details of the translations, see also Skjærvø, "Avestan Quotations in Old Persian," 38 (*vašnā*), 41–43 (*r̥tācā br̥zmaniy*). Also see the review of *Die altpersischen Inschriften der Achaimeniden: Editio minor mit deutscher Übersetzung*, ed. Rüdiger Schmitt, *OLZ* 106 (2011): 327–28. On the connection between (ritual) law and the cosmic order in Avestan and biblical texts, see Kiel, "Young Avestan Model."

In what follows, I will address the broader significance of Xerxes's reference to the "law set down by Ahura Mazda," which can be fully appreciated only in the light of the Avestan tradition. Unlike the law of the king authorized by Ahura Mazda, which participates in a broader discourse found among other ancient Near Eastern cultures, the notion of a "law set down by Ahura Mazda," functions differently and is derived from the Avesta. Skjærvø has demonstrated in this regard that the parallels between the Avesta and the Old Persian inscriptions are not merely thematic—in which case they can essentially be attributed to a common Indo-Iranian heritage or broader ancient Near Eastern patterns—but in some cases indicate a process of literary (but not written) influence of the Old Persian *zand* of the Avesta on the Old Persian inscriptions.[45] Thus, in order to understand Xerxes's conceptualization of the "law set down by Ahura Mazda" we must turn our gaze to the Avestan tradition, in terms of both thematic and lexical parallels.

In the Avesta, while the term *dāta* occasionally refers to secular instructions, it more commonly designates revealed law. In the Young Avesta, "the law of Zarathustra" (*dāta zaraθuštri*) is found in a set list of divine/celestial entities addressed in the *Yasna* liturgy: "the life-giving divine thought" (*maθra spǝnta*),[46] "the law discarding the old/evil gods" (*dāta vīdaēuua*),[47] "the law of Zarathustra" (*dāta zaraθuštri*), "the long Tradition(?)" (*darǝyā upaiianā*), and "the good *daēnā* of those who sacrifice to Ahura Mazda" (*daēnā vaŋʰuhuī māzdaiiasni*)"—all concepts perceived, in one way or another, as manifestations of the Avestan tradition.

Similarly, in Yašt 11.3, "the law of Zarathustra" (*dātǝm zaraθuštri*) is found in a list of sacred utterances that fight (together with Sraoša) against the powers of darkness: the *maθra spǝnta*, the *ahuna vairiia* (the most sacred utterance in Zoroastrianism, uttered for the first time by Ahura Mazda to stun the Evil Spirit),[48] the

---

[45] Skjærvø, "Avestan Quotations in Old Persian," 1–4.

[46] For the *maθra spǝnta* as the chariot of the sun, see Karl Hoffmann, "Zur awestischen Textkritik: Der Akk. Pl. mask. der *a*-Stämme," in *W. B. Henning Memorial Volume*, ed. Mary Boyce and Ilya Gershevitch (London: Lund Humphries, 1970), 187–200, here 200. For the conceptualization of the *maθrō spǝntō* as an embodiment of the divine word, see below.

[47] The "law discarding the old gods" (*dātahe vīdaēuuahe*) refers either to the laws contained in the Young Avestan work carrying this name (the Videvdad) or, more often, to Avestan instructions more broadly. The Avestan name of the Videvdad (*dāta vīdaēuua-*) means "the law, discarding the old gods," or "the law for how to keep the old gods away." It was long assumed that the Avestan name means "the law *against* the old gods/demons," but the prefix *vī-* does not have the meaning "against" but expresses movement to the sides. See Émile Benveniste, "Que Signifie Vidēvdāt," in Boyce and Gershevitch, *W. B. Henning Memorial Volume*, 37–42; Skjærvø, "Videvdad," 106–7. On the *daēuuas* ("the old/evil gods") in general, see the discussion in Skjærvø, "Zoroastrian Dualism," 63–65. For the *daēnā māzdaiiasni* as the cosmic *kusti* (Orion's belt?), see Skjærvø, "Poetic Weaving in the Old Avesta: The *Gāθās* and the Kusti," in *One for the Earth: Prof. Dr. Y. Mahyar Nawabi Memorial Volume*, ed. Mahmoud Jaafari-Dehaghi (Tehran: Markaz-i Dā'irat al-Ma'ārif-i Buzurg-i Islāmī, 1387/2008), 129. For the conceptualization of the *daēna* as an embodiment of the Zoroastrian tradition, see below.

[48] Yuhan Vevaina demonstrated that the later Pahlavi exegetes of the ninth century organized

correctly spoken Word (*aršuxδō vāxš*), and the *daēnā māzdaiiasni*, elements that were, in one way or another, perceived as embodiments or manifestations of the Avestan tradition.

The "law of Zarathustra" (*dātəm zaraθuštri*) thus seems to designate the totality of the Zoroastrian tradition, subsuming under its authoritative wings the sacred utterances mentioned in the passage. It is perhaps the personal attribution to Zarathustra, as the authoritative recipient and mediator of the law set down by Ahura Mazda, that serves to unify the various components of the religious tradition and justify their inclusion in a single coherent notion of textual unity and scriptural revelation.

The idea that the "sacred word" is embodied in scripture is similarly attested in other religious traditions, particularly Brahmanic conceptions of the embodiment of the divine word in the Veda, as well as in ancient Jewish and Christian conceptions of the embodiment of the *logos/memra* and their cognates in Scripture.[49]

---

and schematized the entire corpus of the Zoroastrian religious tradition (which by this point included not merely the Avesta itself but also its traditional Pahlavi translation and commentary, the Zand) based on a parsing of the Ahuna Vairiia prayer (Pahl. Ahunwar) into twenty-one words that are said to encapsulate or embody the twenty-one *nasks* (books) of the Avesta and Zand. See Yuhan Vevaina, "Enumerating the Dēn: Textual Taxonomies, Cosmological Deixis, and Numerological Speculations in Zoroastrianism," *HR* 50 (2010): 111–43, here 118. While this development clearly reaches its fill-fledged articulation only in the Pahlavi literature, I submit that the kernel of this perception is rooted in the Young Avestan tradition.

[49] For the Word embodied in the Veda (and some rabbinic parallels) see, e.g., Barbara A. Holdrege, "Veda and Torah: The Word Embodied in Scripture," in *Between Jerusalem and Benares: Comparative Studies in Judaism and Hinduism*, ed. Hananya Goodman (Albany: State University of New York Press, 1994), 103–78; and, in general, Holdrege, *Veda and Torah: Transcending the Textuality of Scripture* (Albany: State University of New York Press, 1996). On ancient Jewish conceptions, see, e.g., Azzan Yadin, *Scripture as Logos: Rabbi Ishmael and the Origins of the Midrash* (Philadelphia: University of Pennsylvania Press, 2004), 172; Daniel Boyarin, *Border Lines: The Partition of Judaeo-Christianity*, Divinations (Philadelphia: University of Pennsylvania Press, 2004), 128–30; see also Hans Bietenhard, "Logos-Theologie im Rabbinat: Ein Beitrag zur Lehre vom Worte Gottes im rabbinischen Schrifttum," *Principal* 19 (1979): 580–618. In early Christianity, according to Clement of Alexandria, for example, the Logos has not only a carnal manifestation in Jesus Christ, but also a textual manifestation in Scripture: "John, the herald of the Word, besought men to make themselves ready against the coming of the Christ of God. And it was this which was signified by the dumbness of Zacharias, which waited for fruits in the person of the harbinger of Christ, that the Logos, the light of truth, by *becoming the Gospel*, might break the mystic silence of the prophetic enigmas" (*Protr.*, ch. 1, in *ANF*, 2:174). According to Clement, the Logos becomes the gospel, while the gospel functions as a textual manifestation of the incarnated Logos-Jesus, which comes to reveal the true meaning of the Hebrew Bible. For an overview of the place of Logos in Clement's thought, see John Egan, "Logos and Emanation in the Writings of Clement of Alexandria," in *Trinification of the World: A Festschrift in Honour of Frederick E. Crowe in Celebration of His 60th Birthday*, ed. Thomas T. Dunne and Jean-Marc Laporte (Toronto: Regis College Press, 1978), 176–209. The Greek philosophical context of Clement's notion of the Logos is discussed in Salvatore R. C. Lilla, *Clement of Alexandria: A Study*

The *daēnā*, which in the Old Avesta seems to refer primarily to a mental faculty that "sees" in the other world and guides the sacrifices assumes in the Young Avestan texts several additional meanings, one of which is the totality of Ahura Mazda's teachings and traditions (but probably not "religion" as often translated).[50] It is in this sense that the term appears throughout the Videvdad (e.g., 2.1–5; 3.41–42) as the *daēnā māzdaiiasni*. It is possible, therefore, that much of the semantic range of the Pahlavi rendition *dēn* is already presumed in the Young Avestan *daēnā*.[51] Viewed in this light, it is hardly surprising to find the *daēnā* linked to the "law of Zarathustra" in the quoted passage.

That the *daēnā* refers to the totality of traditions and instructions revealed by Ahura Mazda to Zarathustra is known from Videvdad 2.1–2, a passage that forms part of the mythical framework of the main body of ritual legislation contained in this work.[52] To set the stage for the ensuing revelation of the law, the *daēnā* is

---

in *Christian Platonism and Gnosticism*, OTM (Oxford: Oxford University Press, 1971); M. J. Edwards, "Clement of Alexandria and His Doctrine of the Logos," *VC* 54 (2000): 159–77. The notion of Scripture as a manifestation of the Logos is also connected to the notion of *nomos* ("law") as a medium of revelation, an idea that was already developed by Justin Martyr. See Edwin Luther Copeland, "Nomos as a Medium of Revelation, Paralleling Scripture, in Ante-Nicene Christianity," *ST* 27 (1973): 51–61; Willy Rordorf, "Christus als Logos und Nomos: Das Kerygma Petrou in seinem Verhältnis zu Justin," in *Kerygma und Logos: Beiträge zu d. geistesgeschichtlichen Beziehungen zwischen Antike und Christentum; Festschrift für Carl Andresen zum 70. Geburtstag*, ed. Adolf Martin Ritter (Göttingen: Vandenhoeck & Ruprecht, 1979), 424–34; M. J. Edwards, "Justin's Logos and the Word of God," *JECS* 3 (1995): 261–80.

[50] See, e.g., Yasna 46.11, 39.2; Prods Oktor Skjærvø, "Zarathustra: A Revolutionary Monotheist?" in *Reconsidering the Concept of Revolutionary Monotheism*, ed. Beate Pongratz-Leisten (Winona Lake, IN: Eisenbrauns, 2011), 325–58, here 334–35; Mansour Shaki, "Dēn," *EIr* 7.3:279–81: "In the Gathas *daēnā* (which is only 'ahuric') denotes 'vision, conscience, individuality' and, in general, it is 'a theological and metaphysical term with a variety of meanings: the sum of man's spiritual attributes and individuality, vision, inner self, conscience, religion.'" See also Alberto Cantera, "Talking with God: The Zoroastrian ham.parshti or Intercalation Ceremonies," *JA* 131 (2013): 85–138, here 129–31. For visual representations of the *daēnā*, see Michael Shenkar, *Intangible Spirits and Graven Images: The Iconography of Deities in the Pre-Islamic Iranian World*, Magical and Religious Literature of Late Antiquity 4 (Leiden: Brill, 2014), 93–96. From the Young Avestan tradition onward, the *daēnā* also represents the individual's actions in the world embodied as a female figure. She comes to meet the soul of the departed and, pending his religious status, manifests herself either as a beautiful young woman or as an ugly old woman. For the influence of this idea on Manichaean and Islamic thought, see Werner Sundermann, "Zoroastrian Motifs in Non-Zoroastrian Traditions," *JRAS* 18 (2008): 155–65, here 160–62; Shaul Shaked, "'For the Sake of the Soul': A Zoroastrian Idea in Transmission into Islam," *JSAI* 13 (1990): 15–32, here 28–29.

On the anachronistic association of the *daēnā* with "religion," see Skjærvø, "Zarathustra: A Revolutionary Monotheist?," 334–35.

[51] For Pahlavi *dēn*, see Shaki, *EIr* 7.3:279–81; Vevaina, "Enumerating the Dēn," 111–43; Prods Oktor Skjærvø, "The Zoroastrian Oral Tradition as Reflected in the Texts," in Cantera, *Transmission of the Avesta*, 3–48.

[52] Skjærvø has called attention to the mythical basis on which the ritual instructions are

defined in the narrative framework in terms of "the *daēnā* of Ahura Mazda and that of Zarathustra."

> *pərəsaṯ zaraθuštrō ahurəm mazdąm*
> *ahura mazda mainiiō spāništa*
> *dātarə gaēθanąm astuuaitinąm aṣ̌āum*
> *kahmāi paoiriiō mašiiānąm apərəse*
> *tūm yō ahurō mazdā̊*
> *ainiiō mana yaṯ zaraθuštrāi*
> *kahmāi fradaēsaiiō daēnąm*
> *yąm āhūirīm zaraθuštrīm*

> Zarathustra asked Ahura Mazda:
> O Ahura Mazda, most Life-giving Spirit,
> Orderly creator of all things in the world of the living with bones,
> with whom among men did you first converse,
> you, Ahura Mazda,
> other than me, Zarathustra?
> To whom did you exhibit the *daēnā*,
> the one of Ahura Mazda and Zarathustra?

In a number of Young Avestan passages we find the expression "taught by Ahura Mazda, spoken by Zarathustra" (*mazdō.frasāsta zaraθuštrō.fraoxta*) qualifying "the thirty-three divine/ritual models [*ratus*] of Order surrounding Hāuuani [time of the pressing of the *haoma*]," the time of the morning when the *yasna* ceremony was performed to chase darkness and reproduce the day.[53] Thus, the means to abolish chaos and reestablish order via ritual were revealed by Ahura Mazda to Zarathustra. In another Young Avestan text, Videvdad 5.23, the "law of Zarathustra" is praised as being above and beyond all other "words," presumably due to its divine origin.

> *āaṯ mraoṯ ahurō mazdā̊*
> *mąnaiiən bā spitama zaraθuštra*
> *aētəm dātəm yim vīdōiiūm zaraθuštri*
> *upairi aniiāiš srauuāiš*
> *masanaca vaŋhanaca sraiianaca*
> *yaθa zraiiō vouru. kaṣ̌əm upairi aniiā̊ āpō*

> Then Ahura Mazda said:
> Well, Spitama Zarathustra, it is like this,

---

founded by pointing out the compositional sequence of the work. While the laws of purity are the main concern of the Videvdad, the first two chapters are devoted to the unfolding of the Iranian myth of creation, the flood story, God's communication with the antediluvian hero Yima, and finally the revelation of his *daēnā* to Zarathustra. See Skjærvø, "Videvdad," 116–18. For a structural comparison of this work with the Priestly source (P) of the Pentateuch, see Kiel, "Young Avestan Model."

[53] The *ratus* listed in the Yasna, in fact, add up to more than thirty-three.

this law [*dātəm*], the one discarding the old gods [*vīdōiiūm*], in the tradition of Zarathustra,
(is) above and beyond other words
in greatness, goodness, and beauty,
like the Vourukasha Sea is above and beyond other waters.

A later Pahlavi tradition that explicitly identifies the "law of Zarathustra" and the "sacred word" with the Avesta is found in a gloss in Hērbedestān 2.5.

kaṯ dātahe zaraθuštrōiš
abestāg čiyōn dād
maynō mąθrō

"What (part of?) the law of Zarathustra"?
(Pahlavi) "How was the Avesta laid down?"
(as) "the naked divine word."

Here again, the association of the "law of Zarathustra" and "the divine word" with the Avesta appears to have been mediated by the Young Avestan texts we have examined.[54] All in all, the "law of Zarathustra," "the *daēnā* of Zarathustra and that of Ahura Mazda," "the sacred word," and that which was "taught by Ahura Mazda, spoken by Zarathustra" were, in one way or another, linked to the totality of the Avestan instructions revealed by Ahura Mazda to Zarathustra.

We are now in a better position to assess the meaning of Xerxes's allusion to the "law set down by Ahura Mazda." Considering the systematic use of Avestan terminology and conceptions in the Old Persian inscriptions, it is likely that the "law set down by Ahura Mazda" was linked to, even perhaps identified with, the "law of Zarathustra" revealed and taught by Ahura Mazda according to the Avestan tradition. This assumption, however, raises the long-debated dilemma of why Zarathustra is completely absent from the Old Persian inscriptions.[55]

---

[54] Also worthy of note is the Pahlavi interpretation of another Avestan fragment ("and if in search of the *daēnā*") in Hērbedestān (3.3, 3.5, 3.6) in reference to the pursuit of the Avesta.

[55] Several scholars have treated the "divergence" of the Old Persian inscriptions from the Avesta in terms of the relative "orthodoxy" of the Achaemenids and their adherence to Zoroastrianism as defined by the Avestan tradition. See, e.g., Jacques Duchesne-Guillemin, *La religion de l'Iran ancien*, Mana 1.3 (Paris: Presses Universitaires de France, 1962), 165–68; Clarisse Herrenschmidt, "La religion des Achéménides: État de la question," *StIr* 9 (1980): 325–39; Jean Kellens, "L'idéologie religieuse des inscriptions achéménides," *JA* 290 (2002): 417–64; see also Prods Oktor Skjærvø in "The Avesta and Zoroastrianism in Achaemenid and Sasanian Iran," in *The Oxford Handbook of Ancient Iran*, ed. Daniel T. Potts (Oxford: Oxford University Press, 2013), 562–63. It is crucial to understand, however, that the Avesta and the inscriptions represent fundamentally distinct genres: the Avesta is a religious and ritual text, while the Old Persian inscriptions are royal proclamations. In the light of this fundamental distinction, Skjærvø concludes, "There is, therefore, no particular reason to expect any mention in the inscriptions of Zarathustra or the Life-Giving Immortals (*aməša spənta*), who are also absent from the Sasanian inscriptions" ("Achaemenids and the Avesta," 52).

A close examination of the different functions of the king according to the Old Persian inscriptions (first and foremost, sacrifice to Ahura Mazda and the preservation of the cosmic and political Order) against the backdrop of the Avestan roles of Zarathustra, the archetypical sacrificer to Ahura Mazda and preserver of the cosmic Order [Avestan *aṣ̌a-*],[56] has led several scholars to speculate that the king in the inscriptions consciously embodies or represents the Avestan figure of Zarathustra.[57] Viewed in this light, the king became not only the ultimate sacrificer to Ahura Mazda and the preserver of the cosmic Order but also the promoter of "the law set down by Ahura Mazda." Thus, the role of Zarathustra as promoter of the *dāta* and *daēnā* of Ahura Mazda according to the Avesta appears to have been embodied and replicated by the Achaemenid kings. When Xerxes urges his subjects to obey "the law set down by Ahura Mazda," he is likely consciously assuming the role of Zarathustra. As such, Xerxes is not merely participating in a discourse common to other cultures in the ancient Near East, according to which the law of the land established by the king is said to have been authorized by the deity as guardian of justice and dispenser of truth, but is presuming that the king is, in a significant way, subordinate to the law revealed by Ahura Mazda to Zarathustra.

In some respect, the attempt of Xerxes to promote the law (*dāta*) set down by Ahura Mazda by replicating the Avestan figure of Zarathustra informs the attempt of the authors of Ezra-Nehemiah to project the mission of Ezra—in terms of consolidating and codifying pentateuchal law as revealed legislation—back onto the authoritative figure of Moses. In this context, both Ezra and Xerxes similarly embody the respective roles of Moses and Zarathustra, so as to grant authority to their textual and legal missions.

I am *not* arguing that a conscious process of cross-cultural translation is in play according to which YHWH replaces Ahura Mazda, Moses assumes the figure of Zarathustra, and Ezra replicates the mission of Xerxes. What I posit is that the literary reconfiguration of Ezra's mission according to Ezra-Nehemiah in terms of the consolidation and promulgation of Mosaic תורה can be significantly illuminated by the rhetoric that governs the king's self-perception as promoter of the "law set down by Ahura Mazda."

The Avestan construction of the "law of Zarathustra" (and perhaps also its royal subversion by Xerxes) subsumes under its authoritative wings a variety of

---

[56] See, e.g., Yašt 13.87–89; Prods Oktor Skjærvø, "Zarathustra: First Poet-Sacrificer," in *Paitimāna: Essays in Iranian, Indo-European, and Indian Studies in Honor of Hanns-Peter Schmidt*, ed. Siamak Adhami, 2 vols. (Costa Mesa, CA: Mazda, 2003), 1:157–194, here 161–62.

[57] See Clarisse Herrenschmidt, "Histoire du judaïsme à l'époque hellénistique et romaine," *AEPHE.R* 104 (1995–1996): 227–32, here 230; Herrenschmidt, "Writing between Visible and Invisible Worlds in Iran, Israel, and Greece," in *Ancestor of the West: Writing, Reasoning, and Religion in Mesopotamia, Elam, and Greece*, ed. Jean Bottéro, Clarisse Herrenschmidt, and Jean-Pierre Vernant (Chicago: University of Chicago Press, 1996), 67–146, here 115–17; Skjærvø, "Achaemenids and the Avesta," 78–80.

sacred utterances and manifestations of divine revelation. The personal authority of Zarathustra, as the recipient and mediator of the law set down by Ahura Mazda, thus serves to unify and consolidate the different components of the Zoroastrian tradition as well as justify their inclusion in a single coherent framework of textual unity and scriptural authority. The textual and scriptural unity of the Avesta achieved by the promulgation of the "law of Zarathustra [however subverted] set down by Ahura Mazda" would have been a crucial element in the religious undertaking of the Achaemenids.

Similarly, Moses seems to function in Ezra-Nehemiah not merely as a mediator of a single law code revealed by God (as in the preexilic and exilic accounts) but as the thread that unifies and consolidates the various law codes of the Pentateuch and especially those contained in P and D. In fact, it is this novel and inclusive construal of Mosaic תורה that serves to justify the weaving of discrete law codes into a single unity—an undertaking inherent in the Pentateuch and reflected in Ezra-Nehemiah's quotations from the תורה.

Both Xerxes and the authors of Ezra-Nehemiah seem, therefore, to have justified their unprecedented construction of comprehensive scriptural unity underwritten by the weaving of discrete elements known through divine revelation by projecting these undertakings back onto the authoritative and authorial figures of Moses and (a royal subversion of) Zarathustra. Rest assured, we are told, the various components of the religious tradition are contained within the confines of the "Mosaic Torah" revealed by God and the "Law of Zarathustra" set down by Ahura Mazda.

This reconstruction is based not only on thematic affinity and historical probability but also on a distinctive linguistic connection defining the תורה in terms of divine *dāta*. It is particularly this association that suggests that the authors of Ezra-Nehemiah consciously engaged and responded to contemporary Iranian and Persian notions of revelation, codification, and promulgation of divine law. This does not necessitate an active role of the Achaemenid authorities in consolidating pentateuchal law (although the theory of royal authorization of the Pentateuch cannot be altogether excluded) but rather points to the more likely possibility that the authors of Ezra-Nehemiah sought to portray the "Mosaic authority" of Ezra's mission in the image and likeness of contemporary Persian rhetoric and its subversion of Zarathustra.

NEW THIS FALL!

Telling the Old Testament Story

God's Mission and God's People

Brad E. Kelle

While honoring the historical context and literary diversity of the Old Testament, *Telling the Old Testament Story* is a thematic reading that construes the OT as a complex but coherent narrative. Unlike standard, introductory textbooks that only cover basic background and interpretive issues for each Old Testament book, this introduction combines a thematic approach with careful exegetical attention to representative biblical texts, ultimately telling the macro-level story, while drawing out the multiple nuances present within different texts and traditions.

Brad E. Kelle is Professor of Old Testament and Hebrew, School of Theology and Christian Ministry, Point Loma Nazarene University in San Diego, California. He has served as the chair of the SBL's Warfare in Ancient Israel Consultation at the Annual Meeting of the Society of Biblical Literature. He is also the past president and current member at large (executive board) of the Society of Biblical Literature Pacific Coast Region. He is the Old Testament editor for Currents in Biblical Research and has written or edited a variety of works on the Old Testament and ancient Israel.

AbingdonAcademic.com   Abingdon ACADEMIC

Isaiah 31 as a Response to Rebellions against Assyria in Philistia

SHAWN ZELIG ASTER
shawnzelig@gmail.com
Bar-Ilan University, Ramat Gan, 5290002 Israel

Isaiah 31 has been a source of great difficulty for interpreters through the centuries. The chapter contains multiple examples of unusual syntax, vocabulary, and imagery. These difficulties can be solved if the chapter is understood as the prophet's response to a specific episode in the late eighth-century conflict between the Neo-Assyrian Empire and the kingdoms of the Levant. It addresses the quandary the Judean elite faced in approximately 713 BCE in responding to the invitation of Yamani, king of Ashdod, to join a rebellion against Assyria. The chapter references specific figures who took part in earlier anti-Assyrian rebellions in the southern Levant, including Re'u of Egypt and Azuri of Ashdod.

Isaiah 31 opens with a cry against those who rely on Egyptian aid and concludes by prophesying the fall of Assyria by the "sword of no-man." It fits neatly into the debate in Judah in the late eighth century over whether to rebel against Assyrian suzerainty.[1] The uncommon terminology and syntax in some of its verses have posed great difficulties for interpreters. Verses 1-3 use unusual vocabulary, and the meaning of the imagery of the lion and the shepherd in verse 4 and of the the fluttering bird in verse 5 remains an interpretive crux.[2] To resolve some of these

---

[1] For the background of this debate and a full description of the policy of brinksmanship adopted by Hezekiah during the reign of Sargon II, see Gershon Galil, *Israel and Assyria* [in Hebrew] (Haifa: Haifa University Press, 2000), 77–99. All translations from Hebrew and Akkadian are mine.

[2] Brevard S. Childs considers the imagery of these two verses to be "hopelessly incoherent" (*Isaiah*, OTL [Louisville: Westminster John Knox, 2001], 233). To solve these problems, extensive textual emendations have been proposed, for which see ibid., 232; Hans Wildberger, *Isaiah 28–39: A Continental Commentary*, trans. Thomas H. Trapp (Minneapolis: Fortress, 2002), 216; and others. Another explanation for the textual difficulties is offered by the proponents of an "*Assurredaktion*," who propose that the text was extensively reedited in the late seventh century and that the difficulties derived from this process. See Hermann Barth, *Die Jesaja-Worte in der Josiazeit: Israel und Assur als Thema einer produktiven Neuinterpretation der Jesajaüberlieferung*, WMANT 48 (Neukirchen-Vluyn: Neukirchener Verlag, 1977), 77–92; Peter Höffken, "Bemerkungen zu Jesaja

difficulties, I employ the comparative method, which is most appropriate when motifs and phrases similar to challenging biblical ones appear in other ancient Near Eastern texts in which they present no difficulties. In such cases, the linguistic and conceptual difficulties in the biblical text often attest to the borrowing of motifs and phrases.[3]

Verses 4–5 are often considered to be a later accretion to 31:1–3. Many authors note that the prophecies of woe and warning in verses 1–3 contrast with the salvific nature of what follows and that the messenger formula of verse 4 typically begins an oracle.[4] Jan Kreuch notes the literary similarities between 31:1–3 and what he considers to be earlier material in 29:15–30:16. Nevertheless, the continuity of the references to specific characters in 31:1–5, which are detailed below, justifies considering these verses as a single unit.[5] For similar reasons, Reinhard G. Kratz's position, that chapter 31 is "an abbreviation of ch. 30 and a combination with other texts," requires some elaboration.[6] While many of the themes and formulations of chapter 30 are echoed in chapter 31, there are unique references in the latter chapter that require explanation.

I argue below that the key to the interpretation of Isa 31:1–5 lies in recognizing its references to specific characters involved in the political and military turmoil in the southern Levant during the reigns of Sargon II of Assyria and Hezekiah of Judah. The two characters to whom I believe these verses allude were prominent anti-Assyrian rebels during this period, each appearing as a full-fledged character in the narratives of the Assyrian royal inscriptions: Azuri, king of Ashdod—whose actions (in approximately 713 BCE) are described in verses 1–3, in which the root עזר recurs in unexpected lexemes—and Re'u, an Egyptian army commander who abandoned the battlefield in 720 BCE and was scorned in Assyrian

---

31, 1–3," *ZAW* 112 (2000): 230–38. The comparative and historical solution proposed below solves most of the linguistic and conceptual difficulties more simply.

[3] For a fuller discussion of the importance of uncommon biblical phrases and motifs in the biblical text in comparative studies, see Meir Malul, *The Comparative Method in Ancient Near Eastern and Biblical Legal Studies*, AOAT 227 (Neukirchen-Vluyn: Neukirchener Verlag, 1990), 87–93.

[4] Jan Kreuch, *Unheil und Heil bei Jesaja: Studien zur Enstehung des Assur-Zyklus Jesaja 28–31*, WMANT 130 (Neukirchen-Vluyn: Neukirchener Theologie, 2011), 70–76. The division of verses 1–3 from verses 4–5 appears in many earlier commentaries, for example, that of Otto Kaiser, who contrasts the prophecy of woe with that of salvation (*Isaiah 13–39: A Commentary*, trans. R. A. Wilson, OTL [London: SCM, 1974], 311–17). Other commentators, including Ronald E. Clements, consider verse 4 a prophecy of woe and group it with verses 1–4, dividing the unit at verse 5 (Clements, *Isaiah 1–39*, NCBC [Grand Rapids: Eerdmans, 1980], 256–57).

[5] It is entirely possible that 31:4–5 was added to 31:1–3, but since the references to specific characters in verses 1–3 were understood and developed by the author of verses 4–5, little time could have elapsed between the proposed redactional strata.

[6] Reinhard G. Kratz, "Rewriting Isaiah: The Case of Isaiah 28–31," in *Prophecy and Prophets in Ancient Israel: Proceedings of the Oxford Old Testament Seminar*, ed. John Day, LHBOTS 531 (New York: T&T Clark, 2010), 255.

royal inscriptions. This scorn is the basis for the imagery in Isa 31:4, and the repeated use of the noun רע in 31:2 is also a reference to this colorful character.[7] The events of this particular subperiod have been clarified by Andreas Fuchs's publications of Sargon's royal inscriptions and Gershon Galil's important historical discussion of Hezekiah's policy toward Sargon.[8]

Isaiah 31 subverts the imagery used to describe these characters in the Assyrian royal inscriptions in order to undermine Assyrian royal ideology. As Peter Machinist has noted, the author of parts of Isa 1–39 was aware not only of the physical reality of Assyrian power but also of the imagery and motifs known from Assyrian royal inscriptions used to represent that power.[9] As part of the rhetoric of power, Assyrian inscriptions satirize characters who opposed Assyria, and several passages in Isa 31 subvert the Assyrian satire.

I. Linguistic Difficulties in Isaiah 31

The relationship between Isaiah 31 and the Assyrian inscriptions describing these characters is most clearly demonstrated by the linguistic difficulties in verses 1–5.

(1) הוי הירדים מצרים לעזרה על־סוסים ישענו ויבטחו על־רכב כי רב ועל
פרשים כי־עצמו מאד ולא שעו על־קדוש ישראל ואת־י" לא דרשו: (2) וגם־הוא
חכם ויבא רע ואת־דבריו לא הסיר וקם על־בית מרעים ועל־עזרת פעלי און:
(3) ומצרים אדם ולא־אל וסוסיהם בשר ולא־רוח וי" יטה ידו וכשל עוזר ונפל עזר
ויחדו כלם יכליון: (4) כי כה אמר־י" אלי כאשר יהגה האריה והכפיר על־טרפו
אשר יקרא עליו מלא רעים מקולם לא יחת ומהמונם לא יענה כן ירד י" צבאות
לצבא על־הר־ציון ועל־גבעתה: (5) כצפרים עפות כן יגן י" צבאות על־ירושלם
גנון והציל פסח והמליט:

---

[7] This suggestion was first made by Zvi Ilan, "The Name of Azuri King of Ashdod in the Bible" [in Hebrew], *Beit Mikra* 16 (1971): 498–99.

[8] Andreas Fuchs, *Die Inschriften Sargons II. aus Khorsabad* (Göttingen: Cuvillier, 1994); Fuchs, *Die Annalen des Jahres 711 v. Chr. nach Prismenfragmenten aus Ninive und Assur*, SAAS 8 (Helsinki: Neo-Assyrian Text Corpus Project, 1998); Galil, *Israel and Assyria*, 77–99.

[9] Peter Machinist, "Assyria and Its Image in First Isaiah," *JAOS* 103 (1983): 719–39. An extensive discussion of Assyrian activities in the West appears in Angelika Berlejung, "The Assyrians in the West: Assyrianization, Colonialism, Indifference, or Development Policy?," in *Congress Volume: Helsinki 2010*, ed. Martti Nissinen, VTSup 148 (Leiden: Brill, 2012), 21–60. Although Berlejung does not directly engage in textual questions, her study forms an important historical background for these. For the specific question of how these idioms reached Judah in the eighth century BCE, see Shawn Z. Aster, "Transmission of Neo-Assyrian Claims of Empire to Judah in the Late Eighth Century B.C.E.," *HUCA* 78 (2007): 1–44; and, more recently, William Morrow, "Tribute from Judah and the Transmission of Assyrian Propaganda," in *"My Spirit at Rest in the North Country" (Zechariah 6.8): Collected Communications to the XXth Congress of the International Organization for the Study of the Old Testament, Helsinki 2010*, ed. Hermann Michael Niemann and Matthias Augustin, BEATAJ 57 (Frankfurt am Main: Lang, 2011), 183–92.

¹Woe to those who go down to Egypt for help; they rely on horses, and they trust in chariots, for they are numerous, and on charioteers, for they are mighty, and they do not turn to the Holy One of Israel, and they do not seek out YHWH. ²But he, too, is wise, and he brings רע, but he does not remove his word, and he will rise against the בית מרעים and the עזרה of doers of iniquity. ³For Egypt is a man and not a God, and their horses are flesh and not spirit, and when YHWH stretches out his hand, the principal ally and the allied one will fail, and they will all vanish together. ⁴For thus said YHWH to me: just as the lion and the lion-cub roar on their prey, against which all the shepherds were called, but from their voice he does not fear and from their tumult he does not lower himself, so will YHWH of Hosts descend to camp on Mount Zion and on its hill. ⁵Like fluttering birds, so too will YHWH of Hosts defend Jerusalem: defending and saving, protecting and delivering.

In verse 2, the phrase ויבא רע ("and brings disaster") is "somewhat difficult, both grammatically and theologically."[10] In the same verse, the phrase בית מרעים ("house of evildoers") is itself unclear, its referent being obscure. The same is true of the phrase עזרת פעלי און ("helpers of those who work iniquity").[11] Verse 3 contains the clause וכשל עוזר ונפל עזר ("the helper will stumble, and the one helped will fall"), the last word of which is a *hapax legomenon*. Based on the "help" offered by Egypt in verse 1, the עוזר ("helper") appears to refer to Egypt, the word עזר to Israel. The unusual forms of the root עזר—which appears four times in verses 1–3—call for comment.

Verse 4 is generally considered one of the most difficult in the chapter. It draws an analogy between the behavior of a preying lion and that of YHWH. The comparison is unclear, however. YHWH is described as coming down לצבא על Mount Zion: does this mean to "fight against" Mount Zion or to fight upon and defend Zion as the lion defends its prey?[12] One of the key descriptions of the lion is also unclear: does the verb in אשר יקרא עליו מלא רעים ("when a band of shepherds is called out against it," NRSV) denote "be called" or "happen"?[13] The actions of the

---

[10] John N. Oswalt, *The Book of Isaiah, Chapters 1–39*, NICOT (Grand Rapids: Eerdmans, 1986), 571.

[11] The word מרעים is usually interpreted as "evildoers" but can also mean "friends"—as in Judg 14:11. It is used in the former sense in Isa 1:4 and apparently in the latter sense in 14:20. The word עזרת is usually interpreted as "allies," although it is used nowhere else in the Hebrew Bible to designate a group. Furthermore, neither of these groups is identified, and their relationship to those who "go down to Egypt for help [עזרה]" (in v. 1a) is unclear.

[12] Based on Isa 29:7–8 and Zech 14:12, J. J. M. Roberts argues that the phrase means "to fight against" (*First Isaiah: A Commentary*, Hermeneia [Minneapolis: Fortress, 2015], 404). This places 31:4 in direct opposition to verse 5, which describes YHWH protecting Zion. Most commentators interpret the phrase as indicating divine protection of Zion: see Oswalt, *Isaiah*, 574; Joseph Blenkinsopp, *Isaiah 1–39: A New Translation with Introduction and Commentary*, AB 19 (New York: Doubleday, 2000), 427.

[13] Blenkinsopp (*Isaiah 1–39*) and Oswalt (*Isaiah*) opt for the grammatically simpler

shepherds in verse 4 are also very unclear: why does the verse emphasize the voice of the shepherds? Shepherds normally fight predators with weapons (see 1 Sam 17:34–36), and it seems fairly obvious that shouting will not suffice to make lions abandon their prey. Why, then, would anyone expect the lion to react to the voices of shepherds, and why does the passage refer to this action?

As with the root עזר, several different forms of the noun רע are used in this short unit: רע ("evil") and בית מרעים in verse 2 and מלא רעים in verse 4 all contain interpretive difficulties.

The repeated use of עזר and רע in difficult phrases in this chapter raises the question of why they are emphasized. I suggest that they refer to Azuri of Ashdod and Re'u of Egypt, whose importance was noted briefly above.[14] In order to understand the rhetoric of Isa 31:1–4, a short summary of their roles in these rebellions is needed.

II. Re'u and Azuri in Relation to Judah and Assyria in 720–712 BCE

Around the time of the death of Shalmaneser V in 722, a revolt against Assyria developed throughout the Levant, led by Iaubidi (also known as Ilubidi), king of Hamath, and Hanun, king of Gaza, and supported by Shabaka, the ruler of Egypt.[15] Nonroyal elements in Damascus and Samaria also participated. The revolt was subdued by Sargon II in a lightning campaign involving a battle against the northern Syrian elements at Qarqar, the conquest of Samaria, and a battle at Rafiah in

---

translation "gathered," without addressing the nature of the gatherer. Childs translates idiomatically "when the shepherds gather against him" (*Isaiah*), implying that יקרא is to be taken as similar in meaning to נקרא נקריתי in 2 Sam 1:6, where it signifies "happen."

[14] Although oracles rarely mention the name of the individual against whom they are directed, some have been interpreted (correctly, in my view) as referring to specific individuals. Isaiah 14:3–21 is widely regarded as referring to Sargon II due to the "striking concord between the description in vv. 18–19 and information from Assyrian sources on the circumstances of Sargon's death" (Percy van Keulen, "On the Identity of the Anonymous Ruler in Isaiah 14:4b–21," in *Isaiah in Context: Studies in Honour of Arie van der Kooij on the Occasion of His Sixty-Fifth Birthday*, ed. Michaël N. van der Meer et al., VTSup 138 [Leiden: Brill, 2010], 118). For a full list of scholars who support this position, see ibid., n. 41. Van Keulen expounds an interpretation of these verses that I find difficult. A different example of an oracle in Isa 1–39 that refers to specific individuals without mentioning their names is 14:29–31, which alludes to Tiglath-pileser III; see Matthijs J. de Jong, *Isaiah among the Ancient Near Eastern Prophets: A Comparative Study of the Earliest Stages of the Isaiah Tradition and the Neo-Assyrian Prophecies*, VTSup 117 (Leiden: Brill, 2007), 214–15.

[15] For the campaign generally, see K. Lawson Younger, "The Fall of Samaria in Recent Research," *CBQ* 61 (1999): 461–82. For the date of Shabaka's accession, see Dan'el Kahn, "The Inscription of Sargon II at Tang-i Var," *Or* 70 (2001): 1–18, here 12.

southern Philistia. At Rafiah, Sargon engaged and defeated both Hanun of Gaza and Reʾu, sent by Shabaka to aid the revolt. Sargon's inscriptions from Khorsabad describe the Rafiah battle as follows:

> He gave Reʾu, his *turtenu* [second-in-command], to assist him. To do war against me, and battle with me, he went out. By the name of Assur my lord, I defeated him. Reʾu, like a shepherd whose sheep was stolen, fled alone and went away. I seized Hanun [king of Gaza] and brought him in fetters to Ashur, my city. I defeated, destroyed and burned by fire the city of Rafiah.[16]

The ridicule of Reʾu in this inscription contrasts with the trust the rebels placed in him. As the representative of a major power (Egypt), he was expected vigorously to oppose Assyria. The Assyrian scribe who composed the inscription satirizes the rebels' trust by describing Reʾu as a helpless, robbed shepherd. This ridicule of Reʾu was clearly important to the Assyrian scribes: thirteen years after the battle of Rafiah, on a building inscription written in 707 his flight is again adduced:

> Hanun, king of Gaza, together with Reʾu, the *turtenu* [second-in-command] of Egypt, made battle and war against me at Rafiah. I smashed and defeated them. Reʾu feared the noise of my weapons and fled, and his place is not seen.[17]

The shepherd motif plays a role in the 707 inscription as in the earlier one: Reʾu's name is written using the logogram for shepherd. Furthermore, the description of someone fleeing out of fear of noise is unusual in the Assyrian inscriptions.[18] It may be used to highlight the weakness of Reʾu, who fled upon hearing the weapons—even before he saw them. It is easy to understand why the flight of Reʾu would play such a central role in Sargonid propaganda: it marked the end of any challenge from Egypt to Sargon's reestablishing Assyrian dominion over the Levant. The kingdoms of the southern Levant that considered rebellion against Assyrian domination during the reign of Sargon II tended to weigh carefully the likelihood of Egyptian aid in calculating whether to revolt against Assyria.[19] It was therefore important to

---

[16] Cited in Fuchs, *Die Inschriften Sargons II aus Khorsabad*, 90, lines 53–57. The description of the flight of Reʾu leaves no doubt that this is a play on the meaning of the name (which denotes "shepherd" in many Semitic languages), since the cuneiform represents the name with the logogram for "shepherd": *¹Rēʾê* [written as SIPA-e] *ki* ᴸᵁ²*rēʾî ša ṣēnašu ḫabta edanuššu ipparšidma ēli*.

[17] Cited in Fuchs, *Die Inschriften Sargons II aus Khorsabad*, 197–98, lines 25–26. The line describing Reʾu's flight is written: *¹Rēʾê* [written as SIPA-e] *rigim kakkēja ēdurma inabitma lā innamer ašaršu*.

[18] For more typical formulations in Assyrian royal inscriptions describing flight from the "shine" or "fear" of the weapons, see Shawn Zelig Aster, *The Unbeatable Light: Melammu and Its Biblical Parallels*, AOAT 384 (Münster: Ugarit-Verlag, 2012), 89–92, 106–12.

[19] The question arose again in regard to the attempts made by Ashdod, shortly before 712, to enlist Egyptian aid in a revolt in which Judah, Edom, Moab, and other Philistine kings were asked to participate. The episode is recorded in Sargon's inscriptions published in Fuchs, *Die Annalen des Jahres 711 v. Chr.*, 44–46, 73–74. See the discussion below.

publicize Assyria's defeat of Egypt and Egypt's shameful abandonment of the Levantine rebels. Portraying the leader of Egypt's military as a shepherd unable to protect his flock accomplished this.[20]

The events of 720 heavily influenced Judah and surrounding kingdoms, all of whom remained loyal to Assyria at least until 716.[21] In the same year, a building inscription from Calah describes Sargon's subjugation of far-off Judah.[22] Ambassadors from Judah, along with those from Gaza and Moab, also brought their kingdoms' tribute to Sargon at some point—probably between 716 and 713.[23]

Sometime before 712 (712 being Sargon's eleventh year according to the Khorsabad texts), however, another round of rebellions had begun in the southern Levant. Azuri, king of Ashdod, ceased paying tribute and encouraged neighboring kingdoms to do likewise. Sargon replaced Azuri with Ahimti, who was pro-Assyrian. Ahimti did not garner sufficient popular support, and the populace replaced him with Yamani (also known as Yadani). Yamani then did what Hanun of Gaza had done in 720, seeking Egyptian assistance and attempting to widen the circle of anti-Assyrian rebellion. He sent messages to other kings of Philistia, Judah, Edom, and Moab, encouraging rebellion against Assyria. This led to Sargon's eleventh campaign of 712 against Ashdod and the conquest of Ashdod and its satellite cities,

---

[20] This depiction seems to be directly connected to the frequent motif in the royal inscriptions portraying the king of Assyria as a lion. Examples can be found in Sennacherib's inscriptions describing his early battles against Babylon (RINAP 3.1:34, text 1, line 25) and eighth campaign (RINAP 3.1:182, text 22, column v, line 67). The preying animal here vanquishes the shepherd.

[21] In that year, Sargon campaigned on the border with Egypt and received tribute from Osarkon, one of the claimants to the throne of Egypt. See Fuchs, *Die Annalen des Jahres 711 v. Chr.*, 28–29, 57–58; Kahn, "Inscription of Sargon II," 9–10.

[22] The inscription reads, *mušakniš kur Iauda ša ašriša rūqi*, "who defeated the land of Judah whose place is far away." Both the specific formulation and the larger context demonstrate that the goal of the inscription is to describe Sargon's control of the farthest borders of the known world. While not all of the territories described in this inscription were necessarily defeated in a military engagement, all were subjugated by Sargon II. The unusual description of Judah as "far away" may explain the inclusion of Judah in this inscription, which focuses on the expansion of Assyrian control. While Judah is clearly closer to Assyria than Egypt or Rafiah, it was not located on any major road and was therefore a less accessible destination. Highlighting Assyrian domination of Judah seems to be a means of emphasizing Assyrian control even of inaccessible locations. The most recent text edition of this inscription remains Hugo Winckler, *Die Keilschrifttexte Sargons nach den Papierabklatschen und Originalen*, 2 vols. (Leipzig: Pfeiffer, 1889), 2:168–72. Recent translations include an excerpt in Mordechai Cogan, *The Raging Torrent: Historical Inscriptions from Assyria and Babylonia Relating to Ancient Israel* (Jerusalem: Carta, 2008), 100–103, and a fuller translation in Galil, *Israel and Assyria*, 139–41.

[23] Nimrud Letter 16 (ND 2765, IM 64159); see Simo Parpola, *The Correspondence of Sargon II*, 3 vols., SAA 1, 5, 15 (Helsinki: Helsinki University Press, 1987–2001), vol. 1, letter 110. The dating of 716–713, proposed by Galil (*Israel and Assyria*, 86–87), depends on the assumption that the letter was written by Marduk-rimani.

Ashdod-yam and Gath. Sargon claims that he then annexed these cities to Assyria, engaged in two-way deportations, and installed a provincial governor over them.[24]

The events of these years bear directly on the interpretation of Isa 31. Judah was clearly encouraged to rebel against Assyria in the period before 712. Judah

---

[24] The relevant passages are the following:

(1) From the Khorsabad display inscriptions (Fuchs, *Die Inschriften Sargons II aus Khorsabad*, 219–21; Prunkschrift, lines 90–109; my translation):

> Azuri, king of Ashdod, whose heart planned not to bring tribute, therefore sent (messages containing) hostility against the land of Assyria to the kings surrounding him. Because of the crimes he committed toward the people of his land, I changed his rule. I established Ahimti his beloved brother, over them. The people of Hatti, speakers of lies, hated his kingship. They elevated above them Yamani, who had no right to the throne, and like them, did not know how to fear sovereignty [i.e., did not acknowledge Assyrian sovereignty]. Because of my angry heart, I did not gather the mass of my army nor I did summon my camp. With the heroes who do not leave my side, whether in hostile or in friendly territory [translation of this last phrase is based on *CAD* S 104–5], I went to the city of Ashdod. That Yamani from afar heard the movement of my campaign. Into the territory of Egypt near the border of Meluḫḫa [Nubia] he fled, such that his place is not clear. I surrounded and conquered Ashdod, Gath, and Ashdod–yam. I considered as spoil his gods, wife, sons, daughters, property, goods, the wealth of his palace, and the people of his land. I reorganized these cities. I settled there people from the lands I had conquered in the East [lit., from the lands of the rise of the sun]. I placed upon them my official as district governor. I counted them as people of Assyria. They bore my yoke.

(2) From the Khorsabad annals, prepared near the end of Sargon's reign, written in more stylized and less detailed language (Fuchs, *Die Inschriften Sargons II aus Khorsabad*, 132–35 [annals lines 241–255]; my translation):

> Azuri, king of Ashdod, plotted not to deliver tribute … and sent … to the kings of his neighborhood … of Assyria. Because of the crimes he committed against the people of his land, I changed his rule. I appointed Ahimti, his beloved brother, to the kingship. The people of Hatti, speakers of lies, hated his kingship. They elevated above them Yadani, who had no right to the throne, and like them, did not know how to fear sovereignty. In my rage, with my personal chariot and horsemen—who do not leave my side whether in hostile or in friendly territory—I quickly marched to Ashdod, his royal city. I surrounded and conquered Ashdod, Gath, and Ash[dod-yam]. I counted as spoil the gods who dwell in their midst, with the people of his land, gold, silver, and the property of his palace. I settled there people from the lands I had conquered. I placed upon them my official as district governor. I counted them as people of Assyria. They bore my yoke.

(3) The Nineveh annals (Fuchs, *Die Annalen des Jahres 711 v. Chr*, 44–46):

> They appointed Yamani, a *hupšu* soldier, who was not a master of the throne, to the kingship over them, and seated him in the throne of his lordship…. To the kings of Philistia, Judah, Edom, and Moab, who live by the sea, who bear tribute and gifts of the god Assur my lord, (they sent) words of lies and words of treachery, to make them hostile to me. To Pharaoh, the king of Egypt, who will not save, they sent payments seeking help, and asked repeatedly for auxiliaries.

evidently received Yamani's messages shortly before 712 and perhaps had received Azuri's messages somewhat earlier. Both encouraged rebellion against Assyria. The message that Judah certainly received—that of Yamani—also involved a promise of Egyptian help, since Yamani was a sufficiently close ally of Egypt to seek refuge there when his rebellion failed. Important similarities exist between the Ashdod-led rebellions of Azuri and Yamani in the period just before 712 and the rebellion led by Hanun of Gaza in 720. Both sought to build a regional coalition to oppose Assyria in the southern Levant, supported by Egypt. It is reasonable to assume that Judah had the option of participating in the rebellion of 720, but it is entirely certain that Judah was strongly encouraged by Ashdod to participate in at least one of the rebellions in the period just before 712.

III. Interpreting Isaiah 31 Based on Its Historical Background

The prophecy of Isa 31 appears to be counsel to the Judahite elite as they considered the invitation to rebellion led by Yamani issued just before 712.[25] It combines practical political recommendations with theological overtones directed at the elite of Jerusalem. To support these recommendations, the prophecy evokes two earlier memories of putative rebellions that were nipped in the bud by Assyria in which two central figures failed in circumstances similar to those obtaining in 712: (1) the 720 campaign and its disastrous end for the rebels, particularly evoking the memory of Re'u, the failed Egyptian general who deceived the rebels by fleeing from Assyria; and (2) Azuri's attempts to gather allies. The language of the prophecy refers not only to these events but also to the language the Assyrians used to describe them, terminology known from the royal inscriptions and familiar to the Judean political leadership from their interactions with Assyrian officials.[26]

---

[25] Roberts suggests that the literary context of these verses is the crisis created by Hezekiah's rebellion against Sennacherib in the years 705–701 (*First Isaiah*, 401). Yet, because these verses repeatedly point to specific aspects of the political situation in 720 that are similar to the political situation obtaining before 712, it appears preferable to understand its historical context as the period just before 712.

[26] Such interactions took place primarily in annual audiences in Assyrian palaces designed to inculcate loyalty to Assyria. Tribute-bearing representatives of Judah would have been warned against rebellion, and empirical examples of failed rebels very likely were cited along with scorn for these rebels. The Assyrian palace officials who met the tribute-bearing representatives would certainly have known the motifs from the royal inscriptions. For more on the tribute ceremony, see John N. Postgate, *Taxation and Conscription in the Assyrian Empire*, StPohl.SM 3 (Rome: Biblical Institute Press, 1974), 121–28. For the transmission of Assyrian motifs to Judah as a result of these, see Aster, "Transmission of Neo-Assyrian Claims of Empire to Judah"; Morrow, "Tribute from Judah and the Transmission of Assyrian Propaganda," 5.

Isaiah 31:1–3

¹Woe to those who go down to Egypt for help, they rely on horses, and they trust in chariots, for they are numerous, and on charioteers, for they are mighty, and they do not turn to the Holy One of Israel, and they do not seek out YHWH. ²But he, too, is wise, and he brings רע, but he does not remove his word, and he will rise against the בית מרעים and the עזרה of doers of iniquity. ³For Egypt is a man and not a God, and their horses are flesh and not spirit, and when YHWH stretches out his hand, the principal ally and the allied one will fail, and they will all vanish together.

Verse 1 presents a general critique of the Judahites' focus on horses and chariots, contrasting these with reliance on YHWH's power.[27] The final four words go further, however, criticizing the Judahites' lack of regard for YHWH's omniscience.

This emphasis continues in verse 2, the first words of which refer to YHWH. The words ויבא רע are an intentional double entendre: YHWH can bring evil upon Judah, and YHWH is also the motivating force behind Re'u. Unlike the latter, however, whose unreliability became a byword in the Assyrian inscriptions, YHWH does not remove YHWH's words: ואת דבריו לא הסיר. The last half of verse 2 is a declaration of the supremacy of YHWH's power over both of the key parties in the anti-Assyrian alliance formed before 712: YHWH will rise up against the house of the "Re'uites" or Egyptians—indicated by the words בית מרעים—and against Azuri and his supporters. In an apparent calque of Assyrian terms used to designate rebels, Azuri is referred to as עזרת פעלי און.[28]

This emphasis on the qualitative difference between divine and human power continues in verse 3, which highlights the weakness of both Egypt and Ashdod. In the first half of the verse, the apparent advantage that the physical strength of political actors gives them over YHWH is undermined. It is precisely the palpable nature of Egypt's strength that leaves it vulnerable to the might of YHWH, which has no physical boundaries. The last half of verse 3 refers to Ashdod in another double entendre: Judahites are warned that with a swift wave of the hand of YHWH, both the principal ally (עֹזֵר, referring to Azuri) and the allied (עָזוּר, apparently referring to Judah) will vanish.

Each of the actions the prophet attributes to YHWH was accomplished historically by Assyria: the Empire defeated the Egyptians under Re'u in 720,

---

[27] The contrast between military investment and reliance on YHWH is expressed elsewhere in Isa (22:9–11—contrasting Hezekiah's defensive works in Jerusalem with a focus on YHWH) and echoes the Deuteronomic concern with reliance on wealth and strength (Deut 8:12–14). The contrast resembles that between reliance on alliances with Assyria and reliance on YHWH in Isa 10:20, Hos 5:13–6:1.

[28] "Doers of iniquity" is a common way of referring to rebels in Neo-Assyrian royal inscriptions (cf. the reference to Merodach-baladan as *ēpiš lemnêti* in RINAP 3.1:34, text 1, line 25). The description of Azuri and his allies as פעלי און echoes the Assyrian diction.

deposing Azuri some years later. Just as Assyrian royal inscriptions vaunt the military supremacy Assyria enjoyed over all other polities, the prophet in verses 2 and 3 vaunts the qualitative difference between YHWH and the forces of Egypt and Ashdod. The nature of this qualitative difference emphasizes the similarity of all polities, including Ashdod, Egypt, and Assyria. They are all human, their horses being flesh rather than spirit, and always unreliable. This qualitative difference—developed in verse 3—explains the strange opening of verse 2, wherein YHWH is said to "bring evil/bring Re'u." He alone is ultimately capable—and therefore responsible for all political events.

Isaiah 31:4–7

(4) כי כה אמר־י" אלי כאשר יהגה האריה והכפיר על־טרפו אשר יקרא עליו
מלא רעים מקולם לא יחת ומהמונם לא יענה כן ירד י" צבאות לצבא על־הר־ציון
ועל־גבעתה: (5) כצפרים עפות כן יגן י" צבאות על־ירושלם גנון והציל פסח
והמליט: (6) שובו לאשר העמיקו סרה בני ישראל: (7) כי ביום ההוא ימאסון
איש אלילי כספו ואלילי זהבו אשר עשו לכם ידיכם חטא:

[4]For thus said YHWH to me: just as the lion and the lion-cub roar on their prey, against which all the shepherds[29] were called,[30] but from their voice he does not fear and from their tumult[31] he does not lower himself, so will YHWH of Hosts descend to camp on Mount Zion and on its hill. [5]Like fluttering birds, so too will YHWH of Hosts defend Jerusalem: defending and saving, protecting and delivering. [6]Return to the one against whom you have deeply revolted,[32] Israelites! [7]On that day, man will reject his silver idols and his golden idols that your hands made for you as a sin.

Employing the simile of the roaring lion and shouting shepherds, verse 4 continues to draw on the Assyrian concept of the military supremacy of Assyria over Egypt and other polities in order to highlight the qualitative difference between divine power and all human polities. The verse contains both an analogy (between the lion opposing the shepherds and YHWH descending on Jerusalem) and a metaphor (the lion and shepherds). The analogy can be understood only when the metaphor has been interpreted. The lion refers to the power of the Assyrian king, a common

---

[29] Just as מלא כל הארץ כבודו in Isa 6:3 signifies "his presence fills the earth," so יקרא עליו מלא רעים denotes "all the shepherds are called upon him."

[30] The simplest translation of יקרא is that the shepherds were summoned to oppose the lion stealing the sheep. This meaning of the verb in the N-stem appears in Esth 2:14. The image is also fairly simple: one shepherd witnessed the theft of his sheep by a lion but is too scared to confront it so summons others. This is a precise parallel to the actions of the Ashdodite king, who is reluctant to confront Assyria on his own and seeks other partners before instigating a confrontation.

[31] For המון meaning "tumult," see Jer 47:3, Ezek 26:13. The word denotes both "multitude" and "tumult," like the Akkadian *ḫubūru*.

[32] This translation is based on Kaiser, *Isaiah 13–39*, 315.

image in the royal inscriptions.³³ The shepherds are the coalition of potentially anti-Assyrian forces whom the leaders of Gaza and Ashdod repeatedly try to summon, because Hanun, Azuri, and Yamani were too scared to face Assyria on their own. These shepherds oppose the lion with their voices alone, highlighting their lack of confidence and effectiveness. Their ineffective shouting and the lions' refusal to react evoke the Assyrian mocking of Re'u, described in the 707 building inscription as fleeing from the sound of Sargon's weapons. In the simile the prophet constructs by subverting Assyrian metaphors, the supreme unconcern and nonchalance of the lion and its cub are emphasized by their reaction to מלא רעים. The characters in this simile evoke memories of the 720 encounter between Sargon and the Egyptian supporters of the rebels in Philistia, convincingly won by the Assyrians. The lions' lack of concern for the noise of the shepherds here refers to Assyria's indifference to the outmatched military forces of their opponents.

The prophet uses this image of a superior army (Assyria) facing a weaker one (Egypt and its various allies in Philistia) as an analogy for the way in which YHWH will come down to fight against those encircling Mount Zion. His power is qualitatively superior to the forces attacking Mount Zion, and he evinces the same nonchalance in the face of these forces as the Assyrians did in the face of the various rebellions of Hanun, Azuri, and Yamani.

Verse 5 continues to emphasize the divine protection of Jerusalem by subverting another Assyrian image of power. In Assyrian royal inscriptions, birds are consistently used as an image of the enemies of Assyria. They appear in two repeated motifs: (a) the fleeing enemy³⁴ and (b) the defeated enemy, caged like a bird.³⁵

Birds are thus used to evoke the qualitative difference between Assyria's power and that of its enemies. The prophet subverts a motif that originally stands for overwhelming Assyrian power, using it to describe how YHWH will defend Jerusalem: "Thus will YHWH defend Jerusalem: defending and saving, protecting and delivering." The image of the birds in verse 5 is a classic example of a blind motif: it is unclear how a fluttering bird serves to illustrate the protection of a city.³⁶ The use of birds in the Assyrian inscriptions, however, explains the usage in Isa 31:5. In

---

[33] See n. 20 above.

[34] RINAP 1:106, text 42, line 12'; 127, text 48, line 17'; 132, text 49, line r15, with specific reference to Hanun of Gaza fleeing from Egypt, whence he was apparently ejected; RINAP 3.1:134, text 17, column iii, line 92; 177, text 22, column iii, line 65; 184, text 22, column vi, line 29.

[35] RINAP 1:59, text 20, line 11'; 3.1:65, text 4, line 52; 133, text 17, column iii, line 52, in reference to Hezekiah.

[36] A blind motif is a motif that cannot easily be understood in its current context but makes sense in the original context from which it appears to be borrowed; see Jeffrey H. Tigay, "On Evaluating Claims of Literary Borrowing," in *The Tablet and the Scroll: Near Eastern Studies in Honor of William W. Hallo*, ed. Mark E. Cohen, Daniel C. Snell, and David B. Weisberg (Bethesda, MD: CDL, 1993), 255. Roberts interprets "[l]ike birds flying about their nest, Yahweh of Hosts will protect Jerusalem" (*First Isaiah*, 404). The image remains difficult, because birds flying around the nest cannot effectively harm the attackers.

their original context (the Assyrian inscriptions), birds highlight the qualitative difference between Assyria's power and that of its enemies. In the borrowed context (Isa 31:5), the author refers to the original meaning of the symbol, using it to illustrate the imbalance of power between YHWH and those who threaten Jerusalem.

Verses 4 and 5 thus both subvert images of Assyrian power in order to convey that, just as Assyria is a supreme military power, so YHWH's power is qualitatively superior to that of any human polity, including Assyria.

The contrast between YHWH and Assyria inherent in verses 4–5 and in the political context of verses 1–5 is exposed and developed in verses 6–7. Verse 6 calls on Israel to return to YHWH, describing YHWH as "the one against whom you have deeply revolted." This description correlates with those in other Isaianic passages in which Israel's lack of reliance on YHWH is portrayed as related to its veneration of Assyrian power and welcoming of Assyrian suzerainty. This contrast between reliance on YHWH and reliance on Assyria is most prominent in 10:20–21:

(20) והיה ביום ההוא לא־יוסיף עוד שאר ישראל ופליטת בית־יעקב להשען על־מכהו ונשען על־יהוה קדוש ישראל באמת: (21) שאר ישוב שאר יעקב אל־אל גבור:

> [20] On that day, the remnant of Israel and those saved from among the house of Jacob will no longer continue to rely on its smiter but will rely faithfully on the Holy One of Israel. [21] A remnant will return—a remnant of Jacob—to the Powerful God.

In verse 20, Israel's reliance on "its smiter"—a reference to Assyria—is contrasted with its reliance on YHWH; in verse 21, a return to YHWH is predicted following YHWH's defeat of Assyria.[37] Like 10:20–21, 31:6 calls on Israel to cease regarding Assyria as the inevitable suzerain and demands that Israel regard YHWH as such.

---

[37] This contrast is found also in Isa 8:12–13, where the prophet is warned against considering "the מורא" ("fear") of the people to be a מורא or considering it to be a מעריץ ("one who terrifies"). At first glance, this appears to be a caution against fearing the Syro-Ephraimite armies or "all and everything that is surmised to be treason" by the people (Childs, *Isaiah*, 74). Clear philological reasons exist, however, for understanding the warning as directed against reverence of Assyria. The participle מעריץ is best translated as "a conqueror who inspires terror" in light of Ps 10:18 and the related noun in Isa 13:11. While the Jerusalemites may have feared Rezin, he was hardly a successful conqueror. Furthermore, interpreting 8:12b as a warning against fearing the fear of the people is untenable. One would rather expect a warning against fearing that which the people fear—that is, fearing the source of their terror. The word מורא in the Hebrew Bible consistently designates the feeling of terror rather than the source of terror, however. מורא can denote the source of the terror only if the word is a calque on the Akkadian *puluḫtu*. Although *puluḫtu* literally means "fear," it is used as a way of referring to the *melammu* and appears frequently in the Neo-Assyrian royal inscriptions in the phrase *pulḫe melamme*, terror caused by the Assyrian king's reputation for insuperable power (Aster, *Unbeatable Light*, 81–92). Isaiah 8:12b, then, references Assyrian *puluḫtu* by warning the prophet against fearing the people's מורא. It is a warning against sharing their reverence for Assyrian invincibility and against accepting the view

Isaiah 31:7 contains a prediction about humans abandoning idols. At first blush, the shift in topic appears to indicate a move away from the Assyrian historical context. But the abandonment of idols is seen elsewhere in Isaiah as an inherent part of the conflict between reliance on YHWH and reliance on Assyria. The formulation in 31:7 is very similar to that found in Isa 2:20–21, which is part of a passage describing a campaign of YHWH against human arrogance (2:5–22), modeled on Assyrian campaigns against enemies characterized as "proud" (*multarḫu*); it can be dated to the Assyrian period.[38] The prediction of humans abandoning idols in 2:20–21 is part of a recognition of YHWH as the universal sovereign replacing Assyria. In both Isa 2:20–21 and 31:7, the prophet correlates the rejection of idols with the rejection of Assyrian doctrines of omnipotence and universal domination. The motivation for this correlation seems clear: both are false human creations, myths designed to inflate human power and thereby minimize God's control. Just as the replacement of Assyria by YHWH in the campaign narrative in 2:5–22 attracts mention of the rejection of idols in 2:20–21, the message that YHWH, not Assyria, is the ultimate power broker in Judah and Philistia in 31:1–5 attracts mention of the rejection of idols in 31:7.

Verses 6 and 7, then, include motifs that appear elsewhere in Isaiah in passages that clearly contain borrowings from Assyrian sources and that can therefore be dated with certainty to the period in which such motifs were part of the political discourse in Judah (roughly 745–650 BCE). This has consequences for our understanding of the redaction of Isa 31. While it is impossible firmly to disprove the common view that these verses are "secondary additions," their similarity to other eighth-century passages suggests that they derive from, or are modeled on, the original stratum of Isa 1–39. Furthermore, whoever added verses 6–7 to 31:1–5 seems to have understood the political message underlying 31:1–5, namely, that YHWH, rather than Assyria, is responsible for political events and wields ultimate temporal power.[39]

IV. Conclusion

The oracle in Isa 31 extensively references and subverts the imagery used to argue for Assyrian power. It uses the Assyrian rhetoric of supreme power to argue

---

propagated by the Assyrian empire of royal omnipotence and universal rule. Thus, 8:12–13 contrasts regarding Assyria as a terrifying and omnipotent conqueror with attributing these characteristics to YHWH.

[38] Shawn Z. Aster, "The Image of Assyria in Isaiah 2:5–22: The Campaign Motif Reversed," *JAOS* 127 (2007): 249–78.

[39] For this reason, I assign verses 6–7 to the composer of 31:1–5. The distinction Kaiser draws (*Isaiah*, 315) between poetry and prose does not necessarily indicate that the passage is a secondary addition. These verses are discussed further in my *Reflections of Empire in Isaiah 1–39: Responses to Assyrian Ideology*, ANEM (Atlanta: SBL Press, forthcoming).

for the overwhelming power of YHWH, precisely because YHWH is spirit rather than flesh. But the theological message of divine supremacy is tightly linked to a practical political issue. The prophet references the figures of Re'u and Azuri as evidence of the limitation of human power. He dissuades Judah from joining the Yamani-led coalition because this coalition relies on such power. The prophet is neither pro-Assyrian nor anti-Assyrian but rather argues for an alternative to the binary paradigm of Assyria versus local anti-Assyrian coalitions: the Israelites should return to the one to whom they ought to maintain loyalty, against whom they most deeply rebelled (v. 6)—YHWH.

New from
BAKER ACADEMIC

978-0-8010-3089-5 • 240 pp. • $22.99p

"This book is must reading for all serious students of the Bible."

—**TREMPER LONGMAN III**,
Westmont College

978-0-8010-4888-3 • 336 pp. • $29.99p

"Strawn has written a book of urgent practical theology based on prodigious research."

—**WALTER BRUEGGEMANN**,
Columbia Theological Seminary

978-0-8010-4963-7 • 352 pp. • $32.99c

A recognized expert on the Gospels shows that the Sermon on the Mount offers a clear window into understanding God's work in Christ.

B) Baker Academic | bakeracademic.com
Available in bookstores or by calling 800.877.2665

"From a Far Country": Daniel in Isaiah's Babylon

JENNIE GRILLO
jgrillo@div.duke.edu
Duke Divinity School, Durham, NC 27707

This article advances a new proposal for the literary background of the Aramaic Daniel: in crafting a frame for this early collection, the redactor of the tales has created a fictional model of the Babylonian court patterned on the remembered prophecy of Isaiah to Hezekiah in Isa 39:1–7. That ancient threat of royal sons and vessels taken captive to Babylon is conjured up again in the Danielic redactor's opening scene, and it has offered the later writer both a rare window into the "narrative gap" of the exile and a direct precursor to the motif of the Jew at the court of the foreign king. The chronological scaffolding added to the tales reveals further prophetic (and specifically Isaianic) pressure on the redactors' construal of imperial history. This practice of borrowing an earlier scriptural text as a broad canvas for later evocations of Israel's exilic experiences sets the framers of the Aramaic Daniel within a wider Second Temple scribal context, embedding their reading habits in a shared prophecy–fulfillment schema. Their exegesis may be seen as a purposeful engagement with whole scriptural books and with those books' own coherent argumentative and theological structures; perhaps these redactors of Daniel knew Isaiah not as isolated fragments but as an articulated compositional whole.

William Walton's oratorio *Belshazzar's Feast*, first performed in 1931, sets to music the trials and deliverance of Daniel and his friends at the Babylonian court. The libretto is a pastiche of biblical texts drawn together by the poet and novelist Osbert Sitwell: in a brilliantly compressed drama ranging across the Bible, the whole work begins with the words of the prophet Isaiah to King Hezekiah, as a baritone chorus announces, "Thus spake Isaiah – / Thy sons that thou shalt beget / They shall be taken away, / And be eunuchs / In the palace of the King of Babylon," before the other voices join in with Ps 137, "By the waters of Babylon we sat down and wept," and the story of the exiled Judeans at the court of the foreign king begins to unfold.[1] Almost no other modern readers of Daniel have followed Walton and

---

[1] William Walton, *Belshazzar's Feast* (London: Oxford University Press, 1931), first performed at the Leeds Festival under Malcolm Sargent on 8 October 1931 and infamously described

Sitwell in this act of strong imaginative appropriation, in which the specter of Babylon conjured up by the warning voice of Isaiah to Hezekiah becomes the backdrop for the tales of Daniel and his friends. If we follow Sitwell's invitation, however, and set the two texts alongside each other, Isaiah's threatening words to Hezekiah begin to emerge as a close, remembered presence in the opening verses of Daniel, giving prophetic contours to the imaginary geography of the later book. The idea that the book of Daniel opens with Isaiah's prospective onto exile remains a largely unexplored possibility in modern readings of Daniel.[2] In this article, I set out the cumulative case for hearing an echo of Isaiah's words behind the opening verses of the Daniel tales. I examine this textual connection and set it within the larger contexts of postexilic scribal practices in general and the editing of the book of Daniel in particular. The story of Isaiah's warning to Hezekiah is known from two parallel sources, Isa 39:1–7 and 2 Kgs 20:12–18. In establishing a connection between the Isaiah–Hezekiah narrative and the opening of Daniel, I do not distinguish between these two sources, since the differences between them are too small to give us any clues about which version the Danielic redactors might have known. Before concluding, however, I will make a tentative proposal for the greater claim of the book of Isaiah on the attention of those later scribes.

Examining the reading habits of the redactors of Daniel has a longer history in the modern study of the growth of the book. By broad consensus, the opening chapter of the masoretic book of Daniel came into being as a specially designed introduction, originally in Aramaic, to the collection of stories in chapters 2–6. In fastening together treasured tales of Daniel and his companions, the editor of this Aramaic Daniel gave his material a historical and theological frame that accounted for the presence of these exiled Judeans at the Babylonian court. At least since the early work of Reinhard Kratz, an editorial layer has been discerned in the whole tales collection that takes in not only this introductory chapter but also the

---

by *The Times* two days later as "Stark Judaism from first to last"; for the circumstances of Walton and Sitwell's work, see Michael Kennedy, *Portrait of Walton* (New York: Oxford University Press, 1989), 52–61; Stephen Lloyd, *William Walton: Muse of Fire* (Woodbridge: Boydell, 2001), 99–109; Susana Walton, *William Walton: Behind the Façade* (New York: Oxford University Press, 1988), 70–72; and Osbert Sitwell, *Laughter in the Next Room* (Boston: Little, Brown, 1948), 191. For the compact and highly contrastive dramatic character of Sitwell's anthology of biblical texts for *Belshazzar's Feast*, see Lewis Foreman, "Walton's Words," in *William Walton: Music and Literature*, ed. Stewart R. Craggs (Aldershot: Ashgate, 1999), 228–55. When the publishers initially resisted paying Sitwell royalties, arguing that a rearrangement of biblical texts was not an original work, Sitwell was able to convince them otherwise (see Philip Ziegler, *Osbert Sitwell* [London: Chatto & Windus, 1998], 268).

[2] John Goldingay notes in passing a link to Isa 39:7, taken up in the description of the men in Dan 1, but his main source is 2 Chr 36 (*Daniel*, WBC 30 [Dallas: Word, 1989], 7). Klaus Koch suggests that the renaming of the Judeans in Dan 1:7 functions as a fulfillment of the single verse Isa 39:7 (*Daniel: Kapitel 1,1–4,34*, BKAT 22.1 [Neukirchen-Vluyn: Neukirchener Verlag, 1986; repr., 2005], 23).

chronological scaffolding of date notices (1:21; 6:1, 29) and the hymnic snatches interposed throughout the tales (2:20-23, 47; 3:28; 3:31-33; 4:31-34; 6:27-28).[3] A relationship to the book of Isaiah is one strand of the literary filiation of these particular redactors. The Aramaic Daniel bears signs that it has been compiled and edited with an exegetical interest in the figure of Isaiah, echoing narratives about the prophet and words attributed to him. The exegetical evidence for a specific relationship between the opening verses of Dan 1 and the book of Isaiah can be viewed in the wider context of reading the book of Daniel for traces of Isaiah.

I. THE BOOK OF ISAIAH AND THE BOOK OF DANIEL
IN RECENT SCHOLARSHIP

Readers have long observed the influence of the memory of Isaiah and the book called by his name on the book of Daniel.[4] Most of the Isaianic interpretive activity in Daniel has been detected in the later literary stages and the latter chapters of the book, such as the typological identification of Seleucid Syria with Isaiah's Assyria in Daniel's final vision (chs. 10-12). Gerhard von Rad went so far as to describe Dan 7-12 as a pesher on Isaiah, and this focus on the visionary half of the book also characterized the work of Isac L. Seeligman and H. L. Ginsberg.[5] More recently, many examples of exegesis of Isaiah in the later chapters of Daniel have

---

[3] Reinhard G. Kratz, *Translatio imperii: Untersuchungen zu den aramäischen Danielerzählungen und ihrem theologiegeschichtlichen Umfeld*, WMANT 63 (Neukirchen-Vluyn: Neukirchener Verlag, 1991), 35-42, 70-76, 93-96, 148-54, 156-60; see also Klaus Koch, *Das Buch Daniel*, EdF 144 (Darmstadt: Wissenschaftliche Buchgesellschaft, 1980), 63-66, with a summary of the development of this model within older scholarship; and John J. Collins, *Daniel: A Commentary on the Book of Daniel*, Hermeneia (Minneapolis: Fortress, 1993), 35-36, who sustains a very similar schema without accepting all the proposals of the German *Aufstockungshypothese*. There may well have been older collections of these tales (Kratz, *Translatio imperii*, 128-40), but Dan 1 was written to introduce specifically the MT selection and order. The redactional layer I focus on is that of the *Verfasser* of Kratz's Stratum I (Kratz, *Translatio imperii*, 70-76). Although I use a plural to designate the authorship of these editorial materials, they could just as easily come from a single hand, and I make no distinction between the partly overlapping functions of the scribes, editors, redactors, and compilers who are, from the later perspective of the completed Hebrew Bible, themselves biblical authors.

[4] Still influential in this regard are the early studies of H. L. Ginsberg ("The Oldest Interpretation of the Suffering Servant," *VT* 3 [1953]: 400-404, developed by George W. E. Nickelsburg, *Resurrection, Immortality and Eternal Life in Intertestamental Judaism*, HTS 26 [Cambridge: Harvard University Press, 1972], 20-26, 61-66) and Isac L. Seeligmann (*The Septuagint Version of Isaiah: A Discussion of Its Problems*, MEOL 9 [Leiden: Brill, 1948], 82-83; and "Voraussetzungen der Midraschexegese," in *Congress Volume: Copenhagen 1953*, ed. G. W. Anderson, VTSup 1 [Leiden: Brill, 1953], 150-81, esp. 171).

[5] Gerhard von Rad, *Old Testament Theology*, trans. D. M. G. Stalker, 2 vols. (New York: Harper, 1962-1965), 2:314.

been collected by Michael Fishbane, Michael Knibb, Joseph Blenkinsopp, and Andrew Teeter.[6] If it proves plausible that the collection of finished tales that lay before the later authors was itself framed in Isaianic terms, then their style of interpretive composition imitates a scribal leaning already present within the literary deposit on which they built. Conversely, at the older end of the Daniel tradition, a number of scholars have detected borrowings from (in particular) Deutero-Isaiah within the narrative fabric of the tales themselves, such as the language of idol mockery in the stories of the statue and golden image in chapters 2 and 3. In spite of the complicated development of chapter 2, influence from Isaiah can be noted in the earliest versions of the dream and its interpretation.[7] Aage Bentzen saw the tales of deliverance from fire and lions as a *Verkörperung* of sentences such as Isa 43:2.[8] His suggestion echoes the mother of the seven martyrs in 4 Macc 18:12–14, who also links this promise from Isaiah and the tale of the youths in the furnace, reminding her sons that their father "taught you about Hananiah and Azariah and Mishael in the fire.… He reminded you of the scripture of Isaiah, which says, 'Even though you pass through the fire, the flame shall not consume you'" (NRSV). For Peter von der Osten-Sacken, the tales of Dan 1–6 related to Deutero-Isaiah as claims of prophecy fulfilled.[9] John G. Gammie heard the language of Deutero-Isaiah in the hymns that punctuate the tales collection. Some of these pieces are surely editorial and likely belong to the same redactional layer that framed the Aramaic tales collection, but that redactional work may elaborate the Isaianic cadences and tropes of poetic fragments original to the material.[10] The compilers of the Aramaic tales collection thus worked with materials that already used language and motifs learned from the book of Isaiah to retell Israel's exilic experiences.

---

[6] Michael Fishbane, *Biblical Interpretation in Ancient Israel* (Oxford: Oxford University Press, 1985), 489–94; Michael A. Knibb, "'You Are Indeed Wiser than Daniel': Reflections on the Character of the Book of Daniel," in *The Book of Daniel: Composition and Reception*, ed. John J. Collins and Peter W. Flint, VTSup 83 (Leiden: Brill, 2001), 399–411; Joseph Blenkinsopp, *Opening the Sealed Book: Interpretations of the Book of Isaiah in Late Antiquity* (Grand Rapids: Eerdmans, 2006), 14–23, 229–30; D. Andrew Teeter, "Isaiah and the King of Assyria in Daniel's Final Vision: On the Rhetoric of Inner-Scriptural Allusion and the Hermeneutics of 'Mantological Exegesis,'" in *A Teacher for All Generations: Essays in Honor of James C. VanderKam*, ed. Eric F. Mason et al., 2 vols., JSJSup 153 (Leiden: Brill, 2011), 1:169–99.

[7] C. L. Seow, "From Mountain to Mountain: The Reign of God in Daniel 2," in *A God So Near: Essays on Old Testament Theology in Honor of Patrick D. Miller*, ed. Brent A. Strawn and Nancy R. Bowen (Winona Lake, IN: Eisenbrauns, 2003), 355–74; Ida Frölich, "Daniel 2 and Deutero-Isaiah," in *The Book of Daniel in the Light of New Findings*, ed. A. S. van der Woude, BETL 106 (Leuven: Leuven University Press, 1993), 266–70.

[8] Aage Bentzen, *Daniel*, HAT 19 (Tübingen: Mohr Siebeck, 1937), 39, 55.

[9] Peter von der Osten-Sacken, *Die Apokalyptik in ihrem Verhältnis zu Prophetie und Weisheit*, TEH 157 (Munich: Kaiser, 1969), 23–25.

[10] John G. Gammie, "On the Intention and Sources of Daniel I–VI," *VT* 31 (1981): 282–92, esp. 287–89. On the early presence of hymnic material, redactionally developed, see Kratz, *Translatio imperii*, 91–95, 156–60.

Hearing an echo of Isaiah's words in Dan 1:1–4 is itself partly a product of a second reading. The knowing reader is sensitized to that particular literary relationship by the web of Isaianic allusions present in the collection, even as those allusions in turn depend on the opening Isaianic conceit to bring them to prominence. But this is not so much a circular argument as an effect of the book's stages of redactional growth. It is the vestigial presence of Isaiah throughout the tales collection that has determined the selection of Isaianic echoes for its beginning. Daniel 1 stands as the introduction to the whole cycle, and it does so in terms of the book of Isaiah, setting the relationship up for the naïve reader and referring to it for the knowing one. The collecting of the tales of Daniel, then, took place at the midpoint of a process of composition that unfolded under the shadow of Isaiah from the very first to the very last. I turn now to the exegetical evidence for that relationship in the opening verses of the collection.

II. Reading Daniel 1 alongside Isaiah 39/2 Kings 20

In the Daniel author's notice that Nebuchadnezzar has carried Israelite vessels and sons captive to Babylon, several expressions recall the prophecy of Isaiah to Hezekiah reported in Isa 39:1–7/2 Kgs 20:12–19. That prophecy is framed by the story of men "from a far country, from Babylon" coming to visit the king and is taken up by the prophet as a sinister shadow of days to come:

> See, days are coming when everything in your house, and that which your fathers stored up until this day, will be carried to Babylon; not a thing will remain, says YHWH. And some of your sons who go forth from you, whom you beget, will be taken; they will become officials in the palace of the king of Babylon. (Isa 39:6–7/2 Kgs 20:17–18; my translation)

Isaiah's warning has two elements: all the precious things of Hezekiah's ancestral treasuries will be carried away to Babylon (Isa 39:6/2 Kgs 20:17), and sons of the royal house will be taken away to be servants in the palace of the king of Babylon (Isa 39:7/2 Kgs 20:18). The book of Daniel, correspondingly, begins with the news that Nebuchadnezzar has now carried away the vessels of the Jerusalem temple to the treasury of Babylon (1:1–2), along with sons of the royal household[11] taken to serve in the palace of the king (1:3–4). This double fulfillment evokes Isaiah's reported double prophecy. The action proper could equally be said to begin in verse 3, verse 6, or verse 8, but even if verses 1–2 can be formally separated off as a historicizing frame, it is the whole unit of verses 1–7 that does the work of building

---

[11] The phrase מזרע המלוכה refers to "the Jewish royalty and nobility," according to Collins, *Daniel*, 136; Koch has "der Samen des Königtums" (*Book of Daniel*, 3). See too Michael E. Stone, "A Note on Daniel 1:3," *ABR* 7 (1959): 69–71, though this phrase may not refer to an extra group as he suggests.

the necessary network of information for the action recounted in the chapter. Within that section, verses 1–5 carry the descriptive weight of setting the scene, and they do so in Isaiah's terms of stores and sons taken by the king of Babylon to serve in his palace.[12]

According to commentators including James A. Montgomery, Klaus Koch, John J. Collins, John Goldingay, and Louis F. Hartman and Alexander A. Di Lella, Dan 1:1–2 is dependent on 2 Chr 36:5–7. There is less agreement about the possibility that 2 Kgs 24:1 lies behind the confused "third year" of Dan 1:1.[13] A minority of readers prefer a background spread across the final two chapters of the Deuteronomistic History.[14] It is likely that Chronicles was a source: 2 Chr 36:7 has clear similarities to Dan 1:2. Certainly the name of Jehoiakim in Dan 1:1–2 indicates that one of these biblical accounts lay behind the Danielic verses. The Daniel editor's chronological confusion and the imperfect fit of both Chronicles and Kings, however, suggest that neither is a very close source. The Daniel editor's relationship to both Kings and Chronicles is more like half-remembered knowledge than close imaginative engagement. There is no parallel in either history for the narrative backdrop in Dan 1 of king, courtiers, and temple vessels carried together to Babylon in the time of Jehoiakim. 2 Chronicles 36 only speaks of the deportation of the king and the temple vessels in Jehoiakim's time, not of other Judeans (vv. 6–7), and, for the Chronicler, it is only under Zedekiah that Judean citizens go into exile (36:20, with the first use of ויגל, "take into exile"). In 2 Kgs 24–25, there is no deportation in Jehoiakim's reign (24:1–6), and temple vessels and exiles go to Babylon only under Jehoiachin (24:13–16) and Zedekiah (25:11–17). Koch, alternatively, adduces parallels to Jer 39:1 and 25:9–11, both of which passages do refer to Nebuchadnezzar's coming. Jeremiah 39:1, however, speaks not of Jehoiakim but of Zedekiah and only later mentions the deportation of Judeans (v. 9), with no treasures. In Jer 25:9–11 nothing is taken to Babylon and no king is mentioned.[15] In sum, 2 Chr 36:6–7 is the closest background for the situation of Dan 1:1–2, but it

---

[12] See also Kratz, *Translatio imperii*, 35–42, 148–54, for whom verses 1–2 function as a frame within the single redactional piece that is chapter 1, though it contains an older story of the food trial alone.

[13] James A. Montgomery, *A Critical and Exegetical Commentary on the Book of Daniel*, ICC (New York: Scribner's Sons, 1927), 114–16; Koch, *Book of Daniel*, 27, 31; Collins, *Daniel*, 132; Goldingay, *Daniel*, 4; Louis F. Hartman and Alexander A. Di Lella, *The Book of Daniel: A New Translation with Notes and Commentary*, AB 23 (Garden City, NY: Doubleday, 1978), 128. So too Isaac Kalimi, "History of Interpretation: The 'Book of Chronicles' in Jewish Tradition—From the 'Book of Daniel' to Spinoza," *RB* 105 (1988): 5–41.

[14] See, e.g., André LaCoque, *The Book of Daniel*, trans. David Pellauer (Atlanta: John Knox, 1979), 24; Otto Plöger, *Das Buch Daniel*, KAT 18 (Gütersloh: Gütersloher Verlagshaus, 1965); Matthias Henze, "Babylon Remembered: Nebuchadnezzar in the Collective Memory of Ancient Israel," in *With Wisdom as a Robe: Qumran and Other Jewish Studies in Honour of Ida Frölich*, ed. Károly Dániel Dobos and Miklós Kőszeghy (Sheffield: Sheffield Phoenix, 2009), 108–20.

[15] Koch, *Book of Daniel*, 22–23.

is still not very close. One, several, or perhaps all of these historiographic texts must lie somewhere behind the work of the redactor who composed an opening frame for Aramaic Daniel. Since none is an exact fit, none is likely to be an exclusive source: the beginning of Dan 1 has room for another kind of influence from another kind of text.

Alongside these historiographic parallels, a deeper literary *Einklang* is audible between the opening of the book of Daniel and Isaiah's prophecy. The account in Isa 39:6-7/2 Kgs 20:17-18 telescopes the whole protracted downfall of the Judean state into a single event exactly as Dan 1:1-2 does. More natural than the attempts to fit Dan 1 into an earlier, partial deportation is the simple assumption that here is exile. In Collins's words, "The most fundamental aspect of the setting of Daniel 1 ... is the exilic situation."[16] Perhaps the narrative presentation of Isaiah's prophecy originally referred in hindsight only to the events of 598 and predated those of 587, but to the redactor of Daniel, far removed from that catastrophe, the words of the prophet would most naturally point to the entire event of the exile.[17] As the Daniel authors begin to create a setting for their tales, the fictional milieu that they construct bears its closest literary relationship to the narrative of Isa 39/2 Kgs 20. For example, 2 Chr 36:6-7 does not share the term *treasury* (אוצר) with Dan 1:2, whereas we do find treasuries in Isa 39:2, 4/2 Kgs 20:13, 15 (plus the cognate verb in Isa 39:6/2 Kgs 20:17). Likewise, the servants among whom Daniel and his friends find themselves are סריסים (Dan 1:3, 7-11, 18), reflecting the local color of Isaiah's idea of the Babylonian court (Isa 39:7/2 Kgs 20:18). Reading against the background of 2 Chr 36:6-7, Koch notes the addition of divine agency in Dan 1:2, *giving* Jehoiakim into Nebuchadnezzar's power.[18] Koch speculates that this phrasing is imported from 2 Chr 36:17, later in the Chronicler's account, or from Jeremiah's emphasis. Yet a background in the Isaiah story accounts for this within a single narrative, since in Isa 39:5-8/2 Kgs 20:16-19 being taken to Babylon is three times ascribed to YHWH's agency as דבר־יהוה and אמר יהוה.[19] Finally, the naming of Babylon as "Shinar" in Dan 1:2 is not explicable against a background of 2 Chr 36. Most commentators point out the archaizing and pejorative freight of "Shinar," with

---

[16] Collins, *Daniel*, 146; so too C. L. Seow, *Daniel*, WeBC (Louisville: Westminster John Knox, 2003), 21; Montgomery, *Critical and Exegetical Commentary*, 116; Koch, *Daniel*, 25; Bentzen, *Daniel*, 17.

[17] For this reconstruction of the Isaiah material, see R. E. Clements, *Isaiah and the Deliverance of Jerusalem: A Study of the Interpretation of Prophecy in the Old Testament*, JSOTSup 13 (Sheffield: JSOT Press, 1980), 67-68, 103.

[18] Koch, *Daniel*, 33; for this emphasis in Daniel, see Goldingay, *Daniel*, 8-9.

[19] It may be significant in this connection that in Dan 1:2 MT the divine name is אדני, which is supported by Theodotion, who here has κύριος rather than ὁ θεός, which represents האלהים elsewhere in the chapter (some Hebrew manuscripts in fact have יי, but this is probably an inner-Hebrew development from אדני). This usage, unique in the book of Daniel, perhaps echoes יהוה in Isa 39/2 Kgs 20, for which אדני may already have been a substitute.

its connotations of idolatry from the Babel story and from Zech 5:11.[20] LaCoque, however, points out an Isaianic coloring in the echo of the prophecy in Isa 11:11 of the return to Zion of a remnant of the people exiled *in Shinar*.[21] The language and expression of the opening verses of Dan 1, then, have several points of contact with the scriptural memory of Isaiah and his oracle to Hezekiah. I turn now from this web of specific textual connections to examine the way in which the Isaiah oracle provides a larger, almost typological model for the imagined situation of Dan 1.

III. The Silence of Exile and the Fulfillment of Prophecy

The situation briefly forecast in Isa 39/2 Kgs 20 has a more immediate imaginative identity with the world of Dan 1 than do the historians' ways of speaking about exile. Here the life of the exiles as court life is actually envisaged: "they will be taken away and will become officials in the palace of the king of Babylon" (Isa 39:7). Along with the Joseph story, this is one of very few earlier instances of the motif of a Jew at the court of a foreign king that a later writer could invoke.[22] Many scholars have noted what Rainer Albertz called the "yawning gap" of the exilic period in Israel's historical traditions. David M. Carr refers to "one of the most striking absences in the broader Hebrew Bible corpus: the relative lack in the Bible of discourse directly about life during the exile or attributed to figures speaking from the exile."[23] In the backward gaze of historiographic texts, Israel's story

---

[20] So Koch, *Daniel*, 32; Seow, *Daniel*, 23; Bentzen, *Daniel*, 19.

[21] LaCoque, *Book of Daniel*, 26. This is the only one of the lexical connections between Dan 1 and the book of Isaiah that might be affected by the linguistic shift between the earlier text's Hebrew and the redactor's Aramaic: "Shinar" is not usual in Aramaic and tends to be replaced by *bābal* in the targums (although cf. the somewhat different situation in the Samaritan tradition: Abraham Tal, *A Dictionary of Samaritan Aramaic*, HdO 50 [Leiden: Brill, 2000], 915). Koch, correspondingly, ascribes this clause to the Hebrew translator of chapter 1, who in his view is responsible for the scriptural allusions in the opening of the book more generally (*Book of Daniel*, 18–20). That later date would not greatly alter my proposal for allusion to Isaiah within the development of Daniel.

[22] The classic studies of this motif in its biblical instances are W. L. Humphreys, "A Life-Style for Diaspora: A Study of the Tales of Esther and Daniel," *JBL* 92 (1973): 211–23; Susan Niditch and Robert Doran, "The Success Story of the Wise Courtier: A Formal Approach," *JBL* 96 (1977): 179–93; and Lawrence M. Wills, *The Jew in the Court of the Foreign King: Ancient Jewish Court Legends*, HDR 26 (Minneapolis: Fortress, 1990). See also Tessa Rajak et al., eds., *Jewish Perspectives on Hellenistic Rulers*, HCS 50 (Berkeley: University of California Press, 2007); and Tawny L. Holm, *Of Courtiers and Kings: The Biblical Daniel Narratives and Ancient Story-Collections*, EANEC 1 (Winona Lake, IN: Eisenbrauns, 2013), 192–201.

[23] Rainer Albertz, *Israel in Exile: The History and Literature of the Sixth Century B.C.E.*, trans. David Green, SBLStBL 3 (Atlanta: Society of Biblical Literature, 2003), ix, 3–4, 8–11; David M. Carr, "Reading into the Gap: Refractions of Trauma in Israelite Prophecy," in *Interpreting Exile:*

culminates in the moment *of* exile, leaving the reader only on the brink of life *in* exile. In Albertz's words, "only the margins are recorded."[24] 2 Kings 25:27–30 is a rare exception to the silence of this "narrative wreckage,"[25] yet this brief vignette fills in the missing exilic backdrop only for the solitary figure of Jehoiachin.[26] Equally, in the forward projection of prophetic texts and the curses they elaborate, exile is a catalogue of suffering unable to furnish a context for the refined court atmosphere of Dan 1. In Samuel Balentine's phrase, exilic poetry is a "house of sorrow" alongside the historiographical silence.[27] Martien Halvorson-Taylor has traced the process of metaphorization whereby "the Babylonian exile was transformed from a historical experience into a multivalent symbol of physical, mental, and spiritual distress."[28] Exile is darkness, death, catastrophe, dislocation, prison, slavery; the slavery of survivors in 2 Chr 36:20 belongs to this last topos more than it forms a background for the status of "standing before the king" in Dan 1, where equivalent terms for slavery are never used.[29] Jeremiah 29:5–7 modifies

---

Displacement and Deportation in Biblical and Modern Contexts, ed. Brad E. Kelle, Frank Ritchel Ames, and Jacob L. Wright, AIL 10 (Atlanta: Society of Biblical Literature, 2011), 295–308, here 296.

[24] Albertz, *Israel in Exile*, 3; see too Peter R. Ackroyd, *Exile and Restoration: A Study of Hebrew Thought in the Sixth Century B.C.*, OTL (Philadelphia: Westminster, 1968), 31–32, 66–67; B. E. Kelle, "An Interdisciplinary Approach to the Exile," in Kelle, Ames, and Wright, *Interpreting Exile*, 5–38.

[25] Kathleen M. O'Connor (*Lamentations and the Tears of the World* [Maryknoll, NY: Orbis, 2002], 7) borrowed this phrase from Arthur Frank.

[26] This is the difficulty in Meik Gerhards's suggestion that 2 Kgs 25:27–30 is a Deuteronomistic fulfillment notice of the word of Isaiah to Hezekiah ("Die beiden Erzählungen aus 2. Kön 20 und 2. Kön 20,18 als Ankündigung der Begnadigung Jojachins [2. Kön 25, 27–30]," *BN* 98 [1999]: 5–12).

[27] Samuel E. Balentine, "The Prose and Poetry of Exile," in Kelle, Ames, and Wright, *Interpreting Exile*, 345–63; see too Anne-Mareike Wetter, "Balancing the Scales: The Construction of the Exile as Countertradition in the Bible," in Bob Becking, Anne-Mareike Wetter, Wilfred van de Poll, and Alex Cannegieter, *From Babylon to Eternity: The Exile Remembered and Constructed in Text and Tradition*, BibleWorld (London: Equinox, 2009), 34–56.

[28] Martien A. Halvorson-Taylor, *Enduring Exile: The Metaphorization of Exile in the Hebrew Bible*, VTSup 141 (Leiden: Brill, 2011), 41.

[29] For the biblical language of exile as a "lexicography of trauma," see Daniel Smith-Christopher, *A Biblical Theology of Exile*, OBT (Minneapolis: Fortress, 2002), 66, 71–73 for slavery; and his *The Religion of the Landless: The Social Context of the Babylonian Exile* (Bloomington, IN: Meyer-Stone, 1989), 171–74 for prison, although his patterns of exile are themselves partly also generated from the later texts like Daniel. For a close study of the language of exile as death and manifold ills in Deut 28 and Lev 26, see Halvorson-Taylor, *Enduring Exile*, 21–37, and subsequent chapters for its prophetic outworkings in parts of Jeremiah, Isaiah, and Zechariah. For the development of many of the same images of exile in further texts, see Reinhard Müller ("A Prophetic View of the Exile in the Holiness Code" and "Images of Exile in the Book of Judges") and Francis Landy ("Exile in the Book of Isaiah" and "Reading, Writing, and Exile") in *The Concept of Exile in Ancient Israel and Its Historical Contexts*, ed. Ehud Ben Zvi and Christoph Levin, BZAW

the grinding bitterness of the prophetic picture of exile, but this small-town vision of family life is more like home than it is like the exotic court existence imagined in Dan 1.[30] The warning of Isaiah, then, offers what is actually a very rare imagined glimpse into the narrative gap of the exile and into the palace of the king of Babylon where royal sons of Judah stand and serve. As the treasure-house doors close on the departing envoys from a far country, the prophet conjures up a threat that stands directly within the development of the motif of the Jew at the court of the foreign king. Although Ezra, Nehemiah, 1 Esdras, and Esther offer a closer depiction of court life in exile, the imagined Persian settings of those books could at best provide a literary heritage for the *writing* of a text like Dan 1.[31] For the mental journey all the way back to a claimed historical setting in Babylon, the figure of Isaiah is almost the only guide.

By the same token, Isaiah's word offers the authority and thematic relevance of fulfilled prophecy to the redactors of Daniel—George J. Brooke reminds us that "if ever classical prophecy had been about forth-telling, in the Second Temple period it was more clearly perceived by some Jews at least as fore-telling"—whereas a historiographic background like 2 Chr 36 stands at one remove from prophetic prediction and vindication, speaking of the past rather than the future.[32] In fact, both the Chronicler and the author of Dan 1 seem to share a habit of operating inside what in John Barton's typology is a "third mode" way of reading prophecy, that is, as evidence of the plan of God being worked out in historical events. In this context, the figure of the prophet is specially qualified to describe God's action in history, and thus the prophetic witness that a historian can only report is heard firsthand in the words of Isaiah.[33] As a rhetorical resource, the fulfilled prophecy of Isaiah therefore provides the highest level of reassurance that God is in control

---

404 (Berlin: de Gruyter, 2010), 207–28, 229–40, 241–56, and 257–74, respectively; and D. Smith-Christopher ("Reassessing the Historical and Sociological Impact of the Babylonian Exile (597/587–539 BCE") and R. P. Carroll ("Deportation and Diaspora Discourses in the Prophetic Literature") in *Exile: Old Testament, Jewish, and Christian Conceptions*, ed. James M. Scott, JSJSup 56 (Leiden: Brill, 1997), 7–36 and 63–86, respectively; and still Ackroyd, *Exile and Restoration*, 89, for Lev 26:36–39, and 104–6, 117 for Ezekiel.

[30] See Adele Berlin, "Jeremiah 29:5-7: A Deuteronomic Allusion," *HAR* 8 (1984): 3–11.

[31] For these comparisons, see Koch, *Book of Daniel*, 22, and the works cited there.

[32] George J. Brooke, "Prophetic Interpretation in the *Pesharim*," in *A Companion to Biblical Interpretation in Early Judaism*, ed. Matthias Henze (Grand Rapids: Eerdmans, 2012), 235–54, here 239. Goldingay refers to Isaiah's fulfilled prophecy as one of Dan 1's "seeds of hope, partly encouraged by stimuli toward recollection of earlier events and earlier scriptures" (*Daniel*, 22).

[33] See John Barton, *Oracles of God: Perceptions of Ancient Prophecy in Israel after the Exile* (London: Darton, Longman & Todd, 1986), 214–26. According to Barton, the idea that a historian like the Chronicler is also a prophet comes only later in the Second Temple period (21–23, 35–55), even though the converse is true much earlier, as when Chronicles refers to prophets as custodians of history. See also Joseph Blenkinsopp, *A History of Prophecy in Israel* (Philadelphia: Westminster, 1983), 279 n. 75.

even of a world where Judean nobles have become courtiers in Babylon. In this, the redactor of Aramaic Daniel shares his idea of Isaiah with a near contemporary of the later redactors of Daniel. In the words of the grandson of Ben Sira, reading the predictive prophecy of the book of Isaiah in a historicizing mode, "By his dauntless spirit he saw the future, and comforted the mourners in Zion. He revealed what was to occur to the end of time, and the hidden things before they happened" (Sir 48:24–25 NRSV).[34] Within the wider scribal activity of the Daniel tradition, Blenkinsopp has observed the programmatic use of Isaiah's words "destructions are decreed" (כלה ונחרצה, Isa 10:23) as a leitmotif for the book of Daniel; that interpretive borrowing of the later scribes has a special aptness if the book itself has first opened with a fulfillment notice of a destruction decreed by Isaiah.[35] In large patterns of thought as well as in compositional details, then, the opening of the book of Daniel is tied by conceptual and lexical threads to the remembered oracle of Isaiah to Hezekiah.

IV. The Afterlife of Isaiah's Word to Hezekiah: A Narrative Parallel

The Daniel editor's reuse of Isaiah's threat as fulfilled prophecy finds a close parallel in the prophecy's other narrative afterlife, in 2 Kings. Tracing this process furnishes a possible analogue for the textual remembering done by the scribes of Aramaic Daniel. Specifically, 2 Kgs 24:10–17 reports Nebuchadnezzar's siege of Jehoiachin's Jerusalem, his captives, and his looting as the fulfillment of a divine word: "he took out from there all the treasures of the house of YHWH and the treasures of the house of the king; he cut up all the golden vessels in the temple of YHWH which Solomon king of Israel had made, *just as YHWH had spoken*" (v. 13; my translation). What is the divine word that is here fulfilled? When we look in the Deuteronomistic History for a word of YHWH predicting the capture of the royal treasures of Jerusalem by a Babylonian king, the only close correspondence is with Isaiah's oracle to Hezekiah reported in 2 Kgs 20:17 ("See, days are coming when everything in your house, and that which your fathers stored up until this day, will be carried to Babylon; not a thing will remain, says YHWH"; my translation). In the judgment of several commentators, this is the prophecy whose fulfillment is noted in 2 Kgs 24:10–17.[36] Even if the "earlier" passage is in fact inserted into its

---

[34] See Jan L. Koole, "Die Bibel des Ben Sira," *OtSt* 14 (1965): 374–96, here 385; cf. Peter R. Ackroyd, who notes the predominance of exilic allusion and a future, consoling perspective in Sirach's portrait of Isaiah ("Isaiah 36–39: Structure and Function," in *"The Place Is Too Small for Us": The Israelite Prophets in Recent Scholarship*, ed. Robert P. Gordon, SBTS 5 [Winona Lake, IN: Eisenbrauns, 1995], 478–79).

[35] Blenkinsopp, *Opening the Sealed Book*, 15–16.

[36] Mordechai Cogan and Hayim Tadmor, *II Kings: A New Translation with Introduction and*

present position in order to provide an explanation for the events reported in 2 Kgs 24:10–17, the effect created in the finished literary work is a pattern of prophecy and fulfillment.[37] In the Deuteronomistic tradition, then, the Isaianic saying is invoked as a true prediction of the Babylonian captivity in much the same way as the redactor of Aramaic Daniel seems to have borrowed it.

The appeal to the fulfilled words of Isaiah in 2 Kgs 24:13 is also useful evidence that this prophecy was remembered and read as relating to the temple vessels, a relationship that lies submerged beneath the surface in the initial report of the oracle in Isa 39/2 Kgs 20. In that encounter, Isaiah mentions simply "everything in your house, and that which your fathers stored up until this day" (Isa 39:6/2 Kgs 20:17). This gestures back in turn to what Hezekiah has shown the Babylonian envoys, which includes "his treasure-house, the silver, the gold, the spices, the precious oil, his whole armory, and all that was found in his storehouses" (Isa 39:2/ 2 Kgs 20:13), but the temple vessels are not specified. They are theoretically included, if "there was not a thing which Hezekiah did not show them, in his house and in his whole kingdom" (Isa 39:2/2 Kgs 20:13), but the emphasis is on the palace and storehouses (Isa 39:4/2 Kgs 20:15). This appears at first to be a difficulty for the suggestion that the narrative in Isa 39/2 Kgs 20 forms the background to Dan 1, since the vessels in Dan 1:2 are explicitly the temple vessels. This fact is underlined by the parallel cultic purity of Daniel and his friends and by the likely exegetical relationship of this verse to the story of the temple vessels in Dan 5, which it serves to introduce. Isaiah's prophecy is embedded within a pattern in the books of Kings: the loss reported in 2 Kgs 24:10–17 is part of the string of "despoliation notices" running throughout the history of Israel and Judah that threaten the treasures of palace and temple alike. This theme is most often associated with the Chronicler,

---

Commentary, AB 11 (Garden City, NY: Doubleday, 1988), 313; H. G. M. Williamson, *The Book Called Isaiah: Deutero-Isaiah's Role in Composition and Redaction* (Oxford: Oxford University Press, 1994), 208; Peter Höffken, "Zur Eigenart von Jes 39 par II Reg 20,12–19," *ZAW* 110 (1998): 244–49; Eberhard Ruprecht, "Die ursprüngliche Komposition der Hiskia-Jesaja-Erzählungen und ihre Umstrukturierung durch den Verfasser [Dtr] Geschichtswerkes," *ZTK* 87 (1990): 33–66, here 43–44; Gerhards, "Die beiden Erzählungen," 11–12. Marc Zvi Brettler suggests instead that כאשר דבר יהוה refers not to Nebuchadnezzar's activity in the passage but to Solomon's ("2 Kings 24:13–14 as History," *CBQ* 53 [1991]: 541–52, here 545). This, however, would require a prior promise of YHWH that Solomon would make the temple vessels, since the temple itself is an awkward object for עשה ("make") in verse 13 rather than בנה ("build"), and there is no such promise. For Brettler, the oracle of 2 Kgs 20:16–18 cannot be in view here since no sons are mentioned. Yet there is surely an impression of complete deportation in the long list that begins in verse 15 with all Jerusalem and all the סריסים.

[37] This is the reconstruction of Clements (*Isaiah and the Deliverance of Jerusalem*, 66–68, 103), Christof Hardmeier (*Prophetie im Streit vor dem Untergang Judas: Erzählkommunikative Studien zur Entstehungssituation der Jesaja- und Jeremiaerzählungen im II Reg 18–20 und Jer 37–40*, BZAW 187 [Berlin: de Gruyter, 1990], 454–57), and likewise Christoph Levin ("The Empty Land in Kings," in Ben Zvi and Levin, *Concept of Exile in Ancient Israel*, 61–89, here 68).

but it punctuates the Deuteronomistic History too.[38] It is on this basis that the author of 2 Kgs 24:13 can relate the loss of the treasures of palace *and temple* to the word of Isaiah in 2 Kgs 20:17. Isaiah never mentioned the temple treasures, but his threat to the accumulated inheritance of the royal house, "all that your fathers have stored up," is woven by the Deuteronomistic Historian into the larger story of the loss of the riches of the kings of Israel and Judah, including the temple vessels.[39] If this echo of an ancient oracle was assimilated to the broader pattern in its use in 2 Kgs 24:13, we can imagine a similar process of assimilation in the collective remembering that caused Isaiah's prophecy to be heard as a threat spoken over the temple vessels in Dan 1. Exactly this process of assimilation is attested in Pirqe R. El. chapter 52, where Hezekiah shows the Babylonian envoys not only the royal riches but all the treasures of the holy of holies and even the tables of the law.

V. Further Isaianic Redactional Activity in Aramaic Daniel

Other elements of the redaction of Aramaic Daniel also point to the editors' debt to the book of Isaiah. Kratz has suggested that the same collector who gave the narrative frame to the Aramaic tales of Dan 2–6 has likewise provided the tales with a chronological scaffolding in the redactional notices that follow on from 1:1 in 1:21, 6:1, and 6:29.[40] That chronological framework fastens the whole together in a construction of history inherited specifically from the book of Isaiah. I suggest that an Isaianic worldview influences the selection of Cyrus as the marker for historical epochs and shapes the redactor's use of a three-kingdoms grid for the Aramaic tales collection.

First, at the close of the introductory chapter of Daniel (1:21), the redactors signal that their book will share Deutero-Isaiah's Nebuchadnezzar-to-Cyrus chronological frame, in another gesture toward the literary work where Cyrus is most vividly present: "And Daniel was there until the first year of Cyrus the king."[41] Using Cyrus to structure historical time is most often understood as a borrowing from

---

[38] See Isaac Kalimi, *An Ancient Israelite Historian: Studies in the Chronicler, His Time, Place and Writing*, SSN 46 (Assen: Van Gorcum, 2005), 115–23; the classic exposition is Peter R. Ackroyd, "The Temple Vessels: A Continuity Theme," in *Studies in the Religion of Ancient Israel*, VTSup 23 (Leiden: Brill, 1972), 166–81.

[39] See Christopher T. Begg, who further suggests that the silence about the temple vessels comes from deference toward Hezekiah's overall piety in an older oracle that has been taken over by the Deuteronomist ("2 Kings 20:12–19 as an Element of the Deuteronomistic History," *CBQ* 48 [1986]: 27–38). Similarly E. Theodore Mullen, "Crime and Punishment: The Sins of the King and the Despoliation of the Treasuries," *CBQ* 54 (1992): 231–48, here 247.

[40] Kratz, *Translatio imperii*, 19, 84–85, 150–51.

[41] For 1:21 as a redactional bracket, see Koch, *Book of Daniel*, 19, 21.

the Chronicler, and especially from the synchronism in 2 Chr 36 between the accession of Cyrus and the end of exile (2 Chr 36:22–23), which is based on a calculation from Jeremiah's seventy years (2 Chr 36:21; cf. Jer 25:11–12; 29:10).[42] But, as Collins points out, Aramaic Daniel knows nothing of the end of exile, nor are seventy years part of this author's calculation. The collection of Dan 1–6 was of course framed with no knowledge of the later exegesis of Jeremiah's prophecy in Dan 9.[43] Instead, invoking Cyrus at the end of a chapter that began with Isaiah's prophecy of exile to Hezekiah simply follows the arc of history familiar from the shape of the book of Isaiah, where Cyrus is the last in a line of foreign kings to loom over Judah. By using Cyrus in Dan 1 to mark the succession of empires, then, the redactor borrows his history from the book of Isaiah more than from the books of Chronicles.

Second, the entire tales collection also owes its three-kingdoms schema to prophetic, and particularly Isaianic, shaping. According to the redactional model of Kratz, the sequence of Babylon, Media, and Persia that links 1:1 (Babylon), 6:1 (Media), and 6:29 (Persia) has been overlaid onto material that originally had only a two-kingdoms pattern. That original pattern is still visible in the underlying form of Nebuchadnezzar's statue dream (shorn of its expansions, the dream speaks simply of Nebuchadnezzar's kingdom and the one that succeeds it) and in the writing on Belshazzar's wall (where פרסין or פרס most naturally stands for only Persians, with the Medes as a later addition, 5:28).[44] When we look for a source for this new, editorial three-kingdom articulation of the progress of history, we can sense again the pressure of prophecy on the redactors' worldview. As Kratz and others have documented, the book of Daniel's threefold sequence must stem from a traditional Persian motif of the succession of empires from Assyria to Media to Persia. This is known also from Greek sources and can have originated only from Achaemenid royal ideology, notwithstanding other possible sources for the later, four-kingdoms shaping of the Maccabean layer in the tales.[45] But the Daniel redactors have substituted Babylon for Assyria in this traditional scheme. While Kratz argues that this change would have been natural in the redactors' exilic period, pointing to a similar perspective in Chronicles and Jeremiah,[46] the most explicit and purposefully exegetical substitution of Babylon for Assyria in fact lay nearer to hand for the collector, in the book of Isaiah. This change is seen most famously in passages such as the

---

[42] So Koch, *Book of Daniel*, 80; Goldingay, *Daniel*, 15; Kratz, *Translatio imperii*, 148–49; Montgomery, *Critical and Exegetical Commentary*, 90, 137.

[43] Collins, *Daniel*, 145.

[44] Kratz, *Translatio imperii*, 61–62, 84–85, 150–51.

[45] Ibid., 198–201, 210; in particular, the parallel offered by the sequence of empires in the Akkadian Dynastic Prophecy (Assyrian, Babylonian, Persian, Macedonian) is not relevant to this early stage of the book.

[46] Ibid., 69, 211; likewise, he cites the widespread classical historiographical traditions of collapsing the Near Eastern empires together.

oracle against Babylon in Isa 13:1–14:23, which derives part of its force from a saying against Assyria in 14:24–27; or in the delayed threat to Tyre in 23:13, simply, "Look, the land of the Chaldeans! This is the people, it was not Assyria."[47] Whatever the immediate source was for the Medes in the middle of the three-kindgom schema, to a biblically minded redactor this too finds its nearest ideological relationships with prophecy—especially with the book of Isaiah. Neither the Chronicler nor the Deuteronomistic Historian ever mentions the Medes, but the reader meets them most often in the books of Isaiah and Jeremiah.[48] For H. H. Rowley, the book of Daniel owed its "Darius the Mede" to the redactors' belief that the tales of kings that lay before them documented the fulfillment of prophecies about Babylon such as Isa 13:17, "See, I am sending the Medes against them."[49] Echoes of Isaiah have thus exerted an imaginative pressure on the redactors as they fitted their tales within a scripturally constructed historical scaffolding. This, then, is a hint—though no more than a hint—that the opening of their work may also look specifically to the book of Isaiah to create its narrative frame. When we trace the cumulative pattern of all these various textual echoes within the editing of Aramaic Daniel, the literary work that exerts the strongest imaginative pressure on those editors is the book of Isaiah. The allusion to the words of Isaiah in the opening frame of Daniel seems to come not only from traditional memory of the prophet but from the traditions in the book gathered under his name.

VI. Some Possible Implications: Scribal Writing and Reading in Daniel

I have focused especially on the Daniel editors' invitation to their readers to imagine themselves in *Isaiah*'s Babylon, arguing that the fictional exilic setting that the book of Daniel creates is worked on a template familiar from the book of Isaiah. Though their relationship to the book of Isaiah is certainly not an exclusive rela-

---

[47] See Benjamin D. Sommer, *A Prophet Reads Scripture: Allusion in Isaiah 40–66* (Stanford, CA: Stanford University Press, 1998), 92–93. Jacob Stromberg notes the similarity to Daniel's structure of the succession of kingdoms (*An Introduction to the Study of Isaiah* [London: T&T Clark, 2011], 84–93).

[48] See David F. Graf, "Medism: The Origin and Significance of the Term," *JHS* 104 (1984): 15–30, esp. 21–22, though he does not classify Daniel with this prophetic usage.

[49] H. H. Rowley, *Darius the Mede and the Four World Empires in the Book of Daniel: A Historical Study of Contemporary Theories* (Cardiff: University of Wales Press Board, 1935), 57–58. So too R. H. Charles, *A Critical and Exegetical Commentary on the Book of Daniel*, ICC (Oxford: Clarendon, 1929), 141–42, followed in his reasoning for a Mede here by H. F. D. Sparks, "On the Origin of 'Darius the Mede' at Daniel V.31," *JTS* 47 (1946): 41–46. According to Lester L. Grabbe, the fulfillment of prophecy is the standard explanation for the creation of "Darius the Mede" ("Another Look at the *Gestalt* of 'Darius the Mede,'" *CBQ* 50 [1988]: 198–213).

tionship, I suggest here several possible implications of that proposed literary heritage for our wider knowledge of postexilic scribal practice.

Especially noteworthy is the way in which these later scribes have understood the book of Isaiah as a compositional whole, with its own developments and internal relationships: this supports a model of scribal interpretation as holistic rather than atomistic, at least in this particular instance. Using a few echoed verses from Isa 39 to evoke the larger context of that chapter makes use of the overall architecture of the book of Isaiah, in which chapter 39 serves as a pivot into chapter 40 and the Babylonian chapters that follow. The redactor of the Daniel tales has appropriated this hinge piece of Isa 39–40 in exactly its function in both the literary structure and the theological structure of the book of Isaiah: the reference back to Isa 39 in Dan 1 recalls that chapter for just long enough to tip the reader forward into Isa 40, and into the literary setting of the Babylonian exile, where the prophecies of Isa 40–55 are rhetorically located and the tales of Dan 1–6 are fictionally located.[50] As Michael Fishbane has observed of Isa 39, "The nexus between prophecy and fulfilment is sharpened at precisely the point where the eighth- and sixth-century prophecies were joined," and thus "the entire structure of the Book of Isaiah conforms to the prophecy–fulfilment pattern which so preoccupied post-exilic theology in general."[51] Inserted into Daniel, that hinge from Isaiah has corresponding functions in the literary and theological structures of the later book; thus the redactors of Daniel have handled Isaiah with a sense of the book *as a book* and with an understanding of its own narrative arc and the argumentative interactions of its different parts. In this, the framers of Aramaic Daniel may perhaps reflect the same reading habits that Andrew Teeter traces in the work of the last scribes to shape the book of Daniel. Analyzing the use made of Isaiah in Daniel's final vision, Teeter finds the Daniel authors working not with isolated snatches of text but with a whole prophetic book including its overarching organization and argument. In this reading, the composer of Dan 11 is "following hermeneutical trajectories inherent in the composition of his source"; rather than operating atomistically, the exegetical impulse in the final vision "appears to be the product of studied reflection on a prophetic *book* (not fragment), with specific attention to its compositional logic." Earlier texts, then, are not "fragments" to be deciphered, omenlike, by mantic exegesis; rather, "the literary composition of Isaiah has exerted pressure on its imaginative construal."[52] At the beginning of the book of Daniel, as at the end, the book of Isaiah is read in its unfolding plotline, in a metonymic echo where the part carries

---

[50] For the way in which Isa 39 is experienced by the reader as a preface to chapters 40–55, see Peter R. Ackroyd, "Interpretation of the Babylonian Exile: A Study of 2 Kings 20, Isaiah 38–39," *SJT* 27 (1974): 329–52, here 338–42; Christopher R. Seitz, *Zion's Final Destiny: The Development of the Book of Isaiah; A Reassessment of Isaiah 36–39* (Minneapolis: Fortress, 1991), 186, 188; Roy F. Melugin, *The Formation of Isaiah 40–55*, BZAW 141 (Berlin: de Gruyter, 1976), 177.

[51] Fishbane, *Biblical Interpretation*, 496, citing Ibn Ezra.

[52] Teeter, "Isaiah and the King of Assyria," 198–99.

with it traces of the whole and the single story of Isaiah's prophecy to Hezekiah evokes the literary and theological context in which that story has been embedded.

Tracing these roots may also enlarge our understanding of the earliest Daniel editors' sense of their own literary belonging and restore to the text a depth of tradition that has become obscured in recent scholarship. By contrast, in antiquity Isaiah's word to Hezekiah was everywhere invoked as the fulfilled prophecy lying behind Dan 1: those who read the two texts this way include Theodoret, who observes that Daniel chooses his words to remind us of Isaiah's prophecy;[53] and Hippolytus, for whom the correlation with Isaiah is a blessing and a demonstration for the readers of Scripture (*Comm. Dan.* 1.7.2–1.10.1).[54] Josephus perhaps remembers the words of Isaiah when he has the noble Judean youths castrated by the king of Babylon in *Ant.* 10.186. This is how he earlier read Hezekiah's prophecy (*Ant.* 10.33), and Josephus may here be an early witness to the widespread rabbinic tradition that Daniel and his friends were made eunuchs.[55] That motif is based on the rabbis' practice of reading their story through the filter of Isa 39, generally making an explicit exegetical link that is explored most fully in the Babylonian Talmud in b. Sanh. 93b. This intertext is cited as a Jewish reading tradition by Origen and by Jerome.[56] In the earliest traditions of church and synagogue, then, the tales of Daniel were read in Isaiah's Babylon.

Finally, the Daniel editors' use of Isaiah may open a window onto reading practices in one corner of Second Temple literary culture and expose the assumptions about earlier Scripture that underlie those reading practices. As a piece of narrative art, the scenic use of traditions about Isaiah to create a setting has affinities to the large-scale narrative reimaginings of scriptural events that emerge as a discrete genre in this period and, significantly, in the other Aramaic literature, for example, at Qumran. Among the Dead Sea Scrolls a cluster of Aramaic works such as the Genesis Apocryphon, the Aramaic Levi Document, and the parabiblical Danielic texts all exhibit narrative biblical interpretation on a broad scriptural canvas rather than at the lexical level of the pesharim. In a similar way, the use of Isaiah traditions in Dan 1 looks to Scripture to create a narrative world, a stage on which

---

[53] Theodoret of Cyrus, *Commentary on Daniel*, trans. Robert C. Hill, WGRW 7 (Atlanta: Society of Biblical Literature, 2006), 23.

[54] See Hippolytus, *Commentaire sur Daniel*, ed. Gustave Bardy, trans. Maurice Lefèvre, SC 14 (Paris: Cerf, 1947).

[55] See Flavius Josephus, *Judean Antiquities Books 8–10*, translation and commentary by Christopher T. Begg and Paul Spilsbury, FJTC 5 (Leiden: Brill, 2000), 268–69; and Christopher T. Begg, "Hezekiah's Illness and Visit according to Josephus," *EstBib* 53 (1995): 365–85.

[56] See Jay Braverman, *Jerome's Commentary on Daniel: A Study of Comparative Jewish and Christian Interpretations of the Hebrew Bible*, CBQMS 7 (Washington, DC: Catholic Bible Association of America, 1978), 53–71. Nineteenth-century commentators on Isaiah sometimes referred to Dan 1 as a fulfillment of the words of Isa 39:5–7: see Jason A. Alexander, *Isaiah*, 2 vols. (New York: John Miley, 1852), 69; Franz Delitzsch, *Biblical Commentary on the Prophecies of Isaiah*, trans. J. Martin, 2 vols. (Edinburgh: T&T Clark, 1873), 1:126.

familiar characters can be newly scripted.[57] Mark Smith, writing of the particular modes in which Second Temple authors negotiated their literary predecessors, suggests,

> Precisely because such religious texts were considered to be scriptural in this period, they became not simply sites of textual interpretation in a detailed or in some narrow sense. In the Second Temple period, scriptural texts also became the canvases for dramatic, large-scale retellings that reflected the lives of the Second Temple composers and their audiences and the traditions in which they understood themselves.

This observation could apply very precisely to the use of Isa 39 as the canvas for a dramatic re-presentation of traditional tales in Aramaic Daniel.[58] Isaiah's word to Hezekiah establishes at the start of the book of Daniel an open door into the larger narrative world of Deutero-Isaiah, where Israel's exilic experiences can be told anew on an ancient pattern.

---

[57] See Daniel A. Machiela and Andrew B. Perrin, "Tobit and the *Genesis Apocryphon*: Towards a Family Portrait," *JBL* 133 (2014): 111–32.

[58] Mark S. Smith, "What Is a Scriptural Text in the Second Temple Period? Texts between Their Biblical Past, Their Inner-Biblical Interpretation, Their Reception in Second Temple Literature, and Their Textual Witnesses," in *The Dead Sea Scrolls at 60: Scholarly Contributions of New York University Faculty and Alumni*, ed. Lawrence H. Schiffman and Shani Tzoref, STDJ 89 (Leiden: Brill, 2010), 271–98, here 276.

Content and Form: Authorship Attribution and Pseudonymity in Ancient Speeches, Letters, Lectures, and Translations —A Rejoinder to Bart Ehrman

ARMIN D. BAUM
baum@fthgiessen.de
Freie Theologische Hochschule Gießen, 35394 Gießen, Germany

The ancient notion of authorship and forgery can be analyzed in various ancient texts, including embedded texts (e.g., reported speeches) and independent texts, some written under the author's control (e.g., speeches, letters, and history books), as well as others written independently of the author's control (e.g., translations and unauthorized lecture publications). In all cases an authorial attribution was regarded as correct and nondeceptive if either content and wording or just the content of a particular text could be traced back to the author whose name it carried. This prevailing principle of ancient authorship attribution, while often taken for granted and applied without further explanation, was also stated explicitly in several places. These ancient statements are in conflict with the most innovative contribution of Bart Ehrman's otherwise very useful recent book *Forgery and Counterforgery* (2012). Ehrman has rightly joined the growing number of scholars who have raised substantive doubts regarding the once-popular thesis of innocent ancient pseudepigraphy. At the same time, his assertion that in antiquity a text's authenticity was assessed not on the basis of its content but always on the basis of its wording goes one step beyond what the numerous relevant ancient sources reveal.

In Bart Ehrman's recent book on ancient pseudepigraphy, at least three central questions can be distinguished. First, Were pseudepigraphical texts written to deceive and were they regarded as deceptive by their readers? Ehrman gives a positive answer.[1] His second question is, "Did forgers think that lying is something not only right, but divinely sanctioned?" (548). Ehrman's answer is again positive, and

[1] Bart D. Ehrman, *Forgery and Counterforgery: The Use of Literary Deceit in Early Christian Polemics* (Oxford: Oxford University Press, 2012), 529. Page references to this book will be given in parentheses in the text.

there can be little doubt, I believe, that this is exactly what some of the ancient sources indicate.

Third, Ehrman asks what kinds of texts were regarded as pseudepigraphical. His answer to this third question is controversial. Ehrman disagrees with my thesis that "a book that was not authored by the person named is not a forgery if its contents can be traced back directly to that person" (31 n. 6). He does not concur with my observation that the ancients distinguished between the wording and the contents of a text and formed their opinion about its authenticity or inauthenticity on the basis of the origin of its contents (87–88, 90, 110, 116, etc.).[2] Ehrman's counter-thesis is that the decision about a book's authenticity "was not based purely on the question of the contents of a work" (88). A book was regarded as authentic only if it contained the alleged author's "own words" (111). According to ancient standards, a text that did not contain the alleged author's own words was a forgery.

I have already written a short and preliminary reply to Ehrman's counter-thesis.[3] In this article I will defend and improve my earlier interpretation of the ancient notion of authorship in much more detail. For this purpose, I will show how fundamental the ancient distinction between content and form was in many ancient explanations of literary authenticity and pseudonymity. It was applied by various ancient authors to all sorts of texts: independent texts that were produced under their authors' control (I.1) or without their authors' control (I.2) as well as embedded texts (II).

I. Content and Form in Independent Texts

1. Independent Texts Produced under Their Authors' Control

The wording of an independent text of an ancient author could be influenced by others in different ways. (a) Speeches could be composed by professional speech writers. (b) Some ancient correspondents employed secretaries who composed their letters in their own style. (c) Historians could authorize language assistants to improve the Greek style of their books.

a. Speeches Composed by Speech Writers

In Rome, political leaders employed ghostwriters not only for their letters but also for their speeches and proclamations. We are particularly well informed about Roman emperors who made use of this kind of assistance.

---

[2] See Armin Daniel Baum, *Pseudepigraphie und literarische Fälschung im frühen Christentum: Mit ausgewählten Quellentexten samt deutscher Übersetzung*, WUNT 2/138 (Tübingen: Mohr Siebeck, 2001), 195.

[3] See my review of *Forgery and Counterforgery* by Bart D. Ehrman, *NovT* 56 (2014): 428–31.

We learn from Suetonius that, on the one hand, the emperor Nero (54–68 CE) wrote his own verses and did not publish as his own poetry that had been produced by others. On the other hand, Nero was regarded as "first master of the empire to stand in need of borrowed eloquence" (*Nero* 52 [Rolfe, LCL]). As his speech writer he employed Seneca, whose polished style could hardly go unnoticed by those who listened to Nero's speeches. One of the speeches composed by Seneca was Nero's panegyric of Claudius at his precursor's obsequies. According to Tacitus,

> The speech, as the composition of Seneca, exhibited the degree of polish to be expected from that famous man, whose pleasing talent was so well suited to a contemporary audience. (*Ann.* 13.3 [Jackson, LCL])

Later, in 55 CE,

> Nero pledged himself to clemency in a series of speeches, which Seneca, either to attest the exalted qualities of his teaching or to advertise his ingenuity, kept presenting to the public by the lips of the sovereign. (*Ann.* 13.11 [Jackson, LCL])

As these reports demonstrate, at least the style but probably also parts of the content of Nero's speeches were considered the work of his teacher Seneca.

In another case, Tacitus was not sure if a speech of one of Nero's successors had been composed by Otho himself or by his speech writer (*scriptor orationis*) but regarded the second option as more likely (Tacitus, *Hist.* 1.90).[4]

Domitian was also known for having employed speech writers. Suetonius quoted some noteworthy sayings by Domitian but was convinced that "for his letters, speeches and proclamations he relied on others' talents [*alieno formabat ingenio*]" (*Dom.* 20 [Rolfe, LCL]).

In each of these cases, none of which Ehrman has taken into account, the speeches were delivered by the emperors as their own while at least the wording of the speeches came from a speech writer. I am not aware of any ancient complaints that this practice was deceptive.

b. Letters Written by Secretaries

Many modern interpreters of the Pauline epistles have argued that in antiquity it was regarded as legitimate if the author of a letter granted to his secretary much or complete control over its wording. Two scholars have collected and analyzed the most important ancient evidence that supports this widespread assumption. Otto Roller asserted that in some cases ancient secretaries composed letters according to the oral instructions or on the basis of more or less elaborate written drafts of the senders.[5] According to Randolph Richards, an ancient letter writer could employ a secretary (1) as a recorder of his dictated words, (2) as an editor of his detailed

---

[4] Cf. Werner Eck, "Galerius [4]," *DNP* 4:758.

[5] Otto Roller, *Das Formular der paulinischen Briefe: Ein Beitrag zur Lehre vom antiken Brief*, BWANT 58 (Stuttgart: Kohlhammer, 1933), 18–20, 334–41.

notes or instructions, (3) as a coauthor who used his less extensive notes or instructions, or (4) as a composer who was merely asked to write a letter and worked more or less independently.[6]

Ehrman disagrees in two respects (218–22) that pertain to the historicity as well as the legitimacy of the procedures described in categories 2 to 4. On the one hand, he calls into question "the notion that early Christian authors used secretaries who altered the writing style and contributed to the contents of a writing" (218). On the other hand, he doubts that there exists any historical evidence "to suggest that it was acceptable practice … for an 'author' to have someone else write a work for him. If he did commission such a work, this other person would be the author" (248). In our context, only Ehrman's second objection is relevant.

The most supportive evidence for Ehrman's case comes from the letters of Cicero. More than once Cicero asked his friend Atticus to write and send letters in Cicero's name (*Att.* 3.15.8; 11.5.3; 11.13.5). Cicero knew that by this procedure he was deceiving his correspondence partners and therefore asked Atticus to lie about the true origin of these letters:

> Please send letters to any people you think right in my name [*des litteras meo nomine*]. You know my friends. If they notice the absence of my seal or handwriting, please say I have avoided using them owing to the sentries. (*Att.* 11.2.4 [Winstedt, LCL])

Ehrman concludes that the use of independently working secretaries in ancient letter writing was regarded as illegitimate: "Cicero realized the practice was deceitful" (221) and admitted "that it was tantamount to forgery" (222).

This observation is, to a certain extent, correct but does not do full justice to the evidence. The deceptive element in Cicero's procedure was not that he asked Atticus to compose letters in his name but rather that Cicero did not read and authenticate these letters by furnishing them with an autograph postscript or subscription[7] (or his seal[8]) before they were dispatched. This interpretation is confirmed by the remaining historical evidence on letter-composing secretaries, which Ehrman only partially took into account.

We owe an unambiguous remark to Philostratus of Lemnos (third century CE). In his treatise *On Letters*, Philostratus regarded it as possible and legitimate

---

[6] E. Randolph Richards, *The Secretary in the Letters of Paul*, WUNT 2/42 (Tübingen: Mohr Siebeck, 1991), 23–67; see also Hans-Josef Klauck, with the collaboration of Daniel P. Bailey, *Ancient Letters and the New Testament: A Guide to Context and Exegesis* (Waco, TX: Baylor University Press, 2006), 59–60.

[7] See Roller, *Das Formular der paulinischen Briefe*, 72–78; Joram Luttenberger, *Prophetenmantel oder Bücherfutteral? Die persönlichen Notizen in den Pastoralbriefen im Licht antiker Epistolographie und literarischer Pseudepigraphie*, ABIG 40 (Leipzig: Evangelische Verlagsanstalt, 2012), 117–25.

[8] See Roller, *Das Formular der paulinischen Briefe*, 71–72; Luttenberger, *Prophetenmantel oder Bücherfutteral*, 133–44.

that Brutus employed a letter writer who composed his letters and was responsible for their excellent style. Whether Philostratus also distinguished between some letters that Marcus Aurelius wrote himself and others that were composed by secretaries in his name is not completely clear:

> Those who, next to the ancients, seem to me to have used the epistolary style of discourse best are, of the philosophers (Apollonius) of Tyana and Dio (Chrysostomus), of military commanders Brutus or the person Brutus employed to write his letters [Βροῦτος ἢ ὅτῳ Βροῦτος ἐς τὸ ἐπιστέλλειν ἐχρῆτο], of the emperors, the divine Marcus (Aurelius) when he himself wrote (for in addition to his distinction in speech, his firmness of character, too, had been imprinted in his letters).[9]

Ehrman demurs that this evidence may be unhistorical and that we therefore do not know whether the historical Brutus really let a secretary compose his letters (219). But even if Philostratus's report was historically unreliable, we can with certainty deduce that he regarded it as tolerable if the style of someone's letters was the work of his secretary.

The same understanding is expressed in an early Christian statement about two New Testament letters. In an instructive and well-known ancient remark that neither Richards nor Ehrman included, Jerome conjectured that the apostle Peter employed at least two different secretaries who were responsible for the different styles of the two New Testament letters that carry his name:

> Therefore [Paul] had Titus as an interpreter just as the blessed Peter had Mark (as an interpreter), whose gospel was composed with Peter narrating it and Mark writing it down. Further also two letters, which circulate as Peter's, differ from each other in style and character and word order. From this we recognize ... that he used different interpreters. (*Epist.* 120.11.5 [ad Hebediam]; my translation)[10]

For the purpose of this article, the historical plausibility of Jerome's explanation is irrelevant. It demonstrates beyond doubt, however, that the church father did not regard it as deceptive if the author of a letter let secretaries compose his letters in their own words.

While it is true that not all texts adduced by Roller and Richards support with equal clarity their claim that ancient secretaries could legitimately compose the letters of their employers in their own style, the statements of Philostratus of Lemnos and Jerome prove this point beyond reasonable doubt.

c. Texts Improved by Language Assistants

As evidence in support of his hypothesis that in antiquity a book was accepted as orthonymous only if "the alleged author actually wrote the words" (87), Ehrman

---

[9] Philostratus of Lemnos, *De epistulis*, in Abraham J. Malherbe, *Ancient Epistolary Theorists*, SBLSBS 19 (Atlanta: Scholars Press, 1988), 42–43.

[10] For the text, see Isidorus Hilberg, *Sancti Eusebii Hieronymi Epistulae*, CSEL 55 (Vienna: Österreichische Akademie der Wissenschaften, 1996), 507.22–508.4.

refers to a number of ancient statements in which the authenticity of a text is assessed on the basis of its style (88–90, 138–139). Several of Ehrman's prooftexts come from Jerome, who was an experienced style critic. According to Jerome's judgment, some commentaries that carried the name of Theophilus of Antioch did not correspond in style to his uncontested books (Jerome, *Vir. ill.* 25). In addition, a work under Minucius Felix's name, although the work of a talented writer, does not correspond in style to his recognized book *Octavius* (Jerome, *Vir. ill.* 58). Jerome reported that even 2 Peter, on account of the stylistic difference from 1 Peter, is considered by many not to be by the apostle (Jerome, *Vir. ill.* 1). This remark on 2 Peter in particular shows that Jerome's criteria for literary authenticity were more complex than Ehrman wants to admit. As the corresponding statement by Jerome on 2 Peter, quoted above (and omitted by Ehrman), demonstrates, in spite of its un-Petrine style Jerome regarded 2 Peter as authentic because he traced its content back to the apostle Peter and ascribed its style to one of Peter's secretaries. Obviously, while in some cases a different style could be used as a sufficient criterion of authenticity, in other cases it could not.

The rationale behind these different approaches is not difficult to detect. Jerome seems to have presupposed that, as a rule, the authors themselves were responsible for the style of their texts. That is why in many cases he decided on purely stylistic grounds whether a text was authentic. At the same time, Jerome did reckon with the much rarer possibility that an author had employed a language assistant who had developed or at least improved the wording of his book. This was primarily the case if an author felt that he was unable to write or to write in a second language or to write on an appropriate stylistic level. Thus, while Jerome usually assumed that authors "actually wrote the words" of their texts, he was aware of legitimate exceptions and therefore cannot be adduced as an ancient proponent of Ehrman's view. The notion of authorship behind Jerome's and many other ancient statements was a bit more elaborate and consisted of two rules: (a) If a book's content was not the work of its alleged author, it was pseudonymous. (b) If a book's style was not the work of its alleged author, it could be either pseudonymous (if its content was also inauthentic) or orthonymous (if its content was authentic).

Another prooftext that Ehrman quotes in support of his interpretation comes from Galen of Pergamum. In the preface to his treatise *On My Own Books*, Galen relates that in a dispute about the authenticity of a book that carried his name, a man of letters "on reading the first two lines … immediately tore up the inscription saying simply: 'This is not Galen's language—the title is false.'" This erudite reader appears to have made his judgment on the assumption that usually an author himself put pen to paper and wrote his book in his own style. In Galen's case, this assumption was correct because, as Galen himself says later in his preface, he had himself written many of his texts "simply at the request of those individuals, who had desired a written record of lectures they had attended." In the case of the pseudepigraphical books circulating under Galen's name, the supposition that a secretary had paraphrased Galen's teaching in a different style is further excluded by the fact that those books were not "perfectly accurate in their teaching."[11] But to conclude from the style-critical remarks quoted in this preface that Galen would not have been allowed to commission a secretary or language assistant to contribute to the style of his books is a non sequitur.

A third piece of evidence that Ehrman adduces is Dionysius of Alexandria's style-critical observations regarding the Revelation of John. Dionysius did not classify the book as pseudepigraphical writing since, although it was not the work of the apostle John, it nevertheless could be ascribed to a holy and inspired man with the same name (apud Eusebius, *Hist. eccl.* 7.25.7, 12–16). As proof of the nonapostolic authorship of Revelation, Dionysius referred to both its style, which differs from that of the Fourth Gospel and 1 John, and its "thoughts" (νοήματα), which also differ from those of the authentic writings of the apostle John (apud Eusebius, *Hist. eccl.* 7.25.8, 17). In this case also, language does not suffice as a criterion of authenticity. What is more, Dionysius neither says nor implies that the authorial attribution of a book to an author who employed a language assistant was a forgery.

Positive evidence in favor of the legitimacy of the stylistic contribution that language assistants could make to the final shape of an author's work comes from Josephus. In a well-known remark, Josephus discloses that, during the writing of his work on the Jewish War, he enlisted the assistance of several coworkers, who improved the Greek style of his text:

> Then, in the leisure that Rome afforded me, with all my materials in readiness, and with the aid of some assistants [συνεργοῖς] for the sake of the Greek, at last I committed to writing my narrative of the events. (*C. Ap.* 1.50 [Thackeray, LCL])

These language assistants "could have contributed in a variety of ways, ranging from wholesale composition to minor revisions of the Greek, with many intermediate possibilities."[12] It is not possible to determine exactly the extent to which the coworkers contributed to the *Jewish War*, but Josephus's indebtedness to them is apparent in "the uniformly excellent style" of that work.[13] For our purpose, it is not necessary to decide if Henry St. John Thackeray's ingenious hypothesis about the influence of one assistant with a Sophoclean style in *Ant.* 15–16 and of another assistant with a Thucydidean style in *Antiquities* 17–19 is convincing.[14] The point

---

[11] Galen of Pergamum, *De libris propriis*, in *Scripta Minora*, ed. Ioannes Marquardt, Iwan von Müller, and Georg Helmreich, 3 vols., BSGRT (Leipzig: Teubner, 1884–1893), 2:91.1–93.16; translation from Galen, *Selected Works*, trans. Peter N. Singer, World's Classics (Oxford: Oxford University Press, 1997), 3–4.

[12] Josephus, *Against Apion*, translation and commentary by John M. G. Barclay, vol. 10 of *Flavius Josephus: Translation and Commentary*, ed. Steve Mason (Leiden: Brill, 2007), 36.

[13] Henry St. J. Thackeray, *Jewish Antiquities I–IV*, vol. 4 of *Josephus in Nine Volumes*, LCL (London: Heinemann, 1930), xiv–xvii.

[14] See Henry St. J. Thackeray, *Josephus: The Man and the Historian* (New York: Jewish Institute of Religion, 1929), 100–124.

of the matter is that substantial influence of language assistants on the wording of an author's work was regarded as legitimate. Ehrman mentions Josephus's notice in passing (244) but does not draw the necessary conclusion, which militates against one of the major theses of his book.

The ancient notion of literary authenticity and forgery in independent texts that were produced under their authors' control can be summarized in a simple chart:

		Style	
		from the author	from someone else
Content	from the author	authentic	authentic
	from someone else	forged	forged

FIGURE 1. Content and Style in Texts with Authorial Ascription

2. *Independent Texts Produced without Their Authors' Control*

The rule that the authenticity of a text depended on its contents was applied also to independent texts that were produced without authorial control: (a) students published the lectures of their teachers; (b) editors published the knowledge inherited from famous philosophers; and (c) translators rendered texts written by other authors into another language.

a. Lectures Published by Students

The question of authorship attribution also arose when students published the notes they had taken of their teachers' lectures. Not all of Ehrman's relevant prooftexts are in conflict with his thesis, but neither do they substantiate his thesis. Other texts, however, demonstrate that Ehrman's interpretation of ancient authenticity and pseudonymity is untenable.

In the first quarter of the fourth century CE, the Neoplatonic philosopher Iamblichus of Chalcis mentioned books that circulated under the name of Pythagoras but had been composed by his disciples on the basis of his lectures. Iamblichus did not classify these books as pseudepigraphical or deceptive, obviously because he thought that their contents actually came from Pythagoras:

> If, then, it be agreed that some writings now circulated are by Pythagoras, but others were composed on the basis of his lectures [τὰ δὲ ἀπὸ τῆς ἀκροάσεως αὐτοῦ συγγεγράφθαι], and on this account the authors did not give their own names, but attributed them to Pythagoras as his work [εἰς Πυθαγόραν ἀνέφερον αὐτὰ ὡς ἐκείνου ὄντα], it is clear from all these treatises that Pythagoras was sufficiently experienced in all wisdom. (*VP* 29.158)[15]

---

[15] Translation by John Dillon and Jackson Hershbell, *On the Pythagorean Way of Life*, SBLTT 29, GRRS 11 (Atlanta: Scholars Press, 1991), 173. For the text, see Iamblichus, *De vita Pythagorica liber*, ed. Ludovicus Deubner and Udalricus Klein, BSGRT (Stuttgart: Teubner, 1975).

According to Ehrman, Iamblichus regarded as legitimate only the publication of those lecture notes from Pythagoras's oral lectures that "literally contained his own words, not those of the writers" (110–11). But Iamblichus did not say whether the students of Pythagoras published his lectures verbatim or in paraphrase.

In a similar way, when listeners and pupils published some of Quintilian's lectures without their teacher's knowledge and approval they circulated under his name:

> Two books on the art of rhetoric are at present circulating under my name [*sub nomine meo*], although never published by me or composed for such a purpose. One is a two days' lecture which was taken down by the boys who were my audience. The other consists of such notes as my good pupils succeeded in taking down from a course of lectures on a somewhat more extensive scale. (*Inst.* 1 *pr.* 7 [Butler, LCL])

The attribution as such of lecture notes published by a student to his teacher was unproblematic. Again, we do not hear whether Quintilian's pupils published his lectures word for word or more freely. The next passage is more explicit in this respect.

In his letter of dedication introducing his edition of Epictetus's teaching, the historian Arrian of Nicomedia wrote:

> I have not composed these *Words of Epictetus* as one might be said to "compose" books of this kind, nor have I of my own act published them to the world; indeed, I acknowledge that I have not "composed" them at all. But whatever I heard him say I tried to write down, word for word, as best as I could [ταῦτα αὐτὰ ἐπειράθην αὐτοῖς ὀνόμασιν ὡς οἷόν τε ἦν γραψάμενος], endeavouring to preserve it as a memorial, for my own future use, of his way of thinking and the frankness of his speech. (*Epistula ad Lucium Gellium* 1–2 [Oldfather, LCL, slightly modified])

The ancients called the work either Epictetus's discourses as arranged or composed by Arrian,[16] or in an abbreviated way Epictetus's discourses or book[17] (but never Arrian's discourses). Even Arrian in his preface called it the "Words of Epictetus." Therefore, Ehrman is definitely right that "it was widely thought that the written dissemination of a teacher's 'classroom' instruction should be under the teacher's name, since he was the one, after all, who had spoken the words" (114).

On the other hand, Ehrman draws another conclusion from Arrian's letter that is not supported by its context. "If the words did not go back to the teacher himself, this would be forgery" (115). This is a non sequitur. The fact that the ancients regarded it as legitimate to publish a teacher's *words* under his name does not imply that it was illegitimate to publish a paraphrase of his *thoughts* in someone else's style

---

[16] Gellius, *Noct. Att.* 1.2.6: "the first volume of the discourses of Epictetus, arranged by Arrian" (*dissertationum Epicteti digestarum ab Arriano primum librum*) (40.15–16 [Marshall]); 19.1.1; Simplicius, *Commentarius in Epicteti Enchiridion pr.* (J. Mansfield, *Prolegomena: Questions to Be Settled before the Study of an Author, or a Text*, PhAnt 61 [Leiden: Brill, 1994], 110).

[17] Augustine, *Civ.* 9.4 (CSEL 40/1:412.20–21 [Hoffmann]).

under the teacher's name. What the ancients thought of such a literary device has to be derived from source texts that actually speak on this matter.

In the ancient church, Tertullian commented on the authorial attribution of the canonical Gospels in order to affirm the apostolic character of the two Gospels that carried the names of the nonapostolic men Mark and Luke:

> That which Mark edited is stated to be Peter's [*Petri affirmetur*], whose interpreter Mark was. Luke's digest also they usually attribute to Paul [*Paulo adscribere solent*]. It is permissible for the works which disciples published to be regarded as belonging to their masters [*Capit magistrorum videri quae discipuli promulgarint*]. (*Marc.* 4.5.3–4)[18]

According to Tertullian, the two Gospels could be ascribed both to their assumed editors Mark and Luke, who were responsible for their published form, or to their teachers Peter and Paul, who were regarded as the intellectual authors of their contents.

Ehrman is right that historically we have no evidence "that the Second Gospel was ever circulated under Peter's name" (117–18). Neither did Tertullian publish Mark's and Luke's Gospels under Peter's and Paul's names; nor did he say that others had done this. It is also true that Tertullian stopped short of saying that disciples were allowed to publish their *own* ideas under the names of their teachers.

On the other hand, Tertullian did not say simply that the Gospels according to Mark and Luke "represent the views of their teachers" Peter and Paul (52; cf. 76). Rather, Tertullian underscored that it was legitimate to ascribe the books that Mark and Luke had published to their teachers Peter and Paul. The obvious reason was that, for Tertullian, Peter was the author of the *content* of the Second Gospel, which Mark had only edited, and that Paul was the author of the *content* of the Third Gospel, which had only been arranged by Luke. Since Tertullian regarded Mark and Luke only as publishers of their teachers' narratives about the life of Jesus, he would not have considered the Second and the Third Gospels to be deceptive forgeries if they had been attributed to Peter and Paul.

Tertullian does not say whether in his eyes Mark and Luke edited the Jesus narratives of Peter and Paul verbatim. Nor does he say if he regarded only the first alternative as legitimate or both of them. In this respect, another statement sheds more light on the ancient understanding of authorship attribution.

In his homilies on the Letter to the Hebrews, from which Eusebius quoted a lengthy fragment, Origen discussed the secondary attribution of an anonymous letter to Paul that did not conform to the apostle's style. The starting point of Origen's reflections was the observation that, on the one hand, Hebrews is written in a better *style* than the thirteen named letters of Paul, while, on the other hand,

---

[18] Translation by Ernest Evans in Tertullian, *Adversus Marcionem*, 2 vols., OECT (Oxford: Oxford University Press, 1972), 2:270–71 with modifications. For the text, see CCL 1:551.4–9 (Kroymann).

in terms of its theological *content* Hebrews is not inferior to the acknowledged writings of Paul:

> But as for myself, if I were to state my own opinion, I should say that the thoughts [τὰ μὲν νοήματα] are the apostle's, but that the style and composition [ἡ δὲ φράσις καὶ ἡ σύνθεσις] belong to one who called to mind the apostle's teachings and, as it were, made short notes of what his master said. If any church, therefore, holds this epistle as Paul's [εἴ τις οὖν ἐκκλεσία ἔχει ταύτην τὴν ἐπιστολὴν ὡς Παύλου], let it be commended for this also. For not without reason have men of old time handed it down as Paul's. But who wrote the epistle, in truth God knows. Yet the account which has reached us (is twofold), some saying that Clement, who was bishop of the Romans, wrote the epistle, others, that it was Luke, he who wrote the Gospel and the Acts. (Eusebius, *Hist. eccl.* 6.25.11-14 [Oulton, LCL])[19]

Ehrman says that "even though Origen agrees that the contents of the letter to the Hebrews are Pauline, he refuses to call it Pauline.... He refuses to do precisely what Baum's view suggests he should have done: accept the Pauline authorship of the book because of the Pauline contents" (88; cf. 118).

I agree that Origen did not regard Paul as the sender of Hebrews, but that is not the point of the matter. In Origen's eyes, the Letter to the Hebrews with its Pauline content could be attributed in two different ways: (1) If Paul was the sender and therefore personally involved in the writing of Hebrews, it could be ascribed to Paul, who was directly responsible for its theological content and its style. This was a conviction that Origen found in several churches but did not share because of the letter's un-Pauline style. (2) Origen's own view was that Paul was not the sender and therefore not personally involved in the writing of Hebrews, which may have been composed by Clement or Luke. But since this anonymous composer and sender reproduced in it Paul's theology, albeit in his own style, the Letter to the Hebrews could likewise be legitimately "handed down and held as Paul's," that is, ascribed to Paul. According to this statement, Origin shared the ancient view that an authorial ascription was nondeceptive if the named person was at least the author of the text's content.

Elsewhere Origen says without further qualifications that Paul wrote Hebrews.[20] Ehrman suggests as the easiest interpretation that Origen changed his mind on this question (88 n. 66). Yet, in light of what Origen explained in his (above quoted) more elaborate discussion of the authorship of Hebrews, it is just as possible that, in his short references to the letter, Origen felt free to call Paul the author of Hebrews simply because he regarded him as the author of its content.

This interpretation of Origen's statement on the attribution of Hebrews is in line with an earlier statement made by Origen's alleged teacher, Clement of Alexandria. Ehrman mentioned this passage in passing (49) but did not evaluate it in terms

---

[19] GCS NF 6/2:578.13-580.8 (Schwartz/Winkelmann).
[20] Origen, *Princ.* 3.1.10; *Or.* 17; *Comm. Jo.* 2.6; 10.11.

of its relevance for the ancient notion of authorship. According to Eusebius, Clement distinguished between the origin of the letter's stylistic color and the origin of its theological content:

> And as for the Epistle to the Hebrews, he [Clement] says indeed that it is Paul's [Παύλου μὲν εἶναί φησιν], but that it was written for Hebrews in the Hebrew tongue, and that Luke, having carefully translated it, published it for the Greeks; hence, as a result of this translation, the same complexion of style [τὸν αὐτὸν χρῶτα ... κατὰ τὴν ἑρμηνείαν] is found in this Epistle and in the Acts: but that the (words) "Paul an apostle" were naturally not prefixed. For, says he, "in writing to Hebrews who had conceived a prejudice against him and were suspicious of him, he very wisely did not repel them at the beginning by putting his name." (Eusebius, *Hist. eccl.* 6.14.2–3 [Oulton/Lawlor, LCL])

Since he considered Paul to be the author of the letter's contents, Clement says that it would normally have carried his name. From Clement's point of view, Hebrews would not have been pseudonymous or forged if it had been published under Paul's name. Since for Clement Luke, as Paul's translator, was responsible only for the linguistic form of Hebrews, he did not consider ascribing Hebrews to him. (Below the role of the translator will be discussed in more detail.)

As Origen's reflections on the attribution of the Letter to the Hebrews indicate, the oral doctrine of a teacher that was published in paraphrase by his listeners or students could also legitimately be ascribed to the teacher, who was responsible for its content.

b. Inherited Knowledge Published by Editors

One of Ehrman's main targets is my interpretation of ancient school pseudepigraphy. In 2001, I had disputed the prevalent thesis that in ancient philosophical, medical, and Christian schools it was acceptable for pupils to publish *their own ideas* under the names of their famous teachers, for instance, Pythagoras or Hippocrates. After having reviewed the relevant primary sources, I concluded that the understanding of authorship in Greco-Roman schools was compatible with the notion of authenticity in the rest of ancient literature: Pupils had to publish their own philosophical, medical, or theological ideas under their own names. Otherwise they were regarded as literary forgers.[21]

A related result was that pupils were allowed to publish *their teachers' thoughts* under the names of their teachers. This is the point with which Ehrman disagrees. He emphasizes that authors like myself "never cite any sources from the time of the New Testament or of the second century. In no small measure this is because no such evidence exists" (107).

---

[21] See Baum, *Pseudepigraphie und literarische Fälschung*, 51–63.

The above quoted primary sources have already illustrated the problems with Ehrman's interpretation of the ancient evidence. But one statement that Ehrman regards as particularly decisive (87 n. 65; 108–10) has not yet been analyzed. One of the alleged prooftexts for nondeceptive pseudepigraphy in ancient schools that I addressed came from Porphyry. According to Bartel van der Waerden, in a fragment that has been preserved only in an Arabic translation, Porphyry distinguished 280 authentic books by Pythagoras from other books that had been forged under his name. Pythagoras's 280 authentic books consisted of 80 books published by himself and 200 books published by the inheritors of his knowledge under his name.[22] I suggested that Porphyry distinguished the 200 books from the literary forgeries because he regarded them as adequate documentations of Pythagoras's teaching and therefore as nondeceptive.[23]

In his book, Ehrman quotes a new translation of the Arabic fragment. In this new translation, Porphyry does *not* say that the two hundred books by the inheritors of Pythagoras's knowledge were published under Pythagoras's name (109–10). The translation of Porphyry's remarks that Ehrman offers, however, is not complete; it omits the final and most decisive section, in which Porphyry accepted 280 books of the sage as authentic. For this reason, Ehrman can claim that my interpretation of Porphyry's view is mistaken (108–10). In the table on the following page, I offer a synopsis of three modern translations of Porphyry's text: a fragmentary German translation produced by M. Schramm and used by van der Waerden in his Pauly-Wissowa article (1965), a complete English version produced by Marwan Rashed and Carl Huffman (2005), and the incomplete English version produced by Carl Ernst and used by Ehrman in his recent book.[24]

If the full statement of Porphyry is taken into account, he must clearly have been convinced that it was legitimate for pupils who edited the teaching they inherited from a famous teacher to publish it under the teacher's name. What is more, Porphyry did not demand that these edited books be regarded as authentic only if they contained the exact words of Pythagoras.

Apart from the interpretation of Porphyry's statement, Ehrman further argues that, if my reading of the ancient evidence were correct, it would have been impossible to distinguish between authentic and inauthentic texts; it would have been

---

[22] Bartel L. van der Waerden, "Die Schriften und Fragmente des Pythagoras," PWSup 10:843–64, esp. 862–64.

[23] See Baum, *Pseudepigraphie und literarische Fälschung*, 53–57.

[24] M. Schramm, cited in van der Waerden, "Die Schriften und Fragmente des Pythagoras," 862–63. Marwam Rashed, cited in Carl A. Huffman, *Archytas of Tarentum: Pythagoras, Philosopher and Mathematician King* (Cambridge: Cambridge University Press, 2005), 616–17. C. Ernst, cited in Ehrman, *Forgery and Counterforgery*, 109–10. The translations are not published elsewhere.

B. L. van der Waerden (1965) (trans. M. Schramm)	C. A. Huffman (2005) (trans. M. Rashed/C. A. Huffman)	B. Ehrman (2012) (trans. C. Ernst)
(1) (Es gibt 80 von Pythagoras selbst aufgezeichnete Bücher).	(1) As regards the *books of Pythagoras* the sage, in the collection of which Archytas the philosopher from Tarentum distinguished himself, there are eighty books.	(1) But as for the *books of Pythagoras* the sage, which Archytas the Tarentine philosopher collected himself, they are eighty books.
(2) (Es gibt 200 von) *reifen Männern*, welche zur Gruppe des Pythagoras, zu seiner Partei und zu den Erben seines Wissens gehörten (aufgezeichnete Bücher).	(2) As regards those (books), which, at the price of all his efforts, he collected, compiled and gathered, man by man, *from all the men of mature age*, who were of the kindred of Pythagoras the philosopher, of his sect and who inherited his knowledge, their number is two hundred.	(2) But those that he made special effort, with all his strength, to compile, compose, and collect, *from all the old men* who were of the type of Pythagoras the philosopher, his school, and the inheritors of his sciences, man after man, these were two hundred books in number.
(3) (Es gibt zahlreiche) *falsche Bücher* ... dem Weisen in den Mund gelegt und unter seinem Namen geschrieben ... Bücher, welche Fälscher fingiert haben ... andere, die noch hemmungsloser gewesen sind ...	(3) And he who distinguished himself by the clear-sightedness of his understanding and by the putting aside of the *false books*, which were put in the mouth of Pythagoras and circulated under his name and which were invented by unscrupulous individuals ... may he enjoy eternal happiness. Regarding those wicked men who invented those false books which we have mentioned, they are according to the accounts which have reached us, Aristippus the Young, Nikos, who was nicknamed "one eye," as well	(3) And he who was unique in the essence of his intellect [i.e. Archytas] set aside from them the *false books* ascribed to the tongue of the sage and his name, which shameless people fabricated. The criminal individuals who fabricated these lying books that we have mentioned, according to traditions that have reached us, are Aristotle the Younger, Nikos known as the essentially erroneous, one of the

B. L. van der Waerden (*cont.*)	C. A. Huffman (*cont.*)	B. Ehrman (*cont.*)
	as a man of the Cretan people, who is called Konios, and Magillos and FWKHJWAQA [the Arabic is not clear] and others still more impudent. And that which incited them to the invention of these false books, put in the mouth of Pythagoras the philosopher and under his name, was in order to be well received among the moderns and because of that to be honoured, to influence them and to establish personal connection with them.	Cretans called Konios, Megalos, and Fūkhajawāqā [?], along with others even more reprehensible than they. And that was who proposed to them [others?] the fabrication of these lying books with the tongue of the philosopher Pythagoras and his name, so that [these writings] would be accepted among the moderns because of him, so they would honor, prefer, and share them.
(4) (*Von Pythagoras* gibt es 280) Bücher, an denen kein Zweifel besteht; (sie sind) in Vergessenheit geraten, bis sich ihre Existenz bei einer Schar von Weisen, denen guter Vorsatz und Frömmigkeit eigen war, ergab; sie aber haben sie zusammengefasst, zusammengestellt und komponiert, ohne dass sie zuvor in Hellas bekannt gewesen wären, vielmehr wurden sie in Italien aufbewahrt.	(4) Regarding *the books of the sage* which are beyond suspicion, there are two hundred and eighty of them, which were forgotten until the world saw the birth of wise men possessing determination and fervor, who acquired, gathered and compiled them. They were not known previously in the land of Hellas (? Adha), but were preserved in Italy.	

impossible to classify texts as pseudonymous. If two authors who held widely divergent religious views both claimed that the contents of their texts where those of the alleged author, it would be in most cases impossible to adjudicate these claims. "Pseudonymous texts supporting divergent views, on Baum's assessment, would theoretically all have to be seen, historically, as nonproblematic in their authorial claims" (87–88). This, however, is a misunderstanding of my interpretation of the ancient evidence. As Porphyry's statement demonstrates, if two texts that carried the name of the same author contained incompatible ideas, the authorial attribution of at least one of these two texts would be called into question and classified as deceptive. It is certainly true that it could sometimes be difficult to distinguish authentic texts from pseudonymous texts merely on the basis of their contents. But that is not the point of the matter.

c. Texts Translated by Translators

The same understanding of authorship that counted for texts containing posthumously published teaching was applied by ancient translators who rendered texts relatively freely into another language. On the one hand, literal translations were not unknown and in some contexts were highly regarded. This is particularly true of biblical texts, which were presumed to be holy and inspired.[25] On the other hand, some ancient translators took great liberties with the original texts.

Some ancients felt that the producer of a very free translation could himself be considered an author. Consequently, literarily ambitious translations sometimes displayed not only the author's name but also the name of the translator. This led to further discussions as to whether it was adequate to omit the author's name and to mention only the name of the translator. In some cases this did indeed happen, but critical readers classified such a procedure as literary theft. It was not considered legitimate to omit the name of the original author.[26]

Some unambiguous statements about the notion of authorship that are highly relevant in our context have been made by Cicero, Philo, and Jerome. These and many other ancient authors agreed that not just a word-for-word translation but also a *sensu-de-sensu* type of translation was legitimate. Ehrman has apparently not checked his interpretation of the ancient understanding of authorship and forgery against this background.

Cicero translated many Greek texts into Latin and was the most famous Roman who wrote on the art of translating.[27] In 46 BCE, he wrote a preface to his (never written or no longer extant) translation of the orations of Demosthenes and Aeschines in which he also explained his method of translating:

> I did not translate them as an interpreter, but as an orator, keeping the same ideas and the forms, or as one might say, the "figures" of thought [*sententiis isdem et earum formis tamquam figuris*], but in language which conforms to our usage. And in so doing, I did not hold it necessary to render word for word [*non verbum pro verbo*], but I preserved the general style and force of the language [*genus omne verborum*

---

[25] See Markus Mülke, *Der Autor und sein Text: Die Verfälschung des Originals im Urteil antiker Autoren*, UALG 93 (Berlin: de Gruyter, 2008), 111–24. See also Heinrich Marti, *Übersetzer der Augustin-Zeit: Interpretation von Selbstzeugnissen*, STA 14 (Munich: Fink, 1974), 64–81.

[26] Mülke, *Der Autor und sein Text*, 179–201.

[27] Cf. Siobhán McElduff, *Roman Theories of Translation: Surpassing the Source*, Routledge Monographs in Classical Studies 14 (New York: Routledge, 2013), 96–121.

vimque servavi]. For I did not think I ought to count them out to the reader like coins, but to pay them by weight, as it were. (Cicero, *Opt. gen.* 5.14 [Hubbell, LCL])

In his second book on the life of Moses, Philo of Alexandria offered his rendering of the history of the Septuagint.[28] According to Philo, each of the seventy translators translated the books of the Pentateuch under inspiration with exactly the same words that also corresponded exactly to the Hebrew original. The Jewish philosopher contrasted this very literal translation of a biblical text with much freer renderings of other source texts:

> Who does not know that every language, and Greek especially, abounds in terms, and that the same thought can be put in many shapes by paraphrasing more or less freely [ταὐτὸν ἐνθύμημα οἷόν τε μεταφράζοντα καὶ παραφράζοντα σχηματίσαι πολλαχῶς] and suiting the expression to the occasion? (*Mos* 2.38 [Colson, LCL])

Philo did not condemn this less-literal method of translating, which is comparable to the one preferred by Cicero, but simply mentioned it as another approach that he regarded as less appropriate for holy Scriptures but as legitimate as the one chosen by the translators of the Septuagint.

Jerome translated many Old and New Testament books as well as several works of Greek theologians (such as Origen and Didymus) into Latin. In many places in his huge work, he discussed translation theory, most prominently in a letter "On the Best Method of Translating" addressed to Pammachius in 395/396 CE. In it he defended his free translation of a Greek letter of Epiphanius to John of Jerusalem into Latin and responded to the charge that he had "falsified the original" because he had "not rendered word for word" (*Epist.* 57.2.3).[29] In his defense, Jerome referred to the translation practice of secular translators (such as Cicero, Horace, and Terence) (57.5), of other church fathers (namely, the translator of the Life of Antony and Hilary the Confessor) (57.6), of the Gospel authors (57.7–10), and of the translators of the Septuagint (57.11). Jerome conceded:

> For I myself not only admit but freely proclaim that in translating from the Greek (except in the case of the holy scriptures where even the order of the words is a mystery) I render sense for sense and not word for word [*non verbum e verbo, sed sensum exprimere de sensu*]. (*Epist.* 57.5.1–2)[30]

---

[28] See Klaus Otte, *Das Sprachverständnis bei Philo von Alexandrien: Sprache als Mittel der Hermeneutik*, BGBE 7 (Tübingen: Mohr Siebeck, 1968), 32–43; Giuseppe Veltri, *Eine Tora für den König Talmai: Untersuchungen zum Übersetzungsverständnis in der jüdisch-hellenistischen und rabbinischen Literatur*, TSAJ 41 (Tübingen: Mohr Siebeck, 1994), 128–31.

[29] Trans. *NPNF*[2] 6:113; for the text, see *Sancti Eusebii Hieronymi Epistulae*, ed. Isidorus Hilberg, CSEL 54 (Vienna: Österreichischen Akademie der Wissenschaften, 1996), 505.17–18; cf. 57.12–13; see also Gerhardus J. M. Bartelink, *Liber de optimo genere interpretandi (Epistula 57): Ein Kommentar*, MnemosyneSup 61 (Leiden: Brill, 1980), 35–36; and Mülke, *Der Autor und sein Text*, 129–50.

[30] Trans. *NPNF*[2] 6:113; CSEL 54:508.6–18 (Hilberg).

His main argument, which he repeated over and over again, was that because he had just changed the words but not the sense he could not be called a falsifier: "No changes have been made in the sense, nothing has been added, and no other doctrine has been fabricated" (*Epist.* 57.5.1).[31] Jerome argued:

> From all these passages it is clear that the apostles and evangelists in translating the Old Testament scriptures have sought after the meaning, not the words, and that they have not greatly cared for the arrangement and the words, so long as the subjects were clear for the mind [*sensum quaesisse, non uerba, nec magnopere de ordinatione sermonibusque curasse, cum intellectui res paterent*]. (*Epist.* 57.9.8)[32]

Jerome closed his letter of defense with the words that he was content to "stay quiet in my cell and to wait for the day of judgment" (*Epist.* 57.13.2)[33]

Clearly, some of the best-known translators of antiquity were convinced that the legitimacy of a translation must be assessed on the basis of its content, not its wording. Not the translator who departed from the wording or terminology of the source text but only the translator who changed its spirit, sense, or content was considered a falsifier or a forger. The same basic principle is expressed in the above-quoted ancient statements on literary authenticity and pseudonymity in ancient speech writing and letter writing, as well as in the publication of a teacher's lectures and knowledge by his students or editors.

II. Content and Form in Embedded Texts

The distinction between content and form was also applied to embedded texts that were produced without authorial control. Not only in Greco-Roman but also in Old Testament and New Testament historiography, ancient authors regarded it as legitimate to reproduce the content of historical speeches in their own words.

---

[31] Jerome, *Epist.* 57.5.1: *nihil mutatum esse de sensu nec res additas nec aliquod dogma confictum* (CSEL 54:508.6–7); 57.7.3: "though the sense is the same, the words are quite different and differently arranged [*cum sensus idem sit, uerba praepostera sunt et paene diuersa*]" (CSEL 54:513.9–10; trans. *NPNF*² 6:115); 57.7.5: "the divergence of language agrees in oneness of spirit [*et tamen sermonum uarietas spiritus unitate concordat*]" (CSEL 54:514.5–6; my trans.); 57.9.7: "the apostle has not rendered his original word for word, but using a paraphrase, he has given the sense in different terms [*apostolus non uerbum expressit e uerbo, sed παραφραστικῶς eundem sensum aliis sermonibus indicauit*]" (CSEL 54:520.9–11; trans. *NPNF*² 6:117); 57.10.3: "in the scriptures we have to consider not the words but the sense [*non uerba in scripturis consideranda, sed sensus*]" (CSEL 54:522.5–6; my trans.).

[32] CSEL 54:520.19–22; trans. *NPNF*² 6:117 modified.

[33] CSEL 526.14–15.

1. Speeches Reported in Greco-Roman Historiography

The most famous statement on this practice comes from the Greek historian Thucydides, who at the beginning of his work on the Peloponnesian War explains to his readers:

> As to the speeches that were made by different men ... it has been difficult to recall with strict accuracy the words actually spoken.... Therefore the speeches are given in the language in which, as it seemed to me, the several speakers would express, on the subjects under consideration, the sentiments most befitting the occasion, though at the same time I have adhered as closely as possible to the general sense of what was actually said. (1.22.1 [Smith, LCL])

The reason why Thucydides did not reproduce the exact wording of important speeches that had been made during the war was not that he did not want to do it but that, because of the limits of human memory, he could not do it. At the same time, Thucydides did not feel authorized freely to invent his speeches but rather tried to adhere "as closely as possible to the general sense of what was actually said." Although Thucydides could not reproduce the exact words, he nevertheless claimed to have reproduced to a greater or lesser extent the actual content of the historical speeches. In contrast to our modern practice, however, Thucydides offered his own reconstructions of the content of these speeches not in indirect but in direct speech.

Polybius discusses the historian's responsibility regarding the speeches he included in his narrative in much more detail. Like Thucydides, he regarded it as legitimate to present free summaries and paraphrases of historical speeches in direct speech. Going beyond Thucydides, however, Polybius severely criticized other historians who had not reproduced the actual contents of historical speeches but freely invented their own speeches. In his criticism of Timaeus, he applies the well-known distinction between form and content:

> For he [Timaeus] has not set down the words spoken nor the sense of what was really said [οὐ γάρ τὰ ῥηθέντα γέγραφεν, οὐδ' ὡς ἐρρήθη κατ' ἀλήθειαν], but having made up his mind as to what ought to have been said, he recounts all these speeches and all else that follows upon events like a man in a school of rhetoric attempting to speak on a given subject, and shows off his oratorical power, but gives no report of what was actually spoken. (12.25a.5 [Paton, LCL])

The allegation that Timaeus's speech was "neither a transcript nor an accurate résumé of the actual speech" mentions two options that were both legitimate.[34] But, although according to Polybius historians were not expected to render the *wording* of historical speeches, they were obliged to reproduce the *sense* of what had been said. A historian who "passes over in silence the speeches made and the causes of events

---

[34] F. W. Walbank, *Commentary on Books VII–XVIII*, vol. 2 of *A Historical Commentary on Polybius* (Oxford: Oxford University Press, 1967), 386.

and in their place introduces false rhetorical exercises and discursive speeches, destroys the peculiar virtue of history" (12.25b.4 [Paton, LCL]). Polybius therefore charged Timaeus with "deliberate falsification of the truth" (12.25k.1 [Paton, LCL]).

Ehrman believes that, while some ancient historians like Thucydides accepted the invention of speeches in historical narratives, others like Polybius rejected it. Further, Ehrman stresses that "in neither side of the debate, in any event, do we find authors likening the practice to forgery" (58). Therefore Ehrman questions the conviction that "the invention of speeches … in historical documents" is "analogous to literary forgery" (55). Yet the analogy is not difficult to detect. Both ancient historians in their freely invented speeches and ancient pseudepigraphers in their falsely ascribed books put their own ideas into the mouth of someone else. In both cases, the distinction between authentic and inauthentic texts was made on the basis not of wording but of content.

2. Speeches Reported in Old Testament Historiography

In contrast to Greco-Roman authors, Old Testament historians did not explicitly explain their method of speech reproduction. Yet it can be deduced from places where they have quoted someone's speech a second time. In these cases, "verbatim repetition of the original speech, with no omissions or additions whatsoever, is an infrequent occurrence." In only 10 of the nearly 100 instances are the words of the first and the second quotation exactly identical. In 84 quotations, the direct speech has either been shortened or lengthened or paraphrased.[35] "The most frequent changes found in quoted direct speech are paraphrastic in nature.… These range from the simplest kind of morphological variations in verbal forms, to the interchange of synonymous words and phrases, to complete changes in language and syntax."[36] At the same time, "nearly all verifiable quotations are relatively accurate repetitions of the content of the earlier speech."[37]

An utterance by Abraham that is quoted twice in Gen 24 can serve as an example. In the second version the wording is quite different, but the content has not been changed:

| See to it that you do not take my son back there. The LORD, the God of heaven, who took me from my father's house and from the land of my birth, and who spoke to me and swore to me, "To your off spring I | The LORD, before whom I walk, will send his angel with you and make your way successful. You shall get a wife for my son from my kindred, from my father's house. Then you will be free from my kindred, from my father's house. Then you will be |

---

[35] George W. Savran, *Telling and Retelling: Quotation in Biblical Narrative*, ISBL (Bloomington: Indiana University Press, 1988), 29.
[36] Ibid., 33.
[37] Ibid., 35–36.

will give this land," he will send his angel before you, and you shall take a wife for my son from there. But if the woman is not willing to follow you, then you will be free from this oath of mine; only you must not take my son back there. (Gen 24:6–8 NRSV)	free from my oath, when you come to my kindred; even if they will not give her to you, you will be free from my oath. (Gen 24:40–41 NRSV)

In these cases, the reason for the authors' deviation from the wording of the first quotation in the second quotation cannot have been due to their inability to reproduce it.

In the Old Testament, the principle behind the free reproduction of a historical utterance or speech was the same as in Greco-Roman historiography. Since earlier Hebrew historians did not speak about their historical method, however, we must be content with much later Jewish statements. One of the Jewish authors who commented on the reproduction of speeches in the Old Testament was Abraham Ibn Ezra. In his explanation of the differences in wording between the two versions of the Decalogue in Exod 20 and Deut 5, he applied a form–content distinction[38] and wrote:

> Note that words are like bodies and their meanings are like souls. The body is, as it were, a vessel for the soul. Hence all the wise men of all nations are in the habit of preserving the ideas conveyed by a word and are not concerned with changes in wording when the meaning remains one and the same.[39]

3. Reported Speeches in New Testament Historiography

The church fathers made the same distinction when they explained the differences in wording between the differing reproductions of the words and speeches of Jesus in the Synoptic Gospels.

Clement of Alexandria (ca. 150–215 CE) in his treatise *Who Is the Rich Man That Shall Be Saved* quoted Mark 10:17–31 and explained:

---

[38] See Mordechai Cohen, "The Aesthetic Exegesis of Moses ibn Ezra," in *The Middle Ages*, ed. Magne Sæbø, in cooperation with Chris Brekelmans and Menahem Haran, vol. 1, pt. 2 of *Hebrew Bible, Old Testament: The History of Its Interpretation* (Göttingen: Vandenhoeck & Ruprecht, 2000), 282–301, esp. 291–93.

[39] Abraham Ibn Ezra, *Long Commentary on Exodus* 20:1, in *Ibn Ezra's Commentary on the Pentateuch: Exodus (Shemot)*, trans. H. Norman Strickman and Arthur Silver (New York: Menorah, 1996), 399; for similar statements, see Dirk U. Rottzoll, *Parascha Jitro bis Pekudej (Ex 18–20)*, vol. 2 of *Abraham Ibn Ezras langer Kommentar zum Buch Exodus*, SJ 17.2 (Berlin: de Gruyter, 2000), 563–64.

These things are written in the Gospel according to Mark; and in all the recognized gospels the words [τῶν ῥημάτων] vary perhaps slightly everywhere but all show identical agreement in meaning [τῆς γνώμης]. (*Quis div.* 5.1)⁴⁰

Augustine's application of the same distinction between content and form is clearly visible in his discussion of the different reproductions of one of John the Baptist's logia about the Messiah. Whereas in Mark (1:7) and Luke (3:16) John is quoted with the words that he is not worthy *to untie the thong* of Jesus's sandals, in Matthew (3:11) he says that he is not worthy *to carry* Jesus's sandals. According to Augustine, this is not only a difference in wording but also a difference in content. In order to show that "no charge of absolute inveracity should be laid against the evangelists," Augustine did not want to assume that the Baptist had two different statements but rather suggested that both versions of one and the same saying convey the same basic idea of the Baptist's inferiority and the Messiah's superiority. From this example, Augustine deduced a general principle that had to be applied in the interpretation of the Synoptic parallel accounts:

> There is no divergence from truth [*non esse mendacium*], even when they introduce some saying different from what was actually uttered by the person concerning whom the narrative is given, provided that they set forth as his mind precisely what is also so conveyed by that one who reproduces the words. For thus we learn the salutary lesson, that our aim should be nothing else than to ascertain what is the mind and intention of the person who speaks [*ita enim salubriter discimus nihil aliud esse quaerendum quam quid uelit qui loquitur*]. (*Cons.* 2.12.29)⁴¹

III. Conclusion

I have analyzed the notion of authorship and forgery in all kinds of ancient texts, embedded ones (e.g., reported speeches) and independent ones, some of them written under the author's control (e.g., speeches, letters, and history books) and others written without the author's control (e.g., translations and unauthorized lecture publications). Everywhere an authorial attribution was regarded as correct and nondeceptive if either the wording or the content of a particular text could be traced back to the author whose name it carried. To be sure, this prevailing principle of ancient authorship attribution was often taken for granted and applied without further explanation. In several instances, however, it was also stated explicitly. Polybius conceded that a historian did not have to repeat the wording of a speech

---

⁴⁰ Trans. *ANF* 2:592 (modified); for the text, see *Clemens Alexandrinus*, ed. Otto Stählin, 4 vols., GCS 12, 15, 17, 39 (Berlin: Akademie, 1960–1980), 17:163.13–15.

⁴¹ Trans. *NPNF¹* 6.119 (modified); cf. 2.14.31; 2.24.55. For the text, see *De consensu evangelistarum libri quattuor*, ed. Franciscus Weihrich, CSEL 43 (Vienna: Tempsky, 1904), 130.13–19.

that he attributed to a historical figure but demanded that he reproduce the sense of what the speaker actually said. Cicero explained that, in his translation of some Attic orations that were published under the orators' names, he regarded it as legitimate not to render word for word but rather sense for sense. According to Philo, it was common knowledge that the same thought could be correctly paraphrased in many different ways. Much later, Abraham Ibn Ezra stated that when evaluating a text's authenticity, the distinction between its form and its content was a standard for scholars in all languages.

With an eye to these and other ancient statements, I cannot agree with the most innovative contribution of Ehrman's otherwise very useful book. Ehrman has rightly joined the growing number of scholars who have raised substantial doubts regarding the once-popular thesis of innocent ancient pseudepigraphy. At the same time, his assertion that in antiquity a text's authenticity was assessed not on the basis of its content but always on the basis of its wording goes one step beyond what the numerous relevant sources reveal.

Franciscan University Press is now accepting academic manuscripts relating to Catholic studies

— including, but not limited to, theology, philosophy, literature, and the intersection between faith and science.

Send manuscripts, proposals, or questions to
Dr. Stephen Lewis (acquisitionsfup@franciscan.edu).
For full manuscript submission details, please visit franciscan.edu/press.

Did Peter Speak Hebrew to the Servant? A Linguistic Examination of the Expression "I Do Not Know What You Are Saying" (Matt 26:70, Mark 14:68, Luke 22:60)

ERAN SHUALI
shuali@unistra.fr
University of Strasbourg, 67000 Strasbourg, France

In this article I examine the statement "I do not know what you are saying," uttered by Peter according to the Synoptic Gospels as a response to the accusation that he was one of Jesus's men. I examine the Hebrew parallels to this phrase in Tannaitic literature, with special attention to their wording and pragmatic function. Although Tannaitic literature postdates the New Testament, its use of this phrase may shed light on the Synoptic passage. I conclude that Peter's phrase is not likely to have been formulated originally in Greek or Aramaic; it should be understood as reflecting an idiomatic expression in Hebrew.

In recent decades and notably since the discovery of the Dead Sea Scrolls, a growing number of scholars have affirmed that, at the turn of the Christian era, a trilingual reality existed among Jews in the land of Israel.[1] Greek, Aramaic, and Hebrew were all spoken at the time and in the milieu that saw the emergence of the Christian movement. Therefore, it is reasonable to assume that early traditions of this movement—which later found their way into the Synoptic Gospels and other New Testament writings—were formulated in all three of these languages. Yet determining the original language of a specific saying or passage incorporated into the Synoptic Gospels is notoriously difficult. The Hebrew, Aramaic, and Semitized

I would like to thank Jan Joosten, Christophe Rico, Hector Patmore, Avital Grünpeter, Jordash Kiffiak, Rami Arav, and *JBL*'s anonymous reviewer for their remarks on earlier versions of this study.

[1] For a recent survey on this question, see Steven E. Fassberg, "Which Semitic Language Did Jesus and Other Contemporary Jews Speak?" *CBQ* 74 (2012): 263–80. In addition to the abundant bibliographical references provided by Fassberg, see the recent collection of essays *The Language Environment of First Century Judaea*, ed. Randall Buth and R. Steven Notley, Jerusalem Studies in the Synoptic Gospels 2, JCPS 26 (Leiden: Brill, 2014).

Greek spoken at the time in Jewish circles often cannot be differentiated solely on the basis of the Greek text of the Gospels.[2] In order to do so, we need specific relevant insights into these languages from other ancient sources.[3] In this article, I offer one such example, in which the linguistic data at hand do enable us to determine in which language the tradition of the early Christian movement has, in all probability, remembered a certain phrase.

I. Peter's Denial

After having discreetly followed Jesus and his arresters to the house of the high priest, Peter waits outside in the courtyard during his master's trial before the Sanhedrin. While there, he is thrice accused of being one of Jesus's men and thrice he denies this firmly. According to the Gospels of Matthew and Luke, in one of the three denials, he responds sharply, "I do not know what you are saying" (οὐκ οἶδα τί λέγεις [Matt 26:70]; οὐκ οἶδα ὃ λέγεις [Luke 22:60]). In the Gospel of Mark, he replies, "I neither know nor understand what you are saying" (οὔτε οἶδα οὔτε ἐπίσταμαι σὺ τί λέγεις [Mark 14:68]).

In the context of the gospels, the pragmatic function of the phrase is clear: it is a denial. This is stated explicitly in the phrase introducing Peter's words in Matthew and Mark:[4]

ὁ δὲ <u>ἠρνήσατο</u> ἔμπροσθεν πάντων λέγων· οὐκ οἶδα ... (Matt 26:70)
But he <u>denied</u> [it] before all [of them], saying, "I do not know ..." (NRSV)

ὁ δὲ <u>ἠρνήσατο</u> λέγων οὔτε οἶδα ... (Mark 14:68)
But he <u>denied</u> it, saying, "I do not know ..." (NRSV)

---

[2] Three linguistic tests are suggested by Randall Buth in order to establish whether a text in Semitized Greek has been influenced by Hebrew or by Aramaic ("Distinguishing Hebrew from Aramaic in Semitized Greek Texts, with an Application for the Gospels and Pseudepigrapha," in Buth and Notley, *Language Environment of First Century Judaea*, 247-319). Buth states, however, that "it must be recognized and emphasized that these tests are not absolute. They must be done in conjunction with other studies" (318).

[3] See Jan Joosten, "Aramaic or Hebrew behind the Gospels?," *AnBrux* 9 (2004): 88-101, esp. 97-100.

[4] In fact, Matthew and Mark indicate explicitly that all of Peter's three responses are denials: καὶ πάλιν <u>ἠρνήσατο</u> μετὰ ὅρκου ὅτι (Matt 26:72); τότε ἤρξατο <u>καταθεματίζειν</u> καὶ <u>ὀμνύειν</u> ὅτι (Matt 26:74); ὁ δὲ πάλιν <u>ἠρνεῖτο</u> (Mark 14:70); ὁ δὲ ἤρξατο <u>ἀναθεματίζειν</u> καὶ <u>ὀμνύναι</u> ὅτι (Mark 14:71). Luke says this explicitly only in Peter's first response: ὁ δὲ <u>ἠρνήσατο</u> λέγων (Luke 22:57). He introduces Peter's next two responses using simple verbs of speech: ὁ δὲ Πέτρος <u>ἔφη</u> (Luke 22:58); <u>εἶπεν</u> δὲ ὁ Πέτρος (22:60). It seems reasonable to assume that Luke did not reproduce the explicit expressions of denial appearing in his sources in order to avoid repetition and redundancy for a better literary quality.

Furthermore, the fact that this statement uttered by Peter constitutes a *denial* is important in the narrative of the gospels, for this is one of the three times Peter denies Jesus as the latter has foretold.[5]

The exact meaning of these words, however, is rather obscure. What exactly does Peter mean? What precisely does he not know? Does he mean to say he does not know the man of whom the servant speaks, that is, Jesus? Or is it the question itself that he for some reason does not understand? Perhaps he is implying that he does not understand any of what the servant is saying, since her or his accent is strange to his ears? Or rather, is Peter in such a state of stress and confusion that he just mumbles the first thing that comes to his mind and therefore we should not try to find logic in his words?[6] All of these interpretations have been suggested by exegetes.[7]

II. The Parallel Hebrew Expression

It is well known in New Testament scholarship that a Hebrew phrase parallel to the one attributed to Peter by the Synoptic Gospels is found in the Tannaitic literature: איני יודע מה אתה סח ("I do not know what you are saying") occurs five times in the Tannaitic corpus in two different contexts. First, in a legal passage about theft, of which there are parallel versions in the Mishnah and the Tosefta, the phrase is placed on the lips of a man accused of having stolen an ox that had been given into his charge or lent to him.[8] The owner of the animal asks him, "Where is my ox?" to which the man responds, "I do not know what you are saying," thus

---

[5] Matt 26:34, Mark 14:30, Luke 22:34; cf. Matt 26:75, Mark 14:72, Luke 22:61.

[6] W. J. Peter Boyd observes, "If we take the Marcan account seriously as a faithful record of how it all happened, Peter's reply to the maid's question may not seem as 'curious' as it does to the expert linguist with his critical demand for logical consistency. For in daily life people who are suddenly and unwillingly subjected to cross examination usually avoid answering directly. The more unexpected the unwelcome question, the more clumsy any attempt to hedge is likely to be. Peter must have been under considerable stress at the time. The urge to loyalty and the memory of his public avowal, 'Even if I must die, I will never deny you' (v. 31), was opposed by the acute awareness of personal peril, bewilderment at the catastrophe of Jesus' arrest and the apparent failure of all the glorious hopes for the kingdom of God. Such a tension would have been too harrowing to permit clear thought and logical replies" ("Peter's Denial—Mark xiv. 68, Luke xxii. 57," *ExpTim* 67 [1956]: 341).

[7] For a survey of the different interpretations, see Robert H. Gundry, *Mark: A Commentary on His Apology for the Cross* (Grand Rapids: Eerdmans, 1993), 920; Vincent Taylor, *The Gospel according to St. Mark: The Greek Text with Introduction, Notes, and Indexes*, 2nd ed. (London: Macmillan, 1966), 573-74.

[8] According to m. Šebu. 8:2, the man is a שומר חנם, "an unpaid bailee" (Marcus Jastrow, *A Dictionary of the Targumim, the Talmud Babli and Yerushalmi, and the Midrashic Literature* [New York: G. P. Putnam's Sons, 1903], s.v. שׁוֹמֵר). According to m. Šebu. 8:5, he is a שואל, "a borrower." In t. B. Qam. 8:2, 3, it is said that the ox has been *entrusted* to him (שהפקדתי אצלך).

denying the implicit accusation. The sentences in which the expression appears are the following:

m. Šebu. 8:3, 6. איכן שורי, ואמר לו <u>איני יודע מה אתה סח</u>.
"Where is my ox?" And he said to him, "<u>I do not know what you are saying</u>."

t. B. Qam. 8:4 היכן שור שהפקדתי אצלך ואמר לו <u>איני יודע מה אתה סח</u>.
"Where is the ox that I entrusted to you?" And he said to him, "<u>I do not know what you are saying</u>."

t. B. Qam. 8:7 היכן שורי שהפקדתי אצלך אמר <u>איני יודע מה אתה סח</u>.
"Where is my ox that I entrusted to you?" He said, "<u>I do not know what you are saying</u>."

Second, the phrase is used in a midrashic interpretation of Prov 29:24: "The partner of a thief hates his own life; he hears the curse, but discloses nothing" (ESV). In order to illustrate this saying, according to the Tosefta, Rabbi Simeon tells a story (*māšāl*) of a man who sees a thief leaving the house of another, carrying loot. The man asks the thief what is going on, and the thief offers him part of the take in order to persuade him to keep silent. Later, the victim of the theft asks the man to swear that he has not seen anyone leave his house with his possessions. To this, the man says, "(It is) an oath that I do not know what you are saying." The passage is quoted here in full (t. B. Qam. 7:13):

ר' שמעון או' הרי הוא אומ' חולק עם גנב שונא נפשו וגו'. משלו משל. למה הדבר דומה? לאחד שטען כלים ויצא מבית חבירו. מצאו אחר, אמ' לו: "מה זה?" פל' אמ' לו: "ר' טול חלקך ואל תגיד." לאחר זמן מצאו בעל גניבה. א' לו: "משביע אני עליך אם לא ראית אדם שטען כלים ויצא מתוך ביתי." אמ' לו: "<u>שבועה שאיני יודע מה אתה סח</u>." על זה נאמ': "חולק עם גנב שונא נפשו אלה ישמע ולא יגיד."

> R. Simeon says, "Lo, [Scripture says], *The partner of a thief hates his own life; he hears the curse but discloses nothing* (Prov. 29:24). They have made a simile: To what is the matter likened? To someone who is loaded down with utensils and leaving the house of his fellow. His friend came upon him and said to him, 'Now what's going on, Mr. So-and-so?' He replied, 'Take your share and don't squeal!' After some time the one who had been robbed found him and said to him, 'I impose an oath upon you, if you have not seen someone loaded down with utensils and leaving my house.' The other says to him, '[<u>It is</u>] <u>an oath that I do not know what you are saying</u>.' Concerning such a person, it is said, *The partner of a thief hates his own life; he hears the curse* [of an oath] *but discloses nothing*."[9]

The Hebrew phrase in question is evidently a very close parallel to Peter's Greek one. Its wording is identical to the wording of Matthew's version of the saying and very similar to that of Luke and of Mark. Furthermore, the Hebrew and Greek

---

[9] English translation slightly modified from *The Tosefta: Translated from the Hebrew; Fourth Division: NEZIQIN (The Order of Damages)*, trans. Jacob Neusner (New York: Ktav, 1981), 39.

phrases have the same pragmatic function: they are both used to dismiss a claim made by an interlocutor.

Nevertheless, the nature of the Hebrew phrase is much easier to determine: it is an idiomatic expression. Several factors attest to this. First, in the case of the man accused of ox theft, the narrative context does not permit a literal "first-degree" understanding of the phrase, as actually referring to "knowing" or "understanding" something. Unlike Peter, who may claim not to know who Jesus was,[10] it is not likely that the man would claim to have no acquaintance with the ox that has been entrusted to him or that he has borrowed. Similarly, whereas Peter may pretend not to understand the subject matter of the servant's affirmation, the bailee or borrower could hardly claim to be surprised at the self-evident question he is asked by the owner of the ox with whom he is in a business relationship. Finally, there is nothing indicating that the bailee or borrower came from a different region than the owner of the ox and could therefore have difficulties understanding his accent—difficulties such as Peter the Galilean might have understanding a Jerusalemite accent.[11]

Second, in the case of the midrashic interpretation of Prov 29:24, the pragmatics of the man's saying argues against a "first-degree" meaning. His use of the phrase is not a spontaneous reaction to a claim but a direct response, explicitly made under oath, to the demand: "I impose an oath upon you, if you have not seen someone loaded down with utensils and leaving my house." The phrase "(It is) an oath that I do not know what you are saying" is meant to be understood as a resolute rejection of the accusation and not as commentary on the utterance itself.

Last and most important, although the Hebrew and Greek phrases use words that have the same meaning, the Hebrew phrase is distinguished by a lexical particularity. It does not use one of the common verbs meaning "to say," such as the verb אמר or דבר (which are probably as common in Hebrew as the verb λέγω, which is used in Peter's saying in the gospels, is in Greek) but the rather rare verb סח.[12] The rare verb used in all occurrences of the Hebrew phrase is something like an emblem of idiomaticity, for in all languages rare words are often preserved in fixed idiomatic expressions even though they may hardly be used freely in other contexts.

In summary, two points may be noted. First, the simplest and most natural way to understand the phrase pronounced by Peter according to the Synoptic

---

[10] Peter of course does eventually make this claim (see Matt 26:72, Mark 14:71, Luke 22:57).

[11] Gundry, *Mark: A Commentary*, 888.

[12] The verb סח occurs in the Mishnah only in the quoted passages. It can also be found in the Tosefta in Yoma 2:7; Yebam. 14:9; ʿAbod. Zar. 1:14; Nid. 5:3; in Talmud Yerushalmi in Soṭah 19a; Sanh. 42b; in Talmud Bavli in Ber. 18b, 51a; Šabb. 75b; ʿErub. 21b; Pesaḥ. 51a; Yoma 38a, 39b, 67a; Ḥag. 16b; Soṭah 25a; Giṭ. 57b; Sanh. 88a; Menaḥ. 36a, 39a, 109b; Bek. 10b, 38b. Spelled שח, the verb appears in y. Yoma 19b; y. Šeqal. 22b; b. Sukkah 28a; b. Soṭah 44b; b. Ḥul. 27a; b. Bek. 28a.

Gospels is to take it as an idiomatic expression used to vigorously dismiss a claim. This interpretation allows us to take the text at face value, and it is also the understanding adopted by most exegetes and translations.[13] Second, a similar idiomatic expression is attested in Mishnaic Hebrew. We should, of course, be careful not to be led to hasty conclusions by this similarity. Before suggesting that the Greek phrase attested in the gospels reflects a Hebrew expression, we must check two things: Could Peter's phrase actually be a Greek expression used by the authors of the gospels? Could it reflect a similar Aramaic idiom?

III. Is the Phrase a Greek Idiomatic Expression?

There is one exact parallel to Peter's phrase in Greek literature. It appears in the Testament of Joseph in a dialogue between Petephrēs (the Greek name of Potiphar) and a merchant in whose household Joseph was serving. It runs as follows:

> And Petephres ... commanded the merchant to be brought, and he said to him: What is this that I hear, that you steal persons out of the land of the Hebrews, buying them to be servants? Then, the merchant fell on his face and besought him, saying: I beseech you, lord, I do not know what you say [Δέομαί σου, κύριε, οὐκ οἶδα ὃ λέγεις]. (T. Jos. 13:1–2)[14]

Here we have the same words as in Luke's version of Peter's saying, and they are used for the same rhetorical purpose, that is, to energetically dismiss a claim. The uncertain nature of the materials included in the Testaments of the Twelve Patriarchs, however, makes this parallel rather doubtful evidence for linguistic study. In fact, some of the passages in the Testaments likely depend on or have been translated from earlier texts in Hebrew or Aramaic.[15] If this is the case in the

---

[13] The NRSV, the NASB, and the NIV render this phrase using an equivalent idiomatic expression in English: "I do not/don't know what you are talking about!"

[14] Harm W. Hollander and Marinus de Jonge, *The Testaments of the Twelve Patriarchs: A Commentary*, SVTP 8 (Leiden: Brill, 1985), 396.

[15] For a survey of the existing Aramaic and Hebrew materials that are parallel to the Testaments of the Twelve Patriarchs, see Hollander and de Jonge, *Testaments of the Twelve Patriarchs*, 17–29. József Milik thinks that three very small fragments found at Qumran come from an Aramaic Testament of Joseph ("Écrits prééssèniens de Qumrân: D'Hénoch à Amram," in *Qumrân: Sa piété, sa théologie et son milieu*, ed. Mathias Delcor, BETL 46 [Paris: Duculot, 1978], 101-2). For the hypothesis that the Greek text of the Testaments of the Twelve Patriarchs is a translation from a Hebrew or an Aramaic source, see Robert Henry Charles, *The Greek Versions of the Testaments of the Twelve Patriarchs: Edited from Nine MSS together with the Variants of the Armenian and Slavonic Versions and Some Hebrew Fragments* (Oxford: Clarendon, 1908), xxiii–xxxix; Marc Philonenko, *Les interpolations chrétiennes des Testaments des Douze Patriarches et les manuscrits de Qoumrân* (Paris: Presses Universitaires de France, 1960); R. A. Martin, "Syntactical

passage under discussion here, then the quoted phrase actually attests to a Hebrew or an Aramaic expression parallel to the one pronounced by Peter. Furthermore, the Testaments of the Twelve Patriarchs contain many passages that can be ascribed to a Christian author or redactor.[16] If this is the case in the present passage in the Testament of Joseph, then the phrase we have here may have been influenced by Peter's saying in the gospels and may therefore not constitute an independent occurrence of the expression. In view of these uncertainties, we must disregard the occurrence of the phrase in the Testament of Joseph as evidence for its use as an idiomatic expression in Greek.

Apart from the Testament of Joseph, three occurrences of phrases similar to Peter's saying can be found in Greek literature: two in Plato's dialogues and one in Lucian's *Solecist*. When they are read in context, however, it is apparent that their pragmatic use is very different from the phrase attested in the gospels. In Plato and Lucian, these phrases are to be understood literally. They do not constitute idiomatic expressions used to dismiss claims but are simple statements denoting one's incapacity to understand something that has been said.[17] An examination of the relevant passages will show this.

> SOCRATES. Then what can this thing be, which bears the name of figure [τὸ σχῆμα]? Try and tell me. Suppose that, on being asked this question by someone, either about figure or about colour, you had replied: Why, I don't so much as understand what you want, sir, or even know what you are saying [ἀλλ' οὐδὲ μανθάνω ἔγωγε ὅ τι βούλει, ὦ ἄνθρωπε, <u>οὐδὲ οἶδα ὅ τι λέγεις</u>]. He might well have shown surprise, and said: Do you not understand that I am looking for that which is the same common element in all these things? (Plato, *Meno* 74e–75a [Lamb, LCL])

In the imaginary dialogue that Socrates is describing here, Meno uses the phrase that is of interest to us in order to say that he does not understand his interlocutor's abstract question. He does not wish to dismiss it or to express disagreement; he simply does not understand what his interlocutor wants [ὅ τι βούλει] to say.

Evidence of a Semitic *Vorlage* of the Testament of Joseph," in *Studies on the Testament of Joseph*, ed. George W. E. Nickelsburg Jr., SCS 5 (Missoula, MT: Scholars Press, 1975), 105-14; and Anders Hultgård, *L'eschatologie des Testaments des Douze Patriarches*, 2 vols., AUU, Historia religionum 6–7 (Uppsala: Almqvist & Wiksell, 1981), 2:74–79.

[16] This has been emphasized by, among others, Marinus de Jonge in much of his work on the Testaments of the Twelve Patriarchs, e.g., "Christian Influence in the Testaments of the Twelve Patriarchs," in *Studies on the Testaments of the Twelve Patriarchs: Text and Interpretation*, ed. Marinus de Jonge, SVTP 3 (Leiden: Brill, 1975), 193-246, repr. from *NovT* 4 (1960): 182-235; de Jonge, "The Testaments of the Twelve Patriarchs: Christian and Jewish; A Hundred Years after Friedrich Schnapp," in *Jewish Eschatology, Early Christian Christology, and the Testaments of the Twelve Patriarchs: Collected Essays*, NovTSup 63 (Leiden: Brill, 1991), 233-43, repr. from *NTT* 39 (1985): 265-75.

[17] *Pace* Michael Wolter, *Das Lukasevangelium*, HNT 5 (Tübingen: Mohr Siebeck, 2008), 731-32.

CALLICLES. I cannot follow these subtleties of yours, Socrates [Οὐκ οἶδ᾿ ἄττα σοφίζῃ, ὦ Σώκρατες].
SOCRATES. You can, but you play the innocent, Callicles. Just go on a little further, that you may realize how subtle is your way of reproving me. Does not each of us cease at the same moment from thirst and from the pleasure he gets by drinking?
CALLICLES. I cannot tell what you mean [Οὐκ οἶδα ὅ τι λέγεις].
GORGIAS. No, no, Callicles, you must answer him, for our sakes also, that the arguments may be brought to a conclusion. (Plato, *Gorg.* 497a–b [Lamb, LCL])

This passage hardly requires any commentary. The poor Callicles has no objection; he simply does not understand what the two philosophers want. Or in any case, this is what he claims.

SOPHIST. I'm surprised to hear you say I won't be able to recognise a howler [σολοικισμόν].
LUCIAN. How could you recognise one when in your ignorance you've missed three?
SOPHIST. What three?
LUCIAN. Three whole bearded monsters I've just perjured up.[18]
SOPHIST. I think you're joking.
LUCIAN. And I that you don't know when a man makes howlers in his talk.
SOPHIST. How can anyone know when nothing has been said?
LUCIAN. Things have been said and four howlers made, so that you would have achieved a great succession if you had recognised them.[19]
SOPHIST. Not a great one but the minimum requirement now that I've let myself in for this.
LUCIAN. But even now you didn't notice.
SOPHIST. When just now?
LUCIAN. When I talked of your achieving succession.
SOPHIST. I don't know what you mean [Οὐκ οἶδα ὅ τι λέγεις].
LUCIAN. You're right there; you don't [Ὀρθῶς ἔφης· οὐ γὰρ οἶσθα]. Advance forward into the lead then, as you don't want to follow, though you shall be able to understand [συνήσων] if you should wish. (Lucian, *Soleocista* 2 [Macleod, LCL])

Here, too, the phrase is used by the Sophist in order to say that he does not understand what Lucian is aiming at, not that he disagrees with his claim. In addition, Lucian's answer indicates that he takes the phrase as expressing lack of understanding and not disagreement. After affirming that the Sophist does not *know* (οἶδα), he claims that he could have *understood* (συνίημι) if he had wished. "Not knowing

[18] The howler here is the faulty use of the adjective ἀρτιγενείους ("new-bearded") instead of ἀρτιγενεῖς ("newborn"); *Lucian*, vol. 8, trans. Matthew D. Macleod, LCL (Cambridge: Harvard University Press, 1967), 9.

[19] In this English translation, the howler is the use of the word *succession* instead of *success*. The Greek text has ἆθλον ("prize") instead of ἆθλος ("task"); *Lucian*, trans. Macleod, 8:11 n. 1.

what has been said" is equivalent, for the character Lucian, to "not understanding something."

Thus, Greek literature supplies us negative evidence for the existence of an idiomatic expression similar to the one used by Peter according to the gospels. Such an expression is not attested in the Greek corpus, but this does not mean that it did not exist in spoken language. There is one piece of positive evidence, however, in the Synoptic Gospels themselves. As we have seen, Peter's saying has been preserved in two different forms: a long one and a short one. The long form is attested in the Gospel of Mark, and the short one is found in both Matthew and Luke:[20]

οὔτε οἶδα οὔτε ἐπίσταμαι σὺ τί λέγεις (Mark 14:68)
οὐκ οἶδα τί λέγεις (Matt 26:70)
οὐκ οἶδα ὃ λέγεις (Luke 22:60)

Matthew's and Luke's versions of the sayings are almost identical, and the minor difference between them—Luke's use of the relative pronoun ὅ where Mark and Matthew have τί—can easily be explained as Luke's attempt to use "better" Greek. Yet several substantial differences exist between this short form of the saying and the long one we find in Mark. Three such differences should be noted: (1) instead of just one verb of cognition (οἶδα), as in Matthew and Luke, Mark has two (οἶδα, ἐπίσταμαι); (2) instead of a simple negation (οὐκ), Mark has two composite ones (οὔτε ... οὔτε);[21] and (3) in Mark we find the personal pronoun σύ, which is absent from Matthew's and Luke's formulations and which is emphasized by its unusual place in the phrase.

The most striking difference between the long and short form of the saying is Mark's use of two synonymous verbs of cognition where Matthew and Luke have only one. This is far from an isolated case, however. In many places where Mark has duplicate pleonastic expressions, Matthew and Luke retain only one of the two elements, and often it is the same element.[22] There are two ways to explain this phenomenon. First, when using the Markan material, the authors of the Gospels of Matthew and Luke omitted an element they thought to be redundant. Second, the authors of Matthew and Luke had before them a version of the Gospel of Mark

---

[20] Unsurprisingly, these three formulations have exercised influence on one another in the manuscript tradition. Hence, Mark's wording has influenced codices D and Δ of the Gospel of Matthew, where we find ουδε/ουτε επισταμαι added at the end of the phrase. And both Mark's and Matthew's use of τί as a relative pronoun appear also in Luke in codices ℵ and D. For additional information, see NA.

[21] According to BDF §445(2), this use of οὔτε ... οὔτε ... is "inadmissible" and the reading οὐκ ... οὐδέ ... found in some manuscripts is correct. R. T. France seems to disagree with this categorical statement, which disregards most of the manuscript evidence (*The Gospel of Mark: A Commentary on the Greek Text*, NIGTC [Grand Rapids: Eerdmans, 2002], 620 n. 68).

[22] See Frans Neirynck, "Duplicate Expressions and the Original Text of the Gospel," in *Duality in Mark: Contributions to the Study of the Markan Redaction*, rev. ed., BETL 31 (Leuven: Leuven University Press, 1988), 37-44.

that had not the redundant expression but a simple one, which they copied faithfully. In this case, we should assume that a very early redactor of the Gospel of Mark added the duplicate expression after the composition of the Gospels of Matthew and Luke but long before the first textual witnesses we have of this Gospel.

For this argument's sake, it does not matter which of the two hypotheses is closer to the historical reality. What matters is only that a Greek-speaking writer active at the time and in the milieu in which the Synoptic Gospels were composed—either the authors of the Gospels of Matthew and Luke or an early redactor of the Gospel of Mark—radically altered the wording of the phrase put into the mouth of Peter, either by substantially shortening it or adding to it. Considering the fixed nature of idiomatic expressions, this would be an unlikely thing to do, had this writer felt the phrase to be such an expression.[23]

IV. Does the Phrase Reflect an Aramaic Idiom?

To my knowledge, no Aramaic parallel to Peter's phrase is noted in the vast scholarly literature on the Synoptic Gospels. In fact, scholars who thought that this phrase reflects an Aramaic substratum supposed that Peter's original saying was mistranslated from Aramaic to Greek. In the 1930s Charles Cutler Torrey claimed that Peter had said in Aramaic, "I am neither a companion of (יָדַע), nor do I know at all (חָכַם) him of whom you speak (די אמר אנת)."[24] According to Torrey, the mistranslation occurred since the Greek translators mistook the meaning of the Aramaic particle *dī*, which did not mean here "that which," as it most often does, but "he who." Hence, instead of using a masculine relative pronoun in Greek (τίνα/ ὅν[25]), they used a neuter form (τί/ὅ). This hypothesis was later adopted, with minor

---

[23] I am aware that this argument is stronger if the supposed idiomatic expression corresponded to the short form of the saying. It seems to me that doubling the verb of an idiomatic expression would most often destroy its idiomaticity. For example, it is hard to imagine an English-speaking writer transforming the idiomatic expression "What are you **talking** about?!," which has a similar pragmatic function to that of the Greek expression we are studying, into "What are you **talking and speaking** about?" If the supposed expression corresponded to the long pleonastic form, however, a writer might shorten it. For instance, when rewriting the sentence "After all that has happened, we got home **safe and sound**," one might feel that the shorter form is more elegant while conveying the same meaning: "After all that has happened, we got home **safe**." Similar considerations could make one transform the sentence "All she wanted was some **peace and quiet**" into "All she wanted was some **peace**."

[24] This is a summary of Torrey's argument in his *Our Translated Gospels: Some of the Evidence* (London: Hodder & Stoughton, 1936), 16-18, here 16. See also Torrey, *The Four Gospels: A New Translation* (New York: Harper & Brothers, 1933), 296, 303, 314.

[25] Cf. Mark 14:71: οὐκ οἶδα τὸν ἄνθρωπον τοῦτον <u>ὃν</u> λέγετε.

changes, by Matthew Black.²⁶ Although this explanation is possible, it is unduly complicated, since it requires changing the Greek text even though it can make sense.²⁷

An idiomatic expression similar to Peter's phrase is unattested, then, as far as we know, in the written sources we have in Aramaic. Again, however, this cannot prove that such an expression did not exist in the language. This we simply cannot know. Nevertheless, there is one thing that we can have a little more certainty about: the Hebrew idiomatic expression attested in the Tannaitic corpus does not seem to be a calque on an Aramaic expression because of the use of the verb סח in all occurrences of the Hebrew expression. Although this verb was not the most common verb denoting acts of speech in Hebrew, it is well attested in both biblical and postbiblical Hebrew.²⁸ In Jewish Aramaic, on the other hand, this verb is extremely scarce and is attested only a handful of times, mostly in late sources.²⁹ Especially revealing is the fact that in the Targums, with the exception of the late Targum of Job, the Hebrew verb שׂח is never rendered using an Aramaic cognate.³⁰ This verb seems, then, not to be "at home" in the Palestinian Aramaic of the first centuries. If an idiomatic expression similar to Peter's phrase had existed in this dialect of Aramaic, it would probably not make use of the verb סח. It would therefore be surprising for its loan-translation into Hebrew to introduce a rather rare verb not extant in the original form of the expression.

---

²⁶ According to Matthew Black, "A more exact equivalent of the Greek would be *man ʾamar ʾa(n)t*" (*An Aramaic Approach to the Gospels and Acts*, 3rd ed. [Oxford: Clarendon, 1967], 79-80).

²⁷ Torrey writes, "The reading of the Grk. is pure nonsense.... This is a sentence that no author could write" (*Our Translated Gospels*, 16-17).

²⁸ In the Hebrew Bible, the verb is always written with a שׂ. In the rabbinic sources, we find it spelled both with a שׂ and with a ס; see n. 12 above.

²⁹ The following occurrences are noted by Jastrow: b. Ḥag. 5b; Lev. Rab. 26; Tg. Job 7:11 (see below); Tg. Yer. I Num 21:27, 28 (Tg. Prov 8:15 is considered doubtful by Jastrow). To this list should be added the occurrence in b. Ber. 62a, which is parallel to the previous occurrence in the Babylonian Talmud. The verb is probably also used in the Aramaic translation of Job 36:33 in the so-called Targum of Job from Qumran Cave 11 for rendering the Hebrew verb יגיד; 11Q10 XXIX, 10. I thank Hector Patmore for drawing my attention to this occurrence. The verb is not attested in any other dialect of Aramaic. It is possible, however, that it is etymologically related to the root *syḥ*, which is attested in several Semitic languages (see Hans-Peter Müller, "Die hebräische Wurzel שׂיח," *VT* 19 [1969]: 370-71; J. Hausmann, "שׂיח *śyḥ*; שִׂיחָה *śîḥâ*," *TDOT* 14:85).

³⁰ In the Targum of Job, the words אשיחה במר נפשי ("I shall speak in the bitterness of my soul"; Job 7:11) are rendered אשיח במריר נפשי, which has the same meaning. This Targum is dated to the fifth century CE (see Joseph A. Fitzmyer, "Some Observations on the Targum of Job from Qumran Cave 11," *CBQ* 36 [1974]: 503-24, here 516, and references given there). For a recent discussion on the dating of the Targums of the Pentateuch, see Daniel A. Machiela, "Hebrew, Aramaic, and the Differing Phenomena of Targum and Translation in the Second Temple Period and Post-Second Temple Period," in Buth and Notley, *Language Environment of First Century Judaea*, 209-46.

V. Conclusion

The easiest way to interpret Peter's response to the servant's accusation that he is one of Jesus's men—"I do not know what you are saying"—is to consider it to be an idiomatic expression used to vigorously dismiss a claim, much like the English expression "What are you talking about?!" Such an idiomatic expression, however, is attested nowhere else in the corpus of Greek literature. Furthermore, the variation on the form of Peter's phrase in the Synoptic Gospels indicates that at least one of the writers who worked on the texts did not consider it to be an idiomatic expression. In addition, such an idiomatic expression did indeed exist in Mishnaic Hebrew, but nothing of the sort is attested in Aramaic.

From these data, two conclusions follow. First, the oral tradition of the primitive Christian church remembered Peter speaking to servants of the high priest in Hebrew. This would attest both that, according to this tradition, these Jerusalemite servants most commonly spoke Hebrew and that Peter was capable of speaking this language when needed. Second, in the process of the composition of the gospels, the original Hebrew expression attributed to Peter was translated literally into Greek, in a form similar to that in the Gospel of Matthew, possibly with the personal pronoun σύ, as is attested in Mark's version. Subsequently, the author of the Gospel of Luke slightly "polished" the Greek of the expression, whereas the author or, more likely, an early redactor of the Gospel of Mark reworked it more thoroughly.

The Messiah Is "the Holy One": ὁ ἅγιος τοῦ θεοῦ as a Messianic Title in Mark 1:24

MAX BOTNER
botner@em.uni-frankfurt.de
Goethe-Universität, 60323 Frankfurt am Main, Germany

The christological title ὁ ἅγιος τοῦ θεοῦ ("the Holy One of God") appears a total of three times in the New Testament (Mark 1:24, Luke 4:34, John 6:69) and is unattested in other Jewish and Christian literature. While scholars offer a wide range of proposals concerning the background and significance of this title, no one has demonstrated the possibility of a link with messianic traditions. In this article I examine four texts (Ps 88:19 LXX, LAB 59:2, Pss 152, 153) that explicitly refer to the anointed David as God's "holy one" and two additional sources that indicate awareness of the archaic tradition that the oil used to anoint Israel's kings was holy (Ps 89:21 [88:21]; 11QPs^a XXVIII, 11; Josephus, *Ant.* 6.157). Next I explore how the underlying logical connection between "messiah" and "holy one" in these texts illuminates certain features of Mark's Gospel: (1) Jesus's baptism as a messianic anointing and his ensuing wilderness temptation (Mark 1:9–13), (2) the logical connection between the baptism–temptation sequence (1:9–13) and Jesus's first act of public ministry (1:21–28), and (3) the exorcistic connotations surrounding the title "son of David."

It has become almost obligatory to begin a discussion of ὁ ἅγιος τοῦ θεοῦ ("the Holy One of God") by conceding that it "was not a messianic title in Judaism."[1] The

This article has been published within the framework of the Hessian Ministry for Science and Art funded by the LOEWE research hub "Religiöse Positionierung: Modalitäten und Konstellationen in jüdischen, christlichen, und islamischen Kontexten" at Goethe-Universität Frankfurt am Main/Justus-Liebig-Universität Gießen.

[1] Morna D. Hooker, *The Gospel according to St Mark*, BNTC 2 (London: Black, 1991), 64; see also M.-J. Lagrange, *Évangile selon Saint Marc*, 6th ed. (Paris: Librairie Lecoffre, 1942), 22; Vincent Taylor, *The Gospel according to St. Mark: The Greek Text with Introduction, Notes and Indexes*, 2nd ed. (New York: St. Martin's Press, 1966), 174; Howard Clark Kee, *Community of the New Age: Studies in Mark's Gospel* (Philadelphia: Westminster, 1977; repr., Macon, GA: Mercer University Press, 1983), 120; Dieter Lührmann, *Das Markusevangelium*, HNT 3 (Tübingen: Mohr

title never occurs outside the New Testament and, outside of Mark 1:24, it occurs in only two other places (Luke 4:34, John 6:69).² In light of such paltry attestation, some scholars reach the conclusion of Edwin Broadhead that ὁ ἅγιος τοῦ θεοῦ is a "largely inconsequential description."³ Such pessimism is perhaps further warranted by the fact that, despite the efforts of a number of scholars, no compelling explanation for the derivation of this title has been proposed.⁴ Rather, it would

---

Siebeck, 1987), 51; Robert H. Gundry, *Mark: A Commentary on His Apology for the Cross* (Grand Rapids: Eerdmans, 1993), 82.

²Joseph A. Fitzmyer, *The Gospel according to Luke: Introduction, Translation, and Notes*, 2 vols., AB 28, 28A (Garden City, NY: Doubleday, 1981–1985), 1:546. Luke 4:34 is dependent on Mark 1:24; John 6:69 appears to be an alternative version of Peter's christological confession in Mark 8:29; see Craig S. Keener, *The Gospel of John: A Commentary*, 2 vols. (Peabody, MA: Hendrickson, 2003), 1:697.

³Edwin Broadhead, *Naming Jesus: Titular Christology in the Gospel of Mark*, JSNTSup 175 (Sheffield: Sheffield Academic, 1999), 100. See also R. T. France, *The Gospel of Mark: A Commentary on the Greek Text*, NIGTC (Grand Rapids: Eerdmans, 2002), 104; Jack Dean Kingsbury, *The Christology of Mark's Gospel* (Philadelphia: Fortress, 1983), 86–88; Heikki Räisänen, *The 'Messianic Secret' in Mark's Gospel*, trans. Christopher M. Tuckett, SNTW (Edinburgh: T&T Clark, 1990), 173.

⁴The most influential proposal at one time was Otto Bauernfeind's suggestion that Mark had reworked 3 Kgdms 17:18 (*Die Worte der Dämonen im Markusevangelium*, BWANT 3/8 [Stuttgart: Kohlhammer, 1927], 3–18). The collocation of the phrase τί ἐμοὶ καὶ σοί and the vocative ἄνθρωπε τοῦ θεοῦ convinced Bauernfeind that he had located Mark's source. He posited that ὁ ἅγιος τοῦ θεοῦ was a Markan alteration of ἄνθρωπε τοῦ θεοῦ and, by comparing the demon's οἶδα-saying in Mark 1:24 to similar expressions in the Greek Magical Papyri, concluded that ὁ ἅγιος τοῦ θεοῦ signified a θεῖος ἀνήρ. A partial list of scholars who have followed either all or part of Bauernfeind's position includes Erich Klostermann, *Das Markusevangelium*, HNT 3 (Tübingen: Mohr Siebeck, 1950), 17; James M. Robinson, *The Problem of History in Mark*, SBT 21 (London: SCM, 1957), 36; Johannes Schreiber, *Theologie des Vertrauens: Eine redaktionsgeschichtliche Untersuchung des Markusevangeliums* (Hamburg: Furche-Verlag, 1967), 221; Karl Kertelge, *Die Wunder Jesu im Markusevangelium: Eine redaktionsgeschichtliche Untersuchung* (Munich: Kösel, 1970), 53; Kee, *Community of the New Age*, 120; Lührmann, *Das Markusevangelium*, 51; Räisänen, *'Messianic Secret,'* 172–73. In distinction to Bauernfeind, Gerhard Friedrich argued that ὁ ἅγιος τοῦ θεοῦ pointed to Jesus's role as the eschatological high priest who would bind and destroy demons (e.g., T. Levi 18:12) ("Beobachtungen zur messianischen Hohepriestererwartung in den Synoptikern," *ZTK* 53 [1956]: 265–311). This proposal was vigorously attacked by Ferdinand Hahn and has never gained much currency among New Testament scholars (*The Titles of Jesus in Christology: Their History in Early Christianity*, trans. Harold Knight and George Ogg [Cambridge: James Clarke, 1963], 229–35); though see Walter Grundmann, *Das Evangelium nach Markus*, 2 vols., THKNT 2 (Berlin: Evangelische Verlagsanstalt, 1965), 1:43, and to some extent, Joel Marcus, *Mark 1–8: A New Translation with Introduction and Commentary*, AB 27 (New York: Doubleday, 2000), 188. Finally, a group of scholars has suggested that ἅγιος is the result of "wordplay" (*Wortspiel*) on Ναζαρηνός, but their position has been largely rejected as well; see Franz Mussner, "Ein Wortspiel in Mk 1,24?," *BZ* 4 (1960): 285–86; Eduard Schweizer, "'Er wird Nazoräer heissen' (zu Mc 1.24; Mt 2.23)," in *Judentum, Urchristentum, Kirche: Festschrift für Joachim Jeremias*, ed.

appear that the best one can offer is a range of possible connotations that ἅγιος τοῦ θεοῦ might evoke.

In the secondary literature, four scriptural categories are suggested to offer potential points of resonance with Mark 1:24. These can be listed in descending order of popularity. First, many scholars recognize that ὁ ἅγιος τοῦ θεοῦ echoes traditions about two of Israel's most famous charismatic prophets: (1) a widow of Zarephath addresses Elijah, "What have you against me, O man of God?" (τί ἐμοὶ καὶ σοί ἄνθρωπε τοῦ θεοῦ; 3 Kgdms 17:18); and (2) a Shunammite woman describes Elisha as "this man of God [who is] holy" (ἄνθρωπος τοῦ θεοῦ ἅγιος οὗτος, 4 Kgdms 4:9).[5] Second, a number of scholars plausibly suggest resonances with (high) priestly texts (e.g., Ps 106:16 LXX, Sir 45:6).[6] Third, some scholars point to texts that describe YHWH's people as holy (e.g., Deut 7:6, 14:2).[7] Finally, several scholars note that "Holy One (of Israel)" is a common designation for YHWH (see esp. Isaiah).[8] Markedly absent from this list, however, is any indication that ὁ ἅγιος τοῦ θεοῦ may be suggestive of messianic traditions—a curious coincidence in light of the consensus that it functions as a *messianic title* in Mark; that is, it operates within a network of titular designations that unveils Jesus's messianic identity for Mark's audience (Mark 1:24, 3:11, 5:7, 8:29, etc.).[9]

Walter Eltester, BZAW 26 (Berlin: Töpelmann, 1964); Rudolph Pesch, *Das Markusevangelium*, 2 vols., HTKNT 2 (Freiburg im Breisgau: Herder, 1976), 1:122 n. 20.

[5] See Hooker, *Gospel according to St Mark*, 64; Joachim Gnilka, *Das Evangelium nach Markus*, 2 vols., EKKNT 2 (Neukirchen-Vluyn: Neukirchener Verlag, 1978), 1:81. Other notable individuals called ἅγιος in the Jewish Scriptures are Moses (Wis 11:1), Samson (Judg 16:17 LXX B), and Jacob/Israel (Dan 3:35 LXX and θ').

[6] E.g., Marcus, *Mark 1–8*, 188.

[7] Lagrange, *Évangile selon Saint Marc*, 22. Kee points to 1 Enoch (e.g., 1 En. 38:4) (*Community of the New Age*, 120); 1QS and CD use אנשי הקודש ("men of holiness," 1QS V, 13, 18; VIII, 17, 24; CD IV, 6), עצת הקודש ("council of holiness," 1QSa II, 9; 1QS VIII, 21), and עדת הקודש ("community of holiness," 1QSa I, 12–13; 1QS II, 16). John J. Collins notes that the most common referent(s) for holy one(s) in Second Temple literature is (are) angel(s), though he does list some exceptions (*Daniel: A Commentary on the Book of Daniel*, Hermeneia [Minneapolis: Fortress, 1993], 313–18).

[8] M. Eugene Boring, for example, points out that YHWH is called "Holy One (of Israel)" thirty-nine times in Isaiah (*Mark: A Commentary*, NTL [Louisville: Westminster John Knox, 2006], 64). On the wider significance of Isaiah in Mark, see Joel Marcus, *The Way of the Lord: Christological Exegesis of the Old Testament in the Gospel of Mark* (Louisville: Westminster John Knox, 1992), 12–45; Rikki E. Watts, *Isaiah's New Exodus in Mark*, WUNT 2/88 (Tübingen: Mohr Siebeck, 1997).

[9] See William Wrede, *The Messianic Secret*, trans. J. C. G. Greig, Library of Theological Translations (London: James Clarke, 1971), 24–25, 77 n. 75; German original, 1901); Kertelge, *Die Wunder Jesu*, 56; Kingsbury, *Christology of Mark's Gospel*, 86–88; Räisänen, 'Messianic Secret,' 172; Marcus, *Mark 1–8*, 192–93; Elizabeth Struthers Malbon, *Mark's Jesus: Characterization as Narrative Christology* (Waco, TX: Baylor University Press, 2009), 82. In addition, Lukan and Johannine scholars generally agree that the third and fourth evangelists use ὁ ἅγιος τοῦ θεοῦ as an alternative, messianic title; see n. 2 above.

In order to rectify this lacuna, I will first demonstrate that some first-century CE Jews and Christians—perhaps even the evangelist and/or some of his audience—were aware that the designation "the holy one" derived from one's being anointed YHWH's "messiah." In order to make my case, I adduce four texts (Ps 88:19 LXX, LAB 59:2, Pss 152:4, 153:3) that explicitly refer to the anointed David as "the holy one" and two additional texts that demonstrate awareness of the ancient practice of using "holy oil" to anoint Israel's new king (11QPs^a XXVIII, 11; Josephus, *Ant.* 6.157, 165). Second, I examine how the underlying logical connection between messianic anointing and YHWH's holiness in these texts allows us to see certain features of Mark's Gospel in fresh and compelling ways.

I. God's Messiah Is "the Holy One"

My argument that scripturally informed Jews and Christians in the first century could recognize ὁ ἅγιος τοῦ θεοῦ as a messianic designation builds on Matthew Novenson's recent work on "messiah language" in ancient Judaism.[10] Novenson argues convincingly that the linguistic currency of the word *messiah* in antiquity depended on two conditions: (1) "an accessible pool of linguistic resources" (i.e., the Jewish Scriptures) from which an author could clarify what was meant by the term *messiah*, and (2) "a community of competent language users" (i.e., "the Jewish community and their sympathizers").[11] While Novenson appropriately distinguishes between the royal ideologies textualized in the Hebrew Bible and the various messianic aspirations (or lack thereof) among Jewish communities in the late Second Temple period, he rightly concludes that the language used to describe Israel's ancient kings offered the basic building blocks with which members of this linguistic community constructed their messianic ideologies.[12]

If Novenson is correct, it may be misleading to frame our discussion of ὁ ἅγιος τοῦ θεοῦ around the observation that it "was not a messianic title in Judaism,"[13] since this overlooks the possibility that scripturally literate Jews and Christians were aware that "the holy one" was one way of designating Israel's anointed king (i.e., the Davidic "messiah"). The evidence I will present in this section suggests that there was, in fact, an inherent link between messianic/Davidic anointing and the

---

[10] Matthew V. Novenson, *Christ among the Messiahs: Christ Language in Paul and Messiah Language in Ancient Judaism* (Oxford: Oxford University Press, 2012). On the challenges of defining "messiah" and "messianic" texts with reference to much of the secondary literature, see Gerbern S. Oegema, *The Anointed and His People: Messianic Expectations from the Maccabees to Bar Kochba*, JSPSup 27 (Sheffield: Sheffield Academic, 1998), 21–38.

[11] Novenson, *Christ among the Messiahs*, 174; for the full argument, see 41–63.

[12] Ibid., 52–53.

[13] Hooker, *Gospel according to St Mark*, 64.

appellation "the holy one" in the body of linguistic resources from which Jewish and Christian authors derived their messiah language. My proposal is that this link is, in part, responsible for the application of this title to one particular messiah—Jesus Christ.

"Help comes from the Lord, and from the Holy One of Israel, our king" (Ps 88:19 LXX)

Psalm 89 MT (88 LXX) evinces an inherent link between royal anointing and YHWH's holiness: "I [Yhwh] have *anointed* him [David] with *my holy oil*" (בשמן קדשי משחתיו, 89:21 MT; ἐν ἐλαίῳ ἁγίῳ μου ἔχρισα αὐτόν, 88:21 LXX).[14] While the Jewish Scriptures are replete with references to the Davidic king as YHWH's "anointed" (e.g., 1 Sam 16:13, Pss 2:2, 18:50, 132:10), this verse is the lone instance where the oil used to anoint David is specifically classified as "holy."[15] In fact, the construction "with holy oil" (instrumental ב or ἐν + dative) occurs only in two other places in the Jewish Scriptures (Num 35:25, Sir 45:15)—both with reference to the means of high-priestly consecration.[16]

More importantly, the MT and the LXX differ with respect to the referent of "Holy One of Israel" in verse 19. On the one hand, the MT reads, "for our shield *belongs to* YHWH [כי ליהוה מגננו], and our king *belongs to* the Holy One of Israel [ולקדוש ישראל מלכנו]." Both clauses have the subject in final position (מגננו; מלכנו), and both use a possessive *lamed* to indicate *belonging to* YHWH. On the other hand, the LXX reads, "for help comes from the Lord [ὅτι τοῦ κυρίου ἡ ἀντίλημψις], and from the Holy One of Israel, our king [καὶ τοῦ ἁγίου Ισραηλ βασιλέως ἡμῶν]."[17] The syntax of the LXX dictates that τοῦ ἁγίου Ισραηλ is in apposition to βασιλέως ἡμῶν, implying that David is the Holy One of Israel (since βασιλέως cannot function as the subject of the second clause, it is most natural to take ἡ ἀντίλημψις as the subject of both clauses). Some recensions add a copula to clarify this very point:

---

[14] מן שמן קדשי 4QPs^x (4Q98g) 1:3; Hebrew text from Eugene Ulrich, ed., *Psalms–Chronicles*, vol. 3 of *The Biblical Qumran Scrolls: Transcriptions and Textual Variants*, VTSup 134 (Leiden: Brill, 2013), 652–53.

[15] I discuss additional references to David's anointing by holy oil in a later section.

[16] In Priestly literature "holy anointing oil" (שמן משחת־קדש) is used for the consecration of the sancta (e.g., Exod 30:25, 31; 37:29; 38:25), and oil is frequently used to consecrate (high) priests (e.g., Lev 21:10). The specific expression in Ps 89:21 MT//88:21 LXX is rare, however.

[17] Even if one assumes a *Vorlage* equivalent to the MT, there is not enough evidence to detect any recognizable pattern in how the translator renders possessive *lamed*s: (1) לך שמים אף־לך ארץ is rendered σοί [possessive dative] εἰσιν οἱ οὐρανοί καὶ σή [predicate adjective] ἐστιν ἡ γῆ (v. 12); (2) לך זרוע עם־גבורה is rendered σός [predicate adjective] ὁ βραχίων μετὰ δυναστείας (v. 14). The translator's decision to render the possessive *lamed* with a genitive is unique to v. 19 and, whatever the intent, opens the LXX to a different reading from the MT.

sanctus Israel est rex noster.[18] This reading is entirely coherent with the wider context of the psalm: (1) YHWH anoints David with "my holy oil" (ἐν ἐλαίῳ ἁγίῳ μου ἔχρισα αὐτόν, v. 21); (2) YHWH's hand will *help* David (συναντιλήμψεται αὐτῷ, v. 22); and (3) David will cry out to YHWH, "You are my father, my God, and the *helper* of my salvation" (ἀντιλήμπτωρ τῆς σωτηρίας μου, v. 27).[19] Thus, while the underlying message of the LXX remains the same as that of the MT—Israel's help comes from YHWH via YHWH's messiah—the LXX suggests that David is the Holy One of Israel precisely because he is YHWH's messiah.

This shift in referent, while inconsequential for the overall meaning of Ps 88 LXX, has the potential to be very significant for our understanding of ὁ ἅγιος τοῦ θεοῦ in the New Testament. First, although it is clear that none of the earliest Christian writers explicitly cites Ps 88 LXX, there is good evidence that it was an important linguistic resource from which they drew their messianic language.[20] Second, there are a number of places in Mark's Gospel where the language the evangelist uses to describe Jesus "trades on a set of descriptions … similar to those found in the psalm."[21] These are as follows: (1) David's anointing is correlated with his receipt of YHWH's *strength* (Ps 88:20–21 LXX); God's Spirit comes upon Jesus to empower him as ὁ ἰσχυρότερος ("the Stronger One," Mark 1:7–11, 3:23–28);[22] (2) YHWH delegates his cosmic power over the sea to David (88:26 LXX)—the same power YHWH displayed when he slew Yam and Rahab at the *Chaoskampf* (88:10–11 LXX);[23] Jesus exercises the cosmic authority he received from God to rebuke the

---

[18] Bo and Sa are listed in Alfred Rahlfs, ed., *Septuaginta: Psalmi cum Odis*, Vetus Testamentum Graecum 10 (Göttingen: Vandenhoeck & Ruprecht, 1979), 234.

[19] The final clause is missing in 4QPs^x.

[20] By my count, NA^{28} lists twenty-six possible allusions to Ps 89 (88 LXX). On the use of Ps 88 LXX in the New Testament, see esp. Donald Juel, *Messianic Exegesis: Christological Interpretation of the Old Testament in Early Christianity* (Philadelphia: Fortress, 1988), 104–10; Knut M. Heim, "The (God-)Forsaken King of Ps 89: A Historical and Intertexual Enquiry," in *King and Messiah in Israel and the Ancient Near East: Proceedings of the Oxford Old Testament Seminar*, ed. John Day, JSOTSup 270 (Sheffield: Sheffield Academic, 1998), 296–322; Margaret Daly-Denton, *David in the Fourth Gospel: The Johannine Reception of the Psalms*, AGJU 47 (Leiden: Brill, 2000), 245–53; Richard B. Hays, *The Conversion of the Imagination: Paul as Interpreter of Israel's Scriptures* (Grand Rapids: Eerdmans, 2005), 110–11. Although Ps 89 (88 LXX) is less frequent in Jewish messianic texts, there is at least one clear allusion to it in Pss. Sol. 17:4.

[21] J. R. Daniel Kirk and Steve L. Young, "'I Will Set His Hand to the Sea': Psalm 88:26 LXX and Christology in Mark," *JBL* 133 (2014): 333–40, here 338.

[22] Adela Yarbro Collins notes that the "designation of Jesus [as ὁ ἰσχυρότερος] evokes connotations of the divine warrior and his (royal) messiah or other agent in battle" (*Mark: A Commentary*, Hermeneia [Minneapolis: Fortress, 2007], 233).

[23] According to J.-B. Dumortier, "le roi, véritable lieu-tenant de Yahvé sur terre, possède une puissance directement proportionnelle à la puissance divine" ("Un rituel d'intronisation: Le Ps. LXXXIX 2–38," *VT* 22 [1972]: 176–96, here 187); and also, "Yahvé, vainqueur des forces du Chaos … délègue sa domination cosmique à son élu; le roi deviant ainsi le véritable garant de l'order du monde et de sa stabilité toujours menacé" (188). In fact, Dumortier's description of the Davidic

wind and the sea (Mark 4:35–41, 6:45–52);[24] (3) David is described as YHWH's δοῦλος (Ps 88:4, 21, 40, 51 LXX); Jesus's self-giving life and death embody the position of a δοῦλος (Mark 10:44–45); (4) David cries out to YHWH, "You are my Father (πατήρ μου εἶ σύ), my God, and the helper of my salvation!" (Ps 88:27 LXX); at his most vulnerable moment Jesus cries out "Abba, Father" (ἀββὰ ὁ πατήρ, Mark 14:36); [25] and (5) Ps 88 LXX closes with YHWH's messiah (ὁ χριστός σου) being mocked by his enemies (ὀνειδίζειν, 88:52) and pleading with YHWH for deliverance; while Jesus is hanging on the cross he is mocked (ὀνειδίζειν, Mark 15:32) and cries out to God (15:34).[26] Though these points of resonance do not demonstrate—indeed cannot demonstrate—that the evangelist had access to a text form of the psalm in agreement with LXX manuscripts at verse 19, they do open up the distinct possibility that the evangelist had engaged with the psalm and, therefore, that he may have encountered a text describing the Davidic "messiah" as "the *Holy One* of Israel."

"Behold now is this the holy one, the anointed of the Lord?" (LAB 59:2)

In Pseudo-Philo's retelling of 1 Sam 16:6–13, Samuel sets his eye on Eliab, Jesse's firstborn, and inquires, "Behold now is this the holy one, *the anointed of the Lord*?" (sanctus *christus Domini*, LAB 59:2).[27] Scholars propose a number of source

---

king in Ps 89 is remarkably similar to what Joel Marcus says about Jesus at this point in Mark's Gospel (*Mark 1–8*, 338).

[24] So Kirk and Young, "'I Will Set His Hand to the Sea,'" 335–36. Their case is strengthened when we realize that other royal figures in antiquity (e.g., Caesar) claimed to exercise divine authority over the sea. On this point, see Rick Strelan, "A Greater than Caesar: Storm Stories in Lucan and Mark," *ZNW* 91 (2000): 166–79.

[25] Jesus's *Abba* prayer is unique to Mark's Gospel (cf. Gal 4:5, Rom 8:15, Heb 5:7). Joachim Jeremias famously attributed ἀββὰ ὁ πατήρ to Jesus's address of God as "my Father" (*Abba: Studien zur neutestamentlichen Theologie und Zeitgeschichte* [Göttingen: Vandenhoeck & Ruprecht, 1966], 1–67). Although James Barr largely dismantled Jeremias's case, he acknowledged that the ambiguity of *abba* "in its common vocative function" allowed it to signify "my father" ("'Abbā Isn't 'Daddy,'" in *Bible and Interpretation: The Collected Essays of James Barr*, ed. John Barton, 3 vols. [Oxford: Oxford University Press, 2013], 262–80, here 273). Further, while we now know that the address "my father" was not as rare in Palestinian Judaism as Jeremias once thought (see, e.g., Eileen M. Schuller, "The Psalm of 4Q372 1 within the Context of Second Temple Prayer," *CBQ* 54 [1992]: 67–79), this does not necessarily detract from the possibility that some early Christians noticed the connection between Jesus's *Abba* prayer and the Davidic king's invocation in Ps 88:27 LXX.

[26] Jesus's words from the cross are a citation of the opening of Ps 22. Nevertheless, Juel is likely correct that early Christians were reading Ps 89 (88) alongside other psalms that depict the messiah's suffering (e.g., Pss 22, 31, and 69) (*Messianic Exegesis*, 110).

[27] Daniel J. Harrington dates LAB to the mid-first century CE and argues that the Latin text—which is based on a Greek *Vorlage*—ultimately derives from a Semitic *Vorlage* ("The

texts for this verse, but none of the texts provides a direct connection to *sanctus*.[28] It is tempting to speculate that *sanctus* derives from the tradition that the king is anointed with holy oil (cf. Ps 89:21; 11QPs[a] XXVIII, 11; Josephus, *Ant.* 6.157), but one cannot be sure. What is important for our purposes is simply that LAB *assumes* a direct link between *christus* and *sanctus*, namely, that as with Ps 88 LXX "holy one" designates YHWH's messiah.

In addition, Pseudo-Philo manifests a reading strategy for the material subsequent to David's election in 1 Samuel that may shed some light on certain features in Mark. First, the immediate context of LAB links David's status as *sanctus christus Domini* with angelic assistance and antagonism from "beasts": directly after his anointing (LAB 59:3), David bursts into psalmnic praise (*psallere psalmum*), "[God] has delivered me to his angels and to his guardians that they should guard me" (LAB 59:4); while he is still singing he is attacked by "wild beasts" and delivered by God (presumably through angelic mediation; LAB 59:5) in a scene that *anticipates* his triumph over Goliath (LAB 61). In Mark, Jesus is (1) anointed by the Holy Spirit (Mark 1:10–11), (2) immediately launched into a conflict with "beasts" (Mark 1:13), where he (3) receives angelic protection, and (4) emerges victorious in *anticipation* of his victory over Satan.[29] Second, as *sanctus christus Domini*—the recipient of the Lord's spirit (cf. 1 Sam 16:13)—David possesses knowledge of the origin of evil (unclean) spirits (LAB 60:1–3) and predicts a time when "one born from my loins will rule over you."[30] It may be no accident, then, that Jesus *Christ* (1:1)—a

---

Original Language of Pseudo-Philo's *Liber Antiquitatum Biblicarum*," *HTR* 63 [1970]: 503–14). I follow Harrington's English translation throughout, including his italics, which are intended to signal "where the text agrees with a recognizable ancient biblical text (the MT, LXX, Samaritan Pentateuch, etc.)" ("Pseudo-Philo [First Century A.D.]," *OTP* 2:297–378, here 303). The Latin text, including italics, follows Pseudo-Philo, *Les Antiquités Bibliques*, ed. Daniel J. Harrington, trans. Jacques Cazeaux, commentary by Charles Perrot and Pierre-Maurice Bogaert, 2 vols., SC 229, 230 (Paris: Cerf, 1976). Also note that, in distinction to Harrington et al., Howard Jacobson takes *sanctus* adjectivally—"the holy anointed of the Lord" (*A Commentary on Pseudo-Philo's Liber Antiquitatum Biblicarum: With Latin Text and English Translation*, 2 vols., AGJU 31 [Leiden: Brill, 1996], 1:187).

[28] See Jacobson, *Commentary*, 2:1166. In the commentary volume, Perrot and Bogaert list Mark 1:24, Luke 4:34, and John 6:69 as the closest linguistic parallels (*Les Antiquités Bibliques*, 2:230).

[29] Commentators differ as to whether Jesus's "victory" in the wilderness temptation represents the decisive undoing of Satan's power, so that Jesus's exorcisms in the remainder of the Gospel amount to a mere "mop-up" operation (so Ernest Best, *The Temptation and the Passion: The Markan Soteriology*, SNTSMS 2 [Cambridge: Cambridge University Press, 1965], 13–15) or whether it represents but the beginning of an ongoing conflict (so Robinson, *Problem of History*, 33–42). More recently, a very convincing case for the latter position has been presented by Elizabeth Shively, *Apocalytic Imagination in the Gospel of Mark: The Literary and Theological Role of Mark 3:22–30*, BZNW 189 (Berlin: de Gruyter, 2012).

[30] LAB is one of the many traditions that portray David as an adroit exorcist (e.g., 11QApPs[a] V, 4; VI, 3–14; 11QPs[a] XXVII, 9–10; Josephus, *Ant.* 6.166–169; y. Šabb. 6:8b; b. Šebu. 15b; y. ʿErub.

"son of David" (10:47)—begins his public ministry with an *exorcism* as "the Holy One of God" (1:21–28).

"Deliver your holy one from destruction!"
(Ps 152:4 [5 Apoc. Syr. Ps. 4])

The superscription in Ps 152 references the same tradition as LAB 59:5 (1 Sam 17:34–37).[31] At the psalm's midpoint, David cries out, "Spare, O Lord, your *elect one*, and deliver your *holy one* from destruction" (Ps 152:4);[32] and, at its conclusion, he cries out, "Quickly, O Adonai, send from your presence a redeemer; lift me up from the gaping abyss which is seeking to enclose me in its depths" (Ps 152:6). The psalm agrees with Pseudo-Philo in two important ways that go beyond 1 Sam 17:34–36: (1) both texts classify the lion and the bear/wolf as "beasts" (LAB 59:5, Ps 152:5), and (2) both expect that God's holy one will receive angelic assistance when attacked by them (LAB 59:4, Ps 152:6). Finally, the collocation of "elect one" and "holy one" (Ps 152:4), in conjunction with the temporal marker vis-à-vis the psalm's superscription (i.e., *after* David became YHWH's messiah; 1 Sam 16:13), suggests the same logic as Ps 88 LXX and LAB: "holy one" is an alternative way of designating the messiah.

"... and he redeemed his holy one from destruction"
(Ps 153:3 [5 Apoc. Syr. Ps. 5])

Psalm 153 constitutes David's response to God's answering his plea in Ps 152. He celebrates, "For he [God] delivered the physical life of his *elect one* from the hands of death; and he redeemed his *holy one* from destruction" (153:3).[33] David

---

10:26c). Commentators are divided as to whether David's prophecy that his "son" will rule over the evil spirits is a reference to Solomon or to a messianic deliverer (so Jacobson, *Commentary*, 2:1180). The former seems probable (with Harrington, *OTP* 2:373 n. e).

[31] On the basis of its style and its inclusion in a collection with other Syriac psalms whose Hebrew *Vorlagen* have been discovered at Qumran, James H. Charlesworth concludes that "it was probably composed by a Palestinian Jew during the Hellenistic period" ("More Psalms of David [Third Century B.C.–First Century A.D.]," *OTP* 2:609–25, here 615); see also Martin Noth's foundational study, "Die fünf überlieferten apokryphen Psalmen," *ZAW* 48 (1930): 1–23. Alternatively, Patrick W. Skehan argues that the author of Ps 152 was a Nestorian Christian writing in Syriac ("Again the Syriac Apocryphal Psalms," *CBQ* 38 [1976]: 143–58, here 154–55). If Skehan is correct, then Ps 152 indicates that a Syrian Christian author recognized the Davidic "holy one" as a type of the Christ.

[32] Trans. Charlesworth, *OTP* 2:616 (my emphasis). The invocation "rescue your holy one [ḥasāk] from destruction" reflects the language of Psalm 16:10 Peshitta (Skehan, "Again the Syriac Apocryphal Psalms," 153). The author of Luke-Acts claims that Jesus Christ, rather than David, is "the holy one" (ὁ ὅσιος) spoken of in Ps 15:10 LXX (cf. Acts 2:27, 31; 13:35).

[33] Trans. Charlesworth, *OTP* 2:617(my emphasis). The issues with dating Ps 153 are *mutatis mutandis* the same as with Ps 152 (see n. 31 above).

recounts further, "I almost became two parts by two beasts. However, he sent his angel and closed from me the gaping mouths; and redeemed my life from destruction" (153:4b–5). Thus, in agreement with LAB 59:4–5 and Ps 152, Ps 153 transmits a tradition that David, God's "holy one," received angelic assistance when he was attacked by beasts (cf. 1 Sam 17:34–37). Moreover, as in Ps 152, the collocation of "elect one" and "holy one" implies that David is God's messiah.

YHWH's Messiah via "Holy Oil"

Novenson notes that "Jewish readers around the turn of the era will have understood χριστός to signify an anointed person, even if no one had anointed a king or priest for centuries, because they were familiar with the scriptures in Greek."[34] Additionally, we should note that some members of this linguistic community were equally aware that the medium used to conduct this ceremony was *holy oil*.[35] Beyond the singular mention in the MT and LXX (Ps 89:21 MT [88:21 LXX]), the Hebrew version of Ps 151 presents David's first-person account of his anointing as follows: "He [God] sent his prophet to *anoint me* [למושחני], Samuel to make me great.... YHWH God did not choose them [i.e., David's brothers] but sent them to fetch me from behind the flock and *anointed me with holy oil* [וימשחני בשמן הקודש], and made me leader of his people and ruler over the sons of his covenant" (11QPs[a] XXVIII, 7, 10–12).[36] Josephus, too, knows that Israel's kings were anointed with holy oil at the beginning of their reign. On four occasions in *Jewish Antiquities* he describes the unction used to anoint a new king as τὸ ἅγιον ἔλαιον (*Ant.* 6.83, 157; 7.355; 9.106). Most significant for our purposes, Josephus reports that Samuel took τὸ ἅγιον ἔλαιον to the city of Bethlehem (*Ant.* 6.157) and, later, "in the sight of David, he [Samuel] took the oil and anointed him [David] [τὸ ἔλαιον ἀλείφει τ' αὐτόν] and spoke softly into his ear, explaining that God had chosen him to be king" [σημαίνει τοῦθ' ὅτι βασιλεύειν αὐτὸν ὁ θεὸς ᾕρηται]" (*Ant.* 6.165). Thus, while the archaic practice of symbolically demarcating Israel's new king as YHWH's "holy one" through the medium of holy oil had long since passed, we find traces of its remembrance in several Jewish texts roughly contemporaneous with Mark's Gospel.

Awareness of the ancient practice that Israel's kings were made YHWH's messiah by means of holy oil offers an intriguing conceptual parallel to the early

---

[34] Novenson, *Christ among the Messiahs*, 51.

[35] For a brief discussion of the ceremony used to consecrate the king in ancient Israel, see Sigmund Mowinckel, *He That Cometh: The Messiah Concept in the Old Testament and Later Judaism*, trans. G. W. Anderson (New York: Abingdon, 1954; repr., Biblical Resource Series, Grand Rapids: Eerdmans, 2005), 63–64.

[36] Hebrew text from J. A. Sanders, ed., *The Psalms Scroll of Qumran Cave 11: 11QPs[a]*, DJD IV [Oxford: Clarendon, 1965]); the LXX reads "with anointing oil" (τῷ ἐλαίῳ τῆς χρίσεως αὐτοῦ, Ps 151:4 LXX), followed by the Syriac version.

Christian notion that Jesus of Nazareth was appointed God's messiah via the Holy Spirit (e.g., Mark 1:10–11). That is, just as holy oil demarcated the Davidic king as "the holy one," so too the Holy Spirit established Jesus of Nazareth as "the Holy One of God."[37]

Summary

This investigation yields a number of results that could prove fruitful for our understanding of ὁ ἅγιος τοῦ θεοῦ in Mark 1:24 and, potentially, for its other two occurrences in the New Testament (Luke 4:34, John 6:69). First, two texts (Ps 88:19 LXX; LAB 59:2) link "messiah" (χριστός; christus) with "holy one" (ὁ ἅγιος; sanctus), and two more clearly operate under the same assumption ("holy one" and "elect one," Pss 152:4, 153:3). In every instance, the relationship between the two concepts is the same: David is "the holy one" (ὁ ἅγιος/sanctus) because he is YHWH's "messiah" (χριστός/christus). Second, in the literature produced by Mark's linguistic community, we find vestiges of the archaic tradition that Israel's kings were anointed with holy oil. These remnants offer further evidence that the link between messianic anointing and YHWH's holiness was not lost on first-century readers of the Scriptures. Third, while Mark's knowledge of the traditions assessed in this section must remain an open question, it is striking that the designation "the holy one" tends to occur in places that share strong points of resonance with the Second Gospel. For example, three of the four texts retell the events in 1 Sam 16–17, such that, subsequent to his anointing, David—God's "holy one"—received angelic assistance when he was attacked by wild "beasts" (cf. Mark 1:9–13). To this LAB adds that *sanctus christus Domini*—David and, after him, a "son of David"—is also an exorcist par excellence. I now turn to consider how this material might enhance our reading of Mark.

II. Ὁ ἅγιος τοῦ θεοῦ as a Messianic Title in Mark

In this section, I address the following points. First, I explore how the texts examined in the previous section enhance our understanding of the connection between Jesus's baptism and the ensuing wilderness temptation (1:9–13). Second, I demonstrate that these same texts provide a compelling explanation for the connection between the baptism–temptation sequence (1:9–13) and Jesus's first act of public ministry (1:21–28). Finally, I bring both points into conversation with schol-

---

[37] That the early Christians were aware of and played with the metaphorical link between oil and Spirit is highlighted, in particular, by the second-century church father Theophilus of Antioch: "Therefore for this reason we are called 'Christians,' because we are 'christened' with the oil of God" (*Autol.* 1.12); cited from Novenson, *Christ among the Messiahs*, 148.

ars who interpret the title "son of David" in Mark 10:47–48 in light of Solomon-as-exorcist traditions.

The Baptism–Temptation Sequence (Mark 1:9–13)

In the opening line of the Gospel, Mark informs the audience that he sets out to narrate "the good news of Jesus Christ [the Son of God]" (Mark 1:1).[38] The following verses offer evidence of this designation: the composite citation of Exod 23:20//Mal 3:1 and Isa 40:3 introduces the *dramatis personae* (1:2–3); the Baptizer emerges as a "new Elijah" to prepare the "way of the Lord" (1:4–8); and Jesus's baptism by John leads to his anointing by the Spirit and concomitant commissioning by the voice from heaven.[39] The audience thus knows that Jesus of Nazareth is ὁ χριστός because he has been anointed by the πνεῦμα ἅγιον (1:9–11).[40] Matters become more convoluted, however, when τὸ πνεῦμα *immediately* ejects the messiah into the wilderness to be tempted by Satan (1:12), and the situation is complicated further when the evangelist adds the allusive comment "and he [Jesus] was *with the beasts* (καὶ ἦν μετὰ τῶν θηρίων) and *angels were attending him*" (καὶ οἱ ἄγγελοι διηκόνουν αὐτῷ, Mark 1:13). Given the enigmatic nature of verse 13, it is not surprising that scholars have proposed a range of explanations: Jesus is identified as (1) the new Adam, (2) the new Israel, (3) the messiah, (4) the paradigmatic righteous sufferer, and so forth.[41] To varying degrees, each of these ideas is plausible and would

---

[38] There remains significant debate over whether υἱοῦ θεοῦ belongs in the "original" reading of Mark 1:1; see Peter Head, "A Text-Critical Study of Mark 1.1: 'The Beginning of the Gospel of Jesus Christ,'" *NTS* 37 (1991): 621–29; Bart D. Ehrman, *The Orthodox Corruption of Scripture: The Effect of Early Christological Controversies on the Text of the New Testament* (New York: Oxford University Press, 1993) 72–75; Tommy Wasserman, "The 'Son of God' Was in the Beginning (Mark 1:1)," *JTS* 62 (2011): 20–50; Max Botner, "The Role of Transcriptional Probability in the Recent Text-Critical Debate on Mark 1:1," *CBQ* 77 (2015): 467–80.

[39] By having Jesus participate in the same "baptism of repentance" with which John baptized "all Israel" (cf. Mark 1:4–5), Mark locates Jesus of Nazareth within the community of repentant-Israel-awaiting-restoration, so as to align the messiah's anointing with the eschatological turning point in Israel's story: the Spirit that anoints Jesus for ministry is the *same* Spirit that God promised to pour out on Israel at the time of restoration (Mark 1:10, echoing Isa 63:19 [64:1 LXX]).

[40] In keeping with the majority of scholars, I read the dual allusion to Ps 2:7 and Isa 42:1 as an indication that Jesus is being commissioned as Israel's messiah; see Hans-Jörg Steichele, *Der leidende Sohn Gottes: Eine Untersuchung einiger alttestamentlicher Motive in der Christologie des Markusevangeliums*, BU 14 (Regensburg: Pustet, 1980), 135–61; Kingsbury, *Christology of Mark's Gospel*, 60–68; Marcus, *Way of the Lord*, 59–79; Donald Juel, "The Origin of Mark's Christology," in *The Messiah: Developments in Earliest Judaism and Christianity; The First Princeton Symposium on Judaism and Christian Origins*, ed. James H. Charlesworth (Minneapolis: Fortress, 1992), 449–60; Yarbro Collins, *Mark*, 149–51.

[41] Such multivalence is not surprising in light of the overlapping and interlocking of these ideas in Second Temple literature. For an interpretation of Jesus as the new Adam, see Joel Marcus, "Son of Man as Son of Adam," *RB* 110 (2003): 38–61; as the new Israel, see Ulrich W. Mauser,

likely be grasped by some of Mark's audience. My focus, however, is limited to augmenting one current proposal for why the evangelist fuses such a tight link between Jesus's *messianic anointing* and subsequent *conflict* with Satan and "beasts" in the wilderness.

Psalm 91 features as the primary "messianic" text scholars adduce to elucidate Jesus's temptation.[42] The relevant verses read as follows, "For he [God] will command *his angels* concerning you *to guard you* in all your ways. On their hands *they will bear you up*, so that you will not dash your foot against a stone. You will tread on the *lion* and the adder (asp and the basilisk in LXX), the *young lion* and the serpent (lion and the serpent in LXX) you will trample under foot" (91:11–13 MT [90:11–13 LXX]). This approach is influenced by the fact that both Matthew and Luke assume that the messiah is the referent of "you" in the psalm (Matt 4:5–7, Luke 4:10–11). The plausibility of a Markan allusion, however, does not rest on this point alone. First, although Ps 91 lacks a superscription in the MT, the LXX adds "a song of praise by David" (αἶνος ᾠδῆς τῷ Δαυιδ, Ps 90:1 LXX).[43] Second, the version of Ps 91 discovered in Cave 11 near Qumran has been plausibly reconstructed as being attributed to David (11QApPs VI, 2).[44] That this psalm forms the end of a collection used for performing exorcisms may be significant for Mark, since the "beasts" in verse 13 likely represent demons. Third, Émile Puech suggests that this collection of psalms invites the exorcist to embody the role of "Solomon, David's son."[45] If Puech is correct and if Ps 91, in particular, evoked the role "Solomon, son of David," this enhances the possibility that another writer, for example, Mark,

---

Christ in the Wilderness: The Wilderness Theme in the Second Gospel and Its Basis in the Biblical Tradition, SBT 39 (London: SCM, 1963); as the messianic son of God in Ps 2, see Marcus, *Way of the Lord*, 66–69; as the righteous sufferer, see Susan R. Garrett, *The Temptations of Jesus in Mark's Gospel* (Grand Rapids: Eerdmans, 1998), 55–68.

[42] See esp. Jeffrey B. Gibson, "Jesus' Wilderness Temptation according to Mark," *JSNT* 53 (1994): 4–43, here 21–23.

[43] Stephen P. Ahearne-Kroll shows that Mark, like many other New Testament authors, consistently reads psalms with Davidic superscriptions messianically (*The Psalms of Lament in Mark's Passion: Jesus' Davidic Suffering*, SNTSMS 142 [Cambridge: Cambridge University Press, 2007]).

[44] In the preceding column directly following a *vacat*, לדויד indicates the beginning of a Davidic psalm (11QApPsᵃ V, 4); Hebrew text in Florentino García Martínez, Eibert J. C. Tigchelaar, and A. S. van der Woude, eds., *Qumran Cave 11.2: 11Q2–18, 11Q20–31*, DJD XXIII (Oxford: Clarendon, 1998), 198, 202–3.

[45] Puech writes, "Dans la mesure où il été possible d'en restaurer le début et la fin, le deuxième Psaume de 11Q11 appartiendrait à un Psaume davidique et non salomonien, invitant l'exorciste à practiquer l'incantation de David comme le fit Salomon, son fils, qui devint l'exorciste par excellance, ainsi qu'il est bien connu de la tradition ancienne" ("Le paumes davidiques du rituel d'exorcisme (11Q11)," in *Sapiential, Liturgical and Poetical Texts from Qumran: Proceedings of the Third Meeting of the International Organization for Qumran Studies, Oslo, 1998*, ed. Daniel K Falk, Florentino García Martínez, and Eileen M. Schuller, STDJ 35 [Leiden: Brill, 2000], 160–81, here 180).

could apply the text to another "son of David." (To this end, it is noteworthy that Tg. Ps 91 reads vv. 10–13 as a promise God makes to Solomon.)

In addition to Psalm 91, three of the texts I examined in the previous section (LAB 59; Pss 152, 153) also juxtapose angelic protection from wild beasts—the foremost of which is a lion. These texts go beyond the psalm, however, in that they explicitly mention David and assume, whether explicitly or implicitly, that David receives angelic protection from hostile beasts because he is God's messiah. In the case of LAB 59:5, in particular, the angelic protection David receives from beasts occurs *immediately* after he becomes *sanctus christus Domini* (LAB 59:2). A similar logic may be at work in Mark. The Baptist prophesies that the one who comes after him will be a mighty warrior—ὁ ἰσχυρότερος. Jesus then comes to the Baptist (1:9), is anointed God's messiah by the Holy Spirit (1:10–11), and *immediately* faces hostility from God's enemies—Satan and beasts. Just as David received angelic protection because he was *sanctus christus Domini*, so too God's messiah, Jesus, receives assistance from a heavenly entourage and registers a victory that forecasts his ultimate triumph over Satan and demons. Through this process, moreover, the demons come to learn who Jesus of Nazareth truly is—they know that he is the messiah who has been anointed with God's holy unction, the Holy Spirit, and thus they also know that he is the Holy One of God (Ps 88:19 LXX, LAB 59:2, Pss 152:4, 153:3).

"Jesus of Nazareth ... I know who you are!"

A number of scholars recognize the strong intratextual links between the inauguration of Jesus's public ministry at the Capernaum synagogue (Mark 1:21–28) and the themes introduced in the baptism–temptation sequence (1:9–13).[46] Many draw attention to the clear connection, on the one hand, between ὁ ἅγιος τοῦ θεοῦ (1:24) and Jesus's endowment with the Holy Spirit (1:10) and, on the other, between ὁ ἅγιος τοῦ θεοῦ and the more renowned title ὁ υἱὸς τοῦ θεοῦ (e.g., 3:11). Yet no one has explained the logic behind these links. For example, recognition that ὁ ἅγιος τοῦ θεοῦ anticipates ὁ υἱὸς τοῦ θεοῦ led R. T. France to conclude that "the use of ἅγιος here is therefore surprising."[47] If one looks back to Jesus's baptism, however, one may arrive at a conclusion along the lines of Étienne Trocmé that "il y a simplement un contraste voulu entre *le sale esprit* et *le Saint de Dieu*."[48] In other words, the lone function of ὁ ἅγιος τοῦ θεοῦ is to accentuate the difference between the demon's impurity (ἀκάθαρτος) and Jesus's holiness (ἅγιος).

The texts examined in this study suggest that there may be more to the demon's address in Mark 1:24: "What have you to do with us, Jesus of Nazareth? Have you

---

[46] See Robinson, *Problem of History*, 35–38; Marcus, *Mark 1–8*, 190–95; Shively, *Apocalyptic Imagination*, 154–66.

[47] France, *Gospel of Mark*, 104.

[48] Étienne Trocmé, *L'Évangile selon Saint Marc*, CNT 2 (Geneva: Labor et Fides, 2000), 52 (my emphasis).

come to destroy us? I know who you are, the Holy One of God" (τί ἡμῖν καὶ σοί, Ἰησοῦ Ναζαρηνέ; ἦλθες ἀπολέσαι ἡμᾶς; οἶδά σε τίς εἶ, ὁ ἅγιος τοῦ θεοῦ). As we have seen, David's status as ὁ ἅγιος/*sanctus* is the *direct result* of his being made χριστός/*christus*. This suggests the possibility that the *primary* function of ὁ ἅγιος τοῦ θεοῦ is not simply to contrast Jesus with a malevolent spirit that is ἀκάθαρτος but rather to drive home the point that Jesus is ὁ χριστός, christened by πνεῦμα ἅγιον. This may also explain, at least in part, the close association between ὁ ἅγιος τοῦ θεοῦ and ὁ υἱὸς τοῦ θεοῦ, namely, that both titles are initially encountered in relation to God's anointing Jesus ἐν πνεύματι ἁγίῳ (1:10–11). Finally, I suggest that the collocation of the demon's exclamation, "I know who you are, the Holy One of God" (οἶδά σε τίς εἶ, ὁ ἅγιος τοῦ θεοῦ), with the exigent question, "Have you come to destroy us?" (ἦλθες ἀπολέσαι ἡμᾶς;), indicates the demon's awareness that Jesus's baptism marks the ultimate demise of demonic entities: the Holy Spirit is the strength of God (1:7, 3:37) at work in the messiah, who has inaugurated "eschatological holy war" against Satan and demons.[49]

"Son of David" in Mark 10:47–48: Exorcist versus Messiah, or Exorcist and Messiah?

In commenting on the opening line of the Testament of Solomon, Dennis Duling posits that "the address 'Son of David' could be a link between the magical tradition about Solomon and the activity of Jesus as exorcist and healer."[50] Duling's suggestion has been taken up by a number of scholars who argue that blind Bartimaeus's cry, "Son of David, Jesus, have mercy on me!" (υἱὲ Δαυὶδ Ἰησοῦ, ἐλέησόν με, Mark 10:47), indicates that Jesus is an exorcist-healer son of David, *not* a messianic son of David.[51] The results of my study, however, suggest that this group is only partly right.

---

[49] So also Marcus, *Mark 1–8*, 195.

[50] Dennis Duling, "Testament of Solomon (First to Third Century A.D.)," *OTP* 1:935–88, here 960; see also his important study "Solomon, Exorcism, and the Son of David," *HTR* (1975): 235–52.

[51] See Bruce D. Chilton, "Jesus *ben David*: Reflections on the *Davidssohnfrage*," *JSNT* 14 (1982): 88–112; James H. Charlesworth, "The Son of David: Solomon and Jesus (Mark 10.47)," in *The New Testament and Hellenistic Judaism*, ed. Peder Borgen and Søren Giversen (Peabody, MA: Hendrickson, 1995), 72–87; S. H. Smith, "The Function of the Son of David Tradition in Mark's Gospel," *NTS* 42 (1996): 523–39; Ahearne-Kroll, *Psalms of Lament*, 138–44. Another group of important studies does pay attention to the messianic overtones in 10:46–52 but neither recognizes any resonance with Solomon-as-exorcist traditions nor provides a coherent account of how the messianic resonances of "son of David" work with the preceding material; see, e.g., Christoph Burger, *Jesus als Davidssohn: Eine traditionsgeschichtliche Untersuchung*, FRLANT 98 (Göttingen: Vandenhoeck & Ruprecht, 1970), 58–70; Vernon K. Robbins, "The Healing of Blind Bartimaeus (10:46–52) in the Marcan Theology," *JBL* 92 (1973): 224–43; and, to some extent, Marcus, *Way of the Lord*, 130–52 (though Marcus does correct himself in his commentary [*Mark 8–16: A New*

On the one hand, the argument that Mark's audience would hear resonances with Davidic-Solomonic exorcistic traditions in the cry "Son of David" is a perfectly defensible position. In LAB David is both *sanctus christus Domini* (59:2) and the progenitor of a "son" who will rule over demons (60:3). This point of connection becomes even more intriguing when we recognize that the evangelist brackets Jesus's public ministry outside of Jerusalem (1:21–10:52) with two titles: ὁ ἅγιος τοῦ θεοῦ (1:24) and υἱὸς Δαυίδ (10:47–48). These titles are also linked by the designation "Nazarene," which, as Broadhead shows, has been strategically located at various points throughout the Gospel.[52] Inside the frame of 1:9 and 16:6, Jesus is identified by his narrative point of origin in only three other places: (1) at the inauguration of his public ministry (1:24), (2) on his approach to Jerusalem (10:47), and (3) at "Peter's trial" (14:66–72).[53] In every instance where the designation "Nazarene" occurs, it is closely accompanied by information that is central to the audience's perception of Jesus's identity: Jesus is (1) the son of God (1:9–11), (2) the *holy one of God* (1:24), (3) the *son of David* (10:47–48), (4) the messiah son of God and son of Man (14:61–62), and (5) the crucified one who was raised by God (16:6).[54] The combined evidence that ὁ ἅγιος τοῦ θεοῦ (1) resonates with the Davidic-Solomonic exorcistic traditions, (2) occurs at the beginning of Jesus's public ministry *in the context of an exorcism*, and (3) appears to be intentionally linked with υἱὸς Δαυίδ provides additional support for Duling's hypothesis.

Scholars who build on Duling's work, however, tend to assume, incorrectly, that evidence for a Solomon-as-exorcist "son of David" obviates the possibility that Mark's audience would also hear "son of David" as a messianic title.[55] The impetus

---

Translation with Introduction and Commentary, AYB 27A (New Haven: Yale University Press, 2009), 1120]).

[52] Edwin Broadhead, "Jesus the Nazarene: Narrative Strategy and Christological Imagery in the Gospel of Mark," *JSNT* 52 (1993): 3–18.

[53] On the narrative juxtaposing of "Peter's trial" with Jesus's trial, see Donald Juel, *Messiah and Temple: The Trial of Jesus in the Gospel of Mark*, SBLDS 31 (Missoula, MT: Scholars Press, 1997), 67.

[54] I do not have the space to address adequately the arguments scholars propose for why the evangelist *rejects* Jesus's Davidic status. See, e.g., Paul J. Achtemeier, "'And He Followed Him': Miracles and Discipleship in Mark 10:46–50," *Semeia* 11 (1978): 115–45; Elizabeth Struthers Malbon, "The Jesus of Mark and the 'Son of David,'" in *Between Author and Audience in Mark: Narrative, Characterization, Interpretation*, ed. Elizabeth Struthers Malbon, New Testament Monographs 23 (Sheffield: Sheffield Phoenix, 2009), 162–85; Malbon, *Mark's Jesus*, 87–91, 99–101, 159–69. Every argument for why Mark *rejects* the title "Son of David"—including Malbon's narrative analysis—inevitably boils down to the conviction that *Davidssohnfrage* (12:35–37) is the *only* "clear" statement on this topic in the Gospel. To this extent, no recent version of this position has substantially improved upon William Wrede's influential study *Vorträge und Studien* (Tübingen: Mohr Siebeck, 1907), 147–78. The evidence I have provided suggests that Davidic/messianic categories are important to the evangelist's depiction of Jesus of Nazareth and, thus, may be part of a larger argument for why Wrede and others should not be followed on this point.

[55] See, e.g., Chilton, "Jesus *ben David*," 92–97.

behind such a misstep is easily traced back to Duling's study itself, which bifurcates "son of David" into two separate "ideas" that existed in the late Second Temple period (a royal messianic idea, and Solomon-as-exorcist idea). Duling then inquires as to how these two ideas converge or conflict within the history of their transmission.[56] Yet what Duling fails to consider is that Jews and Christians in the late Second Temple period *inherited* a close connection between these two "ideas" within their Scriptures. Indeed, the very same narrative that recounts David becoming YHWH's messiah (ἔχρισεν αὐτόν) and receiving YHWH's spirit (ἐφήλατο πνεῦμα κυρίου ἐπὶ Δαυίδ, 1 Sam 16:13) also presents David as a proto-exorcist (1 Sam 16:14–23).[57] Furthermore, as we have already seen, LAB provides a first-century CE recitation of 1 Sam 16–17 that firmly maintains *both* of these elements. Thus, in my judgment, we have no plausible historical reason for concluding that an exorcist "son of David" is somehow at odds with a messiah "son of David." Rather, the two appear to be inextricably wedded in Mark.

III. Conclusion

The aim of this study has been to rectify the marked absence of messianic traditions in discussions surrounding ὁ ἅγιος τοῦ θεοῦ in New Testament scholarship. The evidence I have adduced makes a plausible case that the designation "the holy one" was among the linguistic resources Jews and Christians had for speaking about an anointed, Davidic king. Thus, I would suggest that ὁ ἅγιος τοῦ θεοῦ functions as a messianic title in Mark and, indeed, in Luke and John because some early Christians were aware of traditions that spoke of the Davidic "messiah" as YHWH's "holy one."

The results of this study may further our understanding of ὁ ἅγιος τοῦ θεοῦ in Luke. Joseph A. Fitzmyer's comments on Luke 4:34 are suggestive: "In the Lucan context Jesus' 'holiness' would have to be explained by his 'sonship' (3:22) and 'anointing' with the Spirit (4:18)."[58] Later, in his second volume, Luke draws a direct connection between God's *servant* David (Δαυὶδ παιδός σου), through whom the Holy Spirit spoke (διὰ πνεύματος ἁγίου, Acts 4:25), and God's *holy servant* Jesus, whom he anointed with the Holy Spirit (τὸν ἅγιον παῖδά σου Ἰησοῦν ὃν ἔχρισας, Acts 4:27). Is it possible that Luke's appropriation of ὁ ἅγιος τοῦ θεοῦ from Mark 1:24 reveals an awareness of the title's messianic resonance? Perhaps the question will be taken up in a further study.

[56] Duling, "Solomon, Exorcism," 250.
[57] So also Yarbro Collins, *Mark*, 66–67.
[58] Fitzmyer, *Gospel according to Luke*, 1:546.

New from Mohr Siebeck

Entangled Worlds: Religious Confluences between East and West in the Roman Empire
The Cults of Isis, Mithras, and Jupiter Dolichenus
Edited by Svenja Nagel, Joachim Friedrich Quack, and Christian Witschel

Did the so-called ›oriental cults‹ form a coherent group? And can they be called ›oriental‹ at all? This collective volume, originating from an interdisciplinary conference at Heidelberg University, answers these questions and deals with their expansion in the Roman Empire, focusing on the three cults of Isis (and Osiris), Mithras and Jupiter Dolichenus.

2017. X, 564 pages (ORA 22).
ISBN 978-3-16-154730-0 cloth
eBook

Herrschaftslegitimation in vorderorientalischen Reichen der Eisenzeit
Hrsg. v. Christoph Levin u. Reinhard Müller

Der Sammelband behandelt Formen und Strategien von Herrschaftslegitimation, die in eisenzeitlichen Königtümern der Levante sowie in Mesopotamien und Ägypten ausgeprägt wurden. Anhand von ikonographischen, textlichen und archäologischen Zeugnissen werden die Grundmuster herausgearbeitet, mit denen in diesen Reichen königliche Herrschaft legitimiert wurde.

2017. XI, 315 pages (ORA 21).
ISBN 978-3-16-154858-1 cloth
eBook

Attilio Mastrocinque
The Mysteries of Mithras
A Different Account

Attilio Mastrocinque explains the mysteries of Mithras in a new way, as a transformation of Mazdean elements into an ideological and religious reading of Augustus' story. The author shows that the character of Mithras played the role of Apollo in favoring Augustus' victory and the birth of the Roman Empire.

2017. 380 pages (est.) (ORA).
ISBN 978-3-16-155112-3 cloth (June)
eBook

Schrift und Material
Praktische Verwendung religiöser Text- und Bildträger als Artefakte im Alten Ägypten
Herausgegeben von Joachim F. Quack und Daniela C. Luft

Texte und Bilder existieren nicht ohne ihr Trägerobjekt. Ihre Verwendbarkeit in unterschiedlichen Kontexten offenbart einen Bedeutungspluralismus, der wieder verstärkt das Individuum in den Fokus rückt. Anhand altägyptischer Quellen werden in diesem Band Grenzen und Chancen archäologischer Rekonstruktion aufgezeigt.

2017. 350 pages (est.) (ORA).
ISBN 978-3-16-155129-1 cloth (August)
eBook

Mohr Siebeck
Tübingen
info@mohr.de
www.mohr.de

Information on Mohr Siebeck eBooks:
www.mohr.de/ebooks

Directly Addressing "Jesus": The Vocative Ἰησοῦ in Luke 23:42

BENJAMIN WILSON
benjamin.wilson@moody.edu
Moody Bible Institute, Chicago, IL 60610

In this article, I examine the use of Jesus's personal name in the penitent criminal's appeal at the crucifixion scene in Luke 23:42. I consider what can be confidently asserted on the basis of the vocative Ἰησοῦ in the criminal's appeal and propose that the use of Jesus's personal name in Luke 23:42 might entail an allusion to the etymology and meaning of that name.

In Luke 23:42, the penitent criminal at the crucifixion scene makes a single plea: "Jesus, remember me when you come into your kingdom." Much attention has been given to the substance of the criminal's entreaty,[1] yet the direct address that precedes the request is equally striking. The criminal does not address Jesus with an honorific title such as "Lord" but rather with Jesus's personal name. What is the significance of this surprisingly personal appeal to Jesus? In this article, I examine the use of the vocative Ἰησοῦ in Luke 23:42, which has yet to receive the

[1] Interpreters tend to focus on the scriptural resonances of the request for remembrance and on the text-critical issue involving the prepositional phrase. The bulk of analysis concerning the broader pericope has understandably centered on Jesus's response to the criminal, "Today you will be with me in paradise." See, e.g., Joseph A. Fitzmyer, "'Today You Shall Be with Me in Paradise' (Luke 23:43)," in *Luke the Theologian: Aspects of His Teaching* (New York: Paulist, 1989), 203–33; Heinz Giesen, "'Noch heute wirst du mit mir im Paradies sein' (Lk 23,43): Zur individuellen Eschatologie im lukanischen Doppelwerk," in *"Licht zur Erleuchtung der Heiden und Herrlichkeit für dein Volk Israel": Studien zum lukanischen Doppelwerk*, ed. Christoph Gregor Müller, BBB 151 (Hamburg: Philo, 2005), 165–75; Pierre Grelot, "Aujourd'hui tu seras avec moi dans le paradis, Luc 23:43," *RB* 74 (1967): 194–214; Ulrike Mittmann-Richert, *Der Sühnetod des Gottesknechts: Jesaja 53 im Lukasevangelium*, WUNT 220 (Tübingen: Mohr Siebeck, 2008), 89–92; Robert H. Smith, "Paradise Today: Luke's Passion Narrative," *CurTM* 3.6 (1976): 328–30; Peter Widdicombe, "The Two Thieves of Luke 23:32–43 in Patristic Exegesis," in *Historica, Biblica, Ascetica et Hagiographica*, vol. 1 of *Studia Patristica: Papers Presented at the Fourteenth International Conference on Patristic Studies Held in Oxford, 2003*, ed. F. Young, M. Edwards, and P. Parvis, StPatr 39 (Leuven: Peeters, 2006), 273–77.

attention it deserves.[2] I begin with what can be confidently asserted regarding the use of the vocative in Luke 23:42, and I will progress to increasingly less certain possibilities of meaning in the criminal's address.

I. Confident Assertions

In the context of the ongoing discourse in Luke 23:39–42, the most obvious function of the vocative Ἰησοῦ in Luke 23:42 is to designate a change of address in the penitent criminal's speech.[3] In verses 40–41, the penitent criminal rebukes the other criminal who has just mocked Jesus: "Do you not fear God, since you are under the same sentence of condemnation? And we indeed justly, for we are receiving the due reward of our deeds; but this man has done nothing wrong." As the criminal then turns to make a request of Jesus in verse 42, it becomes necessary for the narrator to mark the change of address in some way. This is accomplished effectively through the use of the vocative at the beginning of the criminal's appeal: "And he said, 'Jesus, remember me when you come into your kingdom'" (καὶ ἔλεγεν· Ἰησοῦ, μνήσθητί μου ὅταν ἔλθῃς εἰς τὴν βασιλείαν σου). Whereas previously the penitent wrongdoer had been speaking to his fellow criminal, now he speaks to Jesus, and this change of address is introduced to the reader through the vocative Ἰησοῦ, eliminating any possible confusion as to whom the criminal is addressing as he asks to be remembered. Hence, at the practical level, the vocative Ἰησοῦ serves the semantic function of designating a change of address in the criminal's ongoing discourse.

This semantic function, however, does not exhaust the role of the vocative Ἰησοῦ in Luke 23:42. For instance, the change of address could easily have been reported through the narrator's introduction to the criminal's discourse rather than through the use of the vocative within the discourse itself. This could have been accomplished either by means of the dative case (καὶ ἔλεγεν τῷ Ἰησοῦ) or by means of a prepositional phrase (καὶ ἔλεγεν πρὸς τὸν Ἰησοῦν).[4] Both options are amply

---

[2] Previous commentators have briefly noted that the address is strikingly personal, yet few offer more than the tautological claim that the criminal's appeal reflects his knowledge of Jesus's name. For slightly less redundant considerations of the criminal's use of the vocative, see Raymond E. Brown, *The Death of the Messiah: From Gethsemane to the Grave; A Commentary on the Passion Narratives in the Four Gospels*, 2 vols., ABRL (New York: Doubleday, 1998), 2:1005; Giesen, "'Noch heute wirst du mit mir,'" 167; Joel B. Green, *The Gospel of Luke*, NICNT (Grand Rapids: Eerdmans, 1997), 822.

[3] In linguistic parlance, the criminal's use of Jesus's name functions as a "call" to designate the addressee of the criminal's speech (see Arnold Zwicky, "Hey, Whatsyourname!," in *Papers from the Tenth Regional Meeting of the Chicago Linguistic Society*, ed. Michael W. La Galy, Robert A. Fox, and Anthony Bruck [Chicago: Chicago Linguistic Society, 1974], 787–801, here 787–88).

[4] Stephen H. Levinsohn refers to such introductory formulae as "speech orienters" (*Discourse Features of New Testament Greek: A Coursebook on the Information Structure of New Testament*

attested in Luke's Gospel in reports of direct speech.⁵ Indeed, throughout Luke's Gospel, addressees of direct speech are more often designated by one of these constructions than by means of a vocative of direct address. Thus, the use of the vocative in the criminal's appeal to Jesus represents a choice by the narrator. This choice implies some sort of meaning, since the narrator could have chosen otherwise.⁶

The use of Jesus's proper name in Luke 23:42 reflects another choice, since the narrator could just as easily have had the criminal address Jesus with a reverential title (e.g., κύριε, "lord"; ἐπιστάτα, "master"; διδάσκαλε, "teacher") rather than with Jesus's proper name. In fact, when various speakers directly address Jesus throughout Luke's Gospel, they more often employ one of these titles rather than Jesus's proper name.⁷ Speakers do employ the vocative of Jesus's personal name in five instances, yet only in our passage, Luke 23:42, is the vocative Ἰησοῦ unaccompanied by a modifier. Jesus is elsewhere addressed as Ἰησοῦ Ναζαρηνέ ("Jesus of Nazareth," 4:34), Ἰησοῦ υἱὲ τοῦ θεοῦ τοῦ ὑψίστου ("Jesus, Son of the Most High God," 8:28), Ἰησοῦ ἐπιστάτα ("Jesus, Master," 17:13), and Ἰησοῦ υἱὲ Δαυίδ ("Jesus, Son of David," 18:38). In Acts, Stephen addresses the heavenly Jesus as κύριε Ἰησοῦ ("Lord Jesus," 7:59). Only the penitent criminal addresses Jesus simply as Ἰησοῦ. In this regard, the penitent criminal's use of Jesus's personal name is an anomaly otherwise unattested in the canonical gospels.⁸

Greek, 2nd ed. [Dallas: SIL International, 2000], 216). Technically speaking, the vocative does not fit comfortably among the Greek cases, since case involves the syntactical relation of noun phrases to the other elements of a sentence (see Tore Janson, "Vocative and the Grammar of Calls," in *Vocative! Addressing between System and Performance*, ed. Barbara Sonnenhauser and Patrizia Noel Aziz Hanna, Trends in Linguistics: Studies and Monographs 261 [Berlin: de Gruyter, 2013], 219–20).

⁵For the dative, examples include Luke 1:30; 2:10; 3:7, 16; 4:3; 5:10; 6:8; 12:54; 13:14; 17:5. For the use of a prepositional phrase, examples include Luke 1:61; 2:34; 4:21, 23; 5:10; 9:33; 10:29; 12:1; 14:3; 19:8. The latter appears to have been Luke's preferred option, as datives from the Synoptic tradition frequently appear as prepositional phrases in Luke's corresponding parallels. See, e.g., Luke 4:42 (cf. Mark 1:38), Luke 5:22 (cf. Mark 2:8), Luke 5:31, 33–34 (cf. Mark 2:17, 18–19), Luke 6:9 (cf. Mark 3:4), Luke 7:24 (cf. Matt 11:7), Luke 8:21 (cf. Mark 3:33), Luke 9:3 (cf. Mark 6:10), Luke 9:13 (cf. Mark 6:37). The opposite phenomenon, however, does occur as well, e.g., Luke 9:3 (cf. Mark 6:10). On the increasing usage of prepositions in place of cases in Koine Greek, see Murray J. Harris, *Prepositions and Theology in the Greek New Testament: An Essential Reference Resource for Exegesis* (Grand Rapids: Zondervan, 2012), 28; A. T. Robertson, *A Grammar of the Greek New Testament in the Light of Historical Research* (Nashville: Broadman, 1934), 450–53.

⁶See Steven E. Runge, *Discourse Grammar of the Greek New Testament: A Practical Introduction for Teaching and Exegesis*, Lexham Bible Reference Series (Peabody, MA: Hendrickson, 2010), 5–7.

⁷Speakers address Jesus directly in the vocative in forty separate instances in Luke's Gospel. The title employed most frequently is κύριος (seventeen occurrences), followed by διδάσκαλος (eleven occurrences) and ἐπιστάτης (six occurrences).

⁸Brown, *Death of the Messiah*, 2:1005. Among the five occurrences of Jesus's proper name

The extent to which the criminal's address deviates from the stylistic tendencies of the narrator can be seen in the transmission history of Luke 23:42. A number of manuscripts attest to a variant reading in which the narrator introduces Jesus through the dative case, and the vocative of Jesus's proper name is replaced with the vocative κύριε in the plea of the criminal: ἔλεγεν τῷ ’Ιησοῦ· μνήσθητί μου κύριε ὅταν ἔλθῃς εἰς τὴν βασιλείαν σου.[9] Codex Bezae presents another variant reading in which the vocative ’Ιησοῦ is replaced by a prepositional phrase in the introduction to the criminal's plea (πρὸς τὸν κύριον, "to the lord") identifying Jesus as the addressee of the criminal. The best manuscripts attest the reading presented in the critical editions; the variants can be understood as attempts to resolve the problem of how the criminal knows Jesus's name.[10] These variants illustrate the point that the vocative address of Jesus by name in Luke 23:42 is but one of many ways in which the addressee of the criminal's plea could have been designated.

Two choices are therefore reflected in the vocative ’Ιησοῦ in Luke 23:42. First, the narrator has chosen to report the change of address within the penitent criminal's discourse by a vocative of direct address rather than by another construction. Second, against the strong tendency for speakers in Luke's Gospel to address Jesus with reverential titles, the narrator has chosen to present the penitent criminal as addressing Jesus solely by his proper name.

In light of these choices, it is clear that the vocative in Luke 23:42 accomplishes more than the basic semantic function of reporting a change of address in the criminal's discourse. At a minimum, the use of the vocative ’Ιησοῦ in this verse indicates that the narrator has chosen to characterize the criminal as one who knew Jesus's name and addressed him by it.[11] In turn, this awareness of Jesus's name implies some prior knowledge of Jesus on the part of the criminal, yet that prior knowledge may not extend to personal familiarity with Jesus (cf. Luke 17:13, 18:38). This point is supported by what the criminal says about Jesus in the preceding verse—"this man has done nothing wrong." Alternatively, readers might suppose that the criminal has no personal familiarity with this innocent sufferer but that he has simply observed the repeated declarations of innocence by the authorities (cf. Luke 23:4, 14–15) and thus recognizes that the execution of Jesus is a miscarriage

---

in the vocative in Luke's Gospel, the usages in 17:13 and 23:42 are unparalleled, whereas 4:34, 8:28, and 18:38 are paralleled in Mark 1:23, 5:7, and 10:47, respectively. Interestingly, speakers in Matthew's Gospel never address Jesus directly by his proper name (cf. Matt 8:29, 9:27). The same is true for John's Gospel.

[9] The majority of manuscripts attest this alternative reading, including important witnesses A, C², W, as well as some Latin and Syriac witnesses.

[10] Joseph A. Fitzmyer, *The Gospel according to Luke: A New Translation with Introduction and Commentary*, 2 vols., AB 28, 28A (Garden City, NY: Doubleday, 1981–1985), 2:1510.

[11] On the ways in which direct address positions the speaker in relation to the addressee, see Penelope Brown and Stephen C. Levinson, *Politeness: Some Universals in Language Usage*, Studies in Interactional Sociolinguistics 4 (Cambridge: Cambridge University Press, 1987), 107; Zwicky, "Hey, Whatsyourname!," 796–97.

of justice. Thus, a minimalist reading of the vocative simply affirms that the narrator has chosen to tell the story in such a way that the readers can see that the criminal somehow knew Jesus's name.

II. A Probable Hypothesis

Furthermore, the vocative Ἰησοῦ in Luke 23:42 may well recall the previous instances in Luke's Gospel in which speakers call out to Jesus by name.[12] Two of the four other occurrences of Jesus's proper name in the vocative are found on the lips of demons. In Luke 4:34 (cf. Mark 4:24), a demon cries out in a loud voice and interrogates Jesus, "What have you to do with us, Jesus the Nazarene [Ἰησοῦ Ναζαρηνέ]? Have you come to destroy us? I know who you are, the Holy One of God [ὁ ἅγιος τοῦ θεοῦ]." In Luke 8:28 (cf. Mark 5:7, Matt 8:29), another demon asks a similar question of Jesus, "What have you to do with me, Jesus, Son of the Most High God [Ἰησοῦ υἱὲ τοῦ θεοῦ τοῦ ὑψίστου]? I beseech you, do not torment me." In these passages, the demons take care to name Jesus, not just by using his proper name but also by adding descriptors.[13] In 8:28, Jesus responds in turn, asking for the name of the demon (8:30). The prominence of names and titles in these passages may reflect the centrality of naming rites in the practice of exorcisms in antiquity, where names were held to contain a mystical power.[14] At any rate, these encounters between Jesus and the demons are clearly hostile and are therefore unlikely to be fitting parallels for 23:42.

More likely parallels are found in the two other passages in which speakers address Jesus directly by name. In Luke 17:13, a passage unique to the Third Gospel, ten lepers call out to Jesus as he enters into a village on his way to Jerusalem, "Jesus, Master, have mercy on us" (Ἰησοῦ ἐπιστάτα, ἐλέησον ἡμᾶς). In response, Jesus tells them to go and show themselves to the priests, and as they go they are cleansed (17:14). Of the ten lepers, only one—a Samaritan—turns back to praise God, and Jesus commends this pious leper for his faith (17:15–19).

In Luke 18:38, a similar request for mercy is made by the blind beggar on the road to Jericho, "Jesus, Son of David, have mercy on me" (Ἰησοῦ υἱὲ Δαυίδ, ἐλέησόν

---

[12] Commentators who acknowledge some type of a connection between the criminal and other instances in which characters in Luke address Jesus by name include Green, *Gospel of Luke*, 822; I. Howard Marshall, *The Gospel of Luke*, NIGTC (Grand Rapids: Eerdmans, 1978), 872; Michael Wolter, *Das Lukasevangelium*, HNT 5 (Tübingen: Mohr Siebeck, 2008), 760.

[13] Commentators have debated the christological implications of the titles that these demons employ for Jesus, but this debate lies beyond the purview of the present analysis. See the summary remarks of Darrell L. Bock, *Luke*, 2 vols., BECNT (Grand Rapids: Baker, 1994–1996), 2:433.

[14] For a brief discussion and helpful bibliography on the relationship between names and spiritual power in antiquity, see Austin Busch, "Presence Deferred: The Name of Jesus and Self-Referential Eschatological Prophecy in Acts 3," *BibInt* 17 (2009): 521–53, here 523–27.

με). This passage is a part of the triple tradition, and a comparison of Synoptic accounts is illuminating:

Mark 10:47	Matthew 20:30	Luke 18:38
"… Son of David, Jesus, have mercy on me."	"Have mercy on us, Lord, Son of David."	"Jesus, Son of David, have mercy on me."
υἱὲ Δαυὶδ Ἰησοῦ, ἐλέησόν με.	ἐλέησον ἡμᾶς, [κύριε,] υἱὸς Δαυίδ.	Ἰησοῦ υἱὲ Δαυίδ, ἐλέησόν με.

Mark places the proper name of Jesus after the title "Son of David." By contrast, in Luke's version of the beggar's request, the name of Jesus has been brought forward, so that it precedes the reverential title. In Matthew's Gospel, there are two blind men, and they do not use Jesus's proper name to address him. Hence, the name of Jesus is given a distinctive prominence in Luke's account of this incident. Eventually, the beggar's sight is restored, and the healing is attributed to the faith of the beggar (Luke 18:42–43; cf. Mark 10:52, Matt 20:33–34).

Luke 17:13 and 18:38 share several elements. Aside from Luke 23:42, these are the only two instances in Luke's Gospel in which nondemonic characters address Jesus by his proper name. In both passages, the proper name of Jesus is modified by a reverential descriptor in apposition ("Master," "Son of David"), and in both places the name of Jesus is uttered by marginalized figures in the narrative (ten lepers, a blind beggar). Moreover, in each instance the petitioners make the same request for mercy and receive physical healing, and both passages end with Jesus sending away a healed individual with the same affirmation, "Your faith has saved/healed you [ἡ πίστις σου σέσωκέν σε]" (Luke 17:19, 18:42).[15]

In light of these prior requests for mercy, the vocative Ἰησοῦ in the criminal's appeal might characterize the criminal as one like the pious Samaritan leper or the blind beggar on the road to Jericho, a helpless and marginalized suppliant crying out in faith to Jesus for the benefits of his ministry. In addition, the correspondences among the criminal, the ten lepers, and the blind beggar might highlight the continuity in Jesus's ministry to the marginalized all the way to his death. No less at the cross than at earlier phases of Jesus's ministry do the ostracized turn to him in hope.

This intratextual understanding of the penitent criminal's petition is supported by the apparent similarities between the criminal and the earlier supplicants of Jesus. The supplicants share a similarly marginalized status; they address Jesus in a similar way; and Jesus responds in a similarly positive manner toward each of

---

[15] In the case of Luke 17:13–19, the situation is complex, as Jesus commends only the single Samaritan leper who gave praise to God following the healing of all ten lepers. Nonetheless, all ten lepers were healed. Consequently, a problem arises as to whether all ten lepers had faith, since this is the quality to which Jesus attributes the healing. At any rate, the pious leper's identity as a Samaritan in this pericope reinforces the emphasis on Jesus's ministry to the marginalized.

the supplicants. Thus, all three instances in Luke's Gospel in which nondemonic speakers address Jesus by name entail similar requests for mercy from similarly marginalized individuals, and it would be reasonable to understand these passages as connected to one another in some way.

There are, of course, obvious differences between the petition of the penitent criminal and the appeals in Luke 17:13 and 18:38. Whereas the other supplicants address Jesus with honorific titles in addition to his proper name, the criminal simply calls out, "Jesus." In addition, the language and substance of the criminal's request differ from that of the other supplicants. The others ask Jesus for mercy. The criminal asks to be remembered whenever Jesus comes into his kingdom. The requests of the other supplicants appear to be directed primarily toward physical healing, whereas the request of the criminal seems to be directed toward a different form of deliverance. None of these differences is so drastic as to call into question the resonances between the criminal's plea and the previous petitions, but they do reinforce the individuality of the character of the criminal. He is not wholly identical to previous characters, only similar.

III. A Further Possibility

Thus far my interpretation of the vocative Ἰησοῦ in Luke 23:42 is uncontroversial. It seems incontrovertible that the use of Jesus's proper name in the criminal's appeal represents a choice on the part of the narrator, such that the vocative Ἰησοῦ must accomplish more than simply designating the addressee of the criminal's speech. Although some may question the possible parallels with prior passages in which nondemonic characters in Luke's Gospel address Jesus by name, the literary quality of Luke's Gospel supports such intratextual resonances.

In this final section of the article, I will consider a more speculative possibility: Could it be that the use of Jesus's name in the context of Luke 23:39–42 actually plays on the etymology and meaning of the name of Jesus, "God is salvation" or "God saves"?[16] Several factors lend credence to this notion.

1. The Relative Infrequency of Jesus's Name in the Vocative

As the preceding analysis has shown, the vocative Ἰησοῦ in Luke 23:42 is unusual, occurring only ten times in total in the New Testament. Four of the occurrences appear on the lips of demons in two parallel episodes in Mark and Luke

---

[16] The Greek Ἰησοῦς is derived from the theophoric Hebrew name יְהוֹשֻׁעַ through the shortened form יֵשׁוּעַ. On the etymology and meaning of Ἰησοῦς, see W. Foerster, "Ἰησοῦς," *TDNT* 3:289; Margaret H. Williams, "Palestinian Jewish Personal Names in Acts," in *The Book of Acts in Its Palestinian Setting*, ed. Richard Bauckham, vol. 4 of *The Book of Acts in Its First Century Setting*, ed. Bruce W. Winter (Grand Rapids: Eerdmans, 1995), 87.

(Mark 1:24 [cf. Luke 4:34]; Mark 5:7 [cf. Luke 8:28]). Two more of the occurrences appear in prayers addressed to the postresurrection Jesus (Acts 7:59, Rev 22:20). Consequently, only four occurrences of the vocative Ἰησοῦ appear on the lips of nondemonic speakers during Jesus's earthly ministry in the gospels, and all of these appear in the context of petitions for mercy.[17] Thus, the criminal's appeal to Jesus by his name alone in Luke 23:42 is most naturally grouped with the few other places in which nondemonic speakers directly address Jesus by name in petitions for mercy. In itself, this point does not establish that the etymology or meaning of Jesus's name is evoked in Luke 23:42, yet it does show that the vocative Ἰησοῦ in Luke's Gospel should not be grouped with the more common uses of Jesus's proper name as a simple personal referent.[18]

2. The Characteristic Usage of the Vocative in Luke's Gospel

Luke typically uses the vocative of direct address to reveal some element of the speaker's perception of the addressee.[19] Hence, Jesus is addressed most often by a title that describes a specific quality or status of Jesus in relation to the speaker, such as "child" or "teacher" or "master" or "Son of David." Such titles in vocative form do more than simply identify the addressee of the discourse; they also entail some meaning derived from the connotations of the vocative nouns themselves.[20] Indeed, in most instances the vocative is employed despite the fact that the addressee of the discourse is already apparent to the reader. For example, in Luke 9:33, the narrator specifies that Peter is speaking to Jesus (εἶπεν ὁ Πέτρος πρὸς τὸν Ἰησοῦν), yet Peter's discourse begins with the vocative "Master" (ἐπιστάτα), conveying Peter's perception of Jesus's status vis-à-vis the disciples at the transfiguration scene.[21] In such examples, the vocative is semantically unnecessary, since the addressee of the

---

[17] While the available data are certainly limited, the instances of nondemonic speakers directly addressing Jesus by name in the New Testament might point toward a distinctively Lukan use of the proper name of Jesus in the context of petitions for mercy. Luke 17:13 and 23:42 are unparalleled in the other gospels, and in Luke 18:38 the narrator appears to have modified the tradition to give special prominence to the name of Jesus by bringing the name forward to precede the reverential title "Son of David" (cf. Mark 10:47).

[18] Another group of distinct usages of Jesus's name that is well attested in the New Testament is the occurrence of Jesus's proper name in the baptismal formulae, "in/into the name of Jesus" (ἐν/ἐπὶ τῷ ὀνόματι or εἰς τὸ ὄνομα). In these formulae, the name of Jesus is typically accompanied by an additional modifier (κύριος or χριστός), and the consistent baptismal context of these formulae differentiates them from the New Testament usages of the vocative Ἰησοῦ. On the origin and usages of the formulae, see Lars Hartman, "*Into the Name of the Lord Jesus*": *Baptism in the Early Church*, SNTW (Edinburgh: T&T Clark, 1997), 37–50.

[19] On this discourse function of the vocative, see Runge, *Discourse Grammar*, 355.

[20] See Virginia Hill, "Features and Strategies: The Internal Syntax of Vocative Phrases," in Sonnenhauser and Hanna, *Vocative!*, 132.

[21] Other clear examples include Luke 1:30; 3:7; 4:23; 6:42; 11:1; 12:13, 19; 13:15; 15:12; 19:5, 39; 22:48.

discourse has already been identified. The vocative form of address therefore functions purely to reveal an aspect of the speaker's perception of the addressee.

Occasionally, the vocative noun does bear some semantic weight in identifying the addressee.[22] Yet, even where the addressee of the discourse would be unapparent to the reader if not for the vocative, one should not assume that the role of the vocative is limited to its semantic function of identifying the addressee. As we have already seen, the vocative form of address is never a semantic necessity. The addressee could alternatively be reported in the narrator's introduction to the direct discourse, whether through a dative-case noun or pronoun (εἶπεν τῷ Σίμωνι) or through a prepositional phrase (εἶπεν πρὸς τὸν Σίμωνα). Therefore, the use of the vocative still represents a choice by the narrator, even where a need exists to identify the addressee of the discourse. The default assumption should be that the meaning of the vocative noun is not exhausted by any semantic function it might play within the discourse. Interpreters intuitively recognize this point whenever they comment on the significance of various vocatives in the gospels at locations where the vocative bears some semantic weight in designating the addressee of the direct discourse.[23]

In most cases, the vocative is clearly employed for some purpose other than designating the addressee, most often to reveal some aspect of the speaker's perception of the addressee. If this is the most common function of the vocative form of address in Luke's Gospel, then this function may be operative even where the vocative also serves an additional semantic function of reporting the addressee of the direct discourse, as in Luke 23:42.[24] This consideration in itself does not prove that

---

[22] In my estimation, somewhere between 10 and 25 percent of the 107 occurrences of the vocative in Luke's Gospel appear in contexts where the addressee of the direct discourse is not already immediately apparent to the readers, either through contextual considerations or through the explicit remarks of the narrator. Clear examples in which the vocative functions to report the addressee of the discourse include Luke 5:20, 7:14, 8:45, 9:38, 17:13, and 18:38. There are a number of instances in which different readers might disagree as to whether the vocative is employed in order to report the addressee of the discourse, depending on one's assessment of the context.

[23] On the use of the vocative κύριε in Luke 9:54, see C. Kavin Rowe, *Early Narrative Christology: The Lord in the Gospel of Luke*, BZNW 139 (Berlin: de Gruyter, 2006), 124–25.

[24] Surprisingly little attention has been given to the discourse function of the vocative form of address in the New Testament. Although Stanley E. Porter notes, "When used it should be noted," his comments on the vocative are quite brief (*Idioms of the Greek New Testament*, Biblical Languages: Greek 2 [Sheffield: JSOT Press, 1992], 88). Most of the grammars offer only scant remarks, noting that the nominative tends to supplant the vocative and focusing primarily on the significance of the article in relation to the vocative. See, e.g., BDF §§146–47; C. F. D. Moule, *An Idiom-Book of New Testament Greek* [Cambridge: Cambridge University Press, 1959], 31–32; Robertson, *Grammar of the Greek New Testament*, 461–66). Few scholars comment on the discourse-pragmatic function of the vocative, though Runge observes that the vocative often functions to characterize the participants in the discourse (*Discourse Grammar*, 354–55). For a survey of linguistic scholarship pertaining to the vocative outside the realm of biblical studies, see Barbara Sonnenhauser and Patrizia Noel Aziz Hanna, "Introduction: Vocative!," in Sonnenhauser and Hanna, *Vocative!*, 1–23.

the vocative Ἰησοῦ in Luke 23:42 plays on the etymology and meaning of Jesus's name. Nevertheless, if the etymology and meaning of Jesus's name are evoked in Luke 23:42, this would accord with the characteristic use of the vocative throughout Luke's Gospel.

3. *The Significance of Proper Names in Luke-Acts*

Whatever may be said about the function of the proper name of Jesus in Luke-Acts, it is clear that certain occurrences of other proper names in Luke and Acts may be significant. For example, in Luke's account of the Gerasene demoniac (Luke 8:30), when Jesus asks for the name of the man, the man responds that his name is "Legion." The narrator then explains the name by noting that many demons had entered the man. Thus, the meaning of the name is significant for the characterization of the afflicted figure.[25] Similarly, in Acts 4:36, when the narrator introduces Barnabas (Joseph) for the first time, his name is explained as meaning "son of encouragement," a title that is subsequently demonstrated to be fitting for the character.[26] In Acts 13:6–12, Paul and Barnabas have an encounter with a magician and false prophet named Bar-Jesus who opposes their ministry (13:6). The narrator subsequently refers to this individual as "Elymas the Magician," offering the ambiguous explanation, "for thus his name is interpreted [οὕτως γὰρ μεθερμηνεύεται τὸ ὄνομα αὐτοῦ]" (13:8). The narrator's explanation could be taken in multiple ways, but for our purposes what is significant is simply that the narrator has found a correspondence between the meaning of the character's proper name and his narrative function as a magician.[27]

In addition to these overt references to the meaning of proper names, one might detect subtle correspondences in a number of other passages between the meaning of a character's name and the events in the narrative. Consider, for example, the contexts in which one finds the names of Lazarus ("God has helped," Luke 16:19–31), Eutychus ("Fortunate," Acts 20:9–11), and Ananias ("God is gracious," Acts 5:1–11, 9:10–19).[28] Space precludes a detailed discussion of these names and

---

[25] Mark's parallel account is similar but not identical, as the explanation for the name in Mark is placed on the lips of the man rather than reported through a narratival comment, as in Luke (cf. Mark 5:9). Matthew's parallel account does not contain any reference to the name "Legion" (cf. Matt 8:28–34).

[26] Although the real etymology of Barnabas's name seems not to support the explanation of its meaning given by Luke, the meaning assigned to the name remains significant in the narrative. See Williams, "Palestinian Jewish Personal Names in Acts," 101.

[27] The explanation for the name Elymas could mean that the Aramaic Bar-Jesus ought to be translated into Greek as Elymas, or it could mean that Elymas signifies "the Magician."

[28] In the case of Eutychus, a better name could hardly have been chosen for the man Paul resuscitates from a deadly fall. In the case of Ananias, the character's name may add a note of irony to the depiction of God's wrath in Acts 5:1–11, whereas the name coheres with the task that God entrusts to the character who is sent to Saul in Acts 9:10–19.

their contexts, yet the cumulative weight of such examples suggests that the meaning of proper names can be significant in the narrative of Luke-Acts.

4. The Familiarity of the Etymology and Meaning of Ἰησοῦς in the First Century

The etymology and meaning of the name Jesus appears to have been commonly known in the first century. Philo reports that Ἰησοῦς means "safety/salvation of the Lord" (σωτηρία κύριου [*Mut.* 1.121-123; cf. Num 13:16]); Moses's choice of this name for Joshua becomes a springboard for Philo to reflect philosophically on the significance of various names in relation to their bearers.[29] Similarly, in Sir 46:1, the career of Joshua is summarized in terms of his name: "Joshua the son of Nun was mighty in war and was the successor of Moses in prophesying. He became, in accordance with his name, great for the salvation of [God's] elect [ὃς ἐγένετο κατὰ τὸ ὄνομα αὐτοῦ μέγας ἐπὶ σωτηρίᾳ ἐκλεκτῶν αὐτοῦ]." In Matthew's infancy narrative, the angel explains to Joseph that he is to name the child Jesus, "for he will save his people from their sins [αὐτὸς γὰρ σώσει τὸν λαὸν αὐτοῦ ἀπὸ τῶν ἁμαρτιῶν αὐτῶν]" (Matt 1:21).

In the passages cited above, the meaning of the name Ἰησοῦς is consistently connected to the language of salvation (σωτηρία, σῴζω). Neither Sir 46:1 nor Matt 1:21 actually defines the name Ἰησοῦς for the audience. Rather, both passages simply assume that the readers know the meaning of the name. Furthermore, Philo's interest in the meaning of the names of various figures from Israel's history is a good reminder of the significance of personal names in biblical literature.[30]

In contrast to Matthew, Luke does not explain the significance of Jesus's proper name,[31] though Luke's infancy narrative agrees with Matthew in avowing that the name of Jesus was determined by angelic decree (Luke 1:31).[32] The likelihood

---

[29] On the interpretation of this passage in Philo, see Louis H. Feldman, "Philo's Interpretation of Joshua," *JSP* 12 (2001): 165-78, here 171-72.

[30] See François Bovon, "Names and Numbers in Early Christianity," *NTS* 47 (2001): 271-80. A similar interest in the etymology of names can be found at various points in Josephus (e.g., *Ag. Ap.* 1.286; *Ant.* 1.34; 2.92, 228; 5.200; 11.173).

[31] Interestingly, interpreters have occasionally suggested that the use of Jesus's proper name in the inscription above the cross in Matt 27:37 draws on the introduction of that name in Matt 1:21. See Tucker S. Ferda, "The Soldiers' Inscription and the Angel's Word: The Significance of 'Jesus' in Matthew's Titulus," *NovT* 55 (2013): 223-30.

[32] Indeed, the naming of Jesus may stand at the center of the passage in Luke 1:26-38. See Roland Meynet, "Dieu donne son Nom à Jésus: Analyse rhétorique de Lc 1:26-56 et de 1 Sam 2:1-10," *Bib* 66 (1985): 39-72, here 40-42. Following the declaration that the child is to be named "Jesus," the Lukan angel expounds upon the destiny of the child in the terms of Davidic kingship (1:32-33). The child will be great and will be called "Son of the Most High." He will be given the throne of his father David and will possess an everlasting reign over the house of Israel. None of this straightforwardly demonstrates a Lukan understanding of the etymology or meaning of

remains, however, that Luke and his readers would have been familiar with the meaning of the name Ἰησοῦς. An allusion to the etymology and meaning of Ἰησοῦς would therefore have been recognizable for at least some within Luke's readership.

5. Passages in Acts That May Entail Wordplays Involving the Name of Jesus

Two passages in Acts (4:8–12 and 13:23) employ the name Ἰησοῦς alongside the terminology of salvation in such a way that one might suspect an allusion to the meaning of Jesus's name. In Acts 4:8–12, Peter offers a defense of the means by which he has healed a lame man in the temple precincts:

> Rulers of the people and elders, ⁹if we are being examined today concerning a good deed done to a crippled man, by what means this individual has been healed [σέσωται], ¹⁰let it be known to all of you and to all the people of Israel that by the name of Jesus [ἐν τῷ ὀνόματι Ἰησοῦ] Christ of Nazareth, whom you crucified, whom God raised from the dead—by this one [i.e., by this name: ἐν τούτῳ] this man is standing before you healthy. ¹¹This one is the stone that was rejected by you, the builders, which has become the cornerstone. ¹²And there is salvation [σωτηρία] in no one else, for there is no other name [ὄνομα] under heaven given among men by which we must be saved [σωθῆναι].

Peter's explanation for the healing not only prominently features the name of Jesus, but it also exhibits a play on the terminology of salvation in relation to that name.[33] The verb σῴζω ("to save") appears twice in the passage. In the first occurrence (v. 9), the verb refers most naturally to the physical healing of the crippled man. In the second occurrence (v. 12), the verb is employed with reference to a salvation (σωτηρία) that is available to the speaker and apparently to his audience as well (ἡμᾶς).[34] In this way, the passage plays on the semantic flexibility of the verb σῴζω and its cognate σωτηρία; the physical and spiritual nuances of the lexeme are linked together in the passage through the name of Jesus, by which the crippled man has been healed (v. 10; cf. Acts 3:6, 16) and apart from which no one can experience salvation (v. 12).[35]

Jesus's name, but the angel's prediction of Jesus's destiny does anticipate a deliverance for God's people in keeping with Davidic messianic expectations, and later in Luke's infancy narrative this deliverance is described with the terminology of salvation (cf. Luke 1:68–71).

[33] On the prominence of the "name" of Jesus throughout Acts 3 and 4, see Busch, "Presence Deferred," 521–23. On the christological implications of this theme, see Larry W. Hurtado, "Pre-70 CE Jewish Opposition to Christ-Devotion," JTS 50 (1999): 35–58, here 42–43; John A. Ziesler, "The Name of Jesus in the Acts of the Apostles," JSNT 4 (1979): 28–41, here 37–38.

[34] See Robert C. Tannehill, "The Functions of Peter's Mission Speeches in the Narrative of Acts," NTS 37 (1991): 400–414, here 407.

[35] The interest particularly in the "name" of Jesus and the setting of the healing event at the temple may help account for Peter's quotation from Ps 118:22 in this context, since the psalmist will shortly affirm, "Blessed is the one who comes in the name of the Lord, we bless you from the house of the Lord" (Ps 118:26).

When the passage is read with the etymology and meaning of Jesus's name in mind, the close interplay between the name of Jesus and the terminology of salvation is highly suggestive. In Peter's speech, physical and spiritual salvation, available solely by means of the name of Jesus, is related quite naturally to what the name of Jesus actually means.[36]

A second passage from Acts also coordinates the name Ἰησοῦς closely with the terminology of salvation. In Acts 13:23, in the midst of Paul's synagogue sermon at Pisidian Antioch, Paul declares that, from the offspring of David and in accordance with God's promise, God has brought to Israel a savior, Jesus: τούτου ὁ θεὸς ἀπὸ τοῦ σπέρματος κατ' ἐπαγγελίαν ἤγαγεν τῷ Ἰσραὴλ σωτῆρα Ἰησοῦν. In the context of a statement regarding the promised salvation that God has brought to Israel through Jesus, the name Ἰησοῦς is placed in apposition to the title σωτήρ, a title that is used sparingly in Luke-Acts. The title occurs once in Mary's Magnificat with reference to God (Luke 1:47), and it appears with reference to Jesus in the angelic pronouncement to the shepherds at the time of Jesus's birth (Luke 2:11). Aside from these two occurrences, σωτήρ appears only two additional times in Luke-Acts: once in Acts 5:31 with reference to Jesus in a defense speech by Peter, and here in Acts 13:23, where it is followed directly by the name Ἰησοῦς. It is admittedly far from clear whether a play on the meaning of Ἰησοῦς is intended in the current context. Yet, if the verse is read with the etymology and meaning of Ἰησοῦς in mind, the placement of Jesus's proper name in apposition to the title "Savior" is rather suggestive. Jesus's identity as savior is confirmed by his very name, and the meaning of his name speaks to the role that God has chosen for him.

In both Acts 4:8–12 and Acts 13:23, the name of Jesus is placed in close proximity to the terminology of salvation, which suggests a possible allusion to the meaning of Jesus's proper name. If these passages do indeed allude to the meaning of Ἰησοῦς, this would support the plausibility of an allusion to the meaning of Ἰησοῦς in Luke 23:42.

6. *The Prominence of Salvation Terminology in the Immediate Context of Luke 23:42*

Finally, in the surrounding context of the criminal's plea to Jesus, the terminology of salvation is prominent and is closely related to the jeering insults concerning the identity of Jesus. The verb σῴζω appears four times in the three statements by the mockers that immediately precede the words of the penitent criminal (Luke 23:35, 37, 39).[37] In verse 35, the Jewish rulers insist that if Jesus is the "Christ of God, the Chosen One," then he must save himself (σωσάτω ἑαυτόν). Similarly, in verse 37, the mocking soldiers address Jesus directly, "If you are the

---

[36] Regarding the correspondence between the healing efficacy of Jesus's name and its etymology, see Jacques Dupont, "Nom de Jésus," in *DBSup* 6:516, 540.

[37] On the significance of this verb in the present context, see Fitzmyer, "'Today You Shall Be with Me,'" 212.

King of the Jews, save yourself [σῶσον σεαυτόν]." Finally, in verse 39, the blaspheming criminal crucified next to Jesus demands, "Are you not the Christ? Save yourself and us [σῶσον σεαυτὸν καὶ ἡμᾶς]!" In each of these taunts, the speakers appeal sarcastically to different reverential titles for Jesus, maintaining that Jesus must save himself in order to validate his identity as the "Christ," the "Chosen One," and the "King of the Jews."

It is in this context that the penitent criminal directly addresses Jesus, not by any of the titles employed by the surrounding mockers but by his proper name, Ἰησοῦς. The contrast is striking. If one reads the criminal's plea with the etymology and meaning of Jesus's name in mind, then the vocative Ἰησοῦ on the lips of the criminal would affirm precisely what the conflicting voices at the crucifixion scene deny. While others mock Jesus for his inability to save and presume that he cannot truly be a king, the criminal affirms that *Jesus is God's agent of salvation* entering into his kingdom.[38] In this way, the use of Jesus's proper name would subvert the surrounding clamor that questions Jesus's ability to save.

Summary

Could the vocative Ἰησοῦ in Luke 23:42 actually allude to the etymology and meaning of the name of Jesus? The various factors discussed above do provide some provisional indications (1) that the meaning of personal names was a matter of interest for Luke, (2) that Luke was likely aware of the meaning of Jesus's name, and (3) that an awareness of the meaning of Jesus's name may enrich one's reading of multiple passages in Luke-Acts. Indeed, the vocative Ἰησοῦ in Luke 23:42 is highly suggestive in its context when read with the meaning of Jesus's name in mind, and I believe that an allusion to the actual meaning of Ἰησοῦς in Luke 23:42 is a real possibility.

IV. Conclusion

This article has surveyed a spectrum of possible interpretations of the vocative Ἰησοῦ in the penitent criminal's plea in Luke 23:42. At a minimum, the verse shows that the narrator has chosen to characterize the criminal as one who knows the name of Jesus; any number of scenarios might be imagined to account for such knowledge. The vocative Ἰησοῦ in Luke 23:42 also recalls the two other instances in which nondemonic characters in Luke's Gospel address Jesus by name. The ten lepers in 17:13 and the blind beggar in 18:38 call out to Jesus by his proper name

---

[38] That this reading comports well with the immediate context of the passage can be seen by the frequency with which commentators employ the language of "salvation" in their interpretation of the penitent criminal's plea. See, e.g., James R. Edwards, *The Gospel according to Luke*, PilNTC (Grand Rapids: Eerdmans, 2015), 691–92.

in their appeals for Jesus to show them mercy. If the penitent criminal's use of Jesus's name is read in light of these parallels, the vocative Ἰησοῦ in Luke 23:42 may characterize the criminal as a helpless and marginalized supplicant seeking mercy from Jesus in faith. This intratextual resonance might also point toward Luke's sustained interest in the radical inclusivity of Jesus's ministry, as even at the crucifixion scene Jesus is depicted as extending mercy to the marginalized sufferer who calls out to him by name.

More speculatively, the vocative Ἰησοῦ in Luke 23:42 may allude to the etymology and meaning of the name of Jesus, "God is salvation" or "God saves." If so, the use of Jesus's name in the criminal's plea would stand in startling contrast to the mocking voices at the cross who chide Jesus for his inability to save.

Related issues that merit further study include the discourse function of the vocative in the gospels, the significance of onomastic considerations for New Testament exegesis, and the possibility of allusions to the meaning of proper names at various points in Luke-Acts. The latter topic might lead one to explore more thoroughly whether the meaning of proper names is more significant for the interpretation of the New Testament than is typically recognized. Such analyses would surely be useful in their own right, and they would also likely be helpful in assessing what has been set forth provisionally in this article.

NEW IN BIBLICAL STUDIES FROM **EERDMANS**

NEW TESTAMENT APOCRYPHA
More Noncanonical Scriptures
VOLUME 1
TONY BURKE and BRENT LANDAU, editors
FOREWORD BY J. K. ELLIOTT

"*Masterful.... A rigorous but highly accessible volume.*"
— BART D. EHRMAN

ISBN 978-0-8028-7289-0 • 635 PAGES • HARDCOVER • $75.00

SCRIPTURES AND SECTARIANISM
Essays on the Dead Sea Scrolls
JOHN J. COLLINS

"*A must-read for scholars of Second Temple Judaism and early Christianity!*"
— SIDNIE WHITE CRAWFORD

ISBN 978-0-8028-7314-9 • 341 PAGES • PAPERBACK • $45.00

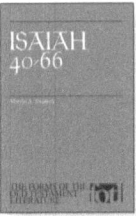

ISAIAH 40–66
MARVIN A. SWEENEY
THE FORMS OF THE OLD TESTAMENT LITERATURE

"*A cutting-edge form-critical study of Isaiah 40–66 for the twenty-first century.*"
— DAVID CARR

ISBN 978-0-8028-6607-3 • 432 PAGES • PAPERBACK • $55.00

TORAH ETHICS AND EARLY CHRISTIAN IDENTITY
SUSAN J. WENDEL and DAVID M. MILLER, editors

"*An incisive treatment of a matter that is of considerable historical, theological, and ethical importance.*"
— BRIAN S. ROSNER

ISBN 978-0-8028-7319-4 • 285 PAGES • PAPERBACK • $35.00

WM. B. EERDMANS
PUBLISHING CO.
2140 Oak Industrial Dr NE
Grand Rapids MI 49505

At your bookstore,
or call 800.253.7521
www.eerdmans.com

JBL 136, no. 2 (2017): 451–465
doi: http://dx.doi.org/10.15699/jbl.1362.2017.186627

A Theology of Glory: Paul's Use of Δόξα Terminology in Romans

SIGURD GRINDHEIM
sgrindheim@gmail.com
Fjellhaug International University College, 0572 Oslo, Norway

According to a common interpretation, Paul's reference to the lack of God's glory in Rom 3:23 alludes to the story of Adam and his loss of God's image. This identification is problematic, however, as most of the evidence that can be cited in its favor is later than Paul. To arrive at a better interpretation, I pay close attention to the development of δόξα terminology in Romans as well as to Paul's use of Israel's Scriptures. In the LXX, δόξα refers to the tangible presence of God, a usage that also is able to explain Paul's terminology. The sixteen occurrences of δόξα in Romans are rich in Septuagintal undertones, in the form of both Septuagintal terminology and more or less clear allusions to the Scriptures of Israel. Against this background, I argue that Paul uses δόξα language in Romans to express his view that God's revelatory presence in Israel has been rejected but is renewed in Jesus Christ.

In Rom 3:23, Paul asserts that "all have sinned and fall short of the glory of God." According to a popular interpretation, the background for Paul's statement is the Genesis account that describes Adam's creation in the image of God. This image, which Paul refers to as the glory of God, was lost when Adam disobeyed the commandment.[1] If this is Paul's understanding of the human predicament, it is

[1] William Sanday and Arthur C. Headlam, *A Critical and Exegetical Commentary on the Epistle to the Romans*, 5th ed., ICC (Edinburgh: T&T Clark, 1950), 84–85; Hans Lietzmann, *An die Römer*, 3rd ed., HNT 8 (Tübingen: Mohr Siebeck, 1933), 49; Otto Michel, *Der Brief an die Römer*, 5th ed., KEK (Göttingen: Vandenhoeck & Ruprecht, 1966), 149; Joseph Coppens, "La gloire des croyants d'après les lettres pauliniennes," *ETL* 46 (1970): 389–92, here 392; C. E. B. Cranfield, *A Critical and Exegetical Commentary on the Epistle to the Romans*, 2 vols., ICC (Edinburgh: T&T Clark, 1975), 1:204; Ulrich Wilckens, *Der Brief an die Römer*, 3 vols., EKKNT 6 (Zurich: Benziger, 1978), 1:188; Ernst Käsemann, *Commentary on Romans*, trans. Geoffrey W. Bromiley (Grand Rapids: Eerdmans, 1980), 94–95; James D. G. Dunn, *Romans 1–8*, WBC 38 (Dallas: Word, 1988), 168; C. K. Barrett, *A Commentary on the Epistle to the Romans*, 2nd ed., BNTC (London: Black, 1991), 71; Douglas J. Moo, *The Epistle to the Romans*, NICNT (Grand Rapids: Eerdmans, 1996), 226; Brendan Byrne, *Romans*, SP 6 (Collegeville, MN: Liturgical Press,

451

natural to understand his description of eschatological salvation in the same light. The future glory of believers (Rom 5:2; 8:18, 21) is then interpreted as the restoration of the divine glory or image with which human beings were endowed at creation.[2]

In this article, I will first examine the Jewish traditions that associate glory with Adam, which will demonstrate that there is no evidence in pre-Pauline sources for the idea that God's glory was attributed to Adam at creation. Second, I will show that Paul's use of δόξα terminology has much in common with a theme that is more broadly attested: the revelatory presence of God in the history of Israel. My thesis is that the eschatological glory of believers, which corresponds to the glory that human beings have forfeited, denotes the impressive manifestation of God's renewed presence. Finally, I will discuss Rom 2:6–10, a passage that may appear to provide a counterindication to my thesis.

1997), 125; Thomas R. Schreiner, *Romans*, BECNT (Grand Rapids: Baker, 1998), 187; N. T. Wright, "The Letter to the Romans," *NIB* 10:393–770, here 470; Eduard Lohse, *Der Brief an die Römer*, KEK 4 (Göttingen: Vandenhoeck & Ruprecht, 2003), 131; Robert Jewett, *Romans: A Commentary*, Hermeneia (Minneapolis: Fortress, 2007), 280. Contra Joseph A. Fitzmyer, who observes that "a reference to Adam here is eisegetical" (*Romans: A New Translation with Introduction and Commentary*, AB 33 [New York: Doubleday, 1993], 347; similarly Leander E. Keck, *Romans*, ANTC [Nashville: Abingdon, 2005], 106). This interpretation was also popular among Protestant interpreters in the time following the Reformation (see Heinrich August Wilhelm Meyer, *Critical and Exegetical Handbook to the Epistle to the Romans*, trans. John C. Moore and Edwin Johnson, 2 vols., Critical and Exegetical Commentary on the New Testament 9–10 [Edinburgh: T&T Clark, 1873–1874], 1:167). Among older commentators, the expression δόξα θεοῦ was often read as a genitive of origin ("glory given by God"), understood as a synonym for the term δικαιοσύνη θεοῦ ("righteousness of God"). See Meyer, *Critical and Exegetical Handbook*, 1:166; Theodor Zahn, *Der Brief des Paulus an die Römer*, KNT 6 (Leipzig: Deichert, 1910), 177; M.-J. Lagrange, *Saint Paul épitre aux Romains*, EBib (Paris: Gabalda, 1916), 74; Karl Barth, *The Epistle to Romans*, 2nd ed., trans. Edwyn C. Hoskyns (London: Oxford University Press, 1968), 101; Adolf Schlatter, *Gottes Gerechtigkeit: Ein Kommentar zum Römerbrief*, 5th ed. (Stuttgart: Calwer, 1975), 142; similarly John Calvin, *Commentary of the Epistle to the Romans*, trans. Francis Sibson (London: Seeley, 1834), 174–75. Some read the expression as an objective genitive ("glory before God"), also in analogy with δικαιοσύνη θεοῦ. See Friedrich Adolph Philippi, *Commentary on St. Paul's Epistle to the Romans*, trans. J. S. Banks, 2 vols., Clark's Foreign Theological Library NS 9 (Edinburgh: T&T Clark, 1878), 1:137; similarly Philip Melanchthon, *Commentary on Romans*, trans. Fred Kramer (1540; St. Louis: Concordia, 1992), 99. Martin Luther also took it as an objective genitive, but interpreted δόξα in an active sense and paraphrased: "They do not have a righteousness of which they can glory before God" (*Luther's Works* [St. Louis: Concordia, 1972], 25:248).

[2] Concerning Rom 5:2, Moo maintains: "As in 3:23, 'the glory of God' is that state of 'God-like-ness' which has been lost because of sin, and which will be restored in the last day to every Christian" (*Epistle to the Romans*, 302). Similarly, Michel, *Der Brief an die Römer*, 178; Cranfield, *Critical and Exegetical Commentary*, 1:260; Käsemann, *Commentary on Romans*, 133; Dunn, *Romans 1–8*, 249; Barrett, *Commentary on the Epistle to the Romans*, 96; Byrne, *Romans*, 170; Schreiner, *Romans*, 255.

I. The Glory of Adam

Especially since the study of Jacob Jervell, there has been broad scholarly agreement that Paul's language in Rom 3:23 refers to the story of Adam and specifically to the image of God.[3] This understanding of the glory of Adam is clearly expressed in Genesis Rabbah, where glory is an inherent quality that Adam lost when he was expelled from the garden of Eden. "The Rabbis maintain: His glory abode with him, but at the termination of the Sabbath He deprived him of his splendour and expelled him from the Garden of Eden, as it is written, *Thou changest his countenance, and sendest him away* (Job XIV, 20)" (Gen. Rab. 11:2).[4]

Jervell's interpretation, however, is problematic in at least two respects: it does not distinguish between the glory of God and the glory of Adam, and his evidence is exclusively from rabbinic sources, mostly from Midrash Rabbah and the targumim.[5] The current consensus is that rabbinic sources do not describe Judaism before the fall of the temple in 70 CE. Without corroborating evidence, these traditions cannot be assumed to have been current in the middle of the first century.[6]

Jervell's work has been supported by James D. G. Dunn, who has amassed evidence from the literature of Second Temple Judaism. Nevertheless, the idea that the divine glory also became inherently Adam's own glory is attested only in the later sources, for example, the Apocalypse of Moses, which is usually dated toward the end of the first century, and by some even later.[7] In Apoc. Mos. 21:6, Adam accuses Eve: "You have estranged me from the glory of God [ἀπηλλοτρίωσάς με ἐκ τῆς δόξης τοῦ θεοῦ]." This glory of Adam presumably corresponds to the glory of Eve, and Eve describes the loss of her glory in Apoc. Mos. 20:1–2:

> And at that very moment my eyes were opened and I knew that I was naked of the righteousness with which I had been clothed. And I wept saying, "Why have you done this to me, that I have been estranged from my glory with which I was clothed [ἀπηλλοτριώθην ἐκ τῆς δόξης μου, ἧς ἤμην ἐνδεδυμένη]?" (trans. J. Priest, *OTP*)

This glory is a glory that is specifically attributed to Eve, as she says that she was clothed with it. Her "glory" is closely associated with her "righteousness," with

---

[3] Jacob Jervell, *Imago Dei: Gen. 1,26f. im Spätjudentum, in der Gnosis und in den paulinischen Briefen*, FRLANT 76 (Göttingen: Vandenhoeck & Ruprecht, 1978).

[4] Quoted from H. Freeman and Maurice Simon, eds., *Genesis*, vol. 1 of *Midrash Rabbah* (London: Soncino, 1939), 83.

[5] Jervell, *Imago Dei*, 100–103.

[6] For the argument that Paul's connection between death and Adam's sin was unattested in earlier sources, see Henry Ansgar Kelly, "Adam Citings before the Intrusion of Satan: Recontextualizing Paul's Theology of Sin and Death," *BTB* 44 (2014): 13–28.

[7] Ibid., 23–24.

which she had also been clothed.[8] A similar idea is reflected in the Testament of Abraham, dated toward the end of the first century or the beginning of the second:

> Abraham asked the Commander-in-chief, "My lord Commander-in-chief, who is this most wondrous man, who is adorned in such glory, and sometimes he cries and wails while other times he rejoices and exults?" The incorporeal one said, "This is the first-formed Adam who is in such glory, and he looks at the world, since everyone has come from him." (Rec. A. 11:8–9). (trans. E. P. Sanders, *OTP*)

The idea of Adam's glory is given a specifically gnostic interpretation in the Apocalypse of Adam, dated toward the end of the first century or later: "Then we became two aeons, and the glory in our hearts deserted us, me and your mother Eve, along with the first knowledge that used to breathe within us" (1:5; trans. G. W. MacRae, *OTP*).

The more relevant evidence is found in the writings from Qumran.[9] There was an expectation that the faithful would enjoy "all the glory of Adam" (1QS IV, 23; CD-A III, 20; 1QH^a IV, 15).[10] The glory of Adam is associated primarily with the gift of everlasting life.[11] According to CD-A III, 20, "Those who remained steadfast in it will acquire eternal life, and all the glory of Adam is for them." In the words of the Thanksgiving Hymns, the works of God include "[forgiving] offence, casting away all their iniquities, giving them as a legacy all the glory of Adam [and] abundance of days" (1QH^a IV, 15). The Community Rule brings the same concepts together: "The reward of all those who walk in it will be healing, plentiful peace in a long life, fruitful offspring with all everlasting blessings, eternal enjoyment with endless life, and a crown of glory with majestic raiment in eternal light" (1QS IV, 6–8).[12] In this last reference especially, the glory in question appears to be the glory

---

[8] Cf. also 3 Bar. 4:16 (Greek); Hist. Rech. 12:3–3a.

[9] James D. G. Dunn, *Christology in the Making: A New Testament Inquiry into the Origins of the Doctrine of the Incarnation*, 2nd ed. (Grand Rapids: Eerdmans, 1989), 106; see also Robin Scroggs, *The Last Adam: A Study in Pauline Anthropology* (Philadelphia: Fortress, 1966), 26–27; and esp. Crispin H. T. Fletcher-Louis, *All the Glory of Adam: Liturgical Anthropology in the Dead Sea Scrolls*, STDJ 42 (Leiden: Brill, 2002), 91–103. Translations of the Dead Sea documents are from Florentino García Martínez and Eibert J. C. Tigchelaar, eds., *The Dead Sea Scrolls Study Edition*, 2 vols. (Leiden: Brill, 1997).

[10] There are also more general references in mostly late apocalyptic literature to the eschatological glory of the righteous. See Dunn, *Romans 1–8*, 168.

[11] Philip R. Davies, *The Damascus Covenant: An Interpretation of the 'Damascus Document,'* JSOTSup 25 (Sheffield: Sheffield Academic, 1983), 141; Émile Puech, *La croyance des Esséniens en la vie future: Immortalité, résurrection, vie éternelle? Histoire d'une croyance dans le judaïsme ancien*, 2 vols., EBib 21–22, (Paris: Gabalda, 1993), 742–43; Stephen J. Hultgren, *From the Damascus Covenant to the Covenant of the Community: Literary, Historical, and Theological Studies in the Dead Sea Scrolls*, STDJ 66 (Leiden: Brill, 2007), 491.

[12] See also 4Q171 III, 1–2, which describes "all the inheritance of Adam" rather than his glory but also associates it with everlasting life: "those who have returned from the wilderness, who will live for a thousand generations, in salva[tio]n; for them there is all the inheritance of

of the righteous. The idea is likely derived from the picture of future resurrection in Dan 12 and the description of the wise: "Those who are wise shall shine like the brightness of the sky, and those who lead many to righteousness, like the stars forever and ever" (Dan 12:3 NRSV).[13] This text does not use the term "glory" (יקר), but the idea is similar and the anticipated splendor is emanating from the wise ones. The glory is apparently their own. But this eschatological glory is not identified as the glory of God, and the concept is quite distinct from that of the creation of Adam in God's image.[14] It is unwarranted to read the concepts of God's glory and Adam's creation in God's image into these texts.[15]

The only early evidence I have found for the connection between Adam's creation and the glory of God is in the Words of the Luminaries, dated in the early or mid-second century BCE.[16] The prayer for the first day of the week makes reference to the first human being: "[... Adam,] our [fa]ther, you fashioned in the image of

---

Adam, and for their descendants for ever." For the association of glory and eternal life in Second Temple Judaism, see Wis 5:16, 1 En. 62:15–16, 2 En. 22:8–9, T. Benj. 4:1, 2 Bar. 51:3.

[13] For the significance of Dan 12 for the resurrection hope at Qumran, see Émile Puech, "Resurrection: The Bible and Qumran," in *The Dead Sea Scrolls and the Qumran Community*, vol. 2 of *The Bible and the Dead Sea Scrolls*, ed. James H. Charlesworth (Waco, TX: Baylor University Press, 2006), 263–81.

[14] Ben Zion Wacholder translates CD-A III, 20: "The people who cling to Him are destined for eternal life and all human glory will be accorded to them" (*The New Damascus Document: The Midrash on the Eschatological Torah of the Dead Sea Scrolls; Reconstruction, Translation and Commentary*, STDJ 56 [Leiden: Brill, 2006], 33). In this translation, there is even less hint of an association with the account of Adam's creation in God's image. Robin Scroggs observes that the ideal state of the eschaton tended to be correlated with the state of creation. Since the community was primarily interested in the eschaton, however, the glory associated with the eschaton would likely have been primary, and any glory associated with creation a secondary development (*Last Adam*, 25–27).

[15] It is also unwarranted to read these texts in light of the traditions regarding the glory shining from Moses's face at Sinai. The Words of the Luminaries makes reference to the face of Moses in the context of describing God's glory (4Q504 6, 10–12), but the text is corrupt and the relation between these two concepts is unclear. As it has been preserved, the text makes no connection between Adam and the glory of Moses. Pace Andrei A. Orlov, "Vested with Adam's Glory: Moses as the Luminous Counterpart of Adam in the Dead Sea Scrolls and in the Macarian Homilies," in *L'église des deux alliances: Mémorial Annie Jaubert (1912-1980)*, ed. Basil Lourié, Andrei Orlov, and Madeleine Petit, Orientalia Judaica Christiana 1 (Piscataway, NJ: Gorgias, 2008), 740–55, here 740–41.

[16] Maurice Baillet, "Un recueil liturgique de Qumrân, grotte 4: 'Les Paroles des Luminaires,'" *RB* 68 (1961): 195–250, here 235–38; Baillet, *(4Q482–4Q520)*, vol. 3 of *Qumrân grotte 4*, DJD VII (Oxford: Clarendon, 1982), 137; Ester G. Chazon, "Is *Divrei Ha-Me'orot* a Sectarian Prayer?" (Ph.D. diss., Hebrew University, 1991), 81–85 (cited from Daniel K. Falk, *Daily, Sabbath, and Festival Prayers in the Dead Sea Scrolls*, STDJ 27 [Leiden: Brill, 1998], 61). Geza Vermes has questioned whether this dating may be exaggeratedly early (in Emil Schürer, *The History of the Jewish People in the Age of Jesus Christ [175 B.C.–A.D. 135]*, rev. ed., ed. Geza Vermes, Fergus Millar, and Martin Goodman, 3 vols. [Edinburgh: T&T Clark, 1973–1986], 3.1:459).

[your] glory [יצרתה בדמות כבוד] [...]" (4Q504 8, 4). The expression is basically a paraphrase of the statement from Gen 5:1 that Adam was made in the likeness of God (בדמות אלהים עשה אתו). This idea is also different from what we find in the eschatological texts surveyed above. According to this prayer, glory is not an inherent quality bestowed on Adam; the glory of God is the model according to which Adam was fashioned.[17] Glory is not specifically attributed to Adam himself.

To be fashioned according to the image of God's glory is associated with other qualities attributed to Adam: life and knowledge. The scroll continues: "[... the breath of life] you [b]lew into his nostril, and intelligence and knowledge" (4Q504 8, 5). As we have seen, the eschatological gift of everlasting life is frequently associated with the glory of Adam, but the concept of Adam's eschatological glory must not be conflated with the concept of God's glory at creation. The idea in the Words of the Luminaries is not that God's glory was inherent in Adam and ensured that he was a living being. Rather, the point is probably that Adam depended on God for the gifts of life and knowledge (Ps 104:29; Job 34:14–15; Eccl 12:7; cf. Job 12:10; 27:3; Isa 42:5; Dan 5:23; 1QH^a X, 23). Accordingly, God's presence was necessary to blow the breath of life "into his nostril" (4Q504 8, 5).[18]

In the Words of the Luminaries, a cultic understanding of the referent of God's glory predominates. Later in the prayer quoted above, God is praised for works of salvation on behalf of the people Israel: "You are in our midst, in the column of fire and in the cloud [...] your [hol]y [...] walks in front of us, and your glory is in [our] midst" (4Q504 6, 10–11). The "glory" refers to the presence of God manifested in the fire and the cloud that accompanied Israel through the wilderness.

As Hanan Eshel has shown, there are some striking parallels between the Words of the Luminaries and the Apocalypse of Weeks (1 En. 93:1–10; 91:12–17). The weeks of the apocalypse correspond broadly to the prayers for the individual days in the Words of the Luminaries.[19] The Apocalypse of Weeks has little to say

---

[17] Fletcher-Louis notes that "Adam is only made in (ב) the likeness of God's Glory" and adds that "the text is too fragmentary to gauge how the relationship was worked out." He goes on to argue that the statement should be interpreted in light of the glory of the high priest in Sir 50:1 (Hebrew), referring to an "embodiment of both God's Glory and divine Wisdom" (*All the Glory*, 93). The Qumran scroll, however, cannot be used as evidence that the glory was understood to be inherently Adam's own glory.

The Hebrew text of Sir 50:1 refers to the high priest (Simon) as the glory of his people. God's glory is not mentioned but must be read into the text. The glory most likely refers to Simon's qualities as the religious leader of the people (Patrick W. Skehan and Alexander A. Di Lella, *The Wisdom of Ben Sira: A New Translation with Notes*, AB 39 [Garden City, NY: Doubleday, 1987], 550).

[18] Concerning the teaching of the texts from Qumran in general, Hermann Lichtenberger observes that the concept of creation in God's image functions not to glorify human beings but to extol God for his works (*Studien zum Menschenbild in Texten der Qumrangemeinde*, SUNT 15 [Göttingen: Vandenhoeck & Ruprecht, 1980], 179–80).

[19] Eshel even argues that the Apocalypse of Weeks likely influenced the Words of the Luminaries ("*Dibre Hameʾorot* and the Apocalypse of Weeks," in *Things Revealed: Studies in Early Jewish*

about creation and makes no reference to the glory of Adam, but it contains a description of "the second eighth week," which is the time of eschatological salvation. In this week, "a house shall be built for the Great King in glory for evermore" (1 En. 91:13). The glory that the apocalypse is anticipating is the presence of God as king.

Later texts explicitly describe Adam's paradisiacal state as enjoyment of God's presence. In 2 Baruch (early second century), God's presence in the temple is compared to his revelation to Adam (4:3), and, according to 2 En. 31:2 (late first century) God created for Adam an open heaven (cf. also 2 En. 71:28; 3 En. 5:12).

The texts surveyed above may be broadly divided into two general categories: the texts that specifically attribute God's glory to Adam and the texts that refer to Adam's own glory. The first category is found only in later works such as rabbinic writings and apocalyptic writings that cannot be dated earlier than the late first century but may be even later. Texts in the second category, which include some writings from Qumran, do not attribute God's glory to Adam but refer to Adam's glory, a glory primarily associated with the gift of eternal life. In these texts, God's glory remains God's own.

II. Glory in Romans

The traditions regarding an inherent Adamic glory are not the most relevant background for understanding Paul's references to God's glory in Romans. It is better to understand Paul in light of the use of δόξα in the Septuagint, which points to the revelatory presence of God, predominantly God's presence at Sinai. Paul's δόξα language has close affinities with this usage.

In the LXX, the use of the term δόξα differs markedly from its use in secular Greek in that the basic meaning "opinion" is not found. Instead, the meaning is shaped by the Hebrew כבוד, referring to the radiance of a theophany.[20] Consequently, the glory of God denotes the impressive display of God's appearance, specifically in the tabernacle and the temple (Exod 29:43; 40:34, 35; Lev 9:23; Num 14:10; 1 Kgdms 4:22; 3 Kgdms 8:11; 2 Chr 5:14; Ezek 8:4; etc.).

---

and Christian Literature in Honor of Michael E. Stone, ed. Ester G. Chazon, David Satran, and Ruth A. Clements, JSJSup 89 [Leiden: Brill, 2004], 149–54, here 153). In any case, the parallels make it likely that these writings reflect similar theological outlooks. The Apocalypse of Weeks may therefore shed some light on the interpretation of the Words of the Luminaries.

[20] Gerhard Kittel and Gerhard von Rad, "δοκέω κτλ.," *TDNT* 2:232–55, here 247; H. Hegermann, "δόξα," *EDNT* 1:344–48, here 345; Jörg Frey, "The Use of Δόξα in Paul and John as Shaped by the Septuagint," in *The Reception of Septuagint Words in Jewish-Hellenistic and Christian Literature*, ed. Eberhard Bons, Ralph Brucker, and Jan Joosten, WUNT 2/367 (Tübingen: Mohr Siebeck, 2014), 85–104, here 86–90. Thomas Wagner concludes that δόξα originated as a cultic term (*Gottes Herrlichkeit: Bedeutung und Verwendung des Begriffs* kabôd *im Alten Testament*, VTSup 151 [Leiden: Brill, 2012], 440).

The story of God's presence in Israel shapes Paul's use of δόξα language as well. Paul presupposes that glory characterizes God.[21] Of the sixteen occurrences of δόξα in Romans, six refer to God's glory (1:23; 3:7, 23; 5:2; 6:4; 9:23) and four to glory given or attributed to God by human beings (4:20, 11:36, 15:7, 16:27). The remaining instances concern human beings seeking glory (2:7) and receiving glory from God (2:10; 8:18, 21; 9:23; cf. 5:2) as well as the glory belonging to Israel (9:4). Two of the references to God's glory also make the point that human beings have forfeited it (1:23) or lack it (3:23). The verb δοξάζω occurs five times in Romans, three times with God as the object (1:21; 15:6, 9).

God's glory belongs to the people of Israel, as Paul affirms in Rom 9:4–5: "They are Israelites, and to them belong the adoption, the glory, the covenants, the giving of the law, the worship, and the promises; to them belong the patriarchs, and from them, according to the flesh, comes the Messiah, who is over all, God blessed forever. Amen" (NRSV). The consensus among commentators is that the glory to which Paul refers is the tangible presence of God.[22] More specifically, Paul may be thinking of the revelation at Sinai, which he describes in 2 Cor 3:7 as having come in glory "so that the people of Israel could not gaze at Moses' face because of the glory of his face" (NRSV).

Yet God's revelation at Sinai—God's glory—was rejected: "Claiming to be wise, they became fools; and they exchanged the glory of the immortal God for images resembling a mortal human being or birds or four-footed animals or reptiles [φάσκοντες εἶναι σοφοὶ ἐμωράνθησαν καὶ ἤλλαξαν τὴν δόξαν τοῦ ἀφθάρτου θεοῦ ἐν ὁμοιώματι εἰκόνος φθαρτοῦ ἀνθρώπου καὶ πετεινῶν καὶ τετραπόδων καὶ ἑρπετῶν]" (Rom 1:22–23 NRSV). This indictment has a universal application, as verse 20 refers to human beings' knowledge of God ever since creation, but Paul's description is inspired by a specific example, the Sinai incident. The language of Rom 1:23 recalls that of Ps 105:20–21 LXX: "And they exchanged their glory for a likeness of a bull calf that eats grass [καὶ ἠλλάξαντο τὴν δόξαν αὐτῶν ἐν ὁμοιώματι μόσχου ἔσθοντος χόρτον]" (NETS). They forgot the God who was saving them, who did great things in Egypt" (cf. also Jer 2:11). Romans 1:23 and the psalm both employ the characteristic terms ἀλλάσσω, δόξα, and ὁμοίωμα, which makes a conscious allusion likely.[23] With the words "a bull calf that eats grass," the psalm makes an

---

[21] Carey Newman observes that δόξα is one of only sixteen words that occur with genitives of both "God" and "Christ" as a qualifier. He concludes, "Glory relates to a field of words like 'spirit,' 'power,' 'word,' 'gospel' and 'presence,' words which sign the presence of God" (*Paul's Glory-Christology: Tradition and Rhetoric*, NovTSup 69 [Leiden: Brill, 1992], 163).

[22] Cranfield glosses this glory as an "outward sign of God's presence with His people" (*Critical and Exegetical Commentary*, 2:461–62; similarly Moo, *Epistle to the Romans*, 563). Dunn understands it as "the theophanies which had been Israel's special privilege as God's people" (*Romans 9–16*, WBC 38B [Dallas: Word, 1988], 526; similarly, Newman, *Paul's Glory-Christology*, 193; Fitzmyer, *Romans*, 546; Frey, "Use of Δόξα in Paul and John," 95).

[23] Similarly, Cranfield, *Critical and Exegetical Commentary*, 1:119; Wilckens, *Der Brief an die Römer*, 1:107; Dunn, *Romans 1–8*, 61; Fitzmyer, *Romans*, 270; Moo, *Epistle to the Romans*, 108;

unmistakable reference to the golden calves that Israel worshiped at Sinai. Perhaps in order not to rule out a universal application, Paul does not include these words. Instead, he expands with the words "images resembling a mortal human being or birds or four-footed animals or reptiles." This expansion of the psalm recalls the language of Deut 4:15–18:[24]

> And guard your souls closely, because you did not notice a likeness [ὁμοίωμα] on the day the Lord spoke to you at Choreb in the mountain from the midst of the fire. Do not act lawlessly and make for yourselves an engraved likeness [ὁμοίωμα], any kind of icon [εἰκόνα]—a likeness [ὁμοίωμα] of male or female, a likeness [ὁμοίωμα] of any animal of those that are on the earth, a likeness [ὁμοίωμα] of any winged bird that flies under the sky, a likeness of any reptile [ὁμοίωμα παντὸς ἑρπετοῦ] that creeps on the ground, a likeness [ὁμοίωμα] of any fish that is in the waters beneath the earth. (NETS)

This passage in Deuteronomy is the only instance in which the terms ὁμοίωμα and ἑρπετόν occur in the same context in the LXX. It would appear that Paul has combined the language of Ps 105 and Deut 4. The effect is to describe Israel's disobedience at Sinai in such a way that it is seen as a direct violation of the commandment. At the same time, the language is sufficiently broad that it may be applied to humanity in general. Once again, the glory of God may be understood in reference to God's revelatory presence at Sinai.[25]

Byrne, *Romans*, 68; Schreiner, *Romans*, 81. Whereas the psalm refers to "their glory," Paul clarifies that the glory is the glory of the immortal God. (Perhaps influenced by the language of Rom 1:23, a few manuscripts also read δόξα θεοῦ in Ps 105:20 LXX.) Cranfield comments, "what is meant by Israel's glory is God Himself ... that self-manifestation of the true God spoken of in vv. 19 and 20" (1:119–20).

[24] Similarly Niels Hyldahl, "A Reminiscence of the Old Testament at Romans i. 23," *NTS* 2 (1956): 285–88, here 285–86; Cranfield, *Critical and Exegetical* Commentary, 1:119; Fitzmyer, *Romans*, 283; Schreiner, *Romans*, 87.

[25] Taking her cue from Nils Hyldahl ("Reminiscence of the Old Testament"), Morna Hooker focuses on the connections to the Adam story in Gen 1. She observes a number of parallels: Adam knew what could be known about God (cf. Rom 1:19); from creation he saw God's attributes (cf. 1:20); he failed to glorify God and became futile and darkened in his mind (1:21); he lost the glory of God (1:23); he gave his allegiance to the serpent, a created being, rather than to the Creator (1:25); and, even though he knew God's decree, he not only violated it but agreed with Eve when she broke it (1:32). See Morna D. Hooker, *From Adam to Christ: Essays on Paul* (Cambridge: Cambridge University Press, 1990), 77–78; similarly Dunn, *Romans 1–8*, 61; and, more cautiously, A. J. M. Wedderburn, "Adam in Paul's Letter to the Romans," in *Papers on the Gospels*, vol. 2 of *Studia Biblica 1978*, ed. Elizabeth Anne Livingstone, JSNTSup 2 (Sheffield: JSOT Press, 1980), 413–33, here 413–19. These parallels are at a general, conceptual level, and there is no shared terminology that can confirm the allusions. What is more, most of the elements in Rom 1:21–32 do not fit Adam's story: Paul mentions knowledge of God through his works of creation (Rom 1:20), but Adam knew God from his verbal encounter with him; the story in Genesis does not report that Adam became futile in his mind, that his senseless mind was darkened, or that he claimed to be wise (1:21–22); and Adam did not lapse into idolatry or worship of creation (1:23,

When Paul picks up the theme in Rom 3:23 of human beings lacking the glory of God, the picture of the wilderness generation from 1:23 is most likely what he has in mind. As in 1:23, the experience of Israel serves as a paradigm for all humanity, so that Paul may affirm: "all have sinned and fall short of the glory of God." They are without the presence of God.[26]

Nevertheless, God's glory or honor is not thwarted, even though it is rejected by God's people. The burden of Paul's letter to the Romans is to show that God's glory still abounds through God's own work, the pinnacle of which is the creation of a people for divine glory. (The term "glory" is not interchangeable with "presence" but refers to the presence as an impressive manifestation). In Romans, God's glory does not describe God in isolation from divine works and divine interaction with creation. God's glory is the glory that results from divine revelation and from divine works. By the Father's glory, Christ was raised from the dead (6:4). In 3:7, Paul emphasizes that God's glory abounds, even through human falsehood, as a result of God's truth.[27] Even more than God's truth, however, God's mercy manifests divine glory. According to Rom 9:23, the riches of God's glory are made known upon the objects of mercy, the ones God previously prepared for glory. These objects consist of those God has called, not only from Jews but also from gentiles (9:24). According to Rom 15:9, when the gentiles bring glory to God, it is precisely in response to divine mercy.

In a reversal of humanity's failure to glorify (ἐδόξασαν) God (1:21) and in imitation of Abraham's giving glory (δόξαν) to God (4:20), the believers in Rome (15:6) and the gentiles (15:9) may glorify (δοξάζω) God. The purpose of Paul's gospel is therefore that God's glory abound. Paul concludes his argument with a doxology in 11:36: "To him be the glory forever. Amen." If 16:25–27 are accepted as authentic, the letter as a whole closes in a similar way: "to the only wise God, through Jesus Christ, to whom be the glory forever! Amen."[28] In 14:1–15:13 Paul

---

[25] or the specific sins that Paul enumerates in 1:26–32. Scroggs correctly concludes that "the δόξα of verse 23 must refer to the glory that shines from God rather than that which rests, or rested, upon Adam" (*Last Adam*, 76).

[26] Fitzmyer concludes, "Estranged from the intimate presence of God by sin, they have been deprived of that enhancing quality which they should have in this life as well as that for which they are destined eschatologically in the presence of God. Hence they fall short of their share in the glory of God" (*Romans*, 347). Similarly, Newman, who notes the connection between Rom 1:23 and 3:23 and understands the expressions "to exchange the glory of God" and "to fall short of the glory of God" to refer to "a ruptured relationship" (*Paul's Glory-Christology*, 225; so also James R. Harrison, "Paul and the Roman Ideal of Glory in the Epistle to the Romans," in *The Letter to the Romans*, ed. Udo Schnelle, BETL 226 [Leuven: Peeters, 2009], 329–69, here 364). Arland Hultgren comments, "To fall short of the glory of God … is to fail to share the perfect communion with God for which humanity was created" (*Paul's Letter to the Romans: A Commentary* [Grand Rapids: Eerdmans, 2011], 155).

[27] The dative ἐν τῷ ἐμῷ ψεύσματι is likely instrumental.

[28] For a thorough discussion, concluding in favor of a later interpolation, see Jewett, *Romans*,

exhorts the believers to glorify God in unity (ὁμοθυμαδόν, 15:6). In 15:7, Paul explains how the church's life can result in the glory of God: "Welcome one another, therefore, just as Christ has welcomed you, for the glory of God" (NRSV). The preposition εἰς must be taken in its telic sense: the goal of the church's welcoming one another is the glory of God. Paul's exhortation to welcome one another must be understood against the background of his entire argument in the epistle, which has been building up to this exhortation: just as the demonstration of God's grace and mercy in Jesus Christ has welcomed both Jews and gentiles into the people of God, so should believers demonstrate grace and mercy in their interactions with one another. Their Christlike community life will then result in the glory of God.

The eschatological glory of believers can therefore not be understood as the restoration of an inherent Adamic glory that once was lost. It is rather related to the renewed presence of God when the relationship between God and God's people is restored.[29] As the manifestation of God's glory is above all a function of divine mercy, the eschaton will reveal that God's people, the objects of mercy, are participating in God's glory.[30] Their glory consists not in having any lost qualities restored to them but in the fact that they are recipients of God's mercy. The glory that belongs to them in the eschaton is a glory that is revealed for their benefit. In Rom 8:18, where Paul refers to the future glory of believers, he says that the glory will be revealed "to us" or "for us." The Greek prepositional phrase εἰς ἡμᾶς is rather unusual. It may be used in a concrete sense, as when someone is coming to us. When the phrase is used with an abstract meaning, the sense is "for our benefit." In a letter to the Alexandrians (P.Lond. 1912), Claudius speaks of their goodwill "toward us" (εἰς ἡμᾶς).[31] In 2 Clem. 3.1, the phrase is used about Christ, who has shown us (εἰς ἡμᾶς) such mercy. The letter of Barnabas discusses whether the covenant is for us or for them (εἰς ἡμᾶς ἢ εἰς ἐκείνους, 13:1). In *Salvation of the Rich* 37, Clement of Alexandria describes God as having sympathy with us (εἰς ἡμᾶς). As

---

997-1005; similarly Dunn, *Romans 9-16*, 912-13; Fitzmyer, *Romans*, 753. Contra Larry W. Hurtado, "The Doxology at the End of Romans," in *New Testament Textual Criticism: Its Significance for Exegesis; Essays in Honour of Bruce M. Metzger*, ed. Eldon Jay Epp and Gordon D. Fee (Oxford: Clarendon, 1981), 185-99; I. Howard Marshall, "Romans 16:25-27—An Apt Conclusion," in *Romans and the People of God: Essays in Honor of Gordon D. Fee on the Occasion of His 65th Birthday*, ed. Sven K. Soderlund and N. T. Wright (Grand Rapids: Eerdmans, 1999), 170-84.

[29] Fitzmyer observes, "Paul formulates the destiny of Christian existence, which he will further specify in time as a share in the 'glory' of God (3:23; 5:2) and in the life of the risen Christ (6:4), i.e., being 'forever with the Lord'" (*Romans*, 302; similarly, Hultgren, *Paul's Letter to the Romans*, 205-6).

[30] Cf. Karl Barth, who concludes, "It is, therefore, always God's self-glorification which is accomplished even in His glorification by the creature" (*The Doctrine of God*, vol. 2.1 of *Church Dogmatics*, ed. G. W. Bromiley and T. F. Torrance, trans. T. H. L. Parker et al. [Edinburgh: T&T Clark, 1957], 672).

[31] Cited from *Non-Literary Papyri: Public Documents*, vol. 2 of *Select Papyri*, trans. A. S. Hunt and C. C. Edgar, LCL (Cambridge: Harvard University Press, 1963), 80-81.

far as I can see, it is therefore unwarranted when the KJV and the NIV translate Rom 8:18 with a reference to the glory that is going to be revealed "in us." Rather, the prepositional phrase is used in the sense "for us," "to us," or "toward us." The future glory of believers does not reside in them. It is a glory that is revealed for them, a glory that is intended for their benefit. This is why Paul can boast in the hope of God's glory (Rom 5:2) without violating the principle of only boasting in the Lord (1 Cor 1:31).

As he says in Rom 8:17, he looks forward to being glorified with Christ. The use of the verb συνδοξάζω with this meaning, as opposed to "holding the same opinion as," appears to be coined by Paul himself.[32] The believers will not be glorified independent of their union with Christ, but they will share in his glory. Just as they suffer with him (συμπάσχομεν), so will they be glorified with him. These sufferings are not just any sufferings that may befall believers in this world but sufferings that they undergo as a direct result of their identification with Christ. It is as if the ill will that is directed at Christ also strikes them by the logic of guilt by association. By analogy, the glory in which they participate is the glory of Christ, a glory that will also be associated with them, provided that they also suffer with him. In the midst of their sufferings, they may therefore "boast in [their] hope of the glory of God" (Rom 5:2).

III. Romans 2:6–10

An apparent exception to the pattern described above is Rom 2:6–10, where glory seems to be a quality human beings are encouraged to pursue:

> For he will repay according to each one's deeds: to those who by patiently doing good seek for glory and honor and immortality, he will give eternal life; while for those who are self-seeking and who obey not the truth but wickedness, there will be wrath and fury. There will be anguish and distress for everyone who does evil, the Jew first and also the Greek, but glory and honor and peace for everyone who does good, the Jew first and also the Greek. (NRSV)

Many commentators find in these words a description of eschatological blessing, but this interpretation needs to be qualified.[33]

The word pair "glory and honor" is well known from the LXX, where it occurs thirteen times (Exod 28:2, 40; 2 Chr 32:33; 1 Macc 14:21; 2 Macc 5:16; Pss 8:6; 28:1; 95:7; Job 37:22; 40:10; Dan 2:37; 4:30; 5:18 Θ). When it is used in a theological sense, it belongs exclusively to God.[34]

---

[32] Dunn, *Romans 1–8*, 456.

[33] Michel, *Der Brief an die Römer*, 115; Cranfield, *Critical and Exegetical Commentary*, 1:147; Wilckens, *Der Brief an die Römer*, 1:126; Dunn, *Romans 1–8*, 88; Moo, *Epistle to the Romans*, 136; Fitzmyer, *Romans*, 302; Jewett, *Romans*, 208–9.

[34] The terms are also used five times in synonymous parallelism (Isa 10:16, 35:2, 2 Macc 4:15,

There is only one example of God giving glory and honor in this more absolute sense to human beings: Ps 8:4–5 praises God who cares for human beings: "What is man that you are mindful of him or son of man that you attend to him? You diminished him a little in comparison with angels; with glory and honor you crowned him" (NETS). Several commentators refer to this psalm as evidence that glory describes what God has in store for human beings.[35]

In the psalm's original context, the term "son of man" was probably a general reference to human beings, but in the early Christian movement the psalm is interpreted christologically.[36] Paul quotes the psalm in 1 Cor 15:25–27 and combines it

---

Wis 8:10, Sir 3:11). The glory and honor in question may be visible splendor that characterizes objects in this world, such as the attire of the high priest (Exod 28:2, 40) and the vessels in the temple (2 Macc 5:16). In a more abstract sense, glory and honor are attributed to people of high status (1 Macc 14:21; cf. Wis 8:10, Sir 3:11, 2 Macc 4:15). When people show honor to someone, they can therefore be said to give them glory and honor (2 Chr 32:33). Glory and honor may characterize earthly kingdoms, such as that of Nebuchadnezzar. In that case, glory and honor are given by God (Dan 2:37, 5:18). When human beings claim glory and honor as their own, God does not approve (Dan 4:30; cf. Isa 10:16, 35:2). Above all, human beings should attribute glory and honor to God (Pss 28:1, 95:7), to whom it belongs (Job 37:22). In Job 40:10, Job is challenged to clothe himself in glory and honor, but the verse is ironic—the point is that these qualities characterize God, and God alone.

[35] Dunn's statement that the expression "'glory and honor,' is familiar enough to Jewish ears as a description of what God desires for man (Job 40:10; Ps 8:5)" is misleading (*Romans 1–8*, 85; similarly Jewett, *Romans*, 208). His two references do not prove the point. Job 40:10 is ironic, and Ps 8:5 was interpreted christologically by Paul (see below).

[36] According to Matt 21:16, Jesus quotes Ps 8 in connection with his triumphal entry, but the quotation does not provide an interpretation of the term "son of man." In the epistle to the Hebrews, the psalm is discussed at some length: "Someone testified somewhere, saying: what is a human being that you remember him, or a son of a human being that you look after him? For a little, you made him lower than the angels, you have crowned him with glory and honor, while subjecting all things under his feet.' When he subjected all things to him, he did not leave anything that was not subjected to him. But now, we do not see that all things are subjected to him. The one who for a little was made lower than the angels, him we see: Jesus, who is crowned with glory and honor because of the suffering of death, so that by the grace of God he might taste death for everyone" (Heb 2:6–10; my translation). It is debatable whether the author has understood "son of a human being" as a double reference both to human beings in general and to Jesus in particular, or if he understood it as exclusively referring to Jesus. For the former interpretation, see William L. Lane, *Hebrews 1–8*, WBC 47A (Dallas: Word, 1991), 47; David A. deSilva, *Perseverance in Gratitude: A Socio-Rhetorical Commentary on the Epistle 'to the Hebrews'* (Grand Rapids: Eerdmans, 2000), 110; Craig R. Koester, *Hebrews: A New Translation with Introduction and Commentary*, AB 36 (New York: Doubleday, 2001), 215. For the latter, see F. F. Bruce, *The Epistle to the Hebrews*, NICNT (Grand Rapids: Eerdmans, 1964), 72–73; George H. Guthrie, "Hebrews," in *Commentary on the New Testament Use of the Old Testament*, ed. G. K. Beale and D. A. Carson (Grand Rapids: Baker Academic, 2007), 946; Gareth Lee Cockerill, *The Epistle to the Hebrews*, NICNT (Grand Rapids: Eerdmans, 2012), 129–30. In any case, however, what is important to the author of Hebrews is the latter point: the son of a human being, who is crowned with glory and honor, is Jesus. See Paul Ellingworth, *The Epistle to the Hebrews: A Commentary on the Greek Text*,

with Ps 110: "It is necessary that he rule as king until 'he puts' all 'his enemies under his feet.' The last enemy to be destroyed is death. 'He has subjected all things under his feet.' When he says: 'all things are subjected,' it is clear that the one who subjects all things to him is excepted" (my translation). In Ps 8:6, the one to whom all things are subjected is the son of man, and in 1 Cor 15:27 it is Jesus.[37] When Paul read Scripture he did not find glory and honor to belong to human beings. When the word pair was used in the qualified sense, Paul saw only a description of God and God's Son.[38]

If honor and glory exclusively belong to God, is it possible that to "seek for glory and honor and immortality" is a synonym for seeking God?[39] Paul's choice of the verb ζητέω ("to seek") lends itself to this interpretation. This verb is never used with glory, honor, and immortality as its object in the LXX. It is often used in its concrete sense, "to look for something." The presupposition is that something is lacking and that it is necessary to seek it or look for it in order to find it. The verb is therefore well suited to having a person as its object. In all these instances, the translation "look for" conveys the sense better in modern English.

Ζητέω is often used in a religious sense, in the context of Israel's relationship with the Lord. In these instances, the object is typically the Lord himself. True, the people may be urged to seek the law (Ezra 7:10, Sir 32:15), the commandments of the Lord (1 Chr 28:8), peace (Ps 33:15, Jer 36:7), faithfulness (Jer 5:1), or (personified) wisdom (Prov 1:28, 8:17, Wis 6:12, Sir 4:11, 6:27, 51:13). In the vast majority of these cases, however, the message is that the people need to seek God or seek God's face.[40] The motivation to look for the Lord is frequently that he is the savior

---

NIGTC (Grand Rapids: Eerdmans, 1993), 152; Harold W. Attridge, *The Epistle to the Hebrews: A Commentary on the Epistle to the Hebrews*, Hermeneia (Minneapolis: Fortress, 1996), 72.

[37] Paul appears to presuppose this reading of Ps 8:6 also in Phil 3:21: "[Jesus Christ,] who will transform our body of lowliness to conform to his body of glory according to the power by which he is also able to subject all things to himself" (my translation). Psalm 8:6 is also quoted christologically in Eph 1:22: "and 'has subjected all things under his feet' and given him as head over all things for the church" (my translation).

[38] In 1 Cor 11:7, Paul says that man is the "image and glory of God" (εἰκὼν καὶ δόξα θεοῦ), but δόξα is used in a more relative sense here. The argument focuses on the differences between man and woman, as man is the "image and glory of God" and woman is the "glory of man." There is no indication that this is a glory that was lost in the fall and is brought to its eschatological restoration. It is a glory that characterizes the man but not the woman (Michael Lakey, *Image and Glory of God: 1 Corinthians 11:2–16 as a Case Study in Bible, Gender and Hermeneutics*, LNTS 418 [London: T&T Clark, 2010], 112). The idea is not that man possesses divine glory, but that his behavior is a display of God's own qualities. Anthony Thiselton comments on this verse: "Man is to exhibit the attributes of God in his life and role" (*The First Epistle to the Corinthians*, NIGTC [Grand Rapids: Eerdmans, 2000], 835).

[39] For the close association between glory and immortality, see Ben C. Blackwell, "Immortal Glory and the Problem of Death in Romans 3.23," *JSNT* 32 (2010): 285–308.

[40] The object of ζητέω is God in Exod 33:7; Deut 4:29; 1 Chr 10:14; 16:11; 21:30; 22:19; 28:9; 2 Chr 11:16; 15:12, 15; 16:12; 18:4, 7; 20:4; 22:9; 26:5; 34:3, 21, 26; 1 Esd 7:13; Ezra 8:22; Pss 23:6;

(Pss 23:5, 26:9, 39:17, 69:5, Lam 3:26). When the term is used in this way, the frame of reference is that of a personal relationship. In the time of need, the Lord is the one who can bring salvation; hence, the need to look for him. Sometimes, the presupposition is that of a ruptured relationship. The Lord is no longer with his people. It is therefore necessary to seek him.

If the word pair "glory and honor" characterizes the personal manifestation of God, and if the verb ζητέω is typically used to describe people seeking the personal presence of God, it is natural to read Paul's statement in Rom 2:7 in this light. To seek glory and honor and immortality is to look for God and to yearn for God's personal presence.

IV. Conclusion

All sixteen occurrences of the term δόξα in Paul's letter to the Romans are best understood against the same background: God's revelatory presence with God's people. Any reference to Adam is at best secondary.

Paul's use of the term presupposes a story: God's presence was with the people Israel but was rejected by them. God's honor was not thwarted, however; it abounds through divine works of mercy, climaxing in the forming of a people consisting of Jews and gentiles. As the recipients of God's mercy, this people are integral to the glorious eschatological manifestation of God's presence. Through them, God's glory is being and will be manifested in an unprecedented way. This people share in God's glory, therefore, not by virtue of their inherent qualities but by virtue of the fact that they serve as a demonstration of God's mercy.

This interpretation has significant implications for our understanding of Paul's theology. In Paul's thought, the preeminent attribute of God is mercy.[41] The people of God are defined accordingly: they are not distinguished by any qualities that may be perceived as their own, not even qualities that are nothing but a gift from God; their only true distinguishing trait is that they are recipients of God's undeserved mercy and favor. Their glory is not their own possession; it is theirs by virtue of their relationship with God.

39:17; 68:7; 69:5; 82:17; 104:3–4; Prov 16:8; 28:5; Wis 1:1; 13:6; Zeph 2:3; Mal 3:1; Isa 51:1; 55:6; 58:2; 65:10; Jer 27:4; 36:13; 43:24; Bar 4:28; Lam 3:25; Ezek 36:37. It is God's face in 2 Chr 7:14; 33:12; Pss 23:6; 26:8; 104:4; Pr Azar 41.

[41] Compare 2 Cor 3:7–11, where Paul insists that the glory of God's life-giving and justifying activity trumps the glory of God's condemning and judging activity.

Congratulations to the 2016 Jordan Schnitzer
BOOK AWARD WINNERS
AWARDED BY THE ASSOCIATION FOR JEWISH STUDIES

Rhinestones, Religion, and the Republic: Fashioning Jewishness in France
KIMBERLY A. ARKIN
Stanford University Press

Protocols of Justice: The Pinkas of the Metz Rabbinic Court, 1771-1789
JAY R. BERKOVITZ
Brill

What's Divine about Divine Law? Early Perspectives
CHRISTINE HAYES
Princeton University Press

Jewish Contiguities and the Soundtrack of Israeli History
ASSAF SHELLEG
Oxford University Press

FINALISTS

Roman Vishniac Rediscovered
MAYA BENTON
DelMonico Books/Prestel/International Center of Photography

Beyond Violence: Jewish Survivors in Poland and Slovakia, 1944-1948
ANNA CICHOPEK-GAJRAJ
Cambridge University Press

Jaffa Shared and Shattered: Contrived Coexistence in Israel/Palestine
DANIEL MONTERESCU
Indiana University Press

Tradition and the Formation of the Talmud
MOULIE VIDAS
Princeton University Press

Support for this program is generously provided by the **Jordan Schnitzer Family Foundation** of Portland, Oregon.

The **Association for Jewish Studies** is the largest learned society and professional organization representing Jewish Studies scholars worldwide. Visit us at **ajsnet.org** to learn more about our work. **Questions?** Contact us at ajs@ajs.cjh.org or (917) 606-8249.

Romans 1:3–4: Beyond Antithetical Parallelism

NATHAN C. JOHNSON
nathan.johnson@ptsem.edu
Princeton Theological Seminary, Princeton, NJ 08540

Scholars universally recognize that Rom 1:3–4, perhaps our earliest christological confession, features parallelism. In describing this feature, many scholars have appealed to Robert Lowth's category of "antithetical parallelism." I question such an approach for two reasons: (1) it often results in setting Davidic descent and divine sonship in antithesis to one another, an unlikely reading based on David traditions in Second Temple Judaism; (2) it fails to take account of the widespread disuse of antithetical parallelism in the contemporary study of biblical parallelism. These shortcomings, which falter on historical and literary grounds, call for a twofold response. First, I survey the evidence from Second Temple Judaism on Davidic descent, concluding that, far from being in antithesis to divine sonship, it was in fact a sine qua non for installation as the son of God. Second, I counter the antithetical reading of Davidic descent on formal grounds by offering a fresh reading of Rom 1:3–4 through the lens of Adele Berlin's critical account of parallelism. The study concludes by providing nuanced alternatives to antithetical parallelism for our understanding of the relationship of the elements in Rom 1:3–4.

In 1753 Robert Lowth delivered his famous Oxford lectures on biblical parallelism. Since then many scholars have applied Lowth's category of "antithetical parallelism" in structuring what is arguably the earliest extant christological confession, Rom 1:3–4:

τοῦ γενομένου ἐκ σπέρματος Δαυὶδ κατὰ σάρκα,
τοῦ ὁρισθέντος υἱοῦ θεοῦ ἐν δυνάμει κατὰ πνεῦμα ἁγιωσύνης ἐξ ἀναστάσεως νεκρῶν

who came from the seed of David according to the flesh,
who was appointed son of God in power according to the Spirit of holiness by the resurrection of the dead.[1]

---

[1] All translations are my own unless otherwise noted.

Such antithetical readings of the structure of the poem have in turn spawned antithetical, pejorative readings of Jesus's Davidic descent. In response to such interpretations, I begin by examining Davidic traditions within the matrix of Second Temple Judaism. After framing the necessary historical background, I then problematize the antithetical argument and work toward bringing the reading of Rom 1:3–4 apace with the contemporary study of biblical parallelism.

I. Davidic Descent in Second Temple Judaism

Although Davidic traditions constituted "the common core of Jewish messianism around the turn of the era,"[2] modern scholars have pointed to the paucity of references to David in the earliest Christian documents, Paul's letters.[3] Paul's strongest reference to Davidic messianism, Rom 1:3, has been excluded from the conversation ever since Johannes Weiss proposed that verses 3b–4a were a pre-Pauline confession.[4] Regardless of whether Paul held Jesus's Davidic descent to be of great significance, what did the early Jesus followers behind Rom 1:3–4 believe?[5]

Ferdinand Hahn, after an otherwise salutary survey of Davidic traditions in Second Temple Judaism, holds that "the title 'son of David' at once denotes 'the messiah in the state of his humanity and lowliness' and thus a specifically Christian sense is stamped upon the Jewish predicate of dignity."[6] This idea that "descent from

---

[2] John J. Collins, *The Scepter and the Star: Messianism in Light of the Dead Sea Scrolls*, 2nd ed. (Grand Rapids: Eerdmans, 2010), 78; similarly Geza Vermes, *Jesus the Jew* (Philadelphia: Fortress, 1973), 131; William Horbury, "The Messianic Associations of 'The Son of Man,'" *JTS* 36 (1985): 34–53; Florentino García Martínez, "Messianic Hopes in the Qumran Writings," in Florentino García Martínez and Julio Trebolle Barrera, *The People of the Dead Sea Scrolls* (Leiden: Brill, 1995), 159–89.

[3] E.g., Rudolf Bultmann, *Theology of the New Testament*, trans. Kendrick Grobel, 2 vols. (London: SCM, 1951–1955), 1:49; Robert Jewett, *Romans: A Commentary*, Hermeneia (Minneapolis: Fortress, 2007), 98 n. 21.

[4] Published posthumously in *Das Urchristentum*, 2 vols. in 1 (Göttingen: Vandenhoeck & Ruprecht, 1917), 86. I am of this view, yet it does not affect my argument to a great degree. Space does not permit interaction with recent reactions, e.g., James M. Scott, *Adoption as Sons of God: An Exegetical Investigation into the Background of υἱοθεσία in the Pauline Corpus*, WUNT 2/48 (Tübingen: Mohr Siebeck, 1992), 221–44; Christopher Whitsett, "Son of God, Seed of David: Paul's Messianic Exegesis in Romans 1:3–4," *JBL* 119 (2000): 661–81, here 680; Robert Matthew Calhoun, *Paul's Definition of the Gospel in Romans 1*, WUNT 2/316 (Tübingen: Mohr Siebeck, 2011), 92–106.

[5] Note that Davidic messianism forms a grand *inclusio* within Romans (1:3, 15:11–12), which suggests its importance (Richard B. Hays, *Echoes of Scripture in the Letters of Paul* [New Haven: Yale University Press, 1989], 72).

[6] Ferdinand Hahn, *Christologische Hoheitstitel: Ihre Geschichte im frühen Christentum*, 5th ed. (Göttingen: Vandenhoeck & Ruprecht, 1995), 253–54, quoting approvingly Günther Bornkamm, *Jesus von Nazareth* (Stuttgart: Kohlhammer, 1956), 206 (my translation).

David ... signifies Jesus' earthly existence and lowliness" still persists.[7] Hahn goes on to note that in Rom 1:3–4, "both son of David and son of God are to a high degree Christianized and are no longer to be understood directly in the light of Jewish tradition."[8] Hahn then famously concludes that Rom 1:3–4 presents a two-stage Christology (*Zweistufenchristologie*) in which Jesus ascends from his lowly human Davidic state to another "mode of existence" as the enthroned son of God, reminiscent of Phil 2:6–11.[9] Hahn's two-stage Christology has been very influential, and he is certainly not the first to read Jesus's Davidic descent in this way. Long before Hahn, Augustine argued that "weakness pertains to David, but eternal life to the power of God."[10]

Contra Hahn and others, I propose that the Christian "stamp" would not have been so indelible, especially if the text was produced at such an early stage in Christian origins, when Jewish-Christian influence was at its strongest. Rather than being read against and apart from Second Temple Judaism, Rom 1:3–4 is better read in its light. Specifically, I contend that the Davidic seed and the son of God are equivalent in a number of texts antecedent to Rom 1:3–4. I will proceed by examining key texts from Israel's Scripture and their subsequent reception in Second Temple Judaism. Thus, my survey will be thematic and intertextual rather than unilinear and diachronic. After reviewing the evidence, I will assess the likelihood that the early Christians who composed the confession in Rom 1:3–4, likely Jewish Christians, would have understood Jesus's Davidic descent as a mark of "lowliness."

Second Samuel 7:12–14 is the biblical *locus classicus* for the Davidic dynasty tradition:

> I will raise up your seed after you, who shall come forth from your body, and I will establish his kingdom. He shall build a house for my name, and I will establish the throne of his kingdom forever. I will be a father to him, and he shall be a son to me.[11]

Three aspects of the passage lend themselves to messianic exegesis: (1) The "seed" from David's body in 2 Sam 7 is singular.[12] (2) The language of "raising up" (הקימתי, ἀναστήσω) would intimate the resurrection (ἀναστάσεως) of David's seed, as it did for many early Christian interpreters.[13] (3) God has a father–son relationship with

---

[7] Arland J. Hultgren, *Paul's Letter to the Romans* (Grand Rapids: Eerdmans, 2011), 49.

[8] Hahn, *Christologische Hoheitstitel*, 258; similarly Matthew Bates, "A Christology of Incarnation and Enthronement: Romans 1:3–4 as Unified, Nonadoptionist, and Nonconciliatory," *CBQ* 77 (2015): 107–27, here 118 n. 32.

[9] Hahn, *Christologische Hoheitstitel*, 255–56.

[10] "Ut infirmitas pertineat ad David, vita vero aeterna ad virtutem dei" (*Ep. Rom. Inch.* 5.7 [PL 35:2091]).

[11] The MT is translated here, though the LXX is roughly equivalent.

[12] Cf. Rom 1:3; Gal 3:16; Acts 13:23; Tertullian, *Carn. Chr.* 22.5. See ἐκ σπέρματος in T. Levi 9:15; T. Jos. 19:8–12; John 7:42.

[13] Lidija Novakovic, *Raised from the Dead according to Scripture: The Role of Israel's Scripture*

David's seed. Since messianic origins, resurrection, and divine filiation were all located in a single text, it is unsurprising that commentators have long linked 2 Sam 7:12–14 and Rom 1:3–4.[14]

One of the earliest comments on 2 Sam 7 is an eschatological pesher from Qumran, 4Q174 (4QFlor):

> I, 10 YHWH [de]clares to you that he *will build you a house. I will raise up your seed after you and establish the throne of his kingdom*
> 11 *[for ev]er. I will be a father to him and he will be a son to me* [2 Sam 7:12–14]. This refers to *the branch of David*,[15] who will arise with the Interpreter of the law who
> 12 [will be raised up] in Zi[on in] the [l]ast days, as it is written: *I will raise up the hut* [סוּכַּת] *of*
> 13 *David which has fallen* [Amos 9:11]. This refers to *the branch* [סוּכַּת][16] *of David which has fall[en, w]hich he will raise up to save Israel*.[17]

The text often advances from one quotation to another by catchword linkages (i.e., *gezerah shawah*). Hence, 2 Sam 7:12–14 is interpreted in light of Amos 9:11 since both use a *hiphil* form of קוּם ("to get up"). This explains the otherwise inexplicable entrance of the "Branch of David" into the text because Jer 23:5 also contains the

---

in the Early Christian Interpretations of Jesus' Resurrection, T&T Clark Jewish and Christian Texts Series 12 (London: Bloomsbury T&T Clark, 2012), 139.

[14] E.g., Tertullian, *Carn. Chr.* 22.6; Lactantius, *Inst.* 14.26; Eusebius, *Dem. ev.* 3.2.39, 6.12.2, 7.3.12–17; Athanasius, *Dion.* 7.2.4; Peter Abelard, *Comm. Ep. Rom.*, on 1:3–4; Guillaume de Saint-Thierry, *Ep. Rom.* 1.11.1–2; Matthew Henry, *An Exposition of the Old and New Testaments*, 5 vols. (New York: Robert Carter, 1860), 5:239; Albert Barnes, *Romans* (New York: Leavitt, 1834), 13; J. W. Colenso, *Romans: Explained from a Missionary Point of View* (New York: Appleton, 1863), 37; M. E. Boismard, "Constitué fils de Dieu (Rom., i.4)," *RB* 60 (1953): 5–17, here 14; C. K. Barrett, *A Commentary on the Epistle to the Romans*, BNTC (London: Black, 1957), 19; Otto Betz, *What Do We Know about Jesus?* (London: SCM, 1968), 87–98; D. C. Duling, "The Promises to David and Their Entrance into Christianity—Nailing Down a Likely Hypothesis," *NTS* 20 (1973): 55–77, here 56; Martin Hengel, *The Son of God: The Origin of Christology and the History of Jewish-Hellenistic Religion*, trans. John Bowden (Philadelphia: Fortress, 1976), 64; P. E. Langevin, "Quel est le 'Fils de Dieu' de Romains 1,3–4?" *ScEs* 29 (1977): 145–77, here 148; Joseph A. Fitzmyer, *Romans: A New Translation with Introduction and Commentary*, AB 33 (New York: Doubleday, 1993), 234; Whitsett, "Son of God," 671; Eduard Lohse, *Der Brief an die Römer*, KEK (Göttingen: Vandenhoeck & Ruprecht, 2003), 66; Richard B. Hays, *The Conversion of the Imagination: Paul as Interpreter of Israel's Scripture* (Grand Rapids: Eerdmans, 2005), 110; Anthony Iffen Umoren, *Paul and Power Christology: Exegesis and Theology of Romans 1:3–4 in Relation to Popular Power Christology in an African Context*, New Testament Studies in Contextual Exegesis 4 (Frankfurt am Main: Lang, 2008), 118; Hultgren, *Paul's Letter to the Romans*, 50. The reception history presents a rare reversal: premodern interpreters were so preoccupied with two-natures Christology in Rom 1:3–4 that modern authors are often better at noting the obvious intertext.

[15] Jer 23:5, 30:8–9, 33:15; cf. Zech 3:8–9; Shemoneh Esreh 14.

[16] Following L. H. Silberman, "A Note on 4Q Florilegium," *JBL* 78 (1959): 158–59, here 158.

[17] Translated from PAM 43.440 in DJD V. On Amos 9:11, see also CD VII, 15–20.

catchword הקימתי: "See, in the days that are coming, proclaims YHWH, *I will raise up* [והקמתי] for David a Righteous Branch." This eschatological figure associated with David is expected "to save [להושיע] Israel."[18] The scroll maintains the paternal formula of 2 Sam 7:14 ("I will be a father to him," etc.), a fact that cannot be said of the targum on this scriptural text.[19] Thus, the author preserves the role of the "seed of David" as God's "son," both key elements in Rom 1:3-4. But what is most surprising is the way in which this Davidic figure is interpreted eschatologically ("[l]ast days"). Thus, the pesher is like a palimpsest, erasing aspects of 2 Sam 7 that would link the "seed" figure to Solomon—David's immediate successor and the builder of the first temple—and overwriting them with visions of the eschatological "Branch of David."[20]

The known reception history of 2 Sam 7 actually begins much earlier than 4Q174 with several instances of inner-biblical exegesis, the most extensive being Ps 89:[21]

> 3   I made a covenant with my chosen one, I swore to David my servant:
> 4   I will establish your seed forever, and I will build your throne for all generations.
> 26 He shall call to me, "You are my father, my God and the rock of my salvation."
> 27 Then I will make him my firstborn, a most high over the kings of the earth.
> 29 I will establish his seed forever; his throne will endure like the days of heaven.
> 36 Once I have sworn by my holiness, I will not lie to David:
> 37 His seed will endure forever, and his throne will endure like the sun before me.
> 38 Like the moon it will be established forever, a faithful witness in the sky.

As in 2 Sam 7, there is in the psalm reference to the singular seed and the father–son relationship, though with the added level of specificity that the Davidic scion is a firstborn son (בכור, πρωτότοκον). The promise of the eternal throne is also expressed metaphorically: it will be "like the sun before" YHWH in its perpetuity. As with 2 Sam 7, many commentators connect it to Rom 1:3-4.[22]

---

[18] The context is clearly eschatological: באחרית הימים ("in the last days") appears in 1:2, 12, 15, and 19.

[19] E.g., Tg. 2 Sam 7:14: "*like* a father [כאב] ... *like* a son [כבר]." Like 4Q174, the targum eschatologizes the promise, adding "the age to come" (7:19).

[20] Jer 23:5, 33:14-18. The "Branch of David" is explicitly messianic and associated with David's singular "seed" in 4Q252 V, 1-4; cf. 4Q285 5 I, 1; b. Sanh. 98b (a rabbinic reaction to Christian readings of Jer 23:5).

[21] Nahum Sarna, "Psalm 89: A Study in Inner-Biblical Exegesis," in *Biblical and Other Studies*, ed. A. Altmann, Philip W. Lown Institute of Advanced Judaic Studies, Brandeis University, Studies and Texts 1 (Cambridge: Harvard University Press, 1963), 35–47.

[22] E.g., Epiphanius, *Test. ex divinis* 7.1; Eusebius, *Dem. ev.* 7.1.145; Giuseppe Ruggieri, *Il figlio di Dio davidico: Studio sulla storia delle tradizioni contenute in Rom 1,3-4*, AnGr 166 (Rome: Pontifical Gregorian University, 1968), 121; L. C. Allen, "The Old Testament Background of

Interest in God's firstborn son was further cultivated at Qumran, as seen in 4Q369. Since the text speaks of a "firstborn son" (בן בכור, 1 II, 6), James Kugel has argued that it refers to Exod 4:22, where Israel is said to be God's "firstborn son" (בני בכרי ישראל).[23] Though his argument has the merit of this significant parallel, these two words are the only verbal linkage between the two texts. The more plausible referent in 4Q369 is a Davidic figure, since both the figure in 4Q369 and the Davidic king share many characteristics.

Both are a "seed."	(1 II, 4 לזרעו; 2 Sam 7:12 and Ps 89:5, זרעך)
Both await an inheritance.	(1 II, 1 נחלתו; Ps 2:8 נחלתך)
Both are promised something eternal.	(1 II, 1, 4; Ps 89:4, 29)
Both are promised something for generations.	(1 II, 4 לדורותם; Ps 89:5 לדר־ודר)
Both are a ruler over the earth.	(1 II, 7; Ps 89:28)
Both receive a crown.	(1 II, 8; Ps 89:20 [v.l.], 40)
Both are God's son.	(1 II, 10 [לבן] כאב; 2 Sam 7:14 לאב ... לבן).

Finally, both are God's "firstborn": "He shall call to me, 'You are my father, my God and the rock of my salvation.' Then I will make him my firstborn [בכור]" (Ps 89:27–28).[24] And the figure most commonly referred to in the Hebrew Bible as God's son is David's son.[25] Thus, the case for a Davidic figure is stronger than Kugel's appeal to Exod 4:22.[26] If the preceding argument is correct, this text is also a witness to the cosmic rule of the Davidic scion, who wears the "c[row]n of the heavens and the glory of the clouds" (1 II, 8). Therefore, the heavenly enthronement of the Davidic king already has precedent in the first century. This is significant for our understanding of Rom 1:3–4, where Jesus is "appointed" or "installed" as the son of God in power.[27]

(ΠΡΟ)ΟΡΙΖΕΙΝ in the New Testament," *NTS* 17 (1970–1971): 104–8, here 108; Duling, "Promises to David," 73; Langevin, "'Fils de Dieu,'" 148; Rudolf Pesch, "Das Evangelium Gottes über seinen Sohn: Zur Auslegung der Tradition in Röm 1,1–4," in *Christus bezeugen: Festschrift für Wolfgang Trilling zum 65. Geburtstag*, ed. Karl Kertelge, Traugott Holtz, and Claus-Peter März, ETS 59 (Leipzig: St. Benno, 1989), 208–17, here 213.

[23] James L. Kugel, "4Q369 'A Prayer of Enosh' and Ancient Biblical Interpretation," *DSD* 5 (1998): 119–48.

[24] For David as both "firstborn" in Ps 89:28 and Jesse's "youngest," see Midr. Ps. 5:4.

[25] See n. 29 below. Indeed, aspects of Israel's sonship would later be applied to a messiah; see Pesiq. Rab. 37:3.

[26] Similarly, Craig Evans, "A Note on the 'First-Born Son' of 4Q369," *DSD* 2 (1995): 185–201, here 197; Florentino García Martínez, *Thematic Studies on the Dead Sea Scrolls*, vol. 2 of *Qumranica Minora*, ed. Eibert J. C. Tigchelaar, STDJ 64 (Leiden: Brill, 2007), 279–80.

[27] David's heavenly enthronement likely derives from conflating Dan 7:13 and Ps 110:1 and the many texts where David is said to be enthroned "before" or "in the presence of" YHWH in

Also speaking of a figure who is "named" the "son of God" is the controversial Aramaic Son of God text, 4Q246 (4QapocrDan ar). Though vastly different identifications for the "son of God" figure have been proposed, the positive messianic proposal championed by John J. Collins and others has, to date, won the most widespread approval.[28] Collins contends that the "son of God" is a messianic figure associated with David since "the individual most often designated as 'the son of God' in the Hebrew Bible is undoubtedly the Davidic king, or his eschatological counterpart."[29] If this is so, 4Q246 would be yet another important witness to divine sonship as an aspect of Davidic messianism.

Recently, Tucker Ferda has seconded Collins's positive messianic reading of the text, though from a different angle. Ferda rightly questions approaches that begin with the titular background of "son of God" for their identifications of the figure. Such approaches can be problematic because "terms are defined by their use, and that means their function in a particular context."[30] Thus, a positive title can be subverted in negative contexts. Form and context, both external and internal to the document, determine meaning. Ferda's argument bolsters the positive identification of the "son of God" by showing the positive rhetorical function of "divine naming" within and outside of the document as a "widespread messianic *topos*."[31]

Collins has made the positive argument on the balance of probabilities that "son of God" most likely refers to a Davidic king; Ferda corroborates the positive reading through divine naming rhetoric and *Tendenzkritik*. If they are collectively correct, 4Q246 is one of the earliest witnesses to the appellative "son of God" being applied to a Davidic figure in a decidedly eschatological and apocalyptic context.[32]

---

heaven. See Ps 89:37; 2 Sam 7:16 (v.l.); 7:29; 1 Kgs 8:25; 1 Chr 6:16; Jer 33:18; 4Q504 2 II, 6–8; "David Apocalypse," in *Synopse zur Hekhalot-Literatur*, ed. Peter Schäfer, TSAJ 2 (Leiden: Brill, 1981) §§122–26.

[28] See summaries in Collins, *Scepter and the Star*, 179–85; Tucker S. Ferda, "Naming the Messiah: A Contribution to the 4Q246 'Son of God' Debate," *DSD* 21 (2014): 150–75, here 153–56.

[29] Collins, *Scepter and the Star*, 183; Seyoon Kim, *The "Son of Man" as the Son of God*, WUNT 30 (Tübingen: Mohr, 1983), 20–22; Géza G. Xeravits, *King, Priest, Prophet: Positive Eschatological Protagonists of the Qumran Library*, STDJ 47 (Leiden: Brill, 2001), 88–89. Fitzmyer famously limits the appellation "messiah" to explicitly eschatological messianic figures, averring that 4Q246 speaks "positively of a coming Jewish ruler, perhaps a member of the Hasmonean dynasty, who be [sic] a successor to the Davidic throne, but who is not envisaged as a Messiah" ("4Q246: The 'Son of God' Document from Qumran," *Bib* 74 [1993]: 153–74, here 173–74). But this is incorrect: one of the greatest difficulties for the Hasmonean dynasty was their lack of Davidic credentials; they *could not* sit on the Davidic throne, as seen in the anti-Hasmonean, pro-Davidic stance of Pss. Sol. 17.

[30] Ferda, "Naming the Messiah," 156.

[31] Ibid., 157.

[32] The "son of God's" judging (4Q246 II, 9) can also be Davidic; see Isa 11:1–10 and its reception (n. 43 below) and 4Q285 5 I, 2–4; 4Q174 1 I, 21; Pss. Sol. 17:24, 29, 35; 1 En. 48:1–3; Rev 19:11; 4 Ezra 13; 2 Bar 36–40; b. Sanh. 93b (Bar Kokhba is rejected for not judging by smell [Isa 11:4; cf. 4Q161 8 III, 22; John 7:24]).

But we may go further. Many have argued that Luke 1:32–35 is influenced "directly or indirectly" by 4Q246.³³ The two are equivalent at several points:

4Q246	Luke 1:32–35
He will be great	He will be great
He will be called the son of God	He will be called the son of God
and they will call him son of the Most High	he will be called son of the Most High

Luke's narrative further aligns with the vision of the son of God's unending rule in 4Q246:

| 4Q246 II, 5 | His kingdom (will be) an eternal kingdom |
| Luke 1:33 | and of his kingdom there will not be an end.³⁴ |

In both texts, the "kingdom" in view is not God's but likely that of the "son of the Most High." Collins rightly calls the correspondences "astonishing."³⁵ Important for our purposes, these son-of-God traditions are fused with Davidic messianism in Luke 1:32:

οὗτος ἔσται μέγας καὶ υἱὸς ὑψίστου κληθήσεται
καὶ δώσει αὐτῷ κύριος ὁ θεὸς <u>τὸν θρόνον Δαυὶδ τοῦ πατρὸς αὐτοῦ</u>.

He will be great and will be called son of the Most High
And the Lord God will give him *the throne of his ancestor David*.

Luke therefore is interpreting the naming of the "son of God" and "son of the Most High" in terms of the Davidic dynasty tradition. To be named "son of God" is to be the Davidic scion, heir to the throne and promise. Luke's use of this tradition does not prove that the author of 4Q246 understood the ברה די אל to be a Davidic figure, but it does demonstrate that this is a probable—and perhaps the only extant—interpretation of 4Q246.³⁶

Davidic and divine elements also appear in 4 Ezra 11–13. In the eagle vision, a roaring lion appears to rebuke Rome (i.e., the eagle), then watches its incineration (cf. Isa 11:4). The identity of the lion is eventually revealed to Ezra by the Most High to be "the messiah (*unctus*, ܡܫܝܚܐ) whom the Most High has kept until the end of days, who will arise from the seed of David" (ܡܢ ܙܪܥܗ ܕܕܘܝܕ, 4 Ezra 12:31–32).³⁷ Thus, the figure here is explicitly Davidic, messianic, and eschatological. The text not only provides us with yet another positive use of "seed of David" but also

---

³³ Collins, *Scepter and the Star*, 177. Fitzmyer's appeal to coincidence here is improbable ("4Q246," 174).

³⁴ Affirmed by Fitzmyer, "4Q246," 164.

³⁵ Collins, *Scepter and the Star*, 173.

³⁶ Similarly Heinz-Wolfgang Kuhn, "Röm 1,3f und der davidische Messias als Gottessohn in den Qumrantexten," in *Lesezeichen für Annelies Findeiss zum 65. Geburtstag am 15. März 1984*, ed. C. Burchard and G. Theissen (Heidelberg: Wissenschaft-theologisches Seminar, 1984), 103–12.

³⁷ Trans. Bruce Metzger, *OTP* 1:550–51.

develops God's promise to David along messianic lines: "I will raise up [David's] seed" (2 Sam 7:12) becomes the messiah "who will arise from the seed of David" (12:32).

Since this entire vision is a reworking of the night vision in Dan 7 (4 Ezra 12:11–12), one would expect the hero of the drama to be the Danielic כבר אנש ("one like a son of man"). Instead, the Judaic and Davidic lion unexpectedly appears. The hero of Dan 7, however, is found in Ezra's next vision, which begins with "something like the figure of a man" flying "with the clouds of heaven [*cum nubibus caeli*]."[38] But just as soon as this Danielic figure appears, he is eclipsed again by Davidic imagery, this time culled from Isa 11. This humanlike figure in 4 Ezra:

1. "sent forth from his mouth as it were a stream of fire, and from his lips a flaming breath [*de labiis eius spiritum flammae*]," adverting to Isa 11:4, where the Davidic scion destroys the impious by the breath of his lips (Vulg.: *spiritu labiorum suorum interficiet impium*), a widespread messianic motif;[39]
2. gathers a peaceable multitude to himself, evoking the peaceable kingdom (Isa 11:5–10);
3. brings back the exiles from Assyria, just as the root of Jesse gathers the exiles of Israel "so that there shall be a highway from Assyria for the remnant that is left of the people" (Isa 11:12–16).

Significantly, the parallels between 4 Ezra 13 and Isa 11 are sequential. Thus, the figure is clearly Davidic.

The figure's positive Davidic identification takes on added importance since he is also the Most High's "son" who "will be revealed ... and he, my son, will reprove the assembled nations" (4 Ezra 13:32, 37). Yet one may aver, as does Michael Stone, that the Latin here (*filius meus*) is derived not from υἱός and בן but from παῖς and עבד.[40] This is unlikely, however, if Ps 2 looms in the background of 4 Ezra 13. In both texts,

1. the Lord's agent goes up on a mountain identified as Mount Zion (4 Ezra 13:35–36, Ps 2:6);
2. the nations are gathered against that man, who is identified as the "anointed one" (4 Ezra 12:31, Ps 2:2); and
3. the nations are repulsed, and the anointed one is named "my son" (4 Ezra 13:32, 37, 52; Ps 2:7).

---

[38] Verbatim of Vulg. Dan 7:13. Elsewhere in the Hebrew Bible, only YHWH rides the clouds (Markus Zehnder, "Why the Danielic 'Son of Man' Is a Divine Being," *BBR* 24 [2014]: 331–47, here 338).

[39] See 1Q28b V, 24–25; Pss. Sol. 17:21–26; 1 En. 62:2; 2 Thess 2:8; Rev 1:16; 2:12; 19:15; 2 Bar. 36–40, 73; Jerome, *Ruf.* 3.31; Pesiq. Rab. 37:4.

[40] Michael E. Stone, *Fourth Ezra: A Commentary on the Book of Fourth Ezra*, Hermeneia (Minneapolis: Fortress, 1990), 207.

Given this allusive framework, *filius meus* in 4 Ezra 13 almost certainly refers to בני /υἱός μου from Ps 2. Thus, 4 Ezra 11–13 gives yet another positive portrayal of the Davidic messiah who is also identified as God's son.[41]

Evidently Irenaeus was correct in writing that many of "the Jews … were eagerly awaiting a messiah ἐκ σπέρματος Δαυίδ ['from the seed of David']."[42] The above survey calls into question readings that cast Davidic descent in a lowly light. Far from forming an antithetical pair, the Davidic scion and the son of God are equivalent in an impressive number of texts, especially those linked with 2 Sam 7 and its offshoots. It should therefore not be surprising that Rom 1:3–4 called to mind these texts, which combine Davidic and divine sonship, for generations of earlier readers.[43]

The evidence, which ranges from exilic to post-temple Judaism, suggests that the son of God is often from the seed of David; conversely, being of the seed of David is a sine qua non for an individual's installation as the son of God.[44] Historically, the relationship is not antithetical but complementary.

II. Literary Issues

Having established that the seed of David could be—and often was—God's son increases the likelihood that Davidic descent was thought of positively in Rom 1:3–4. But the pejorative reading of the Romans text often emerges despite the background of "seed of David" in Second Temple Judaism. Hahn in particular may be inclined to agree with much of our historical survey while still, somehow, maintaining a pejorative, "Christian" reading of ἐκ σπέρματος Δαυίδ κατὰ σάρκα. Most adduce Barn. 12:10 to make this argument, which divorces Davidic and divine sonship:

---

[41] Note too that God addresses "David, my servant" as "my son" (בני) in the recently discovered, turn-of-the-era "Gabriel Revelation" (*Hazon Gabriel: New Readings of the Gabriel Revelation*, ed. Matthias Henze, EJL 29 [Atlanta: Society of Biblical Literature, 2011], 33, 36).

[42] Frag. 27, *Sancti Irenaei, episcopi Lugdunensis, Libros quinque adversus haereses … commentatione perpetua et indicibus variis*, ed. W. Wigan Harvey, 2 vols. (Cambridge: Cambridge University Press, 1857), 2:493.

[43] For Isa 11:1–10 and/or Ps 2:7 among precritical interpreters, see Irenaeus, frag. 47 in *Sancti Irenaei*, 2:510; Tertullian, *Carn. Chr.* 22.6; Eusebius, *Dem. ev.* 3.2.39; John Calvin, *Commentaries on the Epistle of Paul the Apostle to the Romans* (Grand Rapids: Eerdmans, 1948), on 1:3–4; Matthew Poole, *Commentary on the Holy Bible*, 3 vols. (London: Banner of Truth Trust, 1685), 3:479; Hugo Grotius, *Annotationes in Novum Testamentum*, 3 vols. (Paris: Joannem Carolum, 1756), 2:190. On 2 Sam 7 and Ps 89, see nn. 14 and 22 above.

[44] This is not to suggest a uniform *Messiaserwartung* in early Judaism. See further *Judaisms and Their Messiahs at the Turn of the Christian Era*, ed. Jacob Neusner, William Scott Green, and Ernest S. Frerichs (Cambridge: Cambridge University Press, 1988).

> Since they were going to say that the messiah is the son of David, David himself prophesied because he feared and knew the error of the sinners: *The Lord said to my Lord: Sit at my right hand etc.* (Ps 110:1).... Notice how David calls him "Lord" and not "son."[45]

As Joshua Jipp has noted, this negative reading of Jesus's Davidic ancestry is anomalous in the first centuries of Christianity.[46] In addition, the practice of reading Rom 1:3–4 through a later text (Barn. 12:10) is historically dubious in any case. Our survey of Second Temple Judaism shows that the burden of proof is on those who claim that Rom 1:3–4 conceives of Davidic sonship pejoratively, a conception foreign to the thought-world of Second Temple Judaism. Nevertheless, demonstrating that the son of God was often from the seed of David in Second Temple Judaism only establishes the external evidence. This evidence could—unlikely as it is in Rom 1:3–4—be subverted. The situation is analogous to the use of "son of God" in 4Q246: having established the external evidence, we should turn to the text's *Tendenz*. But the situation in Romans is more complex. If Rom 1:3–4 is reckoned a pre-Pauline confession, Paul's writings can be appealed to only as a secondary context for the confession. The Pauline corpus is helpful but not decisive for establishing the earliest attitudes toward the "seed of David." Rather than making an argument on the basis of Paul's attitude toward Davidic messianism, I aim to examine the relationship between "seed of David" and "son of God" primarily within the bounds of Rom 1:3b–4a. Words gain meaning in context, and the literary framework of Rom 1:3–4 is just as important for a positive reading of "seed of David" as the words' historical usage.

Many have already appealed to Lowth's "antithetical parallelism" to answer the question of literary framework.[47] The argument normally begins with the recognition that σάρκα and πνεῦμα form an "antithesis."[48] Once this foundational antithesis is spotted, more apparent antitheses appear, for example, between σπέρματος Δαυίδ and υἱοῦ θεοῦ. From here, many extrapolate and describe the relationship of both lines as "antithetical parallelism" on the basis of these putatively antithetical elements.[49] Antithesis in Rom 1:3–4 has even been used as the basis for discovering

---

[45] Greek text from Michael W. Holmes, ed. and trans., *The Apostolic Fathers: Greek Texts and English Translations*, 3rd ed. (Grand Rapids: Baker Academic, 2007), 420.

[46] Joshua Jipp, "Ancient, Modern, and Future Interpretations of Romans 1:3–4: Reception History and Biblical Interpretation," *JTI* 3 (2009): 241–59, here 254.

[47] See, e.g., James D. G. Dunn, *Romans 1–8*, WBC 38A (Dallas: Word, 1988), 12.

[48] See, e.g., Charles Hodge, *Commentary on the Epistle to the Romans* (Philadelphia: Grigg & Elliot, 1835), 21; William Sanday and Arthur C. Headlam, *A Critical and Exegetical Commentary on the Epistle to the Romans*, ICC (Edinburgh: T&T Clark, 1896), 9. On antithesis, see Aristotle, *Rhet.* 3.9.7; Demetrius, *Eloc.* 22–23.

[49] See, e.g., Frédéric Godet, *Commentaire sur l'épître aux Romains*, 2 vols. (Paris: Grassart, 1883), 1:177.

antitheses throughout the entire epistle.⁵⁰ Thus, antithesis is being used to describe the relationship of words, phrases, entire lines, and even broad patterns within Romans.

In addition to the problem of extrapolating the perceived antithesis of σάρκα–πνεῦμα to the rest of the parallelism, there is also confusion about how parallelism itself functions in Rom 1:3–4. Many argue that parallelism requires that each element of line A have a corresponding element in line B:

> *Andreas Du Toit*: [The addition of ἐν δυνάμει] certainly *disturbs the parallelism* and the cryptic character of this kind of antithetically arranged statement.⁵¹
>
> *James D. G. Dunn*: Some think ἐν δυνάμει is a Pauline addition … on the ground that it *spoils the parallelism* of the clauses.⁵²
>
> *Leander E. Keck*: Because [the phrase "with power"] *clearly mars the symmetry of the lines*, Paul may have added it to the tradition.⁵³
>
> *Robert Matthew Calhoun*: It is hard to imagine why an early christological formula—especially if it is confessional—would prefer γενομένου ἐκ σπέρματος Δαυίδ to γενομένου υἱοῦ Δαυίδ when *the parallel structure calls for the latter*.⁵⁴

On this understanding, line A must match line B element for element for the parallelism to be unspoiled or undisturbed. When an element is out of place, it is liable to the redactional knife. Thus, ἐν δυνάμει is excised on these grounds in many reconstructions of the original confession:⁵⁵

1:3	τοῦ γενομένου ἐκ σπέρματος Δαυίδ	1:4	τοῦ ὁρισθέντος υἱοῦ θεοῦ ἐν δυνάμει
	κατὰ σάρκα,		κατὰ πνεῦμα ἁγιωσύνης ἐξ ἀναστάσεως νεκρῶν.

A final example further demonstrates the confusing uses to which parallelism is put in Rom 1:3–4. Many argue that, if two elements appear in syntactically equivalent places, they should be equivalent in meaning and thus be rendered similarly in English.⁵⁶ Recently, Matthew Bates has argued that, because ἐκ σπέρματος parallels

---

⁵⁰ See, e.g., Nils Alstrup Dahl, *The Crucified Messiah, and Other Essays* (Minneapolis: Augsburg, 1974), 43.

⁵¹ Andreas Du Toit, "Romans 1,3–4 and the Gospel Tradition: A Re-Assessment of the Phrase ΚΑΤΑ ΠΝΕΥΜΑ ΑΓΙΩΣΥΝΗΣ," in *Four Gospels 1992: Festschrift Frans Neirynck*, ed. Frans van Segbroeck et al., 3 vols., BETL 100 (Louvain: Peeters, 1992), 249–56, here 250.

⁵² James D. G. Dunn, "Jesus—Flesh and Spirit: An Exposition of Romans 1:3–4," *JTS* 24 (1973): 40–68, here 41.

⁵³ Leander E. Keck, *Romans*, ANTC (Nashville: Abingdon, 2005), 44.

⁵⁴ Calhoun, *Paul's Definition of the Gospel in Romans 1*, 101–2 (emphasis added to each of the above examples).

⁵⁵ For this outline, see Boismard, "Constitué fils de Dieu," 7.

⁵⁶ See, e.g., Eduard Schweizer: "κατά ist also sicher nicht instrumental zu übersetzen … weil

ἐξ ἀναστάσεως, it should be "construed instrumentally, referring (albeit somewhat obliquely) to *Mary's contribution*":

> An instrumental meaning for ἐκ in Rom 1:3—τοῦ γενομένου ἐκ σπέρματος Δαυίδ ("who came into human existence *by means of* the seed of David")—precisely preserves the parallelism with τοῦ ὁρισθέντος ... ἐξ ἀναστάσεως νεκρῶν ("who was appointed *by means of* the resurrection from among the dead ones") in 1:4, which is more clearly instrumental.[57]

This too is a misapplication of parallelism. Consider, to use a modern analogue, how parallelism functions in T. S. Eliot's "Choruses from 'The Rock'":

> Where is the life we have lost in living?
> Where is the wisdom we have lost in knowledge?
> Where is the knowledge we have lost in information?[58]

Clearly there is a parallel pattern between the lines, driven home by the repetition of "in": in living, in knowledge, in information. Applying Bates's suggestion, every instance of "in" should be grammatically identical because it occurs at the same point in a parallel structure. But such is not the case: "in" has the temporal meaning of "while living" in the first line, but a spatial sense of "within knowledge/information" in the second and third lines. These underlying grammatical differences surface in translations:

> Où est la vie que nous avons perdue *en* vivant ?
> Où est la sagesse que nous avons perdue *dans* la connaissance ?
> Où est la connaissance que nous avons perdue *dans* l'information ?[59]

> Dov'è la Vita che abbiamo sprecato *vivendo* ?
> Dov'è la saggezza che abbiamo perduto *nel* conoscere ?
> Dov'è la conoscenza che abbiamo smarrito *nell'*informazione ?[60]

> Πού είναι η Ζωή πού έχουμε χάσει <u>ζώντας</u>;
> Πού είναι η σοφία πού έχουμε χάσει <u>εν</u> γνώσει;
> Πού είναι η γνώση πού έχουμε χάσει <u>στην</u> πληροφορία;[61]

---

dies im ersten Glied unmöglich wäre.... Man kann *nur* interpretieren 'in der Sphäre des Fleisches— in der Sphäre des heiligen Gottesgeistes'" ("Röm. 1,3f. und der Gegensatz von Fleisch und Geist vor und bei Paulus," *EvT* 15 [1955]: 563–71, here 569).

[57] Bates, "Christology of Incarnation," 117, 120 (emphasis original). Other aspects of the article are salutary, for example, his emphasis on enthronement and a nonpejorative reading of κατὰ σάρκα.

[58] T. S. Eliot, *The Complete Poems and Play: 1909–1950* (New York: Harcourt Brace, 1967), 96.

[59] Trans. Rémi Sussan and Hubert Guillaud, "Pouvons-nous devinir plus intelligents, individuellement comme collectivement?" *Le Monde*, 16 July 2010, https://tinyurl.com/jbl1362a.

[60] Trans. Luigi Berti, *Poesie di Thomas Stearns Eliot* (Bologna: Guanda, 1958), 167.

[61] Trans. Aristoteles Nikolaides, *Τ. Σ. ΕΛΙΟΤ: ΑΠΑΝΤΑ ΤΑ ΠΟΙΗΜΑΤΑ* (Athens: Kedros, 1983), 187.

Grammatical or syntactic parallelism does not lead to equivalent meaning as Bates has suggested. The phenomenon is abundantly common in ancient parallelism.[62] Surface similarities can paper over underlying semantic differences; conversely, equivalence in deep meaning may appear different on the surface.

The examples above show that many have analyzed Rom 1:3–4 on the basis not of how parallelism works but of how they imagine it *should* work. This misapprehension has also guided the quest for the perfect primitive parallelism and produced a preponderance of tradition histories.[63] There are, of course, examples of the type of pure parallelism that many commentators are using as the archetype for their reconstructions. Consider Ps 102:10 LXX:[64]

οὐ κατὰ τὰς ἁμαρτίας ἡμῶν ἐποίησεν ἡμῖν
οὐδὲ κατὰ τὰς ἀνομίας ἡμῶν ἀνταπέδωκεν ἡμῖν.

Not according to our sins did he do to us
nor according to our transgressions did he repay to us.[65]

The pattern is patent and precise: each element in the first line has a correlative in the second, and all are placed in identical sequence.[66] Adele Berlin cautions, however, that "this verse is the exception" and that "the surface structure of the lines is identical in only a small percentage of cases.… More often we find grammatical equivalence: the second line substitutes something grammatically different, but equivalent, for a grammatical feature in the first line."[67] Instead of placing elements in exactly the same place on the surface of the poem, the equivalence between the lines is typically further down; otherwise, parallelism would be tediously tautological. To extend the mathematical metaphor of "equivalence," parallelism rarely presents us with something as banal as: $x = x$. Instead, the sides of the equation can have much greater complexity *while still being equivalent*, as in $6x - 3 = 2x^2 + 1$. The greater the complexity, the more rewarding it is for the reader to unravel the hidden equivalences between the two lines.

At the other end of the spectrum from pure parallelism are structures in which

---

[62] E.g., Sir 6:2, Pss. Sol. 17:17, Luke 2:14, m. 'Abot 1:4; and the LXX in Paul, e.g., Deut 32:21 (Rom 10:19); Isa 65:1 (Rom 10:20).

[63] See, e.g., Robert Jewett's three-level model (*Romans*, 104–6). But why should not precisely paralleling elements be added at later stages (if there were such) to improve the confession; why is it always argued to be a feature only of the earliest stage?

[64] All LXX texts are quoted from *Septuaginta Societatis Scientiarum Gottingensis*, 16 vols. (Göttingen: Vandenhoeck & Ruprecht, 1931–).

[65] Cf. Isocrates, *Helen* 17; Demetrius, *Eloc.* 23.

[66] On precise parallelism, see Lawrence M. Wills, "Scribal Methods in Matthew and Mishnah Abot," *CBQ* 63 (2001): 241–57.

[67] Adele Berlin, *The Dynamics of Biblical Parallelism*, rev. and enl. ed. (Grand Rapids: Eerdmans, 2008), 33, 32, respectively. Many of the biblical examples herein stem from her excellent monograph.

one struggles to discern the correspondence between the two lines, as in Ps 110:5 LXX:

τροφὴν ἔδωκεν τοῖς φοβουμένοις αὐτόν,
μνησθήσεται εἰς τὸν αἰῶνα διαθήκης αὐτοῦ.

Food he gave to those who fear him;
He will remember his covenant forever.

It is difficult to establish any relationship between the lines at a lexical and semantic level. Yet, because the structure invites comparison, the mind still strains to do so. Put differently, the parallelism becomes a metaphor built of two dissimilar clauses. In Ps 110:5 LXX, the reader is invited to wonder how giving is an act of remembering, or how faithfulness in providing food relates to the eternal covenant. As Edward L. Greenstein suggests,

> Parallelism contributes to the meaning of Biblical verse by structuring the ways in which we perceive its content. The presentation of lines in parallelism has the effect of reinforcing the semantic association between them. It has long been observed that when discrete materials appear to us in similar form, we are led to seek, and find, some meaningful correlation between them.[68]

As previously mentioned, Lowth's categories have loomed large in the interpretation of biblical parallelism. The reason scholars have gravitated toward Lowth's divisions for centuries was their utility for describing parallelism with three simple categories:

1. Synonymous, "in which the same sentiment is repeated in different but equivalent words."
2. Antithetic, "in which the parallel members express the opposite sides of the same thought" or "a thing is illustrated by its contrary being opposed to it."
3. Synthetic, "in which the two members contain two disparate ideas, which, however, are connected by a certain affinity between them."[69]

Useful as they may be, Lowth's categories have the disadvantage of seeing more forest than trees. Since the 1980s, most scholars of biblical poetry have eschewed Lowth's framework, and it appears to be time for New Testament scholars to do the same.[70] Instead of the Lowthian reading that has dominated the study of Rom

---

[68] Edward L. Greenstein, "How Does Parallelism Mean?," in *A Sense of Text: The Art of Language in the Study of Biblical Literature* (Winona Lake, IN: Eisenbrauns, 1982), 41–70, here 64.

[69] I. M. Casanowicz, "Parallelism in Hebrew Poetry," *JE* 9:520–22.

[70] The Lowthian model was exploded by James L. Kugel (*The Idea of Biblical Poetry: Parallelism and Its History* [New Haven: Yale University Press, 1981]) and, independently, by Robert Alter (*The Art of Biblical Poetry* [New York: Basic Books, 1985]).

1:3–4, I employ what is arguably the most nuanced and comprehensive approach to date, that of Adele Berlin.

III. Parallelism in Romans 1:3–4

Berlin's comprehensive methodology for analyzing parallelism first appeared in her 1985 monograph, *The Dynamics of Biblical Parallelism*. In the attempt to explain parallelism, many have proposed that it conveys meaning by way of equivalence at different levels: grammatical, lexical, semantic, and phonological. Berlin's approach to parallelism has the advantage of accounting for equivalence on all of these levels. Rather than give a comprehensive introduction to her methodology, I will proceed inductively, applying the aspects of her approach to Rom 1:3–4.[71]

Grammatical Aspect

On the grammatical structure of Rom 1:3–4, all commentators agree that the passage features parallelism. Formally, the parallelism is built on three grammatically equivalent pairs:

| Τοῦ γενομένου | ἐκ σπέρματος | κατὰ σάρκα |
| Τοῦ ὁρισθέντος | ἐξ ἀναστάσεως | κατὰ πνεῦμα[72] |

These grammatical pairs stick up like stepping-stones in the prescript of Romans, and readers have long noticed that this "repetition of syntactic structure" is a formal parallelism.[73] The pattern is clear:

Τοῦ + AORIST GEN. PARTICIPLE | ἐκ + GEN. SG. NOUN | κατὰ + ACC. SG. NOUN.

Κατὰ σάρκα and κατὰ πνεῦμα strengthen the parallelism both metrically, featuring a two-beat rhythm (κα-τὰ σάρ-κα / κα-τὰ πνεῦ-μα), and phonologically through the assonance of "α" (κα-, -τὰ, -κα, -τὰ, -μα). Finally, the prepositions in the lines are arranged in an ABBA pattern (ἐκ, κατὰ / κατὰ, ἐκ).[74] All of these aspects tighten the grammatical parallel, serving as the warp through which other elements of the confession are woven.

Lexical Aspect: Word Pairs

Parallelism is a natural linguistic phenomenon, and we are hard-wired to think in parallel structures. When subjects in an experiment were provided with

---

[71] For a convenient summary, see Berlin, *Dynamics of Biblical Parallelism*, 29.
[72] For the sake of presentation, ἐξ ἀναστάσεως and κατὰ πνεῦμα are transposed.
[73] Greenstein, "Parallelism in Hebrew Poetry," 47.
[74] Bates, "Christology of Incarnation," 125.

the stimulus sentence *The lazy student failed the exam* and were asked to give the first sentence that came to mind, common responses included: *The smart girl passed the test; The industrious pupil passed the course;* and *The brilliant boy studied the paper*, sentences that are all parallel in structure and theme to the stimulus sentence.[75] Just as parallelism is a demonstrably psycholinguistic phenomenon, so too is word pairing. When asked to say the first word that comes to mind, an English speaker will often respond to "dog" with "cat" or to "girl" with "boy." This process of free association is based on a cognitive operation related to the process used to populate the second line of a parallelism after the first has been established.[76] If given "woman," subjects often produce "man" or "girl" since the meaning of these words is only slightly removed from "woman." But they will never respond with "paint" or "Greenland," words that have nothing in common with the stimulus word. Returning to Rom 1:3–4, consider the pair σπέρματος Δαυὶδ / υἱοῦ θεοῦ.[77] Though "seed of David" would likely not elicit "son of God" from a modern subject, we have established that this was entirely possible in the context of Second Temple Judaism. The association of the pair is further tightened because υἱός complements σπέρμα through a phenomenon known as "feature addition"[78]:

σπέρμα = noun → singular → animate → human → descendant
υἱός = noun → singular → animate → human → descendant → child of

The figure in view is not just a descendant at unspecified degrees of remove from his progenitor, but he is a son, one degree from the parent. "Son" specifies the level of relation to the progenitor. By contrast, σπέρμα could address a fuller range of relationships. The movement, then, is toward greater specificity in line B, and this phenomenon contributes to the reader's feeling that line B is repeating yet advancing the content of line A.[79] The relationship between the words in the poem is, to echo Berlin, "dynamic." There is interplay between the two once they are set in a parallel structure, each word of one line exerting force on words of the other, and the result is a sense of heightened specificity from σπέρμα to υἱός that contributes to the poem's sense of movement.

The most contentious word pair in Rom 1:3–4 is σάρκα–πνεῦμα.[80] The crux of

[75] M. P. O'Connor and E. L. Greenstein, "Parallelism," in *The Princeton Encyclopedia of Poetry and Poetics*, ed. Roland Greene and Stephen Cushman, 4th ed. (Princeton: Princeton University Press, 2012), 997.

[76] The classic study is Herbert Clark, "Word Associations and Linguistic Theory," in *New Horizons in Linguistics*, ed. John Lyons (Baltimore: Penguin, 1970), 271–86.

[77] One could object that this is not truly a "pair" since the first element is the object of ἐκ. Yet an analogous Davidic case exists: the personage of Isa 11:1 (ῥάβδος ἐκ τῆς ῥίζης Ιεσσαι) and 11:10 (ἡ ῥίζα τοῦ Ιεσσαι) are one and the same despite the use of ἐκ.

[78] Clark, "Word Associations," 278–79.

[79] Thus Kugel's description of parallelism as "A is so, and *what's more*, B is so" (*Idea of Biblical Poetry*, 8).

[80] The pairing is typical of confessions, e.g., 1 Tim 3:16, 1 Pet 3:18—both lacking κατά. For

the controversy for Rom 1:3–4 is Paul's usage. After a survey of the pairing in Paul's letters, Dunn concludes that seventeen of eighteen usages of κατὰ σάρκα are "phrase[s] of contrast and antithesis."[81] On this basis, he suggests that

> for Paul κατὰ σάρκα in Rom 1:3 carries its normal note of depreciation. For one thing, the physical relationship is precisely that which elsewhere in Romans is Israel's stumbling block—the foundation of her vanity, the source of her faith in works-righteousness, and the cause of her rejecting the Gospel. And for another, κατὰ σάρκα here stands in open antithesis with κατὰ πνεῦμα, and so could hardly lack a pejorative significance in Paul's mind.[82]

This argument displays—and engenders—considerable confusion, not least because Paul's argument on Abrahamic ancestry in Rom 4 is conflated with the messiah's Davidic descent, a requirement for messianic status rather than "the foundation of Israel's vanity."[83] Put differently, Paul may see ethnic descent as problematic when used as a condition of entrance into the Christian community, but it is certainly *not* problematic as a condition for messiahship. Just the opposite is the case: the messiah must belong to Israel κατὰ σάρκα. As noted, it is a sine qua non.

In order to achieve such statistics (i.e., seventeen out of eighteen usages are antithetical), Dunn even reckons the following as a "negative" usage of κατὰ σάρκα:

> They are the Israelites ... and from them comes the messiah κατὰ σάρκα, who is over all, God blessed forever. Amen. (Rom 9:4–5)

This negative reading strains credulity.[84] Κατὰ σάρκα is here applied to the ancestry of the messiah, precisely the context of Rom 1:3 (see Irenaeus, *Haer.* 3.16.3).[85] On historical grounds, I have argued that the earliest Jewish Christians who likely composed Rom 1:3–4 could scarcely have understood Davidic descent as the place where the "pejorative note sounds most clearly." Paul's own *Tendenz* confirms this. As Michael Theobald has shown, in Romans Paul colors the messiah's descent from the nation of Israel κατὰ σάρκα only positively; indeed, Paul's mission "among all the nations" in the very next verse after the confession (1:5) likely springs from his

---

Paul, κατὰ σάρκα and κατὰ πνεῦμα are juxtaposed anthropologically (e.g., Rom 8:4–5, Gal 5:17) but never messianically (cf. Ignatius, *Smyrn.* 1:1b).

[81] Dunn, "Jesus—Flesh and Spirit," 49.

[82] Ibid. (emphasis original), but cf. Dunn, *Christology in the Making: A New Testament Inquiry into the Origins of the Doctrine of the Incarnation* (London: SCM, 1980), 35.

[83] Dunn, "Jesus—Flesh and Spirit," 47: "That which is of decisive significance about [the Christ] is *not* his physical descent. As with Abraham in Rom 4:1, any emphasis on his relationship κατὰ σάρκα is inevitably negative since it obscures the central message of the gospel."

[84] Perhaps even Dunn has tacitly abandoned this position; his article "Jesus—Flesh and Spirit" is conspicuously absent from *Beginning from Jerusalem*, vol. 2 of *Christianity in the Making* (Grand Rapids: Eerdmans, 2009).

[85] Bultmann, *Theology of the New Testament*, 1:237.

conviction that Jesus is the Davidic scion and divine son.[86] The gospel concerning God's son is "to all" (1:16) because the messiah is to be given "the nations as an inheritance" (Ps 2:8) and will "rise up to rule the nations; in him the nations shall hope" (Isa 11:10, Rom 15:12).[87] Far from denigrating Jesus's Davidic descent, Paul, our earliest interpreter of the confession, appears to develop it as one of the bases for his entire mission to the nations.[88]

To summarize the findings on word pairs: (1) "seed of David" could have called to mind "son of God" for a Second Temple author; (2) word pairs are specified and developed in line B ($\sigma\pi\acute{\epsilon}\rho\mu\alpha \rightarrow \upsilon\acute{\iota}\acute{o}\varsigma$); and (3) the juxtaposition of $\sigma\acute{\alpha}\rho\kappa\alpha$ and $\pi\nu\epsilon\tilde{\upsilon}\mu\alpha$ has been overstated in readings of Rom 1:3-4: Paul never uses $\sigma\acute{\alpha}\rho\kappa\alpha$ pejoratively with reference to the messiah.

Semantic Aspect

Since lines are composed not of atomized words and word pairs but of words in relationship to one another, we now direct our attention to features at the level of line and clause.

Semantic aspect is "the relationship between the meaning of one line and its parallel line."[89] It is not the semantic meaning of one line compared with the meaning of the other line, or even of the meaning of the entire parallelism. Rather, it is the *relationship* of the two lines that is crucial.

One useful way to determine the relationship between parallel lines is to consider the conjunction used between them. Of course, there is no single word coordinating or subordinating the parallel lines of Rom 1:3-4, yet I still submit that semantic aspect in general is *the* key issue for understanding Rom 1:3-4. Consider how the addition of a conjunction would clarify the meaning:

He came from the seed of David; *therefore*, he was appointed son of God in power…
He came from the seed of David; *despite this*, he was appointed…
He came from the seed of David, *so that* he might be appointed…

---

[86] Michael Theobald, *Studien zum Römerbrief*, WUNT 136 (Tübingen: Mohr Siebeck, 2001), 102-18.

[87] Ibid., 112-14. On the Davidic messiah's rule over the nations in the eschaton, see Amos 9:11-12 LXX, Pss. Sol. 17:31-34; Josephus, *J.W.* 6.312; Tacitus, *Hist.* 5.13; Seutonius, *Vesp.* 4.5; Hippolytus, *Haer.* 9.3; Gen. Rab. 98:8; Pesiq. Rab. 37:3. Even in the thirteenth century, Meshullam da Pierra expected the son of David to intervene during a Mongol invasion to subdue the nations ("Messianic Movements," *EncJud* 14:120).

[88] See further Whitsett, "Son of God," 669; Larry W. Hurtado, *Lord Jesus Christ: Devotion to Jesus in Earliest Christianity* (Grand Rapids: Eerdmans, 2003), 104 n. 63; Matthew Novenson, "The Jewish Messiahs, the Pauline Christ, and the Gentile Question," *JBL* 128 (2009): 357-73, here 371-72.

[89] Berlin, *Dynamics of Biblical Parallelism*, 90.

Biblical poetry, however, is more often paratactic; "the lines are placed one after another with no connective ... rarely is a subordinate relationship indicated on the surface of the text."[90] This does not rule out the possibility that the type of relationship indicated in the text could be characterized by "therefore," "despite," "so that," or any number of connectives. But the interpreter has to establish and assign this relationship without the explicit help of the text.

One possible relationship is that the second line works to complete the idea of the first (syntagmatic semantic pairing); together the lines would then "contain a semantic continuation, a progression of thought."[91] For example, note the progression in Isa 40:9 LXX:[92]

> ἐπ' ὄρος ὑψηλὸν ἀνάβηθι, ὁ εὐαγγελιζόμενος Σιων·
> ὕψωσον τῇ ἰσχύι τὴν φωνήν σου, ὁ εὐαγγελιζόμενος Ιερουσαλημ·
>
> Ascend upon a high mountain, you who bring good news to Zion;
> Lift up your voice with strength, you who bring good news to Jerusalem.

There is a natural progression between the lines that is both temporal (ascend ... *afterwards*, lift up your voice...) and resultant (ascend ... *so that you can* lift...). The herald must go up a high mountain before lifting his voice aloud. In light of our survey of David traditions in Second Temple Judaism, a syntagmatic relationship is conceivable in Rom 1:3–4, and it could be either (1) temporal or (2) resultant:

1. He came from the seed of David according to the flesh; *then* he was appointed son of God in power...

2. He came from the seed of David according to the flesh *so that* he might be appointed son of God in power...

The former, temporal reading is quite common. It accounts for Hahn's two-stage Christology, Rudolf Pesch's somewhat milder "two stages of existence," and even Hans Windisch's "two births."[93] All conceive of the relationship between the lines as one of progression, of movement from one stage or state or birth to the next. Pejorative readings of Davidic descent can also work in this way (syntagmatically), as when interpreters attempt to map Phil 2:6–11 onto Rom 1:3–4: Jesus was the Son of David in humiliation on earth, *then* the Son of God in exaltation in heaven.[94]

---

[90] Ibid., 6.
[91] Ibid., 90.
[92] Similarly Pss. Sol. 17:36a; m. ʾAbot 1:4, 5.
[93] Pesch, "Das Evangelium Gottes," 215; Hans Windisch, "Zur Christologie der Pastoralbriefe," *ZNW* 34 (1935): 213–16, here 215. Cf. Peter Stuhlmacher's *Dreistufenchristologie* ("Theologische Probleme des Römerbriefpräskripts," *EvT* 27 [1967]: 374–89, here 382–83), common among patristic authors, e.g., Origen, *Comm. Rom.* 1.7.6–7.
[94] This reading stretches back to Origen, *Comm. Jo.* 10.6.23, and Eusebius, *Eccl. theol.* 3.17.14.

But syntagmatic parallelism is less common in biblical poetry than another type, paradigmatic, in which "one thought can substitute for the other."[95] Consider Ps 89:3 MT:[96]

I made a covenant with my chosen one,	כרתי ברית לבחירי
I swore to David my servant.	נשבעתי לדוד עבדי

On its own, the first line would leave the reader wondering to whom "my chosen one" refers. The second line says substantially the same thing as the first but adds specificity by clarifying who "my chosen one" is: David. This is a case of *disambiguation*, in which the first clause does not contain enough information. Disambiguation is typical of nonpoetic discourse as well, as in Teun A. van Dijk's playful example, "Please go to the store and buy me some beer."[97] The second disambiguating clause anticipates and answers possible questions about the request to go to the store: Why do you want me to go? And to which store? Applied to Rom 1:3–4, line A establishes that Jesus is a Davidide ("from the seed of David"). But on its own this is not a completely remarkable claim; many people were or claimed to be descendants of David.[98] Thus, it is further disambiguated by τοῦ ὁρισθέντος υἱοῦ θεοῦ ἐν δυνάμει. Read this way, the second line restates and clarifies the first: "the one who came from the seed of David, *that is*, the one appointed son of God in power."

Apropos of the paradigmatic view, one possibility is that the lines can be different on the surface—in their grammatical, lexical, and phonological aspects—while still having an equivalent "deep structure." Berlin explains:

> To take a mundane example, the questions *How are you?*, *How are things?*, *How do you feel?* could be said to be different realizations of the same underlying semantic entity. The notion of paraphrases—that the same thought can be expressed through different words and forms—is based on the existence of a semantic deep structure.[99]

In Berlin's example (*How are you?*, etc.), the interrogatives have very little in common syntactically. One may even add *What's up?*, which has nothing formally in common with *How do you feel?* save that it too is a question. Yet, for all their differences, the clauses are equivalent in meaning.

In Rom 1:3–4, the parallel lines could be regarded as semantically equivalent.

---

[95] Berlin, *Dynamics of Biblical Parallelism*, 90. Note that Berlin's usage of "paradigmatic" and "syntagmatic" differ from the grammatical concepts of "parataxis" and "syntaxis/hypotaxis."

[96] See also 4Q246 I, 9–II, 1; Luke 1:32a; 2 Cor 6:2b; Phil 2:9; m. ʾAbot 1:7.

[97] Teun A. van Dijk, *Text and Context: Explorations in the Semantics and Pragmatics of Discourse* (London: Longman, 1986), 58–60.

[98] Many "discovered" their Davidic ancestry, e.g., Hillel (Gen. Rab. 98:7), R. Hiyya (b. Ket. 62b), and the Babylonian Exilarch (b. Sanh. 38a). Jesus's family was purportedly persecuted on account of Davidic descent (Eusebius, *Hist. eccl.* 3.12; 3.32; 20.1–6).

[99] Berlin, *Dynamics of Biblical Parallelism*, 93.

This reading would account for the relationship between "seed of David" and "son of God" that I have outlined on historical grounds, since the two are often synonymous in Second Temple Judaism. This line of interpretation is encouraged also by what is likely our earliest extant reception of Rom 1:3–4, the creed in 2 Tim 2:8:[100]

Μνημόνευε Ἰησοῦν Χριστὸν
    ἐγηγερμένον ἐκ νεκρῶν,
        ἐκ σπέρματος Δαυίδ,
κατὰ τὸ εὐαγγέλιόν μου

Remember Jesus Christ,
    raised from the dead,
        from the seed of David,
That is my gospel.

In 2 Tim 2:8 the resurrection is put before Davidic descent; the confession reverses these aspects of line A and B in Rom 1:3–4. Further, 2 Tim 2:8 cannot be read temporally: the resurrection cannot come before Jesus's Davidic origin.[101] Thus, 2 Tim 2:8 problematizes readings that expect the parallelism of Rom 1:3–4 to advance temporally (i.e., syntagmatically).[102] If Rom 1:3–4 progresses along a time line from birth to resurrection, then 2 Tim 2:8 would make little sense. It would be analogous to "(B) The car started (A) then she turned the key" or "(B) He bought groceries (A) then entered the supermarket." Elements B and A are temporally unidirectional and only make sense as A → B. Thus our earliest reception outside of Romans of the confession destabilizes linear antithetical readings that move from Jesus's "lowly" status as seed of David to his exalted status as risen son of God. In brief, Rom 1:3–4 likely cannot follow the movement of Phil 2:6–11 from humiliation to exaltation,[103] nor is there necessarily a progressive temporal movement from Davidic descent to divine sonship. 2 Tim 2:8 complicates such readings.

Yet, though there is a deep level of correspondence and equivalence between the lines, it would be reductionistic to imply that the second line is simply a restatement of the first *in toto*. Entire elements are unaccounted for and underemphasized by the equivalence argument (e.g., ἐξ ἀναστάσεως νεκρῶν). So is the relationship

---

[100] On Rom 1:3–4 being the earlier of the two, see Hanna Stettler, *Die Christologie der Pastoralbriefe*, WUNT 2/105 (Tübingen: Mohr Siebeck, 1998), 168–70.

[101] The resurrection cannot come first temporally unless becoming a Davidide was tantamount to being enthroned in heaven.

[102] See, e.g., Eta Linnemann, "Tradition und Interpretation in Röm 1,3f," *EvT* 31 (1971): 264–76, here 268: "Zwischen Davidssohnschaft und Gottessohnschaft besteht kein Sphärenunterschied, sondern eine Zeitdifferenz. Davidide ist Jesus von Geburt—oder er wäre es nicht. Seine Einsetzung zum Messias erfolgt dagegen nicht schon mit seiner Geburt, sondern erst mit seiner Auferstehung von den Toten." Rather, 2 Tim 2:8 is connecting rising "from the dead" with "from the seed of David," a fitting echo of 2 Sam 7:12: "I will raise up your seed after you."

[103] Rightly critiqued by Theobald, *Studien zum Römerbrief*, 112–13.

between the lines syntagmatic or paradigmatic? Does the second line develop or restate the first? Berlin perceptively questions such questions:

> We expect a poem to have a unity of theme and we expect its parts to relate to one another—and parallelism contributes to the unity of the parts. But at the same time the terseness of the poem and the parataxis of parallel lines do not permit the unity among the parts to be spelled out directly. So we are left very often with ambiguity or polysemy in regard to semantic relationships. But this, after all, is the core of poeticalness and the crux of poetic interpretation.[104]

Given the choice between syntagmatic and paradigmatic, Berlin often affirms both. For Rom 1:3–4, I conclude that the center of gravity inheres in the second line: there is a discernible crescendo in the poem. At the same time, however, the second line draws us back to a rereading and reappreciation of the first. In this way, the lines are held together in generative tension, exhibiting both development and equivalence.

One final note: In the preceding discussion, the emphasis on identifying equivalent elements has sidelined ἐξ ἀναστάσεως νεκρῶν. Indeed, on formal grounds readers may expect the parallelism to end at κατὰ πνεῦμα, since all other elements of the parallelism have already been paralleled. This is showcased by the way in which ἐξ ἀναστάσεως νεκρῶν stands awkwardly aloof in common arrangements of the lines:

> came from the seed of David   in terms of the flesh
> designated Son of God (in power)   in terms of the Spirit of holiness
> as from the resurrection of the dead[105]

Yet despite this, ἐξ ἀναστάσεως νεκρῶν is rarely on the redactional chopping block, perhaps because it has a rough grammatical equivalent in ἐκ σπέρματος Δαυίδ.[106] In any case, its presence serves as a reminder that parallelism is not a rigid code but a protean structure. Berlin suggests,

> Not every part of the first line need be paralleled in the second, and, in fact, it rarely is. But it is a mistake to perceive such parallelisms as "incomplete" or otherwise defective. The words which are gapped or left unparalleled are those which the verse wants to deemphasize; the emphasis is on the words that are repeated or paralleled.[107]

---

[104] Berlin, *Dynamics of Biblical Parallelism*, 102.
[105] Outline and translation from Dunn, *Christology in the Making*, 34.
[106] This is exactly how it functions in Jewett's first redactional stage (*Romans*, 104; cf. Augustine, *Ep. Rom. Inch.* 5.5):

3b τοῦ γενομένου   4a τοῦ ὁρισθέντος υἱοῦ θεοῦ
3c ἐκ σπέρματος Δαυὶδ   4d ἐξ ἀναστάσεως νεκρῶν.

[107] Berlin, *Dynamics of Biblical Parallelism*, 96.

Her point reinforces yet again that the quest for a pure parallelism behind Rom 1:3–4—in which every element of line A precisely corresponds to an element in line B—is certainly a cul-de-sac. Yet the scenario in Rom 1:3–4 is in many ways the opposite of what Berlin addresses: the second line does not subtract but adds. The placement of ἐξ ἀναστάσεως is prominent. After the normal structure, it bursts in unexpectedly; it extends beyond what readers anticipate—like the resurrection itself.[108] In doing so, it also draws the reader back up to its grammatically equivalent twin, ἐκ σπέρματος Δαυίδ.[109] The creatively charged relationship of the two ἐκ clauses reminds readers that the one who has risen from the dead is from the seed of David, just as YHWH promised to "raise up David's seed" (2 Sam 7:12). Instead of deemphasizing the unparalleled expression, Rom 1:3–4 draws attention to it by placing it, like the resurrection itself, as the surprising last word.

IV. Conclusion

My approach to Rom 1:3–4 has been twofold. First, I established that the Davidic dynasty tradition is often bound together with divine sonship in Second Temple Judaism. Next, I questioned the aptness of labeling Rom 1:3–4 an antithetical parallelism. Far from being antithetical, many elements of the lines are equivalent; for example, being from the seed of David can be restated as being God's son. Romans 1:3–4 uses parallelism in a way that accents equivalences between Davidic descent and divine sonship and startles readers with the surprising fact of resurrection.

Applied to Rom 1:3–4, Berlin's categories challenge regnant readings, such as the quest for a pristine *Urbekenntnis* with pure parallelism. Further, this study has pointed out that the precise relationship between the lines is *the* critical question in the debate on Rom 1:3–4. I suggest that there is a dynamic interplay of equivalence and development between seed of David and son of God rather than a firm antithetical barrier.

The study of biblical parallelism has come a long way since Robert Lowth's seminal eighteenth-century lectures, and these advances merit further application in New Testament studies in order to yield more nuanced readings of Christianity's earliest poems. The polysemy of poetry demands no less.

---

[108] Here I agree with Ambrosiaster: "Paul did not say 'by the resurrection *of Jesus Christ*' but 'by the resurrection *of the dead*,' because the resurrection of Christ leads to the general resurrection" (*Comm. Rom.* 1.3.17–19 [CSEL 81:16]). Similarly, Augustine, *Exp. quaest. Rom.* 1.1; *Ep. Rom. Inch.* 5.11; S. H. Hooke, "The Translation of Romans 1:4," *NTS* 9 (1963): 370–71.

[109] Similarly Theobald, *Studien zum Römerbrief*, 113.

JBL 136, no. 2 (2017): 491–510
doi: http://dx.doi.org/10.15699/jbl.1362.2017.156767

Is It Pesher? Readdressing the Relationship between the Epistle of Jude and the Qumran Pesharim

BLAKE A. JURGENS
bjurgens@fsu.edu
Florida State University, Tallahassee, FL 32306

The observed midrashic qualities of Jude 5–19 have led many scholars to claim that the author of the epistle is engaging Scripture in ways common to early Jewish exegesis. Some have even gone so far as to claim that, because of its extensive similarities to the Qumran pesharim in both form and hermeneutic perspective, this portion of Jude is actually an example of pesher exegesis akin to texts such as the Habakkuk Pesher. Because a number of new studies have been published on both Jude and the pesharim in the past two decades, it is appropriate to offer a new assessment concerning the validity of this claim. In this study I will analyze pesher as a genre in order to ascertain which features are necessary and sufficient components of pesher exegesis and then address whether Jude 5–19 possesses these essential characteristics and therefore should be referred to as an example of pesher exegesis.

In the past several decades, it has become increasingly common for scholars to situate the epistle of Jude within a "Palestinian-Christian" or "Hellenistic Jewish" compositional milieu.[1] The epistle's use of esoteric Jewish text traditions, the

Most of the research for this study was generously funded by the Fulbright-Kommission and facilitated by Ludwig-Maximilians-Universität München. An earlier version of this article was presented at the Southeastern Commission for the Study of Religion in Nashville, Tennessee, in March 2015. Many thanks to Loren Stuckenbruck, who was instrumental in refining earlier drafts of this article, as well as to Carson Bay, Matthew Goff, Jacob Lollar, and David Skelton for their helpful comments.

[1] For a thorough discussion of Jewish and Hellenistic elements in both Jude and 2 Peter, see Anders Gerdmar, *Rethinking the Judaism-Hellenism Dichotomy: A Historiographical Study of Second Peter and Jude*, ConBNT 36 (Stockholm: Almqvist & Wiksell, 2001); Jörg Frey, "Der Judasbrief zwischen Judentum und Hellenismus," in *Frühjudentum und Neues Testament im Horizont Bibilscher Theologie*, ed. Wolfgang Kraus and Karl-Wilhelm Niebuhr, WUNT 162

491

presence of Semitisms, and the employment of a pseudonymous author recognizable in a Judean context are features that suggest a Jewish Christian background to the epistle.[2] One of the other prominent features mentioned in this discussion is the particular way Jude utilizes Scripture, an approach often referred to as "midrashic." One of the first scholars to make this observation was E. Earle Ellis, who wrote that Jude contains exegetical techniques "common to first century Judaism" and employs "not only quotations but also explicit and implicit midrashim on the Old Testament as their authoritative texts."[3] Many of Ellis's ideas about Jude were subsequently taken up and developed by Richard Bauckham, who in recent years has been the principal proponent of the midrashic structure and form of the body of the epistle (vv. 5–19). According to Bauckham, many of the exegetical techniques employed by the epistle's author are formally similar to features found in the Qumran pesharim. Bauckham finds this resemblance between the epistle and the pesharim so striking that he goes so far as to say that the epistle of Jude is a tangible example of "pesher exegesis."

The issue in this study is the accuracy of this association of Jude with the pesharim. First, I will offer a summary of the main points proposed by Bauckham to support his assessment of Jude as "pesher exegesis." Second, I will provide a brief survey of recent scholarship on the pesharim with a particular focus on discussions concerning their form, content, and overall hermeneutical perspective. Third, I will critique Bauckham's points, concluding that, although Jude is not an example of pesher exegesis, there are still some fruitful avenues of comparative research to explore regarding the epistle and the Qumran pesharim.

(Tübingen: Mohr Siebeck, 2003), 180–210 (Eng. trans.: "The Epistle of Jude Between Judaism and Hellenism," in *The Catholic Epistles and Apostolic Tradition*, ed. Karl-Wilhelm Niebuhr and Robert W. Wall [Waco, TX: Baylor University Press, 2009], 309–21).

[2] See, among others, J. N. D. Kelly, *The Epistles of Peter and of Jude*, BNTC (London: Black, 1969), 233–34; Roman Heiligenthal, *Zwischen Henoch und Paulus: Studien zum theologiegeschichtlichen Ort des Judasbriefes*, TANZ 6 (Tübingen: Francke, 1992); J. Daryl Charles, *Literary Strategy in the Epistle of Jude* (Scranton, PA: University of Scranton Press, 1993), 65–89; Andrew Chester and Ralph P. Martin, *The Theology of the Letters of James, Peter, and Jude*, New Testament Theology (Cambridge: Cambridge University Press, 1994), 66; Peter H. Davids, *The Letters of 2 Peter and Jude*, PilNTC (Grand Rapids: Eerdmans, 2006), 12–14; Gene L. Green, *Jude and 2 Peter*, BECNT (Grand Rapids: Baker Academic, 2008), 12–16; Donald P. Senior (1 Peter) and Daniel J. Harrington (Jude and 2 Peter), *1 Peter, Jude and 2 Peter*, SacPag 15 (Collegeville, MN: Liturgical Press, 2008), 172–82.

[3] E. Earle Ellis, *Prophecy and Hermeneutic in Early Christianity: New Testament Essays*, WUNT 18 (Tübingen: Mohr Siebeck, 1978), 220. Ellis clarifies that his use of the term *midrash* is not equivalent to its use for works of rabbinic midrashim, though such clarification does not negate the ambiguity of his terminology and its shortcomings.

I. Jude as Pesher: The Approach of Richard Bauckham

Although Bauckham does not advance one distinct argument identifying Jude as an example of pesher exegesis, throughout many of his publications on the epistle he reiterates the same four basic points supporting his identification of Jude as a form of pesher exegesis. He recognizes three formal features and one hermeneutical perspective that are shared by the epistle and the Qumran pesharim.

A. *A "Text"-Interpretation Formal Structure*

First, according to Bauckham both Jude and the pesharim follow a pattern in which a scriptural quotation directly precedes the author's interpretation of that lemma. Bauckham claims that, like the pesharim, the epistle of Jude provides a series of so-called text citations (vv. 5–7, 11, 14–15, 17–18), each of which is subsequently followed by a "passage of interpretation" (vv. 8–10, 12–13, 16, 19).[4] Along these lines, verses 5–19 consist of four main sections of "text" and corresponding commentary, with each commentary identifying the false teachers as the present-day subject of their respective "texts."[5] Bauckham does acknowledge that this comparison has its difficulties. First, unlike the pesharim Jude does not directly quote from any text of the Hebrew Bible (much less the Septuagint) and offers only one specific text citation—1 En. 1:9 in verses 14–15.[6] Second, while the pesharim direct their interpretive attention solely to prophetically oriented Scripture, Jude interprets two sets of paraphrased historical typologies (vv. 5–7, 11) alongside the quotation from 1 Enoch (vv. 14–15) and an apostolic prophecy (v. 17–18). Bauckham ultimately admits that these two formal deviations significantly hinder a direct comparison between the pesharim and Jude, yet he nonetheless asserts that "the structure of text and commentary is in every other respect too clear for the anomalous character of the actual 'texts' to outweigh" their comparison.[7]

---

[4] Richard Bauckham, *Jude, 2 Peter*, WBC 50 (Waco, TX: Word, 1983), 4. Cf. Ellis, *Prophecy and Hermeneutic*, 220–26. Bauckham places quotation marks around the term *"text"* in order to signify that the portion of Jude being interpreted is distinguishable from an actual scriptural quotation. See also Bauckham, *Jude and the Relatives of Jesus in the Early Church* (Edinburgh: T&T Clark, 1990), 182.

[5] Richard Bauckham, "James, 1 and 2 Peter, Jude," in *It is Written: Scripture Citing Scripture; Essays in Honour of Barnabas Lindars, SFF*, ed. D. A. Carson and H. G. M. Williamson (Cambridge: Cambridge University Press, 1988), 303–17, here 304–5.

[6] Outside the explicit quotation of 1 Enoch, the epistle also alludes to 1 En. 67 and 80. See Carroll D. Osburn, "*1 Enoch* 80:2–8 (67:2–5) and Jude 12–13," *CBQ* 47 (1985): 296–303. More on the epistle's use of 1 Enoch can be found in sections below.

[7] Bauckham, *Jude and the Relatives of Jesus*, 182.

B. The Use of Οὗτοι Clauses as Introductory Formulae

Bauckham identifies Jude's use of clauses separating the citation of "texts" from their interpretations as roughly parallel to the פשר introductory formulae of the pesharim. Specifically, Jude's use of οὗτοι ("these") throughout the exegetical section serves as a formulaic marker distinguishing the text from its alternating commentary:[8]

v. 8: Ὁμοίως μέντοι καὶ οὗτοι ("Yet in the same way these ...")
v. 10: Οὗτοι δὲ ("But these ...")
v. 12: Οὗτοί εἰσιν οἱ ("These are ...")
v. 16: Οὗτοί εἰσιν ("These are ...")
v. 19: Οὗτοί εἰσιν οἱ ("It is these ...")

According to Bauckham, these formulae—especially the last three instances—are comparable to the standard "This is"/"These are" formulae found in the interpretation sections of apocalyptic dreams visions (e.g., Dan 5:25–26; Zech 1:10, 19–21; 4:10, 14; Rev 7:14; 11:4; 14:4; 1 En. 18:14, 15; 21:6; 22:4; 46:3; 4 Ezra 10:44; 12:10, 30, 32; etc.). In these instances, the demonstrative pronouns often refer back to something (or someone) witnessed in the vision, which is subsequently interpreted by an angelic being or God. This same quotation formula is also used at times in the pesharim, both without the word פשר (4QpIsa[a] III, 7, 9, 10, 12; 4QpIsa[b] II, 6–7, 10; 4QFlor I, 2, 3, 11, 12, 17) and accompanied by it (1QpHab X, 3; 4QpNah II, 2; IV, 1; 4QpPs[a] II, 5; III, 12; IV, 1, 23; CD IV, 14). This formulaic resemblance leads Bauckham to conclude that such similarities are not accidental but stem from a shared Near Eastern background of dream and oracle interpretation fundamental to both the Qumran pesharim and Jude's exegetical segment.[9] Although Jude's use of the demonstrative expository formula does not strictly follow the "pesher formulae" of the Dead Sea Scrolls—especially in its lack of any word equivalent to פשר—Bauckham determines that this omission may simply be "accidental" and is not indicative of a formal deviation from the exegetical techniques of the pesharim.[10]

---

[8] Bauckham, *Jude, 2 Peter*, 44–45 (cf. Ellis, *Prophecy and Hermeneutic*, 225); Bauckham, "James, 1 and 2 Peter, Jude," 304.

[9] Bauckham, *Jude and the Relatives of Jesus*, 203–4: "The fact that he [the author of Jude] is writing commentary rather than vision virtually requires that his use of the οὗτοι formulae must derive from a tradition of scriptural commentary similar to that of the Qumran sect."

[10] Bauckham, *Jude and the Relatives of Jesus*, 151, 204. A helpful list of all the commentary and citation formulae appearing in the pesharim can be found in C. D. Elledge, "Appendix: A Graphic Index of Citation and Commentary Formulae in the Dead Sea Scrolls," in *The Dead Sea Scrolls: Hebrew, Aramaic, and Greek Texts with English Translations; Pesharim, Other Commentaries, and Related Documents*, ed. James H. Charlesworth, PTSDSSP 6B (Tübingen: Mohr Siebeck, 2002), 367–77.

C. The Employment of Jewish Exegetical Techniques

Bauckham claims that Jude, like the Qumran pesharim, employs a number of Jewish exegetical techniques.[11] His most prominent example is the utilization of catchwords either linking textual citations to their interpretation or associating one text citation with another, a feature that Bauckham refers to as a rough equivalent of the rabbinic *gĕzērâ šāwâ*.[12] For instance, in the first citation section the words κύριος ("lord," v. 5) and σαρκός ("flesh," v. 7) are alluded to in the corresponding interpretation in verse 8, which correlates the unbelieving Israelites and Sodomites with the "dreamers" who "also defile the flesh" (σάρκα μὲν μιαίνουσιν) and "reject authority" (κυριότητα δὲ ἀθετοῦσιν).[13] Bauckham also points out instances where catchwords link a text with the interpretation of an alternate citation, such as the appearance of ζόφον τετήρηκεν ("kept in darkness," v. 6) and αἰωνίου ("eternal," v. 7) in the first "text" citation, which then reemerge in v. 13 (ὁ ζόφος τοῦ σκότους εἰς αἰῶνα τετήρηται, "the deepest darkness has been reserved forever" [NRSV]).[14] Another midrashic exegetical technique Bauckham identifies in both Jude and the pesharim is the use of a secondary quotation.[15] As in some of the pesharim (e.g., 4QFlor I, 4, 12–13, 15–17; 4QpIsa^e), the epistle's author, during his second "text"-commentary section (vv. 8–10), refers to a supplementary "text" episode (v. 9) from the Testament or Assumption of Moses.[16] While Bauckham admits that these

---

[11] See Ellis, *Prophecy and Hermeneutic*, 225; D. J. Rowston, "The Most Neglected Book in the New Testament," *NTS* 21 (1975): 554–63, here 558–59.

[12] This includes (1) the root ἀπωλ- ("destruction," vv. 5, 11; texts 1 and 2); (2) ἀσεβ- ("impiety," vv. 15, 18; texts 3 and 4); (3) κύριος/κρίσιν ("lord"/"judgment," vv. 5–6, 9, 14–15; texts 1, 1a, 3); and (4) πλάνη/πλανῆται ("error"/"lead astray," vv. 11, 13; text 2). See *Jude and the Relatives of Jesus*, 207.

[13] Bauckham, *Jude and the Relatives of Jesus*, 207–8. This type of catchword connection also appears with βλασφημίας ("slander") and κύριος in v. 9 (βλασφημοῦσιν: vv. 8, 10; κυριότητα: v. 8) and with ἐλάλησαν ("have said") in verse 15 corresponding with λαλεῖ ("speak") in verse 16. He also includes the repetition of πλάνη/πλανῆται in verses 11 and 13.

[14] Bauckham, *Jude and the Relatives of Jesus*, 208. He notes also the use of the verb ἐπορεύθησαν ("they go") in verse 11 and the participle πορευόμενοι in verse 16 and the similar phrases found in verse 16 (κατὰ τὰς ἐπιθυμίας ἑαυτῶν, "[they indulge] their own lusts") and verse 18 (κατὰ τὰς ἑαυτῶν ἐπιθυμίας πορευόμενοι, "indulging their own lusts").

[15] Bauckham, *Jude, 2 Peter*, 45; Bauckham, "James, 1 and 2 Peter, Jude," 304–5. See also Maurya P. Horgan, *Pesharim: Qumran Interpretations of Biblical Books*, CBQMS 8 (Washington, DC: Catholic Biblical Association of America, 1979), 95; and George Brooke, *Exegesis at Qumran: 4QFlorilegium in Its Jewish Context*, JSOTSup 29 (Sheffield: JSOT Press, 1985), 130–33, 145–47, 304–5.

[16] A good summary of the debate concerning the Mosaic text and tradition behind verse 9 can be found in John Muddiman, "The Assumption of Moses and the Epistle of Jude," in *Moses in Biblical and Extra-Biblical Traditions*, ed. Axel Graupner and Michael Wolter, BZAW 372 (Berlin: de Gruyter, 2007), 169–80. See also Bauckham, *Jude, 2 Peter*, 65–76; Green, *Jude and 2 Peter*, 80–84.

techniques "are by no means unique to Qumran" as a whole, he understands Jude's adept application of catchwords and a secondary quotation as further evidence supporting his argument that the exegetical section of Jude is formally akin to the Qumran pesharim.[17]

D. A Shared Prophetic Hermeneutical Perspective

In addition to these three formal characteristics shared by the pesharim and Jude, Bauckham also proposes that underlying both is a similar hermeneutical perspective. For Bauckham, both the pesharim and Jude possess "the same conviction that the ancient texts are eschatological prophecy" which is then applied to the current events experienced by their respective exegetes.[18] For example, Bauckham notes that all four of the "text" citations in Jude explicitly deal with the judgment of the wicked, either by means of typology (vv. 5–7, 11), the quotation of an ancient prophecy (vv. 14–15, quoting 1 En. 1:9), or the quotation of an apostolic prophecy (Jude 18). In turn, all four of these citations are marked by corresponding shifts in verb tenses distinguishing the "text" citation from the commentary; the "texts" contain verbs in the past tense (corresponding to the "prophetic perfect") or the future tense to show the expectation of the prophecy, while the commentary (which provides the present-day fulfillment of the presage) always contains verbs in the present tense.[19] Both of these features lead Bauckham to conclude that, like the pesharim, the commentary composed by Jude's author is intent on showing that the prophetic foretellings of the past are being fulfilled in the reality experienced by the letter's recipients. Thus, the rise of the false teachers, their rebellious and morally suspect behavior, and their foretold consequential judgment at the parousia are the historical events being prophetically described in the eschatologically oriented commentary on the "texts."[20] Bauckham reasons that Jude's eschatological

---

[17] Bauckham, *Jude and the Relatives of Jesus*, 208.

[18] Bauckham, *Jude, 2 Peter*, 5. See also Bauckham, *Jude and the Relatives of Jesus*, 152. Bauckham refers to this interpretive perspective as one that understands the current age as one of "eschatological fulfillment." A similar view is articulated by Green, *Jude and 2 Peter*, 39–41. See also Robert L. Webb, "The Eschatology of the Epistle of Jude and Its Rhetorical and Social Functions," *BBR* 6 (1996): 139–51. On Jude's apocalyptic perspective, see Kelley Coblentz Bautch, "'Awaiting New Heavens and a New Earth': The Apocalyptic Imagination of 1–2 Peter and Jude," in *Reading 1–2 Peter and Jude: A Resource for Students*, ed. Eric F. Mason and Troy W. Martin, RBS 77 (Atlanta: Society of Biblical Literature, 2014), 63–82.

[19] Bauckham, *Jude, 2 Peter*, 4–5, 78, 94.

[20] Bauckham, "James, 1 and 2 Peter, Jude," 303–5. A recent treatment of Jude's conception of judgment at the *parousia* and its relationship to prophetic witness is the detailed work of Christian Blumenthal, *Prophetie und Gericht: Der Judasbrief als Zeugnis urchristlicher Prophetie*, BBB 156 (Göttingen: V&R Unipress, 2009).

interpretive perspective is, in fact, "the same principle [that] enabled the Qumran community to see its enemies portrayed in Habakkuk and Isaiah."[21]

In summary, Bauckham concludes that these three formal features—the "text"-interpretation formal structure, the use of introductory οὗτοι formulae, and the employment of Jewish exegetical techniques—along with a shared eschatologically and prophetically oriented hermeneutical approach to interpreting "texts," ultimately confirm his appraisal of Jude 5–19 as exegetically analogous to the Qumran pesharim. Bauckham therefore goes so far as to claim that Jude is aligned "more closely with the Qumran pesharim than with other examples of Jewish exegesis."[22] The combination of these features leads Bauckham to conclude that the author of Jude was "a highly accomplished practitioner of pesher exegesis" whose work constitutes "the most elaborate and complex early Christian example of commentary in the style of the Qumran pesharim."[23]

II. The Qumran Pesharim: Three Approaches

In order to assess Bauckham's argument for the identification of Jude 5–19 as pesher, it is prudent to offer first a working definition of pesher or the pesharim. There has been no shortage of publications in the last several decades dedicated to identifying what the pesharim are and determining what features define them.[24] In order to offer an accurate picture of where this discussion stands currently, I will survey three of the more recent attempts to define the Qumran pesharim.

First, in his monograph on the pesharim, Timothy Lim seeks to delineate what factors distinguish pesher from other forms of scriptural exegesis, yet he simultaneously wishes to avoid classifying pesher as its own genre of scriptural interpretation, viewing such a thing as a "scholarly construct."[25] Despite this, Lim still offers a basic summation concerning what he means when he speaks of pesher:

---

[21] Bauckham, *Jude, 2 Peter*, 10.
[22] Bauckham, "James, 1 and 2 Peter, Jude," 305.
[23] Bauckham, *Jude and the Relatives of Jesus*, 221; see also 233.
[24] Arguably, the most influential has been George J. Brooke, "Qumran Pesher: Towards the Re-definition of a Genre," *RevQ* 10 (1981): 483–503. Other earlier works addressing this question include Karl Elliger, *Studien zum Habakuk-Kommentar vom Toten Meer*, BHT 15 (Tübingen: Mohr, 1953); Cecil Roth, "The Subject Matter of Qumran Exegesis," *VT* 10 (1960): 51–68; L. H. Silberman, "Unriddling the Riddle: A Study in the Structure and Language of the Habakkuk Pesher (1QpHab)," *RevQ* 3 (1962): 323–64; W. H. Brownlee, *The Midrash Pesher of Habakkuk: Text, Translation, Exposition with an Introduction*, SBLMS 24 (Missoula, MT: Scholars Press, 1979); Horgan, *Pesharim*; Devorah Dimant, "Pesharim, Qumran," *ABD* 5:244–51; Dimant, "Qumran Sectarian Literature," in *Jewish Writings of the Second Temple Period: Apocrypha, Pseudepigrapha, Qumran Sectarian Writings, Philo, Josephus*, ed. M. E. Stone, CRINT 2.2 (Philadelphia: Fortress, 1984), 483–550.
[25] Timothy Lim, *Pesharim*, Companion to the Qumran Scrolls 3 (Sheffield: Sheffield

As a genre, the pesher reflects a common exegetical approach to the scriptural texts: the consecutive citation of verses from a section of biblical passages is interspersed with comments, much like the way some modern commentaries present their verse-by-verse exposition by first quoting and then commenting on each biblical verse.[26]

While these features are relevant to delineating the formal characteristics of the pesharim, Lim admits that classifying the pesharim solely according to these exegetical features is problematic.[27] If it was the case that such features alone were sufficient identifiers, then according to Lim there would be very little to effectively distinguish the pesharim from rabbinic midrashim, targumim, and some of the interpretations of Scripture found in the New Testament. For Lim, what distinguishes the pesharim from other types of biblical interpretation is not the *form* but rather the *content* of the pesharim, that is, "its emphasis upon prophetic literature (including the Psalms), eschatological orientation, contemporizing tendencies and the special role that it confers upon a continuous revelation and the Teacher of Righteousness."[28] Like George Brooke before him, Lim asserts that the pesharim cannot be understood or defined unless both *form* and *content* are simultaneously considered.

Lim's concern for both form and content is further explored by Shani Berrin (now Tzoref), who defines pesher as:

> a form of biblical interpretation peculiar to Qumran, in which biblical poetic/prophetic texts are applied to post-biblical historical/eschatological settings through various literary techniques in order to substantiate a theological conviction regarding divine rewards and punishment.[29]

One of the strengths of Berrin's definition is that instead of relying solely on form or content, her definition also brings motive and method into the discussion.[30] For

---

Academic, 2002), esp. 44–53, here 53. He bases this claim on (1) the fact that no ancient lists of the pesharim exist, nor any manuscript that possesses the word *pesher* in its title; and (2) the features shared by all the documents labeled "pesharim" are not as numerous or substantial as scholars suggest.

[26] Ibid., 52. He adds that all the continuous pesharim share (1) continuous quotation of biblical texts; (2) the technical term *pesher* in the introductory formulae of the interpretation; and (3) the identification of a figure within the biblical text with a contemporaneous figure. This stands alongside a prevalent, but not always explicitly stated, eschatological orientation (40).

[27] Cf. Brooke, "Qumran Pesher: Towards the Re-definition of a Genre," 485–91.

[28] Lim, *Pesharim*, 52.

[29] Shani Berrin, "Qumran Pesharim," in *Biblical Interpretation at Qumran*, ed. Matthias Henze, SDSSRL (Grand Rapids: Eerdmans, 2005), 110–33; this definition is derived from her earlier work, *The Pesher Nahum Scroll from Qumran: An Exegetical Study of 4Q169*, STDJ 53 (Leiden: Brill, 2004). See also Shani Berrin, "Pesharim," in *The Encyclopedia of the Dead Sea Scrolls*, ed. Lawrence H. Schiffman and James C. VanderKam (Oxford: Oxford University Press, 2000), 644–47.

[30] This is drawn out in more detail in Berrin, *Pesher Nahum Scroll*, 9–19.

Berrin, pesher *formally* is identified by "a citation of a biblical text (the 'lemma'); an introductory formula using the word *pesher* (such as 'its *pesher* concerns...'); and an application of the text to a historical, eschatologically significant reality, outside its original context."[31] Regarding *content*, Berrin identifies pesher as possessing a prophetic biblical base text *or* a historical/eschatological application to a particular piece of Scripture.[32] Next, Berrin understands the *method* of the pesharim as a synthesis of "revelation" (due to the connections of פשר with dream interpretation) and "exegesis" (due to the usage of certain exegetical techniques) such that the scriptural interpretation of biblical prophecy presupposes both the revelatory receptiveness of the human interpreter and the cryptic nature of the text.[33] Finally, the *motive* of the pesharim, according to Berrin, is the unveiling of the esoteric meaning and truths hidden in past Scriptures concerning the reality of the present day.[34] Thus, the pesharim draw out the fulfillment of biblical prophecies in what their interpreters identify as the eschatological age.[35] Like Lim, Berrin understands pesher as the amalgamation of many features, each of which contributes to the full understanding of the identity of pesher.

One of the more nuanced perspectives on the pesharim is that of Robert Williamson, who, after noting the various shortcomings of previous attempts to define the pesharim, offers a cognitive model of the genre of pesher.[36] Following the lead of genre theorists like Alastair Fowler and Daniel Chandler, Williamson attempts to locate the *center* of the genre from which any particular text may be more or less closely aligned.[37] In his approach to the pesharim, Williamson distinguishes three types of generic features: *compulsory features*, which can call into question a text's genre membership if absent (e.g., continuous quotation of scripture, use of technical term פשר, contemporization of biblical figures);[38] *default*

---

[31] Berrin, "Qumran Pesharim," 111–13, here 111.

[32] Ibid., 114–22. She specifies that, while the use of an eschatologically significant prophetic or poetic base text is a "typical" and possibly "essential" feature, it is the eschatological application of the base text that is "certainly essential" to the pesharim (122).

[33] Shani Berrin Tzoref, "Pesharim," in *The Eerdmans Dictionary of Early Judaism*, ed. John J. Collins and Daniel C. Harlow (Grand Rapids: Eerdmans, 2010), 1050–55, esp. 1051.

[34] Berrin, "Qumran Pesharim," 130–33.

[35] Berrin, *Pesher Nahum Scroll*, 11.

[36] Cf. the comparable approach taken by Benjamin G. Wright, "Joining the Club: A Suggestion about Genre in Early Jewish Texts," *DSD* 17 (2010): 260–85.

[37] Robert Williamson Jr., "Pesher: A Cognative Model of the Genre," *DSD* 17 (2010): 307–31, esp. 312–17. Williamson is heavily influenced by the philosophy of Wittgenstein in that his approach admittedly runs close to Wittgenstein's concept of family resemblance (313–14). In this way, as Williamson writes, "texts that participate more fully in the repertoire may be considered to be more central members of the genre (part of the 'nuclear family,' so to speak), while those that participate only sparingly in the repertoire can be considered more distantly related (a 'second cousin,' perhaps)."

[38] By *compulsory*, Williamson ("Cognitive Model of the Genre," 318) means "elements that occur in all fifteen of the continuous pesharim" as identified by Lim, *Pesharim*, 40.

features, which belong to the prototype of the genre but which may or may not be displayed by all the texts of that genre (e.g., verse-by-verse commentary, short citation of Scripture lemma, use of certain literary devices/techniques);[39] and finally *optional features*, which account for the idiosyncratic elements of individual texts (e.g., recitation of scriptural lemma).[40] Having determined which of these features are prototypical of the pesharim, Williamson goes on to offer a definition:

> Pesher is a genre of biblical interpretation in which the prophetic passages of the Bible are viewed as mysteries of God (רזין) concerning history contemporary to the author of the pesher; as such, the biblical text is understood to be properly interpreted only by one specially endowed by God to unravel (פשר) its meaning. This interpretation, so understood, consists of a *Gestalt* structure in which: (1) the scriptural citation is linked to (2) a contemporary referent by means of (3) an interpretation understood as an "unraveling" of "mysteries," generally (though not always) introduced by the technical term פשר.[41]

Thus, while some default features may or may not be apparent in all the individual texts that could be included in the pesher genre, the deviations do not disqualify a text from being identified as a pesher but instead indicate whether a text is a "more central member of the genre" or simply "a peripheral participant in the genre."[42] Like Berrin's and Lim's definitions of pesher, Williamson's consolidates form, content, and overall hermeneutic into one general conception of what it means for a text to be considered a pesher. Moreover, Williamson's definition also successfully avoids confounding pesher with other forms of early Jewish literature that merely employ similar exegetical techniques. Formal features are not necessarily compulsory features but may be default or optional features whose absence or presence does not necessitate accepting or rejecting a certain text as a pesher.[43]

What is pertinent for the task at hand is not to determine which of these definitions may be the most accurate but rather to explore where the definitions of Lim, Berrin, and Williamson overlap. All three of these definitions of pesher seek a solution that does not rely solely on the formal features of the pesharim but includes elements such as content, hermeneutical perspective, and even motive. Despite the variance of their approaches, however, the definitions are similar in delineating *which formal features are indicators of the pesher genre*: a tripartite scriptural lemma–formula (usually with the term פשר)–commentary structure strung together by "midrashic" exegetical techniques and underlined by an eschatological hermeneutic that perceives contemporary figures and events as being foretold in prophetically significant sections of Scripture. These formal features for all three scholars would fall under Williamson's category of *compulsory* features, making

---

[39] Williamson, "Cognitive Model of the Genre," 319–20. His list of default features is mostly derived from Horgan's list of formal features and literary devices (*Pesharim*, 229–59).
[40] Williamson, "Cognitive Model of the Genre," 320.
[41] Ibid., 327.
[42] Ibid., 328.
[43] Ibid., 331.

each a crucial and necessary feature of a text identified as pesher. Although these scholars bring up significant points in their individual methodological analyses of the pesharim, the fact that all three agree on which formal features are basic to the pesharim will serve as a point of reference throughout the rest of this study.

III. Reassessing Jude's Status as Pesher Exegesis

Having laid out both Bauckham's points of comparison and a brief survey of what scholars mean when they talk about the pesharim and pesher exegesis, this final section will assess whether Bauckham's comparative analysis justifies his assessment of the epistle as an example of pesher exegesis.

A. *The "Text"-Commentary Formal Structure*

While Bauckham feels that it is insignificant that the "texts" of Jude are, in reality, paraphrastic collages of biblical narrative and an apostolic prophecy with only one true scriptural quotation (1 En. 1:9),[44] it seems that none of the pesherists would have considered such a thing to be insignificant. Both Lim and Berrin emphasize the importance of the *citation* of Scripture in the pesharim as opposed to a paraphrase or allusion. Similarly, Williamson classifies the "quotation of sections, large and small, of a biblical text" to be a compulsory and thus prototypical feature of the pesharim.[45] According to Brooke, "base text" and "commentary" are not separate entities in the pesharim but exist in a "symbiotic relationship" such that the commentary inherits its authority from the base text and the authority of the base text is endorsed by virtue of its being commented upon.[46] The fact that the contemporizing interpretation of the pesherists relies heavily on the specific words of the prophetic texts that they decrypt suggests that mere paraphrases, allusions, or summaries of the words of Scripture would not adequately serve their purpose.[47]

---

[44] Unlike Bauckham, I do not see any issue with referring to 1 Enoch as an authoritative scriptural text, despite its extrabiblical status. Considering the influence of Enochic literature on both first-century Judaism and early Christianity, and the fact that no conception of canon would have restricted the author of Jude from embracing 1 Enoch as being sacred, it seems unnecessary and unsubstantiated to exclude it as a citation of an authoritative text.

[45] Williamson, "Cognitive Model of the Genre," 348.

[46] George J. Brooke, "Some Comments on Commentary," *DSD* 19 (2012): 249–66, here 255.

[47] Others who share this view include Alex P. Jassen, "The Pesharim and the Rise of Commentary in Early Jewish Scriptural Interpretation," *DSD* 19 (2012): 363–98, here 366–70; George Brooke, "The Pesharim and the Origins of the Dead Sea Scrolls," in *Methods of Investigation of the Dead Sea Scrolls and the Khirbet Qumran Site: Present Realities and Future Prospects*, ed. Michael O. Wise et al.; Annals of the New York Academy of Sciences 722 (New York: New York Academy of Sciences, 1994), 339–53; Michael Fishbane, "Use, Authority and Interpretation of Mikra at Qumran," in *Mikra: Text, Translation, Reading, and Interpretation of the Hebrew Bible in Ancient Judaism and Early Christianity*, ed. Martin J. Mulder, CRINT 2.1 (Assen: Van Gorcum,

Although minor variations and deliberate alterations do occur in the cited Scripture of the pesharim, such changes never dramatically morph the source text from a scriptural citation into a loose abridgment or paraphrase.[48] Therefore, while Bauckham finds Jude's use of "texts" as opposed to actual citations of Scripture to be nonconsequential, according to the scholars surveyed above the absence of explicit scriptural quotations in Jude diverges significantly from the formal tendencies of the pesharim.[49]

B. The Use of Introductory Formulae in Jude and the Pesharim

On the one hand, much like the pesher formulae in the pesharim, the οὗτοι formulae of Jude do separate and distinguish its biblical allusions (i.e., "texts") from their respective expository sections. In this way, both the οὗτοι formulae and the pesher formulae share this specific functional trait. This does not, however, entail that the introductory formulae of Jude thereby mimic *every* functional feature of the pesher formulae.[50] The most obvious formal discrepancy between the two, noted even by Bauckham, is the absence of a term equivalent to פשר throughout the epistle. Like the explicit citation of Scripture, the use of פשר is viewed by a majority of Qumran scholars to be an essential or distinctive feature of the pesher genre.[51] Linguistically, the Hebrew פשר (cf. פתר in Gen 40–41) is related to the Akkadian *pašāru* ("to loosen, dissolve"), which takes on the meaning "to interpret" in its frequent appearances in dream and omen interpretations.[52] The use of the

---

1998), 339–77, here 362. It is also prudent to note that the tendency for the pesharim to isolate certain elements of the lemma from their surrounding scriptural context (referred to by earlier scholars as "atomization") as well as utilize numerous text-exegetical techniques seems to imply that the biblical text does play a substantial role that would not be satisfied by simple paraphrase or allusion.

[48] Lim's analysis of the variant readings in the biblical quotations of the continuous pesharim reveal that there is an overall 11 percent variation rate compared to the MT and that most of the variants consist of orthographical differences such as full versus defective spellings (*Holy Scripture in the Qumran Commentaries and Pauline Letters* [Oxford: Clarendon, 1997], 89–94).

[49] Cf. Berrin, "Pesharim", 1051–52.

[50] It is even debatable whether the οὗτοι formulae were intended to distinguish between "text" and interpretation or were primarily used to distinguish between the letter's recipients (the plural "you") and the ungodly opponents (the "these"). Arguments supporting the rhetorical effect of the latter have been made most notably by J. Daryl Charles, "'Those' and 'These': The Use of the Old Testament in the Epistle of Jude," *JSNT* 38 (1990): 109–24; and Stephen J. Joubert, "Persuasion in the Letter of Jude," *JSNT* 58 (1995): 75–87.

[51] See, e.g., Asher Finkel, "The Pesher of Dreams and Scriptures," *RevQ* 4 (1964): 357–70; Isaac Rabinowitz, "*Pesher/Pittaron*: Its Biblical Meaning and Its Significance in Qumran Literature," *RevQ* 8 (1973): 219–32; Horgan, *Pesharim*, 230–37; Lim, *Pesharim*, 40; Berrin, "Qumran Pesharim," 111; Williamson, "Cognitive Model of the Genre," 348; Jassen, "Pesharim and the Rise of Commentary," 391–96.

[52] Martti Nissinen, "Pesher as Divination: Qumran Exegesis, Omen Interpretation, and Literary Prophecy," in *Prophecy after the Prophets? The Contribution of the Dead Sea Scrolls to the*

Aramaic cognate פשר in the book of Daniel reveals a similar confluence of meaning in episodes where Daniel acts as the interpreter of dreams and omens (Dan 2:31–45; 4:16–27; 5:25–28; 7:2–24; 9).[53] As such, the use of the term פשר is a theologically significant move, as its usage entails and explicates that the pesharim are not simply scriptural commentary but *inspired* scriptural commentary that relies just as heavily on divine revelation as it does on certain exegetical patterns. In this sense, the pesherists are not *interpreting* the text as much as they are *deciphering, unraveling,* or *unveiling* the cryptic meaning behind the prophetic oracles and omens of the past that apply to their constructed "historical" reality.[54] Theologically, this makes the appearance of the term פשר a crucial element to the pesharim—as Lim, Berrin, and Williamson all confirm—for it unequivocally indicates this dual exegetical-revelatory background of the pesharim. Bauckham's claim, therefore, that the absence of the term פשר in Jude's formulae is "insignificant" fails to articulate how essential its presence actually is in the pesharim.

Furthermore, while Bauckham is correct that the pesharim at times do use demonstrative pronouns *in lieu* of more typical pesher formulae, he neglects to note that they do so *only* in conjunction with formulae that include the term פשר. For example (as Bauckham notes), 4QpIsa[b] II contains two occurrences of demonstrative clauses introducing the interpretation of Scripture (II, 6–7: אלה הם ... אשר; II, 10: היא ... אשר) but only does so under the heading of the first line of the column, which indicates that the following column is "the *pesher* of the matter concerning the last days…" (II, 1: … פשר הדבר לאחרית הימים). Daniel Machiela confirms this and notes that other pesharim also employ demonstrative pronouns as introductory formulae but do so primarily in connection with interpretations of secondary and subordinate citations of text as opposed to the interpretation of a central

---

Understanding of Biblical and Extra-Biblical Prophecy, ed. Kristin De Troyer and Amin Lange, CBET 52 (Leuven: Peeters, 2009), 43–60; see also A. Leo Oppenheim, *The Interpretation of Dreams in the Ancient Near East, with a Translation of an Assyrian Dream Book*, TAPhS NS 46.3 (Philadelphia: American Philosophical Society, 1956; repr., Piscataway, NJ: Gorgias, 2008), 217–25; Uri Gabbay, "Akkadian Commentaries from Ancient Mesopotamia and Their Relation to Early Hebrew Exegesis," *DSD* 19 (2012): 267–312.

[53] See esp. Daniel A. Machiela, "The Qumran Pesharim as Biblical Commentaries: Historical Context and Lines of Development," *DSD* 19 (2012): 313–62, esp. 336–44; Horgan, *Pesharim*, 230–37; Jassen, "Pesharim and the Rise of Commentary," 385–96, esp. 391–96.

[54] Jutta Jokiranta, *Social Identity and Sectarianism in the Qumran Movement*, STDJ 105 (Leiden: Brill, 2013), 117–18. Jokiranta tempers this later, noting that the pesharim do not function primarily as symbolic historical repositories; rather, their primary function centers on group codification and identity construction (209–13). For more on the somewhat tenuous relationship between the pesharim and history, see Bilhah Nitzan, "The *Pesher* and Other Methods of Instruction," in *The Teacher of Righteousness: Literary Studies*, part 2 of *Mogilany 1989: Papers on the Dead Sea Scrolls Offered in Memory of Jean Carmignac*, ed. Zdzisław Jan Kapera (Kraków: Enigma, 1991), 209–20; John J. Collins, "Prophecy and History in the Pesharim," in *Authoritative Scriptures in Ancient Judaism*, ed. M. Popović, JSJSup 141 (Leiden: Brill, 2010), 209–26.

quotation of a base text, which is introduced by the typical pesher formula.[55] Although the pesharim may not use the term פשר in every instance of interpretation, its absence in certain situations does not indicate that it was an unnecessary or secondary element of the pesher genre.[56]

C. *The Employment of Catchwords and a Secondary "Text"*

In contrast to the previous two points, Bauckham's remark that Jude employs techniques such as catchwords and the use of a secondary text as in the pesharim is a valid observation. At a closer look, however, the significance of these formal features is rather muted. Taking up Williamson's work with cognitive genre theory, if Jude's use of catchwords and a secondary quotation are indeed sound arguments for classifying Jude as an example of pesher exegesis, such an observation would offer only a *default* feature in the case of catchwords and an *optional* feature in the use of a secondary quotation.[57] Unless these exegetical techniques are coupled with more determinative features of pesher exegesis—say, the use of prophetic texts and the appearance of pesher formulae—the appearance of catchwords and the utilization of a secondary "text" are relatively ineffective identifiers. As Williamson notes, unless a text possesses most, if not all, of the *compulsory* features and at least *some* of the *default* features, it should not be classified as being part of that particular genre. Therefore, even if we do accept Bauckham on this particular observation, its overall bearing on the identification of Jude 5–19 as pesher exegesis is minimal.

D. *Prophetic Hermeneutical Perspective*

Finally, also problematic is Bauckham's claim that Jude and the pesharim share a similar hermeneutical perspective that understands their interpretation of "texts" as the contemporizing of ancient prophecies in reference to the eschatological

---

[55] Machiela, "Qumran Pesharim as Biblical Commentaries," 324 n. 34. See also Moshe Bernstein, "Introductory Formulas for Citation and Re-Citation of Biblical Verses in the Qumran Pesharim," *DSD* 1 (1994): 30–70.

[56] Thus, while both the continuous pesharim and the thematic pesharim at times use introductory formulae lacking the term פשר, none of the pesharim completely lacks any instances where the word is used within an introductory formula (minus those which are exceedingly fragmentary). See Berrin, "Qumran Pesharim," 111–13; Lim, *Pesharim*, 40. See also Williamson, "Cognitive Model of the Genre," 348 n. 45, although I disagree with Williamson's relegation of the use of the term פשר to a default feature while the "pesher relationship" between the text and interpretation is what is ultimately compulsory.

[57] Williamson, "Cognitive Model of the Genre," 320. Williamson explicitly categorizes the use of specific literary devices as a default feature. He does not mention the use of secondary text citations, though he does classify the recitation of a base text as an optional feature. Such secondary quotations are not frequent in the pesharim, and, according to Williamson's model, this device would be termed an optional feature.

present. While both the pesharim and Jude have eschatological concerns, what problematizes Bauckham's proposition is that the "texts" Jude cites for the most part do not lend themselves to the same prophetic interpretive interaction that occurs in the pesharim. Although both the pesharim and Jude share an eschatological orientation, the particular way this worldview is played out in the respective texts is much different.

First, while the two typological sets of verses—5–7 and 11—serve as examples of divine judgment over the paradigmatic promulgators of wickedness, neither of these "texts" offers an explicit prophecy pertaining to the eschatological present, much less an oracle, unfulfilled blessing, or curse that is oriented to the future.[58] The first "text"—the unfaithfulness of post-exodus Israel, the inordinate activities of the fallen angels, and the sexual immorality of Sodom and Gomorrah—does not present itself as a prophecy being fulfilled but rather stands as an *example* of both extreme wickedness and divine justice.[59] This is affirmed in v. 8, where the phrase Ὁμοίως μέντοι ("yet in the same way") begins the proposed expository section of previously presented "text," suggesting not that unfaithful Israel, the Watchers, and Sodom and Gomorrah are being *prophetically fulfilled* by the present salacious acts of the opponents but rather that the misdeeds of the opponents and their expected judgment *are akin to* these previously mentioned paradigms of ungodliness and thus destined for the same divine retribution.[60]

---

[58] Examples of the latter in the Hebrew Bible include Jacob's final blessing in Gen 49, Balaam's final oracle in Num 24, and many of the Davidic psalms. Often these texts were viewed as "prophetic" due to the eschatologically florid character of their language and subject matter; for example, both Gen 49:1 and Num 24:14 contain the phrase באחרית הימים ("in the last/latter days"), which was often taken eschatologically at Qumran and in other Second Temple literature. See Annette Steudel, "אחרית הימים in the Texts from Qumran," *RevQ* 16 (1993): 225–46. By the late Second Temple period, the psalms also acquired prophetic attributes, especially those associated with David (e.g., 11QPs[a] 27; cf. Josephus, *Ant.* 8.109–110; Acts 1:16; 2:30–31; Barn. 12.10). See, e.g., Peter Flint, "The Prophet David at Qumran," in Henze, *Biblical Interpretation at Qumran*, 158–67.

[59] This is indicated by the use of the word δεῖγμα ("example") to describe the Sodomites in verse 7. See E. K. Lee, "Words Denoting 'Pattern' in the New Testament," *NTS* 6 (1961–1962): 166–73; see also Jerome H. Neyrey, *2 Peter, Jude: A New Translation with Introduction and Commentary*, AB 37C (New York: Doubleday, 1993), 58–60, 72–73; Harrington, *1 Peter, Jude and 2 Peter*, 194–212, both of whom refer to the scriptural allusions as "examples" as opposed to "types." For other appearances of the Israel-Watchers-Sodomite paradigm of ungodliness and divine judgment, see Sir 16:7–10; 3 Macc 2:4–7; T. Naph. 3:4–5; Jub. 20:2–10; CD II, 17–III, 12; m. Sanh. 10:3; 2 Pet 2:4–8.

[60] See Robert L. Webb, "The Use of 'Story' in the Letter of Jude: Rhetorical Strategies of Jude's Narrative Episodes," *JSNT* 31 (2008): 53–87, esp. 55. Webb's perspective is similar to mine in that he views "texts" 1 and 2 not as fulfilled prophecy but as truncated allusions to scriptural narratives that serve as examples of divine judgment. He writes, "The sins of those judged in the examples [i.e., the 'texts'] provide points of *comparison* between the scriptural traditions and Jude's opponents" (64; emphasis mine). Further affirming this point is the use of καί ("also") here, which

Similarly, the second "text" also does not contain an explicit prophecy but instead compares the "way of Cain," Balaam's error "for the sake of gain," and Korah's rebelliousness (v. 11) to the frivolous and disastrous ways of the opponents (vv. 12–13).[61] Although verse 11 is structured as a woe oracle—which, according to Bauckham, "implies prophetic consciousness on the part of the speaker or writer"[62]—this does not require that the "text" in Jude be interpreted in the same way that the pesharim interpret prophetic Scriptures. While verse 11 does prescribe future judgment for those who emulate these woefully unsavory characters in misleading others into sin and rebellion, again the author of Jude does not view the opponents as the *prophetic fulfillment* of these villains. Rather, the epistle states that the opponents follow the *example* of these dissolute paradigms.[63] In this way, neither "text" 1 nor "text" 2 is a prophetic text whose interpretation points to its contemporary fulfillment. Instead, "texts" are paradigmatic examples that both indicate the severity of the adversaries' wickedness and hint at the general sort of judgment that those who are grossly ἀσεβεῖς will face.[64]

---

depicts the present-day events of verse 8 as similar to the examples of verses 5–7 as opposed to being *identified as* the figures of verses 5–7.

[61] In contrast to verse 8, there is no explicit indication of this apart from the use of the demonstrative and reflexive pronouns in verse 12. A further complication of identifying "text" 2 as pesher is the fact that referring to the opponents as οἱ ἐν ταῖς ἀγάπαις ὑμῶν σπιλάδες συνευωχούμενοι ἀφόβως ("blemishes on your love-feasts, while they feast with you without fear, feeding themselves") seems to have very little to do with the mention of Cain, Balaam, and Korah. This is unlike the pesharim, whose interpretation is interconnected with its scriptural quotation by exegetical techniques.

[62] Bauckham, *Jude, 2 Peter*, 78. For a detailed assessment of Jude 11 and its woe oracle, see Blumenthal, *Prophetie und Gericht*, 278–301. For a general assessment of woe oracles and their context in the Hebrew Bible, see Waldemar Janzen, *Mourning Cry and Woe Oracle*, BZAW 125 (Berlin: de Gruyter, 1972).

[63] I have intentionally avoided using the terms *type* and *typology* to explain Jude's use of biblical tradition for two reasons. First, the word τύπος or any of its cognates never appears in Jude. Second, typology is not a uniform system but rather a multivalent method that can connote "examples" (e.g., 1 Cor 10:6, Phil 3:17, 1 Thess 1:7, 1 Pet 5:3), "patterns" or "archetypes" (Acts 7:44, Heb 8:5), a "norm" (Rom 6:17) or the "prefigurations" of prominent figures from the Hebrew Bible (e.g., Rom 5:14). While Jude's use of biblical traditions does contain some of the ideas articulated in the above passages, it is unclear whether all the "texts" of Jude function in the same way.

[64] The most substantial argument for the prophetic nature of the examples of Jude 5–7 and 11 is the statement concerning the opponents in verse 4: οἱ πάλαι προγεγραμμένοι εἰς τοῦτο τὸ κρίμα ἀσεβεῖς ("people who long ago were designated for this condemnation as ungodly"). Bauckham concludes that this phrase indicates that "the false teachers and their condemnation have been prophesied in pre-Christian prophecy, either in the form of the OT types of vv. 5–7, 11 or in the book Enoch" (*Jude, 2 Peter*, 36). Even if this is the case, however, the fact that the author of Jude does not specifically cite any prophetic texts condemning these ungodly ones (apart from 1 En. 1:9) seems again to argue against Jude's status as pesher exegesis, especially since no shortage of Scripture passages exists that would have satisfied this end. Moreover, even if Jude 5–19 is prophetic in nature, nothing essentially requires Jude to use prophecy in the same way as the

Second, like "texts" 1 and 2 of the epistle, the fourth and final "text"—the quotation of one of "the predictions of the apostles of our Lord Jesus Christ" (v. 17: τῶν ῥημάτων τῶν προειρημένων ὑπὸ τῶν ἀποστόλων τοῦ κυρίου ἡμῶν Ἰησοῦ Χριστοῦ)—suggests a very different hermeneutical stance from that of the pesharim. The apostolic prediction of verse 17 is explicitly prophetic and also identifies the opponents as the fulfillment of the prophecy.[65] In this way, the prophetic character of the apostolic warning and its depiction of the opponents as the object of the prophecy do offer some similarities to the pesharim. On the other hand, however, there is one clear feature of verses 17–18 that stands in stark contrast to the hermeneutical perspective of the pesharim—an apostolic prophecy is a *modern* prophecy, *not an ancient one*.[66] While the pesherists did understand their inspired deciphering of Scripture as a continuation of the ongoing process of prophetic revelation,[67] their progressive approach to the text was always anchored *in the ancient texts themselves*.[68] The pesharim take the meaning and context of Scripture and, with revelatory insight, discern how the cryptic words of the past actually foretell the events of the present or future. In this sense, much of the power behind the pesherists' interpretation lies in the prophetic base text itself. Although the apostolic status of the ῥημάτων τῶν προειρημένων may give it authority, its authority is that of contemporaneous figures, not of ancient prophets as in the pesharim.[69] Again, this

---

pesharim. Following his analysis of Jude's status as midrash/pesher and the epistle's use of "οὗτοι-Aussagen," Blumenthal concludes that "Jud 5–19 nicht als Midrasch zu bezeichnen" and instead should be viewed as "ein Überführen der Gegner als ἀσεβεῖς zu verstehen, welches dann wiederum eine prophetische Unheilsankündigung begründen kann, die Judas in V. 11 über seine Gegner ausspricht: οὐαὶ αὐτοῖς" (*Prophetie und Gericht*, 338; see also 313–46, esp. 313–22).

[65] See Harrington, *1 Peter, Jude and 2 Peter*, 218. In contrast to verses 5–13, which Harrington views as examples of judgment, he understands verses 14–19 to be two prophecies that are fulfilled by the opponents.

[66] See Bauckham, *Jude and the Relatives of Jesus*, 184. A further issue lies in whether verses 17–19 should be included in the body of the letter as the appearance of the phrase Ὑμεῖς δέ, ἀγαπητοί ("But you, beloved"), which parallels the appearance of ἀγαπητοί in verse 3, appears to suggest that verse 17 is the start of a new section of the epistle rather than the final part of an exegetical section. See Davids, *Letters of 2 Peter and Jude*, 85.

[67] See the chapter "Revelatory Exegesis at Qumran," in Alex Jassen, *Mediating the Divine: Prophecy and Revelation in the Dead Sea Scrolls and Second Temple Judaism*, STDJ 68 (Leiden: Brill, 2007), 343–62.

[68] Berrin, *Pesher Nahum Scroll*, 12–19. See also George J. Brooke, "Biblical Interpretation at Qumran," in *The Bible and the Dead Sea Scrolls: The Second Princeton Symposium on Judaism and Christian Origins*, ed. James H. Charlesworth, 3 vols. (Waco, TX: Baylor University Press, 2006), 1:287–319, esp. 314–17; Jassen, *Mediating the Divine*, 345–47.

[69] Interestingly, the dependent presentation of this apostolic prophecy in 2 Pet 3:2–4 adds the phrase ὑπὸ τῶν ἁγίων προφητῶν ("by the holy prophets") and thus attributes the prophecy to both the apostles and the prophets. Similar eschatological prophecies include Acts 20:29–30 and 1 Tim 4:1–3. See David E. Aune, *Prophecy in Early Christianity and the Ancient Mediterranean World* (Grand Rapids: Eerdmans, 1983), 288–90.

contradicts what we see in the pesharim, which do not *replace* the meaning of their base texts but simply *reinterpret* their perceived hidden meanings and apply them to their current situation. The old meanings *remain intact* but are simply supplemented with a hidden presage.[70]

The one "text" whose form and ideological foundation seem most comparable to the pesharim is the quotation of 1 En. 1:9 in Jude 14–16.[71] The citation of 1 Enoch is an actual scriptural lemma, as opposed to the other three so-called texts. By writing that Enoch "prophesied" about these opponents (προεφήτευσεν ... καὶ τούτοις),[72] the author of the epistle makes it explicitly clear that Enoch is to be viewed as a prophetic figure and that the opponents are the contemporary object of his ancient, antediluvian prophecy.[73] In turn, out of all the "texts" surveyed above, the structure of verses 14–16 is most similar to the overall structure of the pesharim—it offers a quotation of prophetic Scripture (vv. 14b–15) followed by a formulaic clause (v. 16: Οὗτοί εἰσιν), which separates the "text" citation from its subsequent interpretation of judgment on the wicked, including the present-day bombastic opponents of the epistle.[74] Moreover, as with the use of Scripture in the pesharim, 1 En. 1:9 is lexically

---

[70] See George J. Brooke, "Genre Theory, Rewritten Bible and Pesher," *DSD* 17 (2010): 361–86. He writes that, while the pesharim are not concerned with "modernizing pastness" as seen in rewritten Scripture, they are intent on incorporating the actualization of prophecy into authoritative Scripture in such a way that the prophetic meaning behind the text still exists alongside this hidden fulfillment of the text (373). See also Berrin, "Qumran Pesharim", 320–29, and esp. 332.

[71] On the source behind Jude's use of 1 Enoch, see Edward Mazich, "'The Lord Will Come with His Holy Myriads': An Investigation of the Linguistic Source of the Citation of *1 Enoch* 1,9 in Jude 14b–15," *ZNW* 94 (2003): 276–81; Anton Vögtle, *Der Judasbrief, Der Zweite Petrusbrief*, EKKNT 22 (Zurich: Benziger; Neukirchen-Vluyn: Neukirchener Verlag, 1994), 71–77; Bauckham, *Jude, 2 Peter*, 94–96. For more on Jude's use of 1 Enoch and other pseudepigraphic material, see J. Daryl Charles, "Jude's Use of Pseudepigraphical Source-Material as Part of a Literary Strategy," *NTS* 37 (1991): 130–45; Jeremy F. Hultin, "Bourdieu Reads Jude: Reconsidering the Letter of Jude through Pierre Bourdieu's Sociology," in *Reading Jude with New Eyes: Methodological Reassessments of the Letter of Jude*, ed. Robert L. Webb and Peter H. Davis, LNTS 383 (London: T&T Clark, 2008), 32–53, esp. 43–48; James C. VanderKam, "*1 Enoch*, Enochic Motifs, and Enoch in Early Christian Literature," in *The Jewish Apocalyptic Heritage in Early Christianity*, ed. James C. VanderKam and William Adler, CRINT 3.4 (Assen: Van Gorcum, 1996), 33–101, esp. 35–36, 63.

[72] The nearest antecedent of καὶ τούτοις in verse 14 is the opponents, who are metaphorically being described in verse 13. This affirms that, like verse 13, the prophecy of Enoch is referring to these opponents. See Green, *Jude and 2 Peter*, 109.

[73] For Enoch's emerging role as prophet in the first centuries of Christianity, see Annette Yoshiko Reed, "Pseudepigraphy and/as Prophecy: Continuity and Transformation in the Formation and Reception of Early Enochic Writings," in *Revelation, Literature, and Community in Late Antiquity*, ed. P. Townsend and M. Vidas, TSAJ 146 (Tübingen: Mohr Siebeck, 2011), 25–42, esp. 36–39; Nicholas J. Moore, "Is Enoch Also among the Prophets? The Impact of Jude's Citation of *1 Enoch* on the Reception of Both Texts in the Early Church," *JTS* 64 (2013): 498–515.

[74] According to George W. E. Nickelsburg, 1 En. 1:9 encapsulates the preceding oracle of judgment in chapter 1 of 1 Enoch by summarizing both God's theophanic arrival with angelic

linked to its interpretation, tying the "hard speech" (τῶν σκληρῶν ὧν ἐλάλησαν) of the Watchers to the "bombastic speech" (λαλεῖ ὑπέρογκα) of the opponents.[75]

These formal and ideological similarities, however, are by no means perfect matches. As Lim, Berrin, and Williamson note, one of the key structural features of the pesharim is its continuous verse-by-verse commentary on Scripture, something that Jude 5–19 obviously does not offer. Although there are cases in which isolated pesher units appear in non-pesher texts,[76] what argues against identifying vv. 14–16 as such a case is its lack of a specific term equivalent to פשר, which, as I stated earlier, is a significant formal omission that carries equally significant theological baggage. It is the term פשר that formally marks pesher exegesis as the unveiling of hidden prophetic meaning through divine revelation. In contrast, Jude does not offer any indication that this dual revelatory-exegetical approach underlies either its interpretation of "texts" or its solitary engagement with the quotation of 1 En. 1:9. In this fashion, Jude's depiction of the opponents as the fulfillment of 1 En. 1:9 does not concretely exhibit the same ideological presuppositions that stand behind the pesharim, and in many ways Jude's interpretation differs little from the prophetic fulfillment found in Paul's epistles, the Gospels, and Revelation.

IV. Conclusion

A number of the alleged formal similarities shared by the Qumran pesharim and Jude are not as conclusive or clear as has been previously suggested by Bauckham.[77] The "text"-commentary structure of Jude differs markedly from the way that the pesharim use Scripture. The epistle predominantly uses paraphrase as opposed to citation and lacks an equivalent to the formulaic term פשר, which complicates the situation both formally and ideologically. Moreover, despite a shared concern and expectation of general eschatological judgment, there are problems regarding Jude's purported prophetic hermeneutic, including the epistle's use of "texts" as examples and paradigms of divine judgment rather than as ancient prophecies fulfilled by the epistle's opponents, Jude's use of a contemporary apostolic prophecy, and the lack of any explicit indication that Jude understood its

---

beings and his subsequent judgment upon the wicked. See *1 Enoch 1: A Commentary on the Book of 1 Enoch, Chapters 1–36, 81–108*, Hermeneia (Minneapolis: Fortress, 2001), 143, 148–49; see also James C. VanderKam, "The Theophany of Enoch I 3b–7, 9," *VT* 23 (1973): 129–50.

[75] Bauckham states that the idea of speech is the primary topic of verses 14–16 (*Jude, 2 Peter*, 97, 99).

[76] E.g., 1QS VII, 12–16; CD I, 13–14; III, 21–IV, 6; VII, 14–18; 4Q252 V, 1–7; 4Q379 22 II, 7–15. See Dimant, "Pesharim, Qumran," 247.

[77] See Frey ("Epistle of Jude between Judaism and Hellenism," 312 n. 15), who notes that Bauckham's comparison of Jude with the pesharim is "a rather far-fetched analogy."

reading of "texts" as the unraveling of mysteries hidden in ancient prophecies. Jude 5–19 does not uniformly equate its opponents with the contemporary fulfillment of the hidden meaning of prophetic texts. Rather, verses 5–19 use a variety of techniques—examples of wickedness, an apostolic foretelling, Enochic prophecy—and scriptural traditions in order to portray its present-day opponents as prime examples of ungodliness while simultaneously encouraging its righteous readers and hearers to stand firm in faith, knowing that the tribulations brought on by these iniquitous adversaries are signs of the ἐσχάτου χρόνου ("the last time"), which will culminate in God's divine judgment. By embracing biblical paradigms in connection with Enoch's prophecy concerning the Lord's arrival and judgment of the wicked, and with the apostolic prophecy about the final days, Jude equates the opponents with timeless exemplars of iniquity doomed for perdition while contextualizing them within the present eschatological age, buttressing his claims with the authoritative prophecies of both ancient Enoch and one of the apostles.

In conclusion, while the few elements shared by Jude and the pesharim admittedly fall short of proving that the works can be classified as belonging to the same genre, it is surprising that no one has yet written anything about what is arguably the clearest similarity between the pesharim and Jude—the intention of producing propagandistic accounts of an "out-group" in order to solidify the "in-group." While scholars have examined the use of polemic and rhetoric in Jude[78] and the sociological traits of the pesharim,[79] no one has ventured to compare how the use of language, rhetoric, and imagery in these respective texts serves them in their common goal of distinguishing those viewed as deviant and dangerous from the authors and those whom they consider pious. Although such a study would presumably come no closer to proving a generic relationship between the pesharim and Jude, it would offer valuable insight into how group ideology and eschatology come to fruition in ancient literature addressing conflict.

---

[78] In addition to works cited above, see J. Daryl Charles, "Polemic and Persuasion: Typological and Rhetorical Perspectives on the Letter of Jude," in Webb and Davis, *Reading Jude with New Eyes*, 81–107; Lauri Thurén, "Hey Jude! Asking for the Original Situation and Message of a Catholic Epistle," *NTS* 43 (1997): 451–65; Frederik Wisse, "The Epistle of Jude in the History of Heresiology," in *Essays on the Nag Hammadi Texts: In Honour of Pahor Labib*, ed. Martin Krause, NHS 6 (Leiden: Brill, 1975), 133–43.

[79] See, e.g., Jokiranta, *Social Identity and Sectarianism*; and Jokiranta, "Pesharim: A Mirror of Self-Understanding," in *Reading the Present in the Qumran Library: The Perception of the Contemporary by Means of Scriptural Interpretations*, ed. Kristin De Troyer and Armin Lange, SymS 30 (Atlanta: Society of Biblical Literature, 2005), 23–34; Berrin Tzoref, "Pesharim," 1052.

New and Recent Titles

SBL PRESS

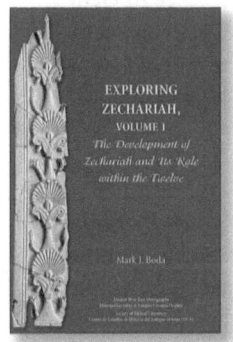

EXPLORING ZECHARIAH
Mark J. Boda
Volume 1: The Development of Zechariah and Its Role within the Twelve
Paperback $37.95, 978-1-62837-162-8   290 pages, 2017   Code: 062814
Hardcover $52.95, 978-0-88414-199-0   E-book $37.95, 978-0-88414-198-3
Ancient Near Eastern Monographs 16

Volume 2: The Development and Role of Biblical Traditions in Zechariah
Paperback $46.95, 978-0-88414-200-3   270 pages, 2017   Code: 062815
Hardcover $61.95, 978-0-88414-202-7   E-book $46.95, 978-0-88414-201-0
Ancient Near Eastern Monographs 17

SENSING WORLD, SENSING WISDOM
The Cognitive Foundation of Biblical Metaphors
Nicole L. Tilford
Paperback $34.95, 978-1-62837-175-8   258 pages, 2017   Code 062634
Hardcover $49.95, 978-0-88414-220-1   E-book $34.95, 978-0-88414-219-5
Ancient Israel and Its Literature 31

LIFE IN KINGS
Reshaping the Royal Story in the Hebrew Bible
A. Graeme Auld
Paperback $39.95, 978-1-62837-171-0   330 pages, 2017   Code 062632
Hardcover $54.95, 978-0-88414-212-6   E-book $39.95, 978-0-88414-211-9
Ancient Israel and Its Literature 30

FAMILY RELIGION IN BABYLONIA, SYRIA AND ISRAEL
Continuity and Change in the Forms of Religious Life
Karel van der Toorn
Paperback $64.95, 978-1-62837-168-0   500 pages, 2017   Code: 069575
Brill Reprints 75   Studies in the History and Culture of the Ancient Near East 7

A HISTORY OF ANCIENT NEAR EASTERN LAW
Raymond Westbrook, editor
Paperback $149.95, 978-1-62837-179-6   1240 pages, 2017   Code: 069581
Brill Reprints 81   Handbook of Oriental Studies 72

SBL Press • P.O. Box 2243 • Williston, VT 05495-2243
Phone: 877-725-3334 (toll-free) or 802-864-6185 • Fax: 802-864-7626
Order online at www.sbl-site.org/publications

Errata

Due to a technical error, the article "The Ground That Opened Its Mouth: The Ground's Response to Human Violence in Genesis 4," by Mari Jørstad (pages 705–15 in *JBL* 135.4), incorrectly identified one of the verbal roots in Gen 1:28. The verbal root is כבש, not שכב. The online version of the article has been updated with this correction. We regret the error.

The article "Creation, Destruction, and a Psalmist's Plea: Rethinking the Poetic Structure of Psalm 74," by Nathaniel E. Greene (pages 85–101 in *JBL* 136.1), incorrectly described part of the Ugaritic Baal Cycle on p. 98, reading "Yamm is then proclaimed king." It should read, "Baal is then proclaimed king." The online version has been updated with this correction. We regret the error.

NEW THIS FALL!

While honoring the historical context and literary diversity of the Old Testament, *Telling the Old Testament Story* is a thematic reading that construes the OT as a complex but coherent narrative. Unlike standard, introductory textbooks that only cover basic background and interpretive issues for each Old Testament book, this introduction combines a thematic approach with careful exegetical attention to representative biblical texts, ultimately telling the macro-level story, while drawing out the multiple nuances present within different texts and traditions.

Brad E. Kelle is Professor of Old Testament and Hebrew, School of Theology and Christian Ministry, Point Loma Nazarene University in San Diego, California. He has served as the chair of the SBL's Warfare in Ancient Israel Consultation at the Annual Meeting of the Society of Biblical Literature. He is also the past president and current member at large (executive board) of the Society of Biblical Literature Pacific Coast Region. He is the Old Testament editor for Currents in Biblical Research and has written or edited a variety of works on the Old Testament and ancient Israel.

AbingdonAcademic.com **Abingdon ACADEMIC**